Humanizing Education

Humanizing Education

Edited by

GRETCHEN BRION-MEISELS
KRISTY S. COOPER
SHERRY L. DECKMAN
CHRISTINA L. DOBBS
CHANTAL FRANCOIS
THOMAS NIKUNDIWE
CARLA SHALABY

HARVARD EDUCATIONAL REVIEW
REPRINT SERIES NO. 46

Library of Congress Control Number 2009942749

ISBN 978-0-916690-50-2

Published by Harvard Educational Review,
an imprint of the Harvard Education Publishing Group

Harvard Educational Review
8 Story Street
Cambridge, MA 02138

Cover Design: Sarah Henderson

Cover art: detail from the mural "The Best of All Possible Worlds,"
created by students at The Pollard Middle School, Needham,
Massachusetts, in 1996, directed by David Fichter.

The typefaces used in this book are New Baskerville for text and
Adobe Myriad Pro for display.

Contents

Editors' Introduction

> Within history, in concrete, objective contexts, both humanization and dehumanization are possibilities for a person as an uncompleted being conscious of their incompletion. But while both humanization and dehumanization are real alternatives, only the first is the people's vocation. This vocation is constantly negated, yet it is affirmed by that very negation. It is thwarted by injustice, exploitation, oppression, and the violence of the oppressors; it is affirmed by the yearning of the oppressed for freedom and justice, and by their struggle to recover their lost humanity.
>
> —Paolo Freire, *Pedagogy of the Oppressed*

In *Humanizing Education* we recognize the people's vocation and continue a *Harvard Educational Review* (*HER*) tradition of forefronting ideals and illustrations of education that celebrate praxis, "the action and reflection of men and women upon their world in order to transform it" (Freire, 1970c, p. 36). In an important sense, this work began in 1970 with the publication of two articles by Paolo Freire and has continued through various contexts, methods, actors, and voices on the pages of *HER*. For Freire, authentic humanizing education is the dialogic relationship between understanding the world and transforming it. In his first *HER* essay, "The Adult Literacy Process," Freire (1970a) insists that "there is no other road to humanization—[the oppressed's] as well as everyone else's—but authentic transformation of the dehumanizing structure" (p. 211).

In this collection of articles published in *HER* over the last forty years, we offer reflections of Freire's call for authentic transformation. From Dayton, Ohio, to Puerto Rican Chicago to Barcelona, Spain, this book carries readers to places where people have first imagined—and then organized—their own educational responses to dehumanizing practices and conditions. The collection spotlights teachers insisting on pedagogies of love, communities enacting pedagogies of solidarity, and young people demanding pedagogies of recognition. In preschool classrooms and in prisons, on college campuses and on the roads of Caswell County, North Carolina, the contributors offer examples of hopeful and humanizing educational spaces and movements. From them we glean a definition of humanizing education as a process through which people come to understand their power, discover and create avenues through which to use that power, and ultimately transform their contexts, themselves, and each other through relationships of solidarity. A humanizing education is an empowering, participatory, and hopeful education.

In contrast to this liberating vision, many scholars suggest that current trends in education have a different purpose, one that functions to maintain and reproduce the status quo of social inequalities in our society (Apple, 1995; Giroux, 1997). Bill Ayers (2009) states that such environments are often likened to factories that view "education as a commodity rather than a right" and that our schools "too often teach indifference, emotional and intellectual dependency, provisional self-esteem, and the need to submit to certified authority" (390). Indeed, we recall our own schooling experiences, which often favored individualism and competition, were focused on education as a product rather than a process, and were decontextualized from our family and community lives. To add to this depiction, we considered the wealth of research focused on race- and class-based educational disparities. This work reveals the daily microaggressions and static macrostructures that indoctrinate students to expect a life of mediocrity, disempowerment, and inferiority (Anderson, 1988; Anyon, 1997; Fine, 1991; Lipman, 1998; MacLeod, 1995; Payne, 2008). Together, these commonplace images of education portray the learning process as an experience devoid of humanity.

Perhaps equally disconcerting, in response to these abysmal conditions, a long history of educational "reform" shows that scholars, policy makers, and educators alike continually gravitate toward remedies that appear to address the symptoms of the problems within our schools without truly shaking the core. Whether in the name of progressive or conservative ideals, these efforts tend to focus on changing the technical aspects of schools, such as lengthening the school day and making class and school sizes smaller. Thus, they emphasize outcome-based measures such as high-stakes test scores, push a back-to-basics instructional agenda, and reward individual teachers based on "merit" (Apple, 1995; Au, 2009; Elmore, 2007). Some of these efforts even give families the illusion of school choice (Apple & Pedroni, 2005; Au, 2009).

A reflection on our status quo in education, along with an examination of efforts that seek to revolutionize it, could not be timelier. The election of Barack Obama in November 2008 inspired a sense of hope and change throughout our country, igniting new conversations about our nation's most pressing foreign and domestic issues. Obama's views on race and relentless corporate control, his community-organizing background, and his progressive attitudes toward social services during the campaign gave many Americans the sense that his ideals would usher in a new era of school reform that would honor the people and practices that create rigorous and engaging teaching and learning. Indeed, during his presidential campaign Obama passionately criticized the most egregious aspects of reform stemming from the 2001 No Child Left Behind Act that overemphasized test scores by threatening sanctions on low-performing schools and deprioritizing nontested academic subjects. And he argued that such policies, largely underfunded throughout the country, only served to perpetuate inequalities in schools and in society (Au, 2009).

Yet one year into the new presidency, critics of Obama's plans for educational reform observe that his administration's policies are almost in lockstep with the status quo in place over the last several decades. Most recently, the administration's Race to the Top program—a $4.35 billion initiative that allows individual states to compete for cash prizes that will fund their school reform efforts—prioritizes standards, more testing, teacher performance pay, and school choice (Fuhrman, Resnick, & Shepard, 2009; Wall Street Journal, 2009) while neglecting a focus on instruction that empowers and humanizes students. Ultimately, this "new" federal initiative appears to be an echo of our past, moving along an unpromising trajectory of educational reform.

Indeed, what such efforts ultimately do—even if they make some temporary headway in increasing achievement outcomes—is reinforce a failing school system (Tyack & Cuban, 1995) and an unjust social order (Bowles & Gintis, 1976) instead of transforming the overall dehumanizing structure of schools. Scholars suggest that what is missing in our discourse of reform is adequate attention to the human relationships that form the crux of genuine learning processes; without attending to the human side of reform, we might only succeed in perpetuating both educational and societal inequities (Payne, 2008).

In a context of continued calls for such educational reform, the articles in this volume do more than challenge dehumanizing forms of education; these stories and voices from the past forty years revolutionize our understanding of education. In doing so, they seek to inspire a collective imagination for critical alternatives in education. Each piece articulates what it means to participate in a humanizing pedagogy, one that engages youth and adults together in an ongoing process of transforming selves and the world. Here, authors engage readers in conceiving of education as a communal effort inclusive of learners, families, community leaders, and educators. By traveling the country, partnering with community centers, or bringing classrooms to remote corners of the world, the people featured here dismantle the school walls that so often seem to constrain the realization of a humanizing education. As a result, the learning process is contextualized in students' lived experiences, providing them with the opportunity to see themselves, their families, and their communities in the content with which they engage.

Similarly, these articles illustrate how educators who align themselves with students can develop reciprocal, collaborative relationships that simultaneously impact students' learning experiences and teachers' beliefs and instruction. While traditional philosophies of school reform favor unilateral decisions of how teachers and administrators can improve student learning, the pieces here realize a vision of education that emerges from action in solidarity. Indeed, the adults featured throughout this reprint actively listen to their students, develop relationships with them and their families and communities, and stand beside them as they pursue learning and justice. Moreover, the educators attest to their own individual growth and transformation by engaging in a participatory, reciprocal process instead of a unidirectional one. From these efforts emerges a shifted ideology that no longer views students as passive receptors of their schooling experiences but instead as people who exercise agency over what they learn and how they learn it.

These selections portray transformations in education among the groups most dehumanized by our educational institutions. Adults struggling to read and write, incarcerated women, and children of color who are living in poverty form the centerpiece of the collection. The stories about their quest for education provide a new vision of what is possible for those whom our society often views through a lens of brokenness and deficit (Tuck, 2009). Though many of the educational efforts featured in this collection are large in scale, they are hardly ever replicable—primarily because they are built on the particular needs, desires, and strengths of each community. Yet the lessons from these small-scale efforts are worth heeding; they show that the change for which people are fighting is not always external but also internal—transforming individual minds and hearts and fostering a sense of intellectual and personal freedom.

In *Humanizing Education*, readers will encounter transformation at three interdependent levels of society: individuals, communities, and larger systems. Consistently, these transformations happen as people critically examine their contexts and then work in solidarity with others to intentionally interact with and act on these contexts. In his second *HER* essay, Freire (1970b) explicated this phenomenon: "*Consciousness of* and *action upon* reality are, therefore, inseparable constituents of the transforming act by which men become beings of relation" (p. 453). Humanity shines through dialogic relationships, whether it is between a counselor and a three year old or a band of *brigadistas* and 400,000 Nicaraguan villagers. It is our hope that by putting these pieces together, by synthesizing examples of humanizing practice at different levels with different people in different contexts, we might spark a reimagining of a purpose of education that alights with the life vocation of being more fully human.

In the essay that opens this volume, Maxine Greene (1986) calls on readers to "make audible again the recurrent calls for justice and equality" (p. 440), resurrecting a legacy of collective struggle to envision an educational revolution for today. Echoing this call, Obama's 2008 campaign for the U.S. presidency was characterized by hopeful idealism and a slogan of "change we can believe in." In the 2009 special issue of the *Harvard Educational Review*, commissioned to mark the historic occasion of Obama's election, scholars, practitioners, and students considered the implications for education as this new administration began working to implement an agenda of change and justice. Though it is difficult to say now what the legacy of the Obama presidency will ultimately be, we believe that calls for activism and justice must be explored whenever they come to the forefront and searched for when absent. Therefore, this reprint collection highlights historical examples of educational spaces, practices, and movements that embody *contemporary visions* of hope and change. After all, these calls drive our hope and commitment to build an educational system that "restores democracy, ensures equity, and reflects the worth and dignity of our young people" (Editors, 2009). Thus, this collection is bookended with two essays by Maxine Greene—the first from 1986 and the second from 2009—both of which argue for the need to imagine a more humanizing educational system. Similarly, each of the three sections of the book begins with a 2009 theoretical framing piece from an Obama issue contributor and includes a collection of historic articles that bring the theoretical vision to life with examples of lived practice.

Part I: Insurrectionary Generation is framed by a provocative essay that likens our current educational system to the U.S. slave system. Jay Gillen makes the argument that it will be the youth living in poverty who lead the insurrection necessary for our society to reach its potential for equity and justice. *Part II: Participatory Democracy* is framed by Bill Ayers, who, in his stirring essay, calls for a reclaiming of education by the very people who are in the midst of it. Finally, Jeff Duncan-Andrade frames *Part III: Critical Hope* by rejecting false hope and evoking an authentic, painful, unifying hope in his inspired essay addressed to educators of the oppressed. These framing essays are beautiful constructions of the *reflective* aspect of Freire's notion of praxis. Critical examinations of the world, these selections serve as a call to action for all those who would do the difficult work of humanizing our society. The articles that follow in each section illustrate the *action* that Freire insists is necessary for the critical consciousness that precedes the transformation of ourselves and our world.

By gathering these works into a single collection, we intend to both review and continue the dialogue started many years ago, documenting the ongoing educational struggle to reclaim a humanity lost amid reforms that include a relentless focus on test scores, time spent on task, longer school days, and performance pay for teachers. The beautiful, instructive episodes of teaching and learning included on the pages of this book have continued to take place despite this context of dehumanizing reform, and there is much to be learned by studying the struggles of these educators and students alongside one another. Perhaps, more importantly, we audaciously hope that this book will lead readers toward the praxis exemplified by the teachers and learners in these many spaces and places. As our hope is realized, we look forward to filling the next five decades of *HER*'s pages with a new collection of critical alternatives to educational reform.

References

Anderson, J.D. (1988). *The education of blacks in the South, 1860-1935.* Chapel Hill, NC: University of North Carolina Press.

Anyon, J. (1997). *A political economy of urban educational reform.* New York: Teachers College Press.

Apple, M. W. (1995). *Education and power* (2nd ed.). New York: Routledge.

Apple, M. W., & Pedroni, T. C. (2005). Conservative alliance building and African American support of vouchers: The end of Brown's promise or a new beginning? *Teachers College Record, 107*(9), 2068–2105.

Au, W. (2009). Obama, where art thou? Hoping for change in U.S. educational policy. *Harvard Educational Review, 79*(2), 309–321.

Ayers, W. (2009). Barack Obama and the fight for public education. *Harvard Educational Review, 79*(2), 385–395.

Bowles, S., & Gintis, H. (1976). *Schooling in capitalist America: Educational reform and the contradictions of economic life.* New York: Basic Books.

Editors. (2009). Editors' introduction. *Harvard Educational Review, 79*(2), 177–178.

Elmore, R. F. (2007). *School reform from the inside out: Policy, practice and performance.* Cambridge, MA: Harvard Education Press.

Fine, M. (1991). *Framing dropouts: Notes on the politics of an urban public high school.* Albany: State University of New York Press.

Freire, P. (1970a). The adult literacy practice as a cultural action for freedom. *Harvard Educational Review, 40*(2), 205–225.

Freire, P. (1970b). Cultural action and conscientization. *Harvard Educational Review, 40*(3), 452–477.

Freire, P. (1970c). *Pedagogy of the oppressed.* New York: Herder and Herder.

Fuhrman, S. H., Resnick, L., & Shepard, L. (2009). Standards aren't enough. *Education Week.* Retrieved January 7, 2010, from http://www.edweek.org/ew/articles/2009/10/08/07fuhrman.h29.html?tkn= VLRCPAw8p8uUP2zz3wkGxsil88r5TnrwH%2FNe

Giroux, H. A. (1997). *Pedagogy and the politics of hope: Theory, culture, and schooling.* Boulder, CO: Westview Press.

Greene, M. (1986). In search of critical pedagogy. *Harvard Educational Review, 56*(4), 427–441.

Greene, M. (2009). Coda: Slow fuse of change. *Harvard Educational Review, 79*(2), 396–398.

Lipman, P. (1998). *Race, class and power in school restructuring.* Albany: State University of New York Press.

MacLeod, J. (1995). *Ain't no makin' it: Aspirations and attainment in a low-income neighborhood* (Expanded ed.). Boulder, CO: Westview Press.

Payne, C. M. (2008). *So much reform, so little change: The persistence of failure in urban schools.* Cambridge, MA: Harvard Education Press.

Tuck, E. (2009). Suspending damage: Letter to communities. *Harvard Educational Review, 79*(3), 409–427.

Tyack, D., & Cuban, L. (1995). *Tinkering toward utopia: A century of public school reform.* Cambridge, MA: Harvard University Press.

Wall Street Journal. (2009, July 30). Obama's 'race to the top': Who'll blink first: The unions or the White House? *Wall Street Journal Opinion.* Retrieved January 6, 2009 from http://online.wsj.com/article/SB10001424052970204886304574308442726348678.html

In Search of a Critical Pedagogy

MAXINE GREENE

In what Jean Baudrillard describes as "the shadow of silent majorities" in an administered and media-mystified world, we try to reconceive what a critical pedagogy relevant to this time and place ought to mean.[1] This is a moment when great numbers of Americans find their expectations and hopes for their children being fed by talk of "educational reform." Yet the reform reports speak of those very children as "human resources" for the expansion of productivity, as means to the end of maintaining our nation's economic competitiveness and military primacy in the world. Of course we want to empower the young for meaningful work, we want to nurture the achievement of diverse literacies. But the world we inhabit is palpably deficient: there are unwarranted inequities, shattered communities, unfulfilled lives. We cannot help but hunger for traces of utopian visions, of critical or **dialectical**[a] engagements with social and economic realities. And yet, when we reach out, we experience a kind of blankness. We sense people living under a weight, a nameless inertial mass. How are we to justify our concern for their awakening? Where are the sources of questioning, of restlessness? How are we to move the young to break with the given, the taken-for-granted — to move towards what might be, what is not yet?

Confronting all of this, I am moved to make some poets' voices audible at the start. Poets are exceptional, of course; they are not considered educators in the ordinary sense. But they remind us of absence, ambiguity, embodiments of existential possibility. More often than not they do so with passion;

[a] While there are a number of definitions and interpretations of **dialectics**, for the general purposes of critical pedagogy, this concept refers to the interconnecting and contradicting relationships that constitute a particular phenomenon, for example, among the economic, political, social, and cultural dimensions of society. A dialectical analysis is also often used to show how every idea or force has its opposite/contradiction. For example, the dialectic of "oppressor" is the reality of the "oppressed." Such an analysis holds both "opposing" concepts together at once to see how they interconnect and play off each other.

Harvard Educational Review Vol. 56 No. 4 November 1986

and passion has been called the power of possibility. This is because it is the source of our interests and our purposes. Passion signifies mood, emotion, desire: modes of grasping the appearances of things. It is one of the important ways of recognizing possibility, "the presence of the future as *that which is lacking* and that which, by its very absence, reveals reality."[2] Poets move us to give play to our imaginations, to enlarge the scope of lived experience and reach beyond from our own grounds. Poets do not give us answers; they do not solve the problems of critical pedagogy. They can, however, if we will them to do so, awaken us to reflectiveness, to a recovery of lost landscapes and lost spontaneities. Against such a background, educators might now and then be moved to go in search of a critical pedagogy of significance for themselves.

Let us hear Walt Whitman, for one:

> I am the poet of the Body and I am the poet of the Soul,
> The pleasures of heaven are with me and the pains of
> hell are with me.
> The first I graft and increase upon myself, the latter I translate into a
> new tongue.
>
> I am the poet of the woman the same as the man,
> And I say it is as great to be a woman as to be a man,
>
> . . . .
>
> I chant the chant of dilation or pride.
> We have had ducking and deprecating about enough,
> I show that size is only development.
>
> Have you outstript the rest? are you the President?,
> It is a trifle, they will more than arrive there every one,
> and still pass on.[3]

Whitman calls himself the poet of the "barbaric yawp"; he is also the poet child going forth, of the grass, of comradeship and communion and the "en masse." And of noticing, naming, caring, feeling. In a systematized, technicized moment, a moment of violations and of shrinking "minimal" selves, we ought to be able to drink from the fountain of his work.

There is Wallace Stevens, explorer of multiple perspectives and imagination, challenger of objectified, quantified realties — what he calls the "ABC of being . . . the vital, arrogant, fatal, dominant X," questioner as well of the conventional "lights and definitions" presented as "the plain sense of things." We ought to think of states of things, he says, phases of movements, polarities:

> But in the centre of our lives, this time, this day,
> It is a state, this spring among the politicians
> Playing cards. In a village of the indigenes,
> One would still have to discover. Among the dogs
> and dung,
> One would continue to contend with one's ideas.[4]

One's ideas, yes, and blue guitars as well, and — always and always — "the never-resting mind," the "flawed words and stubborn sounds."

And there is Marianne Moore, reminding us that every poem represents what Robert Frost described as "the triumph of the spirit over the materialism by which we are being smothered," enunciating four precepts:

> Feed imagination food that invigorates.
> Whatever it is, do with all your might.
> Never do to another what you would not wish done to yourself.
> Say to yourself, "I will be responsible."
>
> Put these principles to the test, and you will be inconvenienced by being over-trusted, overbefriended, overconsulted, half adopted, and have no leisure. Face that when you come to it.[5]

Another woman's voice arises: Muriel Rukeyser's, in the poem "Käthe Kollwitz."

> What would happen if one woman told the truth about her life?
> The world would split open[6]

The idea of an officially defined "world" splitting open when a repressed truth is revealed holds all sorts of implications for those who see reality as opaque, bland and burnished, resistant both to protest and to change.

Last, and in a different mood, let us listen to these lines by Adrienne Rich:

> A clear night in which two planets
> seem to clasp each other   in which the earthly grasses
> shift like silk in starlight
>   If the mind were clear
> and if the mind were simple   you could take this mind
> this particular state and say
> *This is how I would live if I could choose:*
> *this is what is possible*[7]

The poem is called "What Is Possible," but the speaker knows well that no mind can be "simple," or "abstract and pure." She realizes that the mind has "a different mission in the universe," that there are sounds and configurations still needing to be deciphered; she knows that the mind must be "wrapped in battle" in what can only be a resistant world. She voices her sense of the contrast between the mind as contemplative and the mind in a dialectical relation with what surrounds.

They create spaces, these poets, between themselves and what envelops and surrounds. Where there are spaces like that, desire arises, along with hope and expectation. We may sense that something is lacking that must be surpassed or repaired. Often, therefore, poems address our freedom; they call on us to move beyond where we are, to break with submergence, to transform. To transform what — and how? To move beyond ourselves — and where? Reading such works within the contexts of schools and education, those of us still preoccupied with human freedom and human growth may well find our questions more perplexing. We may become more passionate about the possibility of a critical pedagogy in these uncritical times. How can we (decently, morally, intelligently) address ourselves both to desire and to purpose and obligation? How can we awaken others to possibility and the need for action in the name of possibility? How can we communicate the importance of opening spaces in the imagination where persons can reach beyond where they are?

Poets, of course, are not alone in the effort to make us see and to defamiliarize our commonsense worlds. The critical impulse is an ancient one in the Western tradition: we have only to recall the prisoners released from the cave in *The Republic,* Socrates trying to arouse the "sleeping ox" that was the Athenian public, Francis Bacon goading his readers to break with the "idols" that obscured their vision and distorted their rational capacities, David Hume calling for the exposure of the "sophistries and illusions" by which so many have habitually lived. In philosophy, in the arts, in the sciences, men and women repeatedly have come forward to urge their audiences to break with what William Blake called "mind-forg'd manacles." Not only did such manacles shackle consciousness; their effectiveness assured the continuing existence of systems of domination — monarchies, churches, land-holding arrangements, and armed forces of whatever kind.

The American tradition originated in such an insight and in the critical atmosphere specific to the European Enlightenment. It was an atmosphere created in large measure by rational, autonomous voices engaging in dialogue for the sake of bringing into being a **public sphere.**[b] These were, most often, the voices of an emerging middle class concerned for their own independence from anachronistic and unjust restraints. Their "rights" were being trampled, they asserted, rights sanctioned by natural and moral laws. Among these rights were "life, liberty, and the pursuit of happiness," which (especially when joined to justice or equity) remain normative for this nation: they are goods *to be* secured. Liberty, at the time of the founding of our nation, meant liberation from interference by the state, church, or army in the lives of individuals. For some, sharing such beliefs as those articulated by the British philosopher John Stuart Mill, liberty also meant each person's right to think for himself or herself, "to follow his intellect to whatever conclusions it may lead" in an atmosphere that forbade "mental slavery."[8]

[b] **Public spheres** in the critical sense are public arenas for citizens in which political participation, outside of direct government and economic influence and intervention, is enacted through dialogue and debate. Schools are envisioned by critical pedagogues as "public spheres," wherein classrooms are active sites of public intervention and social struggle, rather than mere adjuncts of corporate and partisan interests. Because mainstream society is constituted by particular oppressive ideologies, these critical spheres are also referred to as "counterpublics."

The founders were calling, through a distinctive critical challenge, for opportunities to give their energies free play. That meant the unhindered exercise of their particular talents: inventing, exploring, building, pursuing material and social success. To be able to do so, they had to secure power, which they confirmed through the establishment of a constitutional republic. For Hannah Arendt, this sort of power is kept in existence through an ongoing process of "binding and promising, combining and covenanting." As she saw it, power springs up between human beings when they act to constitute "a worldly structure to house, as it were, their combined power of action."[9] When we consider the numbers of people excluded from this process over the generations, we have to regard this view of power as normative as well. It is usual to affirm that power belongs to "the people" at large; but, knowing that this has not been the case, we are obligated to expand the "worldly structure" until it contains the "combined power" of increasing numbers of articulate persons. A critical pedagogy for Americans, it would seem, must take this into account.

For the school reformers of the early nineteenth century, the apparent mass power accompanying the expansion of manhood suffrage created a need for "self-control" and a "voluntary compliance" with the laws of righteousness.[10] Without a common school to promote such control and compliance, the social order might be threatened. Moreover, the other obligations of the school — to prepare the young to "create wealth" — could not be adequately met. Even while recognizing the importance of providing public education for the masses of children, we have to acknowledge that great numbers of them were being socialized into factory life and wage labor in an expanding capitalist society. Like working classes everywhere, they could not but find themselves alienated from their own productive energies. The persisting dream of opportunity, however, kept most of them from confronting their literal powerlessness. The consciousness of objectively real "open" spaces (whether on the frontier, "downtown," or out at sea) prevented them from thinking seriously about changing the order of things; theoretically, there was always an alternative, a "territory ahead."[11] It followed that few were likely to conceive of themselves in a dialectical relation with what surrounded them, no matter how exploitative or cruel. As the laggard and uneven development of trade unions indicates, few were given to viewing themselves as members of a "class" with a project to pull them forward, a role to play in history.

The appearance of utopian communities and socialist societies throughout the early nineteenth century did call repeatedly into question some of the assumptions of the American ideology, especially those having to do with individualism. The founders of the experimental colonies (Robert Owen, Frances Wright, Albert Brisbane, and others) spoke of communalism, mental freedom, the integration of physical and intellectual work, and the discovery of a common good. Socialists called for a more humane and rational social arrangement and for critical insight into what Orestes Brownson described as the "crisis as to the relation of wealth and labor." He said, "It is useless to shut our eyes to the fact and, like the ostrich, fancy ourselves secure because we have so concealed our heads that we see not the danger."[12] Important as their insights were, such people were addressing themselves to educated humanitarians whose good offices might be enlisted in improving and perfecting mankind. Critical though they were of exploitation, greed, and the division of labor, they did not speak of engaging the exploited ones in their own quests for emancipation. No particular pedagogy seemed required, and none was proposed, except within the specific contexts of utopian communities. Once a decent community or society was created, it was believed, the members would be educated in accord with its ideals.

There were, it is true, efforts to invent liberating ways of teaching for children in the larger society, although most were undertaken outside the confines of the common schools. Elizabeth Peabody and Bronson Alcott, among others, through "conversations" with actual persons in classrooms, toiled to inspire self-knowledge, creativity, and communion. Like Ralph Waldo Emerson, they were all hostile to the "joint-stock company" that society seemed to have become, a company "in which the members agree, for the better securing of his bread to each shareholder, to surrender the liberty and culture of the eater."[13] Like Emerson as well, they were all hostile to blind conformity, to the ethos of "Trade" that created false relations among human beings, to the chilling routines of institutional life. It is the case that they were largely apolitical; but their restiveness in the face of an imperfect society led them to find various modes of defiance. Those at Brook Farm tried to find a communal way of challenging the social order: Fuller found feminism; Emerson, ways of speaking intended to rouse his listeners to create their own meanings, to think for themselves.

The most potent exemplar of all this was Henry David Thoreau, deliberately addressing readers "in the first person," provoking them to use their intellects to "burrow" through the taken-for-granted, the conventional, the genteel. He wanted them to reject their own self-exploitation, to refuse what we would now call **false consciousness**[c] and artificial needs. He connected the "wide-awakeness" to actual work in the world, to projects. He knew that people needed to be released from internal and external constraints if they were to shape and make and articulate, to leave their own thumbprints on the world. He understood about economic tyranny on the railroads and in the factories, and he knew that it could make political freedom meaningless. His writing and his abolitionism constituted his protests; both *Walden* and *On Civil Disobe-*

[c] Linked to the notion that social institutions like schools are agents of ideological control that work to maintain dominant beliefs, values, and forms of oppression, **false consciousness** is the point at which members of society buy into their own exploitation and subordination, and become uncritical tools of production and consumption. More contemporary concepts referring to similar phenomena are: *domestication, mystification of reality, dysconsciousness, anesthetized, the social construction of not seeing, manufactured consent,* and *colonization of the mind.*

dience function as pedagogies in the sense that they seemed aimed at raising the consciousness of those willing to pay heed. His concern, unquestionably, was with his "private state" rather than with a public space; but he helped create the alternative tradition in the United States at a moment of expansion and materialism. And there are strands of his thinking, even today, that can be woven into a critical pedagogy. Whether building his house, hoeing his beans, hunting woodchucks, or finding patterns in the ice melting on the wall, he was intent on *naming* his lived world.

There were more overtly rebellious figures among escaped slaves, abolitionists, and campaigners for women's rights; but the language of people like Frederick Douglass, Harriet Tubman, Sarah Grimke, Susan B. Anthony, and Elizabeth Cady Stanton was very much the language of those who carried on the original demand for independence. The power they sought, however, was not the power to expand and control. For them — slaves, oppressed women, freedmen and freedwomen — the idea of freedom as endowment solved little; they had to take action to *achieve* their freedom, which they saw as the power to act and to choose. Thomas Jefferson, years before, had provided the metaphor of *polis* for Americans, signifying a space where persons could come together to bring into being the "worldly structure" spoken of above. Great romantics like Emerson and Thoreau gave voice to the passion for autonomy and authenticity. Black leaders, including Douglass, W. E. B. Du Bois, the Reverend Martin Luther King, Jr., and Malcolm X, not only engaged dialectically with the resistant environment in their pursuit of freedom; they invented languages and pedagogies to enable people to overcome **internalized oppression.**[d] Struggling for their rights in widening public spheres, they struggled also against what the Reverend King called "nobodiness" as they marched and engaged in a civil disobedience grounded in experiences of the past. Du Bois was in many ways exemplary when he spoke of the "vocation" of twentieth-century youth. Attacking the industrial system "which creates poverty and the children of poverty . . . ignorance and disease and crime," he called for "young women and young men of devotion to lift again the banner of humanity and to walk toward a civilization which will be free and intelligent, which will be healthy and unafraid."[14] The words hold intimations of what Paulo Freire was to say years later when he, too, spoke of the "vocation" of oppressed people, one he identified with "humanization."[15] And the very notion of walking "toward a civilization" suggests the sense of future possibility without which a pedagogy must fail.

Public school teachers, subordinated as they were in the solidifying educational bureaucracies, seldom spoke the language of resistance or transcendence. It is well to remember, however, the courageous ones who dared to go

[d] **Internalized oppression** occurs when a member(s) of an oppressed group, after a period of abuse and criticism, comes to believe the dominant group's description of them as "inferior."

south after the Civil War in the freedmen's schools. Not only did they suffer persecution in their efforts to invent their own "pedagogy of the oppressed" — or of the newly liberated; they often fought for their own human rights against male missionary administrators and even against the missionary concept itself.[16] It is well to remember, too, the transformation of the missionary impulse into settlement house and social work by women like Jane Addams and Lillian Wald. Committing themselves to support systems and adult education for newcomers to the country and for the neighborhood poor, they supported union organizations with an explicitly political awareness of what they were about in a class-ridden society. They were able, more often than not, to avoid what Freire calls "malefic generosity" and develop the critical empathy needed for enabling the "other" to find his or her own way.

For all the preoccupations with control, for all the schooling "to order," as David Nasaw puts it,[17] there were always people hostile to regimentation and manipulation, critical of constraints of consciousness. Viewed from a contemporary perspective, for example, Colonel Francis Parker's work with teachers at the Cook County Normal School at the end of the nineteenth century placed a dramatic emphasis on freeing children from competitive environments and compulsions. He encouraged the arts and spontaneous activities; he encouraged shared work. He believed that, if democratized, the school could become "the one central means by which the great problem of human liberty is to be worked out."[18] Trying to help teachers understand the natural learning processes of the young, he was specifically concerned with resisting the corruptions and distortions of an increasingly corporate America. In the Emersonian tradition, he envisioned a sound community life emerging from the liberation and regeneration of individuals. And indeed, there were many libertarians and romantic progressives following him in the presumption that a society of truly free individuals would be a humane and sustaining one.

This confidence may account for the contradictions in the American critical heritage, especially as it informed education within and outside the schools. Structural changes, if mentioned at all, were expected to follow the emancipation of persons (or the appropriate molding of persons); and the schools, apparently depoliticized, were relied upon to effect the required reform and bring about a better world. If individual children were properly equipped for the work they had to do, it was believed, and trained to resist the excesses of competition, there would be no necessity for political action to transform economic relations. The street children, the tenement children, those afflicted and crippled by poverty and social neglect, were often thrust into invisibility because their very existence denied that claim.

John Dewey was aware of such young people, certainly in Chicago, where he saw them against his own memories of face-to-face community life in Burlington, Vermont. Convinced of the necessity for cooperation and community support if individual powers were to be released, he tried in some sense to recreate the Burlington of his youth in the "miniature community" he hoped to see in each classroom.[19] In those classrooms as well, there would be continuing and open communication, the kind of learning that would feed into practice, and inquiries arising out of questioning in the midst of life. Critical thinking modeled on the scientific method, active and probing intelligence: these, for Dewey, were the stuff of a pedagogy that would equip the young to resist fixities and stock responses, repressive and deceiving authorities. Unlike the libertarians and romantics, he directed attention to the "social medium" in which the individual growth occurred and to the mutuality of significant concerns.

Even as we question the small-town paradigm in Dewey's treatment of community, even as we wonder about his use of the scientific model for social inquiry, we still ought to be aware of Dewey's sensitivity to what would later be called the **"hegemony,"**[e] or the ideological control, implicit in the dominant point of view of a given society. He understood, for instance, the "religious aureole" protecting institutions like the Supreme Court, the Constitution, and private property. He was aware that the principles and assumptions that gave rise even to public school curricula were so taken for granted that they were considered wholly natural, fundamentally unquestionable. In *The Public and Its Problems,* he called what we think of as ideological control a "social pathology," which "works powerfully against effective inquiry into social institutions and conditions." He went on, "It manifests itself in a thousand ways: in querulousness, in impotent drifting, in uneasy snatching at distractions, in idealization of the long established, in a facile optimism assumed as a cloak, in riotous glorification of things 'as they are,' in intimidation of all dissenters — ways which depress and dissipate thought all the more effectually because they operate with subtle and unconscious pervasiveness."[20] A method of social inquiry had to be developed, he said, to reduce the "pathology" that led to denial and to acquiescence in the status quo. For all his commitment to scientific method, however, he stressed the "human function" of the physical sciences and the importance of seeing them in human terms. Inquiry, communication, "contemporary and quotidian" knowledge of consequence for shared social life: these fed into his conceptions of pedagogy.

His core concern for individual fulfillment was rooted in a recognition that fulfillment could only be attained in the midst of "associated" or intersubjective life. Troubled as we must be fifty years later by the "eclipse of the public," he saw as one of the prime pedagogical tasks the education of an "articulate public." For him, the public sphere came into being when the consequences of certain private transactions created a common interest among people, one

[e] **Hegemony**, as derived from the work of Italian theorist Antonio Gramsci, is used to express how certain groups manage to dominate others. An analysis of hegemony is especially concerned with how the imposition of particular ideologies and forms of authority results in the reproduction of social and institutional practices through which dominant groups maintain not only their positions of privilege and control, but also the consensual support of other members of society.

that demanded deliberate and cooperative action. Using somewhat different language, we might say that a public emerges when people come freely together in speech and action to take *care* of something that needs caring for, to repair some evident deficiency in their common world. We might think of homelessness as a consequence of the private dealings of landlords, an arms build-up as a consequence of corporate decisions, racial exclusion as a consequence of a private property-holder's choice. And then we might think of what it would mean to educate to the end of caring for something and taking action to repair. That would be *public* education informed by a critical pedagogy; and it would weave together a number of American themes.

Certain of these themes found a new articulation in the 1930s, during the publication of *The Social Frontier* at Teachers College. An educational journal, it was addressed "to the task of considering the broad role of education in advancing the welfare and interests of the great masses of the people who do the work of society . . . those who labor on farms and ships and in the mines, shops, and factories of the world."[21] Dewey was among the contributors; and, although it had little impact on New Deal policy or even on specific educational practices, the magazine did open out to a future when more and more "liberals" would take a critical view of monopoly capitalism and industrial culture with all their implications for a supposedly "common" school.

In some respect, this represented a resurgence of the Enlightenment faith. Rational insight and dialogue, linked to scientific intelligence, were expected to reduce inequities and exploitation. A reconceived educational effort would advance the welfare and interests of the masses. Ironically, it was mainly in the private schools that educational progressivism had an influence. Critical discussions took place there; attention was paid to the posing of worthwhile problems arising out of the tensions and uncertainties of everyday life; social intelligence was nurtured; social commitments affirmed. In the larger domains of public education, where school people were struggling to meet the challenges of mass education, the emphasis tended to be on "life-adjustment," preparation for future life and work, and "physical, mental, and emotional health."

There is irony in the fact that the progressive social vision, with its integrating of moral with epistemic concerns, its hopes for a social order transformed by the schools, was shattered by the Second World War. The terrible revelations at Auschwitz and Hiroshima demonstrated what could happen when the old dream of knowledge as power was finally fulfilled. Science was viewed as losing its innocence in its wedding to advanced technology. Bureaucracy, with all its impersonality and literal irresponsibility, brought with it almost unrecognizable political and social realities. It took time, as is well known, for anything resembling a progressive vision to reconstitute itself; there was almost no recognition of the role now being played by "instrumental rationality,"[22] or what it would come to signify. On the educational side, after the war, there were efforts to remake curriculum in the light of new inquiries into knowledge structures in the disciplinary fields. On the side of the general public, there were tax revolts and rejections of the critical and the controversial, even as the McCarthyite subversion was occurring in the larger world. Only a few years after the Sputnik panic, with the talent searches it occasioned, and the frantic encouragement of scientific training, the long-invisible poor of America suddenly took center stage. The Civil Rights Movement, taking form since the Supreme Court decision on integration in 1954, relit flames of critical pedagogy, as it set people marching to achieve their freedom and their human rights.

Viewed from the perspective of a critical tradition in this country, the 1960s appear to have brought all the latent tendencies to the surface. The civil rights movement, alive with its particular traditions of liberation, provided the spark; the war in Vietnam gave a lurid illumination to the system's deficiencies: its incipient violence; its injustices; its racism; its indifference to public opinion and demand. The short-lived effort to reform education and provide compensation for damages done by poverty and discrimination could not halt the radical critique of America's schools. And that many-faceted critique — libertarian, Marxist, romantic, democratic — variously realized the critical potentialities of American pedagogies. Without an Emerson or a Thoreau or a Parker, there would not have been a Free School movement or a "deschooling" movement. Without a Du Bois, there would not have been liberation or storefront schools. Without a social reformist tradition, there would have been no Marxist voices asking (as, for instance, Samuel Bowles and Herbert Gintis did) for a "mass-based organization of working people powerfully articulating a clear alternative to corporate capitalism as the basis for a progressive educational system."[23] Without a Dewey, there would have been little concern for "participatory democracy," for "consensus," for the reconstitution of a public sphere.

Yes, the silence fell at the end of the following decade; privatization increased, along with consumerism and cynicism and the attrition of the public space. We became aware of living in what Europeans called an "administered society";[24] we became conscious of technicism and **positivism**[f] and of the one-dimensionality Herbert Marcuse described.[25] Popular culture, most particularly as embodied in the media, was recognized (with the help of the critical theorist Theodor Adorno) as a major source of mystification.[26] The

[f] Associated with the Enlightenment and modernism, **positivism** refers to a belief system or paradigm that makes claims to objectivity, truth, and certainty in defense of a scientific basis for the study of culture. As such, knowledge and reason are seen as neutral and universal, rather than as social constructions that reflect particular interests and ideologies. This uncritical call to science has resulted in an obsession with finding and using the "right" technique to understand a phenomenon or solve a problem. For example, "technocratic" models, which conceptualize teaching as a discrete and scientific undertaking, embrace depersonalized methods for educating students that often translate into the regulation and standardization of teacher practices and curricula, and rote memorization of selected "facts" that can easily be measured through standardized testing. As such, the role of the teacher is reduced to that of an uncritical, "objective," and "efficient" distributor of information.

schools were recognized as agents of **"cultural reproduction,"**[g] oriented to a differential distribution of knowledge.[27] Numerous restive educational thinkers, seeking new modes of articulating the impacts of ideological control and manipulation, turned towards European neo-Marxist scholarship for clues to a critical pedagogy. In an American tradition, they were concerned for the individual, for the subject, which late Marxism appeared to have ignored; and the humanist dimension of **Frankfurt School**[h] philosophies held an unexpected appeal. Moreover, what with its concern for critical consciousness and communicative competence, Frankfurt School thinking held echoes of the Enlightenment faith; and, in some profound way, it was recognized.

There is, of course, an important sense in which the Frankfurt School has reappropriated philosophical traditions (Kantian, Hegelian, phenomenological, psychological, psychoanalytical) which are ours as well or which, at least, have fed our intellectual past. But it also seems necessary to hold in mind the fact that European memories are not our memories. The sources of European critical theory are to be found in responses to the destruction of the Workers' Councils after the First World War, the decline of the Weimar Republic, the rise of Stalinism, the spread of fascism, the Holocaust, the corruptions of social democracy. As climactic as any contemporary insight was the realization that reason (viewed as universal in an Enlightenment sense) could be used to justify the application of technical expertise in torture and extermination. Europeans saw a connection between this and the rationalization of society by means of bureaucracy, and in the separating off of moral considerations long viewed as intrinsic to civilized life. The intimations of all this could be seen in European literature for many years: in Dostoevsky's and Kafka's renderings of human beings as insects; in Musil's anticipations of the collapse of European orders; in Camus's pestilence, in Sartre's nausea, in the Dionysian and bestial shapes haunting the structures of the arts. We have had a tragic literature, a critical literature, in the United States. We need only recall Twain, Melville, Crane, Wharton, Hemingway, Fitzgerald. But it has been a literature rendered tragic by a consciousness of a dream betrayed, of a New World corrupted by exploitation and materialism and greed. In background memory, there are images of Jeffersonian agrarianism, of public spheres, of democratic

[g] Critical social theorists argue that dominant ideologies and knowledge are built into social institutions that both privilege and exclude particular perspectives, voices, authorities, and representations. Within theories of **cultural reproduction**, schools, educators, and curricula are generally viewed as mechanisms of ideological control that work to reproduce and maintain dominant beliefs, values, norms, and oppressive practices. This reproductive process is mediated, in part, through the "hidden curriculum" — the hidden agenda of maintaining the status quo through specific schooling practices.

[h] This German institute of social research, frequented by the likes of Marcuse, Fromm, Horkheimer, Adorno, Habermas, Arendt, Brecht, Lukacs, and a great many others, had an enormous impact on the sociological, political, and cultural thought of this century. It was in this institute that the term "critical theory" and its ideas evolved.

and free-swinging communities. We do not find these in European literature, *nor* in the writings of the critical theorists.

One of the few explicit attempts to articulate aspects of the Western tradition for educators has been the courageous work of Freire, who stands astride both hemispheres. He has been the pioneer of a pedagogy informed by both Marxist and existential-phenomenological thought; his conception of critical reflectiveness has reawakened the themes of a tradition dating back to Plato and forward to the theologies of liberation that have taken hold in oppressed areas of the Western world. His background awareness, however, and that of the largely Catholic peasants with whom he has worked, are not that of most North Americans. It must be granted that his own culture and education transcend his Brazilian origins and make him something of a world citizen when it comes to the life of ideas. Like his European colleagues, however, he reaches back to predecessors other than Jefferson and Emerson and Thoreau and William James and Dewey; his social vision is not that of our particular democracy. This is not intended as criticism, but as a reminder that a critical pedagogy relevant to the United States today must go beyond — calling on different memories, repossessing another history.

We live, after all, in dark times, times with little historical memory of any kind. There are vast dislocations in industrial towns, erosions of trade unions; there is little sign of class consciousness today. Our great cities are burnished on the surfaces, building high technologies, displaying astonishing consumer goods. And on the side streets, in the crevices, in the burnt-out neighborhoods, there are the rootless, the dependent, the sick, the permanently unemployed. There is little sense of agency, even among the brightly successful; there is little capacity to look at things as if they could be otherwise.

Where education is concerned, the discourse widens, and the promises multiply. The official reform reports, ranging from *A Nation at Risk* to the Carnegie Forum's *A Nation Prepared,* call for a restructuring of schools and of teacher education to the end of raising the levels of literacy in accord with the requirements of an economy based on high technology.[28] The mass of students in the schools, including the one-third who will be "minorities," are to be enabled to develop "higher order skills" in preparation for "the unexpected, the nonroutine world they will face in the future."[29] The implicit promise is that, if the quality of teachers is improved (and "excellent" teachers rewarded and recognized), the majority of young people will be equipped for meaningful participation in an advanced knowledge-based economy wholly different from the mass-production economy familiar in the past.

On the other hand, there are predictions that we will never enjoy full employment in this country, that few people stand any real chance of securing meaningful work. If the military juggernaut keeps rolling on, draining funds and support from social utilities, daycare centers, arts institutions, schools and universities, we will find ourselves devoid of all those things that might make life healthier, gentler, more inviting, and more challenging. At once we are reminded (although not by the authors of the educational reports) of the dread of nuclear destruction (or of Chernobyls, or of Bhopal) that lies below the surface of apparent hope for the future. This dread, whether repressed or confronted, leads numbers of people to a sense of fatalism and futility with respect to interventions in the social world. For others, it leads to a sad and often narcissistic focus on the "now." For still others, it evokes denial and accompanying extravagances: consumerism increases; a desire for heightened sensation, for vicarious violence, grows. And for many millions, it makes peculiarly appealing the talk of salvation broadcast by evangelists and television preachers; it makes seductive the promise of Armageddon.

As young people find it increasingly difficult to project a long-range future, intergenerational continuity becomes problematic. So does the confidence in education as a way of keeping the culture alive, or of initiating newcomers into learning communities, or of providing the means for pursuing a satisfying life. Uncertain whether we can share or constitute a common world, except in its most fabricated and trivialized form, we wonder what the great conversation can now include and whether it is worth keeping alive. Michael Oakeshott spoke eloquently of that conversation, "begun in the primeval forests and extended and made more articulate in the course of centuries." He said it involves passages of argument and inquiry, going on in public and in private, that it is an "unrehearsed intellectual adventure. . . ." Education, for him, "is an initiation into the skill and partnership of this conversation," which gives character in the end "to every human activity and utterance."[30] We know now how many thousands of voices have been excluded from that conversation over the years. We know how, with its oppositions and hierarchies, it demeaned. As we listen to the prescriptions raining down for "common learnings" (which may or may not include the traditions of people of color, feminist criticism and literature, Eastern philosophies) and "cultural literacy," we cannot but wonder how those of us in education can renew and expand the conversation, reconstitute what we can call a common world.

Yes, there are insights into humane teaching in the latest reports; but, taking the wide view, we find mystification increasing, along with the speechlessness. We have learned about the diverse ways we Americans interpret our traditions: about those who identify with the old individualism, those who yearn for old communities, those who seek new modes of justice, those who want to lose themselves in a cause.[31] We know something about the persistence of a commitment to freedom, variously defined, and to the idea of equity. At once, we are bound to confront such extremes as a moral majority usurping talk of intimacy and family values, while neoliberals seek out technocratic, depersonalized solutions to quantified problems and speak a cost-benefit language beyond the reach of those still striving for public dialogue.

People have never, despite all that, had such vast amounts of information transmitted to them — not merely about murders and accidents and scandals, but about crucial matters on which public decisions may some day have to be made: nuclear energy, space vehicles, racism, homelessness, life-support systems, chemotherapies, joblessness, terrorism, abused children, fanatics, saints. There are whole domains of information that arouse frustration or pointless outrage. All we need to do is think of the persecution of the sanctuary-movement leaders, of children living in shelters, of the *contras* in Honduras, of adolescent suicides, of overcrowded jails. At the same time, no population has ever been so deliberately entertained, amused, and soothed into avoidance, denial, and neglect. We hear the cacophonous voices of special interest groups; we hear of discrete acts of sacrifice and martyrdom; we seldom hear of intentionally organized collaborative action to repair what is felt to be missing, or known to be wrong.

Complacency and malaise; upward mobility and despair. Sometimes we detect feelings of shame and helplessness perceived as personal failure. To be dependent, to be on welfare, is to be certified as in some manner deviant or irresponsible since good Americans are expected to fend for themselves. Even as oppressed peasants internalize their oppressors' images of them as helpless creatures, so unsuccessful Americans (young or old) internalize the system's description of them as ineffectual. They are unable to live up to the culture's mandate to control their own lives and contribute to the productivity of the whole. Our institutional responses are ordinarily technical (and we are drawn to technical solutions out of benevolence, as well as out of helplessness). Yet we know that to think mainly in terms of techniques or cures or remedies is often to render others and the earth itself as objects to be acted upon, treated, controlled, or used. It is to distance what we believe has to be done (efficiently, effectively) from our own existential projects, from our own becoming among other incomplete and questing human beings. It is to repress or deny the prereflective, tacit understandings that bind us together in a culture and connect us to our history.

Having said all this, I must ask again what a critical pedagogy might mean for those of us who teach the young at this peculiar and menacing time. Perhaps we might begin by releasing our imaginations and summoning up the traditions of freedom in which most of us were reared. We might try to make audible again the recurrent calls for justice and equality. We might reactivate the resistance to materialism and conformity. We might even try to inform with meaning the desire to educate "all the children" in a legitimately "common" school. Considering the technicism and the illusions of the time, we need to recognize that what we single out as most deficient and oppressive is in part a function of perspectives created by our past. It is a past in which our subjectivities are embedded, whether we are conscious of it or not. We have reached a point when that past must be reinterpreted and reincarnated in the light of what we have learned.

We understand that a mere removal of constraints or a mere relaxation of controls will not ensure the emergence of free and creative human beings. We understand that the freedom we cherish is not an endowment, that it must be achieved through dialectical engagements with the social and economic obstacles we find standing in our way, those we have to learn to name. We understand that a plurality of American voices must be attended to, that a plurality of life-stories must be heeded if a meaningful power is to spring up through a new "binding and promising, combining and covenanting." We understand that the Enlightenment heritage must be repossessed and reinterpreted, so that we can overcome the positivism that awaits on one side, the empty universalism on the other. But we cannot and ought not escape our own history and memories, not if we are to keep alive the awarenesses that ground our identities and connect us to the persons turning for fulfillment to our schools.

We cannot negate the fact of power. But we can undertake a resistance, a reaching out towards becoming *persons* among other persons, for all the talk of human resources, for all the orienting of education to the economy. To engage with our students as persons is to affirm our own incompleteness, our consciousness of spaces still to be explored, desires still to be tapped, possibilities still to be opened and pursued. At once, it is to rediscover the value of care, to reach back to experiences of caring and being cared for (as Nel Noddings writes) as sources of an ethical ideal. It is, Noddings says, an ideal to be nurtured through "dialogue, practice, and confirmation," processes much akin to those involved in opening a public sphere.[32] We have to find out how to open such spheres, such spaces, where a better state of things can be imagined; because it is only through the projection of a better social order that we can perceive the gaps in what exists and try to transform and repair. I would like to think that this can happen in classrooms, in corridors, in schoolyards, in the streets around.

I would like to think of teachers moving the young into their own interpretations of their lives and their lived worlds, opening wider and wider perspectives as they do so. I would like to see teachers ardent in their efforts to make the range of symbol systems available to the young for the ordering of experience, even as they maintain regard for their vernaculars. I would like to see teachers tapping the spectrum of intelligences, encouraging multiple readings of written texts and readings of the world.

In "the shadow of silent majorities," then, as teachers learning along with those we try to provoke to learn, we may be able to inspire hitherto unheard voices. We may be able to empower people to rediscover their own memories and articulate them in the presence of others, whose space they can share. Such a project demands the capacity to unveil and disclose. It demands the exercise of imagination, enlivened by works of art, by situations of speaking and making. Perhaps we can at last devise reflective communities in the interstices of colleges and schools. Perhaps we can invent ways of freeing people to feel and express indignation, to break through the opaqueness, to refuse the silences. We need to teach in such a way as to arouse passion now and then; we need a new camaraderie, a new en masse. These are dark and shadowed times, and we need to live them, standing before one another, open to the world.

Notes

1. Jean Baudrillard, *In the Shadow of Silent Majorities* (New York: Semiotexte, 1983).
2. Jean-Paul Sartre, *Search for a Method* (New York: Knopf, 1968), p. 94.
3. Walt Whitman, *Leaves of Grass* (New York: Aventine Press, 1931), pp. 49–50.
4. Wallace Stevens, *Collected Poems* (New York: Knopf, 1963), p. 198.
5. Marianne Moore, *Tell Me, Tell Me* (New York: Viking Press, 1966), p. 24.
6. Muriel Rukeyser, "Käthe Kollwitz," in *By a Woman Writt,* ed. Joan Goulianos (New York: Bobbs Merrill, 1973), p. 374.
7. Adrienne Rich, *A Wild Patience Has Taken Me This Far* (New York: Norton, 1981), p. 23.
8. John Stuart Mill, "On Liberty," in *The Six Great Humanistic Essays* (New York: Washington Square Press, 1963), p. 158.
9. Hannah Arendt, *On Revolution* (New York: Viking Press, 1963), pp. 174–175.
10. Horace Mann, "Ninth Annual Report," in *The Republic and the School: Horace Mann on the Education of Free Men,* ed. Lawrence A. Cremin (New York: Teachers College Press, 1957), p. 57.
11. Mark Twain, *The adventures of Huckleberry Finn* (New York: New American Library, 1959), p. 283.
12. Orestes Brownson, "The Laboring Classes," in *Ideology and Power in the Age of Jackson,* ed. Edwin C. Rozwenc (Garden City, NY: Anchor Books, 1964), p. 321.
13. Ralph Waldo Emerson, "Self-Reliance," in *Emerson on Education,* ed. Howard Mumford Jones (New York: Teachers College Press, 1966), p. 105.
14. W. E. B. Du Bois, *W. E. B. Du Bois: A Reader,* ed. Meyer Weinberg (New York: Harper Torchbooks, 1970), pp. 153–154.
15. Paulo Freire, *Pedagogy of the Oppressed* (New York: Continuum, 1970), pp. 27 ff.
16. Jacqueline Jones, "Women Who Were More Than Men: Sex and Status in Freedmen's Teaching," *History of Education Quarterly, 19* (1979), 47–59.
17. David Nasaw, *Schooled to Order* (New York: Oxford University Press, 1981).
18. Colonel Francis Parker, *Talks on Pedagogics* (New York: Harper, 1894).
19. John Dewey, "The School and Society," in *Dewey on Education,* ed. Martin Dworkin (New York: Teachers College Press, 1959), p. 41.
20. John Dewey, *The Public and Its Problems* (Athens, OH: Swallow Press, 1954).
21. Lawrence A. Cremin, *The Transformation of the School* (New York: Knopf, 1961), pp. 231–232.
22. Jürgen Habermas, *Knowledge and Human Interests* (Boston: Beacon Press, 1972).
23. Samuel Bowles and Herbert Gintis, *Schooling in Capitalist America* (New York: Basic Books, 1976), p. 266.
24. Herbert Marcuse, "Some Social Implications of Modern Technology," in *The Essential Frankfurt School Reader,* ed. Andrew Arato and Eike Gebhardt (New York: Urizen Books, 1978), pp. 138–162.
25. Herbert Marcuse, *One-Dimensional Man* (Boston: Beacon Press, 1966).
26. Theodor Adorno, "Cultural Criticism and Society," in *Prisms* (London: Neville Spearman, 1961), pp. 31–32 ff.
27. See Pierre Boudieu and Jean-Claude Passeron, *Reproduction* (Beverly Hills: Sage, 1977).
28. The National Commission on Excellence in Education, *A Nation at Risk: The Imperative for Educational Reform* (Washington: U.S. Department of Education, 1983); and Carnegie Forum on Education and the Economy, *A Nation Prepared: Teachers for the 21st Century* (New York: Carnegie Forum, 1986).
29. Carnegie Forum, *A Nation Prepared,* p. 25.
30. Michael Oakeshott, *Rationalism in Politics and Other Essays* (London: Methuen, 1962), pp. 198–199.

31. Robert N. Bellah, Richard Madsen, William M. Sullivan, Ann Swidler, and Steve M. Tipton, *Habits of the Heart: Individualism and Commitment in American Life* (Berkeley: University of California Press, 1985).
32. Nel Noddings, *Caring: A Feminine Approach to Ethics and Moral Education* (Berkeley: University of California Press, 1984).

PART I

Insurrectionary Generation

"The Discipline of the Radical Alternative"

PART I

Insurrectionary Generation

"The Discipline of the Radical Alternative"

The four articles in this section invite readers to consider the power and potential of our nation's youth to bring about change. Students rarely factor into the current dominant discourse of school reform; when they do, it is generally with a narrow emphasis on their "achievement" as measured by performance on high-stakes tests. Even when achievement is coupled with a consideration of student voice and power, the conversation is overwhelmingly focused on how educators can give voice to and empower students—where schools, administrators, and teachers are assumed to be the agents of change on behalf of young people. In this section, we see that students already have voice and power and need not wait for either to be given to them. The authors remind us that it is young people themselves who have the greatest potential to reform the educational landscape, and it is with them that power and hope reside. In the articles and interview that follow, youth acquire the discipline and political consciousness necessary to act collectively, reflect critically, and make demands for an authentic educational and social transformation.

Reflecting Maxine Greene's call for humane and relevant education, Jay Gillen's 2009 essay introduces "the discipline of the radical alternative" by asserting that young people are "constitutionally romantic . . . visionaries not yet sure where they are going but with determination to create and establish new institutions of equity and justice." Considering whether the election of Barack Obama will spur change in education, Gillen argues that change will only come when it is called for by youth living in poverty—the "insurrectionary generation." Through comparisons to slavery and the "march toward freedom," Gillen argues that young people have the power to demand a radical alternative to traditional schooling and that the insurgency toward true democracy is beginning to surface in their demands for more equitable education.

Capturing such a demand for equity, the second piece in this section demonstrates the power of insurrection through a 1972 interview with Arthur Thomas, who was the director of the Center for the Study of Student Citizenship, Rights, and Responsibilities in Dayton, Ohio. Thomas describes helping young people and their families understand and mobilize against the dehumanizing treatment and oppression of Black children in schools. Such alliance between youth and adults is also central to the third article, in which Nancy Murray and Marco Garrido describe Project HIP-HOP (Highways into the Past: History, Organizing and Power) and the program's 1994 summer journey from Boston to key sites of the civil rights movement in the South. An organizer and a youth participant respectively, these authors tell a moving story of transformation as youth discover themselves, one another, and the power of individuals to ignite civic change against injustice.

Finally, in an article from 1996, Wendy Ormiston presents a transformative struggle for equity championed by a small group of college students. Fighting against the university to bring a transgender speaker to commencement, Ormiston reflects on the oppression of a system that imposes diametrical binary definitions of male and female.

Together, these four pieces demonstrate the potential, the curiosity, and the boldness of young people as they acquire the discipline and the critical consciousness required to ignite an insurrection and demand the recognition of their humanity.

An Insurrectionary Generation

Young People, Poverty, Education, and Obama

JAY GILLEN

> Democracies require earned insurrections.
>
> *Robert Moses, 2007*

The extent to which an Obama presidency changes American education will be determined by young people in poverty. They are still far from equal, and far from free. There is no place for them to participate in the decisions that affect their lives, as there was no place for sharecroppers in the racist South. Their struggle for freedom and dignity is not different from but is a part of the unfinished, many-sided struggle that made the election of a black president possible.

Consider the status of poor students. The following list describes widespread strategies for managing working-class young people in public schools, but it comes almost verbatim from historian Vincent Harding's (1981) description of how the slave system treated human beings. I have replaced Harding's *slaves* with *students* and *master* with *school*, and have marked one additional change in italics:

1. The establishment of strict discipline over the students; the development of unconditional submission.
2. The development within the students of a sense of personal inferiority, especially in relation to their *ancestry, economic status, and maturity.*[1]
3. The development of raw fear, to awe them with a sense of the school's enormous power (Of course, behind the power of the school stands the power of local and national government.)
4. The establishment within the students of a sense that the school's welfare is really synonymous with their own.

5. The creation of a willingness within the students to accept the school's standards of conduct as their own.
6. The development within the students of a habit of perfect dependence upon those who claim to be their masters. (pp. 105–106)

The purpose of these strategies is to convince the oppressed that freedom is both too much to ask for and too much to handle. In strikingly similar arguments, racists in the past asserted the impracticality of black freedom, just as schooling today asserts the impracticality of freedom for youth. Schools proclaim young people's dangerous wildness, especially the wildness of young people in poverty; they cannot be trusted because they are undisciplined, morally and intellectually immature, overly emotional, hypersexual, and lacking in self-control. What can no longer be said openly of a race is not at all unacceptable to say of adolescents, and adolescents in poverty are particularly vulnerable to the mistreatment that results. Money protects middle-class and wealthier youth, who are able to tolerate an extended dependency for at least a decade past puberty if they have enough stimulation, amusement, food, phones, and cars. But poor youth, for whom survival is a pressing issue, experience something much closer to the oppression of slavery; they are continually treated like children by schools, while being monitored as dangerous and threatening. They are neither autonomous nor protected. Commanded, they must obey. If they choose not to obey, they risk literal starvation, homelessness, or shackles in prison. They are far from free.

Many of my students are not sure when they will eat next and worry that they will have nowhere to sleep at night. Many have already been to jail and know others who are either locked up now or constantly under threat of imprisonment. These are not abstract or theoretical insecurities. Life is tenuous in poverty. Life expectancy in Baltimore's poorest neighborhood is twenty years below life expectancy in the city's richest (Baltimore City Health Department, 2008). The fear of dying is real at the subsistence levels of poverty, and this fear gives leverage to schooling's strategies of control.

Young people—sixteen, seventeen, or eighteen years old—are, however, physically and intellectually capable of self-reliance. Fifty years ago many adolescents could leave school even before graduation and begin to earn enough money to survive. A high school diploma, showing little more than rudimentary literacy, was sufficient for employment that could support a family. But the technological revolution has ruined economic opportunity for older adolescents. Decent employment now requires many years of education beyond minimal literacy, resulting in the extended childhood of middle-class and wealthier youth subsidized all the way into their mid-twenties. But young people in poverty have no subsidy and find themselves trapped: treated as children but without the economic support children need to survive; too badly educated to earn a real living but too poor to afford to stay in school.

This economic problem, combined with the partial success of the freedom struggle, makes education the political battleground it is today. Before the Second World War, school issues were simpler, both because the American caste system allowed fewer options to the poor and because lack of education was a much less significant barrier to employment. Now, however, the pressure on education is extreme. Each family seeks good schools to try to prepare its children for employment and to avoid disintegration and dislocation. But the country, too, uses the promise of educational opportunity as its safety valve for preserving the appearance of equality. Without our paying lip service to equal educational opportunity, the caste system would be officially impermeable; we imagine that caste is not absolutely determined by birth only because of the potential for public education to create social mobility. Of course, education as it exists today alleviates none of the economic peril in poor communities and moves relatively few children out of poverty. President Obama's own private schooling and the private school he has chosen for his daughters are small reminders that the promise of equal opportunity through public education is not yet realized. But we draw up our battle lines based on whom we blame for this fact.

Brown v. Board of Education marks the ironic turning point. From Reconstruction until 1954, the principle that public education was the responsibility of government was widely accepted. If schools for different races were separate and unequal, the authorities were clearly to blame. Since 1954, however, this certainty has blurred, and the argument that education is largely the responsibility of parents is now widespread. Blaming parents for educational failure is, in fact, the caste system's evolutionary adaptation to *Brown*. It is now second nature to us, a part of our consensus as a people, that parents of sufficient means will move their families to wealthier jurisdictions with better schools—schools, and often the jurisdictions themselves, created by white flight in response to legally enforced desegregation. If parents cannot afford these wealthier jurisdictions and better schools, well, this is America: Whose fault is it but theirs? And don't they have their own public schools in the urban jurisdictions left behind? Nothing prevents poor parents from involving themselves passionately in their children's schools as wealthier parents do. If poor parents cared, their children would learn.

Charter schools, vouchers, school choice, and the shadow system of private education all lend themselves to the same argument: parents as individual agents determine the quality of their child's education, not the collective agency of a people united by common purpose and principles. Defenders of public schools cling to the unifying promise of *Brown* despite the country's geographic resegregation by caste, but parental choice is an extremely powerful, if ultimately circular, argument. Parents *rightly* bear responsibility for their children's education; families *should* be free to live where they choose. The circularity is just that of inherited caste: where families choose to live depends on their wealth; their wealth depends on what they inherit and on what they earn; what they earn depends largely on the quality of education they received; the quality of education they received depends on where their family chose to live or could afford to send them to school.

Bob Moses (2008) succinctly summarizes how public accommodations were extricated from the caste system through the student sit-ins in the early 1960s. Access to electoral power was extricated from the caste system through the voting rights movement and the opening up of the Democratic Party (developments of which President Obama is the clear beneficiary). But the system of public education has yet to be extricated from the caste system and is bound to it with the same cords and same tension that bind parents to their children and to their children's children.[2]

Neither parents nor government will untie these knots. The educational system will not be pried apart from the caste system by adults. But young people in poverty inherit a legacy of struggle that one day they will claim. An insurrectionary generation will challenge the caste system for the same reason that insurrectionary generations have challenged the caste system before: human beings do not lightly accept subjugation, and the young cannot bear insults. As they change from children to adults, adolescents naturally, biologically, experience an awakening of consciousness, an awareness that the world is bigger than it seemed to them before, that the horizon is wider, that their own powers are greater, that possibilities and openings are more numerous and more meaningful. This puzzles them, and the new landscape frightens some into accepting submission. But many pursue the troubling, exhilarating questions. They challenge whatever contorts or limits their expanding sense of self. They ask why their parents and teachers have made or accepted such shameful arrangements. They wonder why other people their age can go here and there and enjoy this or that privilege denied them. They spend long hours thinking and talking and rhyming about freedom.

President Obama may have scaled his heights by knowing how to work inside the system and not give offense, but he acknowledges that his opportunity was won by people who gave a great deal of offense, by people who were scorned, dispossessed, disenfranchised, jailed, brutalized for fashioning the political insurrection that eventually set him free. Those earlier insurgents, often very young and often led by other young people, analyzed the strategies used to subjugate them and rebelled. They resisted the patterns Harding enumerates, choosing defiance over obedience; equality over subordination; adventure over fear; their own interests over their oppressor's interests; their own speech and song over the oppressor's lying hymns; self-reliance and reliance on each other over humiliating dependence on the master. We are wrong to teach that the time for insurrection has passed or that the strategy of bringing tension to the surface is now counterproductive. Schooling for young people in poverty uses the same strategies to crush the spirit that the slave system and the sharecropper system did before, and young people are as right today as the earlier generations of insurgents we now lionize were right to challenge the oppression of caste. Our role as older people may be to mediate to some degree, to temporize and wait for opportunities; but young people's role is certainly different. Our tame teachings alienate the idealistic, horizon-seeking center of their experience and persuade them only that we are old. They crave drama and conflict not for the thrill alone but because conflict represents externally the life-giving struggle inside them between their sense of developing power and the cold, grown-up shadows of limitations and impossibilities.

We should recall that the slaves who wanted most badly to be free were often considered by their fellow slaves to be foolhardy and self-destructive; in many cases, by unimaginative standards, those runaways and rebels accomplished nothing. We should also recall that in the 1950s and 1960s the young people who forced the discussion of civil rights out into the open were often considered by their parents and teachers to be presumptuous, dangerous, and rash. Won't any serious, idealistic challenge to our racialized caste system tempt disaster? Shouldn't that upstart Obama himself have known not to run for president, since he risked a backlash of white rage and even violence? But the world is strange and beautiful, and from time to time, reality sides with romantics against realists.

Young people are constitutionally romantic; they are biologically presumptuous, dangerous, and rash. They do not yet see as a collective how to dare their insurrection, and they have not yet earned the discipline and commitment they will need to win. But the example of Obama brings their victory nearer, not because of his caution but because of his boldness, which is an imitation of the boldness of the slaves who struggled to create new institutions of freedom and of the boldness of the young freedom fighters all over the world who resist oppression with their imagination and their love of life.

So the question of Obama's effect on education boils down to this: What lesson will young people in poverty take from his election? Will they conclude that if they only work hard in school, follow directions, test well, jump through hoops for diplomas, and quiet their more arrogant questions, then they can achieve success as President Obama has? Or will they conclude instead that the insurrectionary youth who are their ancestors were right to fight against injustice, to form alliances against oppressors, to take great risks in struggling to transform the world, and that Obama is living proof those young ancestors' insolence was fruitful, pragmatic, and wise?

There is a discipline required in both alternatives. One is the classical discipline that accepts hierarchies as they are and works to perfect the existing forms within the existing social structure. Today, unfortunately, this choice requires acceptance of the lie that the current structure is more or less the best we can do. The discipline of the radical alternative, in contrast, chooses justice and our common humanity as masters. It requires no less work, no fewer postponements of gratification; but the work is new, its forms not already molded or established. This discipline that young people must acquire to fashion their insurrection is a discipline of creation and invention and truthfulness to an ideal. It suits the age of Obama. It fits the American narrative of the march toward freedom led by visionaries not yet sure where they are going but with determination to create and establish new institutions of equity and justice.

Many young people have already begun to learn the discipline of this coming insurgency. Many more will join in because of Obama's breakthrough, possibly misinterpreting his personal classicism but sensing that he, too, is a part of the river to freedom—the river whose deepest, strongest currents overwhelm preexisting forms and make things new. The individual acts of resistance number in the millions, as in slave times: students in poverty choose not to go to school, to cut class, to drop out, to set fires, to vandalize, to defy, to disobey. But in addition to these individual acts, the developing insurgency shows itself wherever young people organize to demand an arrangement that is in their own interest rather than in the interest of the institutions that attempt to break them. These organized demands are growing in many places, and the first skirmishes have begun now all across the country: in New York, Los Angeles, Baltimore, New Orleans, Philadelphia, Miami, Denver, Chicago, Houston, Oakland, Detroit. Students organize to demand adequate funding, freedom of speech, respect for their languages and cultures, richer curriculum, the end of police brutality and of forced relocations. But the cohesiveness and thoroughness needed are not yet here. Many older people stand ready to help, but the young will determine whether change comes sooner or later. We do not yet know when they will rise up together to expose the caste system's insult to freedom, its betrayal of the learning free human beings crave. But young people in poverty will not suffer the insult forever. The day will come when they force the invention of a new education that promotes values other than dominance, values other than the dominion of the high over the low, of the high test score over the low test score, of the rich over the poor.[3] They will show us that a black president, as our new president acknowledges, represents only one current to freedom among many necessary currents and that young people's roiling of the water will play a crucial role in the eventual coming of democracy to America.

Notes

1. The last portion of Harding's original item number 2 reads, "especially in relation to their African ancestry." Harding based his list on Kenneth H. Stampp's analysis in *The Peculiar Institution* (New York: Vintage Books, 1956), pp. 144–148. Many of my arguments and my use of the river image throughout this essay are derived from Harding.
2. Robert Moses is the source of many ideas in this essay, especially the general topic of student insurrection in the context of civil rights history. See, for example, "Shaping Demand" in Moses and Cobb (2001, pp. 161–193).
3. Education that promotes values other than dominance is Bertrand Russell's notion from *Power: A New Social Analysis* (London: Allen & Unwin, 1938).

References

Baltimore City Health Department. (2008). *Neighborhood health profiles.* Retrieved January 15, 2009, from http://www.baltimorehealth.org

Harding, V. (1981). *There is a river: The black struggle for freedom in America.* New York: Harcourt Brace Jovanovich.

Moses, R. (2007, April). Keynote address made at Long Island University. *Creating balance in an unjust world.* Brooklyn, NY.

Moses, R. (2008, July). Remarks made at Jackson State University. *Raising the floor: Quality public school education as a constitutional right.* Jackson, MS.

Moses, R., and Cobb, C. (2001). *Radical equations.* Boston: Beacon Press.

Community Power and Student Rights

An Interview with Arthur E. Thomas

Law has traditionally influenced education through the precedent-setting power of key judicial decisions. The Tinker[1] *and Serrano*[2] *judgments, to name only two, have generated new concepts of what student rights and educational equality might mean. Within this framework, a citizen petitions the courts with the expectation that the decision will affect individuals across the country with similar grievances. Judicial decisions can thus be used as instruments to initiate large-scale changes in policy.*

During the past year, the Center for the Study of Student Citizenship, Rights, and Responsibilities in Dayton, Ohio has been exploring additional strategies for using the law to promote significant social and educational changes. Rather than relying on the legal profession to secure rights for others, the Center relies on the ability of students, parents, and citizens in the community to understand and use the law for themselves. This gives the phrase "taking the law into their own hands" a new meaning: by learning to handle the law, people can gain a sense of efficacy in dealing with their present situation and can envision new possibilities for their individual and collective futures. In this way, the law is transformed from an alien tool that controls and represses to a resource for self-construction and for confrontation with the social and political world.

Our interview with Dr. Arthur E. Thomas, founder and director of the Center, follows.[3]

Art Thomas himself began to teach in an elementary school in Dayton in 1962. In his first school, in the center of the Black community, he found himself faced with a conflict between his impulse to "paddle" his "disruptive" students to keep order and his desire to become involved in the concerns and lives of his students. When three years later he had become an eighth grade teacher and a coach in track and football, he had given up paddling. "I refused to believe that my eighth graders could not learn and could not behave; the results were that they did learn and that they did behave." He had begun to reconsider other things too—and began helping his students to get scholarships, to get out of jail, to think about their own futures, and to begin to "love, trust, and respect" themselves. He also instituted a series of Black History Lectures, which he was allowed to conduct after school. In 1967, he was promoted to assistant principal of MacFarlane Elementary School, where for a year he attempted to create an environment in which students and their parents could learn and could establish an atmosphere of mutual trust with teachers.

In September, 1969, when the Dayton School System began to integrate its schools, Thomas was Director of the Model Cities Education Program. He and others from both the Black and white communities had warned that sudden integration in the racially tense city would be dangerous, but the school administration persisted in sending students from an all-Black urban community to an all-white Appalachian school. Severe trouble erupted at the school and one Black student was seriously hurt. On the next day, Thomas accompanied the Black students to school and attempted to help officials and parents keep order. Informed of the possibility of more violence, school officials promised to send a bus to take the Black students home. The bus did not arrive and tensions between Black and white students increased. Hoping to avoid more physical confrontations, Thomas persuaded the Black students to walk with him to safety in the administration building. When he returned to the school to collect a few Black students who still remained there, he was arrested—along with several of the Black students. Thomas left the jail only after all the Black students were released. He was subsequently fired by the Dayton Board of Education for "exceeding his authority."

Thomas decided to appeal the Board's decision and with the help of Dr. Ruth Burgin and three lawyers—the late Mr. Charles S. Bridge, Ms. Jean Camper Cahn and Dr. Edgar Cahn, he argued his case before administrative hearings. After three months of hearings, the Board of Education ruled against him.

No longer permitted to teach and work in the public school system of Dayton, Thomas began to consider alternative strategies for continuing his work with Black and poor children in the public schools. "The night the board ruled against me, we sat down and carefully analyzed my role; Dr. and Ms. Cahn kept reminding me that I had been an advocate for the children ever since the first day I had started teaching. Ms. Cahn, who had had long conferences with parents and students in the community, told me that the children perceived me as their advocate—someone who would stand behind them to defend their rights, no matter what. She said that no genuine advocate could work effectively from within the school system, that the system tends to mediate to the point where it co-opts all positions of advocacy, and that only in the legal system is it permissible to be an advocate. We decided on an O.E.O. legal services program led by an educator."

What has been the strategy behind the Center?

The Center was developed with several strategies in mind.[4]

Our overall purpose was to educate students and parents about their human and constitutional rights as they relate to the institution called school.

This goal in itself might have led us in several directions, but we had one thing in particular that we had to deal with first. After the Dayton Board of Education and the school administration fired me, they wanted to prevent me from working with the students and parents. I was too effective from their point of view. School boards have a record of trying to eliminate teachers who seriously challenge them. They kept trying to secure court orders to bar me from the children. Therefore we—all the parents and children and lawyers who were involved—decided that we needed a way for my skills and support to be useful to the community, even if I couldn't work directly in the system.

So we chose to develop the role of parent ombudsman who would be in continuous touch with the schools—the teachers, administration, counselors—and with the children and their families. Now the important thing to note about the way this strategy developed is that, though we started out from a simple need to replace me, we've ended up with a stronger, long range strategy. For one thing, while it is relatively easy to stop one individual, it is difficult to stop a growing number of informed, determined people.

Even more important, we now have begun a process through which we have our ten ombudsmen teaching others—parents and students—in the community. We're creating a ripple effect that will prepare many people to understand and deal effectively with the types of physical and psychological violence imposed upon the children by the school system and its agents. It's impossible for community people to have a lawyer with them whenever a child is injured. Our idea is to get the students and their parents to be their own lawyers—to help them have some control over their fate.

Another strategy was to make sure that the Center would be an independent institution. Students have learned the variety of forms of oppression that come down from the school system; one of the reasons they're beginning to trust us is because they know we stand completely apart from it.

As we work now, our lawyer develops legal tactics to deal with the inequities that are pointed out by me and our ombudsmen. What we're trying to do is to make the rights guaranteed by the Constitution real to and for children. The *Tinker* decision was important for this in theory—it said that your constitutional rights don't stop at the school door. We're trying to bridge the gap between theory and practice.

But how can you explain to students about their rights?

Many children seven years old, or nine years old, or fifteen years old, don't have any idea what basic rights are all about. They don't know what a Constitution is, or what a Declaration of Independence is. They don't have a conception of a right because the school teaches them that the only right they have when they walk into a school is to sit down and do as they are told. As the Cahns[5] point out, this situation affects the child's whole conception of what chance he or she has for fair play, for justice, for reciprocal relationships in the wider world. They, like Coleman, say that even the child's academic performance is influenced by his sense of whether he has any chance to control his own destiny.

When you start communicating to a young child or to a 16-year-old that he has certain basic rights, you're saying that he is human and that with that humanness comes real power for him to begin to have some control over his whole life. We tell him, "Look, you have certain basic constitutional rights. There are certain things that a teacher *can* do and *can't* do. We don't want you to react violently, we don't want you to use this information to start dehumanizing or destroying the teacher. But you do have certain control of your fate. Come to us and we will help you." Now he can begin to control what happens to him. He feels differently. Sometimes by teaching a student a basic right you get him into reading, sometimes you interest him in college, in medicine, in the law—you teach him to love, trust, and respect himself and his fellow man.

How then do you begin to help students implement their rights?

The first thing you do is teach them to love, trust, and respect themselves. Then you teach them to study the oppressor, the school, and its agents. For example, we start educating children and parents and teachers about the fact that words are sometimes used violently and that words sometimes result in a child's not wanting to learn, or in a child's not wanting to be anything, or in a child's not believing that he can be anything. They learn that the word thing has to be changed. Therefore we say that if you've been called dumb that is verbal abuse and there's an Ohio statute that protects you from verbal abuse. If you are suspended you are entitled to a hearing. You have the right to face your accusers. If you are not learning anything from eight o'clock in the morning until three o'clock in the afternoon then somebody has to be held accountable for the fact that you are not learning anything. *You* have a responsibility also—you have to get in there and try to learn. But if you are in that building from eight o'clock in the morning until three o'clock in the afternoon, and your teacher is forcing you to read a racist book that destroys your self-worth or that is not preparing you for the real world, you are not in school—you are in prison. It is a violation of the Constitution of the United States to incarcerate a person unless he has committed a crime.

We are going to have to institute various methods of accountability. I think you can deal with it very basically. No matter how bad his home conditions are, a child should know more at 3 o'clock in the afternoon than he knew at 8 o'clock in the morning. He should know more in June than he knew the preceding September, and he should certainly know more in 1972 than he knew in 1967. I think that the critical thing is that we have to stop assigning blame to the child. When we say, "The child is culturally deprived; the child is culturally disadvantaged," we are merely stereotyping a child; we are not blaming the institution. I am saying there is something wrong with the *school*, not the *child*.

As William Ryan says, we have to stop *Blaming the Victim*. A rapist is looked upon in this society very negatively. So is an embezzler, right? So is a murderer. So is a robber. But teachers who dehumanize? What about them? We are experts at making children the criminals, and adults and penal institutions, like schools, the saints. We hear people say, "The reason that the society is so messed up is because of the young." We've got to start assigning criminal names to criminals—and I'm not talking *only* about institutions because we've been doing that for too long. We say, "It is the school *system*," and that is correct—the oppression *is* systemic. But how do you identify who's wrong *within* an institution? From the child's perspective, it is the principal or the teacher who is destroying him or her, not the system.

Let me give you a very specific example of how this thing operates. A second grader was going around a school with the zipper down on his pants. Now the principal said that the child, a second grader, had "deviant sexual behavior." Now, a little research showed that his mother was on welfare, and his mother did not have enough money to buy him some pants, or even to buy him a zipper. She was trying to feed him. And the reason that he was in school was because his mother had impressed upon him the need to go to school every day so that he could *be somebody*, so that he could make some money. Therefore he was in school and he did not have a zipper on his pants. The principal sent him home and said that he was going around exposing himself and that that was deviant sexual behavior. The principal had no basic concept of what it was like to be poor. He did not have sense enough to ask the child if he had another pair of pants at home. That kind of behavior, in my opinion, means that the principal is guilty of *misfeasance*, *malfeasance*, and *incompetence*. What we're saying is those kinds of acts of atrocity have to be eliminated. Potentially, that child could be the doctor with the cure for cancer. Teachers who see his office card marked "deviant," however, will treat him like a criminal, not like a future M.D.

How does your work at the Center attempt to deal with examples like this?

When we can develop a strategy whereby teachers and administrators are held criminally responsible for the kinds of atrocities they are guilty of creating and implementing in the public schools, then we'll get to protecting that child's right to an education. What we're trying to develop is a legal strategy for actually documenting and charging that teacher or principal or administrator with being an accessory to whatever crime the child commits in later life as a result of a teacher's or administrator's cruelty. Lawyers will always say, "Why, that's ridiculous." Many lawyers have been programmed into thinking a certain way, too. But I see no basic difference between a warden in a prison and a principal. There are psychological dimensions of violence and I think that the law and lawyers and the courts have got to redefine violence.

It's violent to dehumanize a person. You can be very violent with words. You can be very violent with nonverbal types of communication. To refuse to touch a child is a form of violence. We have a case in our files where a teacher was a very effective teacher in terms of teaching the skills—reading, writing, arithmetic, etc.—and that's hard to find today. But she was getting no results with fourth graders because every morning she went into the room and sprayed disinfectant. She was just a clean teacher who liked everything to be perfect and she was very methodical. But the point is, the children perceived that as being a negative thing and they perceived that she felt that they were dirty and that she was much better than them. Therefore they responded to her negatively. Our staff is working with her now. She put the disinfectant can down and she's working a lot more effectively with the children.

Then you don't always go to court with the problem?
No. Our strategies have to be flexible. The most important thing is for us to communicate effectively to the oppressed what their rights are. The only way that we're really going to have the kind of impact we need is for everybody to have the same kind of information so that they can start affecting what happens to them.

Knowledge is power—so when a nine-year-old or an eleven-year-old comes to me and says, "I'm tired of that teacher yelling at me. Next time she does it, I'm going to knock her down," I say, "Listen. The next time that teacher is mean to you, be cool. Just sit there in the classroom and don't say anything for 20 minutes. Then, when you are completely calm and in control, raise your hand. When she calls on you, tell her coolly and calmly, 'Ms. Jones, what you did a few minutes ago, the way you talked to me, has psychologically dehumanized me, has made me feel like an animal, like a stupid animal. If that happens often enough, a child like me grows up thinking of himself as stupid and ugly and he can never function as a human being again. So unless you refrain from treating me in such a manner, I may have no alternative but to take you to the U.S. District Court and explain all this to the judge. And let me remind you, Ms. Jones, that there is a good possibility that I can win a $100,000 damage suit against you if I charge you with a psychological tort.'"

We work on this statement and practice it just like practicing for the Christmas play. We've tried this. It works. The child develops a new sense of power and fate-control. The teacher develops a new sense of responsibility relative to her behavior.

This is quite a different consequence from what usually happens. When Ms. Jones hollers at him, his immediate reaction is to holler back at her, or Ms. Jones hollers at him, and his immediate reaction is to put his head down and turn off everything that has happened, or Ms. Jones hollers at him, and he internalizes it and goes out on the playground and slaps another student and then gets into trouble in another way. Then Ms. Jones, the oppressor, has won, and there is no way of letting her know that she may have started an armed robbery that will occur in two years or five years or that she may have contributed to that child's graduation to Attica or San Quentin, or dope or welfare or psychological death.

Imagine the impact we could have if we could show this kind of example on television or film or even on recordings. We could get to the students—and maybe even the teachers.

I'm trying to work on other examples of using the law—like taking a tort, and phrasing it in a way that a young child, a second grader, can understand. So that he can then start explaining these things to the teacher. I strongly believe that one of the basic problems is that teachers do not understand children. Teachers do not understand the child's perception and only a child can teach the teacher how he feels and in that way change the teacher's behavior towards that child.

Let me give you another example of how we try to teach law to the brothers and sisters as a tool to protect them. An eighteen-year-old brother came into our office last year and said, "Look, Art, that jive teacher keeps messing with me and I am going to knock him down if he doesn't get off my back."

I said, "Dig, Brother, if you hit the teacher he can sue you for assault and battery and he might be able to have you arrested." I said, "Why don't you just lay back and be cool, and let him hit you and when and if he does, don't hit him back—just get your witnesses together and then you can sue *him.*"

He came into our office one day. He was smiling and he said, "Hey, Art, you are a jive cat. I waited all year for that dude to hit me and he didn't hit me and I was planning on suing the dude so I could use the money to buy me a short [car]." He is in college now—so you can see that our approach is useful in many different ways.

Of course another effective way to deal with the problem is to take those individuals responsible for racism, dehumanization, and oppression to the courts or to the public and hold them accountable for their atrocities against children. We do not need to look for scapegoats in the poor Black community or the poor white community, or the Indian community, or the Puerto Rican community or the youth community. The policy makers and the administrators of that policy must be held accountable.

But suppose you don't win in court?

But, look, I'm dealing with another thing. Even if the case doesn't get one inch in a courtroom, what we're doing is re-defining what a criminal is. It's not the child who is the criminal—it's the teacher or administrator who destroys the child's humanness that is the criminal. The word game is very important. By assigning criminal definitions to what so-called educators are doing, I'm trying to get both the oppressed and the oppressor to see that certain acts committed by school people are criminal.

But won't you have to prove premeditation—and isn't that a hard thing to prove?

Yes. This idea is a very radical, even unsound strategy, as the law is now used. But I'm saying that there is premeditation. Black and poor children are being deliberately destroyed so that they cannot compete with middle class and rich white children for jobs.

I'm also saying that this country has a habit of responding very quickly in some situations and responding very slowly in others. For example, as a result of the rebellions that occurred in the 60's and 70's, many state governments and the federal government moved swiftly to pass legislation that dealt with restricting the right to freedom of assembly, inter-state travel, etc. A great deal of this legislation dealt with limiting the young or protecting institutions from the young, the poor, the Black—the oppressed.

If it was logical to deal with a crisis situation in order to preserve institutions in the manner I just described, then is it not logical to deal with the physical and psychological destruction of children, which in my opinion is in the crisis stage, by redefining our concepts of who the criminals really are and what the consequences of criminal actions are relative to the survival of our children?

Furthermore, at no time in the near future will all oppressed children be able to have their own lawyers. Therefore, it is very important that we find ways to communicate to children and their parents that *they* are not the criminals. If we do not do this, the self-fulfilling prophecy will once again force them to act like criminals and later to become criminals. On the other hand, we have to develop a strategy to protect their right not to be destroyed. We have tried everything from money to sensitivity sessions to in-service training for teachers to performance contracts to get accountability. Why not try criminal statutes? Teachers are not doing children a *favor* if they teach them effectively and treat them as human beings—that's their *job.* We have tried moral persuasion already, and it hasn't worked well. But nobody wants to be fined or to go to jail.

We have to develop strategies for massive attitudinal change. The oppressed have to change their attitudes and behavior toward self and the oppressor. The oppressors have to change their attitudes and behavior toward the oppressed.

So part of the strategy is that you're redefining who the criminal is. Are you also redefining who the defenders of the law should be?

Yes. Chief Justice Burger and others in the legal profession are talking about the fact that the administration of justice is reaching a crisis stage because of tremendous case loads, administrative problems, new regulations, etc. Jean and Edgar Cahn have stated that there are many things that citizens or trained technicians can do to take the pressure off the courts and to enhance the possibility of more people receiving justice. Like Thomas Jefferson said (even though he wasn't talking about Black people), educate the masses and tyranny and oppression will disappear!

What we are trying to do is to take mothers on welfare, take young students and provide the opportunity for them to develop their own survival strategies.

We are trying to get young students who understand the kinds of oppression that are going on to teach the community what's going on. It's a matter of teaching, it's a matter of effective communication.

It's a matter of the so-called professional learning from the people as well as teaching the people. It's a matter of loving, trusting, and respecting the people and it's a matter of doing *with* rather than doing *for* the people.

It's also a matter of winning.

We are trying to get our ombudsmen to orient themselves thoroughly to how some principals and teachers lie and deliberately deceive people. We want parents to always move from a *child advocacy* perspective. The principals and teachers have associations to protect their rights. This is a society of checks and balances, so children should also have an association to protect their rights. We hope that the parent ombudsmen check the "new sovereign immunity" that the "public servant" has over the child, the parents, and the community.

So the ombudsmen are the real link with the community?

Yes, but not just that. Because the ombudsmen are deeply involved, sometimes they come up with the most important legal points, just as some of the best criminal reform law has come from prisoners and not the dudes that sit in the big law firms. The jailhouse lawyer type dudes are living what's going on—not reading about it. For example, Ms. Robinson, one of our ombudsmen, is a state chairman of the Welfare Rights Organization (NWRO). She's been working with me for quite some time—since way back in '62. The only way we could get results then was to picket, shout at, and threaten the oppressor. Now by sitting in sessions with the lawyers, analyzing school law, and studying the oppressor, she and other ombudsmen have developed other strategies for dealing with the establishment. Let me give you an example—it wasn't our lawyer but Ms. Robinson who read the school code, the Ohio State Statute as it related to school expulsions. She said, "Look, this thing says that if a child is expelled, he has a right to a hearing." When one of her children was expelled she pointed out the rule to our lawyer. The Center is probably one of the few places where the oppressed can go and read law books. You usually have to be a lawyer to get into the law library downtown. Many of our people don't have access to or know how to use the library. But at the Center we have law books right in the community and people come in and read those books. So Ms. Robinson read the book and it said, "If a child is expelled, he is entitled to a hearing."

Now, let me tell you what the school administration's strategy was. Whenever a child was expelled, the assistant superintendent in charge of pupil personnel would send out a copy of the part of the regulation which dealt with his right to expel a child. But he did not send out the section of the regulation which dealt with the child's right to a hearing before the Board of Education. As a result of Ms. Robinson's discovery, the staff attorney asked for a hearing before the Board of Education. The Board of Education held the hearing and the Board of Education directed the assistant superintendent in charge of pupil personnel to review its expulsion policy. There had been a number of expulsions from the Dayton School System in the previous eighteen months and the Board of Education sensed that the Student Rights Center could very easily bring *every* child that had been expelled in for a hearing before the Board of Education. That would take a lot of time and effort and energy on the part of the school board and administrators.

They don't expel many students anymore. Now what they do is suspend them. They always change their strategy—and so will we. That's another reason that we have to be very careful—as you get freedoms for the young brothers and sisters, the administrators and teachers find other ways, maybe more subtle ways, to oppress them.

Why do you think they concentrate so much on getting the children out of school?

Some of it is just overt racism. Some of it is institutionalized racism. Subconsciously they feel, "Dirty nigger, I don't want you in here anyway. So get out." That's what it boils down to. Other reasons are connected to administrative convenience. Some administrators don't necessarily hate children, but they see children as inconveniences. They see a child who is mistreating another child as a problem who has to be sent home so they can do their quarterly reports. Or they see a child who cuts a class as somebody that is walking around the hall that should be sent home so that he won't pull the fire alarm. I'm convinced, I'm totally convinced that if you explain to a child the reason why you want him to do something, he will respond positively.

But most administrators don't feel that they have any obligation to explain anything to a student. They don't treat students as consumers or customers; they treat them as criminals or as prisoners of war or as the enemy.

The child who is extorting money from another child did not have that ability to extort when he came out of his mother's womb. It was obviously taught by someone. It was probably taught by an adult. But do the teachers attempt to deal with the problem of extortion? Hell, no! They're too busy dealing with Columbus discovering something that some Indian brothers had already inhabited, and telling lies about Abraham Lincoln freeing us when he really pawned us. Now wouldn't it be more practical, in terms of the seriousness of conflict situations in our society, for a teacher to deal effectively with the problem of mistreating one's fellow man? But the reality of it is that teachers do not know *how* to deal with those things.

In not dealing with the problem the teacher implicitly contributes to it. The teacher has no information or strategy or knowledge whatsoever in solving the problem of extortion. She sends the child home so he can then go to another school on the way home to extort from another child. Rather than teaching this child that it is important that he learn to love, trust, and respect the other child, she sends him home. Instead of sending the child home she could go through a thing like "Stand up here, Johnny. Now, three of you go up and take

Johnny's money. Just take Johnny's money from him. Now, how do you feel about that, Johnny?" That doesn't happen. That never happens.

No programs are developed to teach the young brothers and sisters how to relate to each other. No. Because it's very simple for teachers to open that one textbook, say "Read Chapters 3 and 4," and that's it. Sit down and be a good *boy* and you can pass—stand up and try to be a *man* and you get kicked out.

What we are doing is attempting to develop an entire society of robots. But a society of robots or yes-men doesn't correspond with our stated objective of democracy. As Barbara Sizemore says in her testimony before the Mondale Committee, if we don't get about the business of establishing systems for participatory democracy in institutions that socialize our children for a so-called democracy, there will be little chance for having a real democracy.

Ermon O. Hogan has written in *Racial Crisis in American Education*, "Although our schools have provided a quasicommon heritage, they have not provided a common experience out of which youth could learn to develop the responsibilities of freedom, to respect universal equality, and to acquire the skills necessary to guarantee prosperity through the years to come."

Some students are learning, though. They are learning that teachers make mistakes, they are learning that administrators lie, they are learning that some of our institutions are oppressive. They are responding by trying to free themselves so that they can free others, so we can build a free society.

I believe that some children condition themselves to take out the anger and frustration that they feel toward a teacher or an administrator or a parent on other children rather than the adult. Experience has taught them that they will lose in a confrontation with an adult. Children, like any oppressed group, sometimes behave like the oppressor. Any individual who is being oppressed has developed a way to get back at something or someone. If he doesn't, he may easily lose his sanity.

The child learns that the principal is always right, even when the child knows that he is wrong. The child knows that the principal will always say that the teacher is right even when the child knows that the teacher is wrong. And often the child's parents will make the same assumption.

Why would the parents tend to assume that the child is always wrong?

Parents are sometimes very repressive. In fact they are in many respects just as repressive as teachers. They don't do this intentionally—it's because they see education as the one thing that can improve the conditions in life for their children. They want their children to do well in life so they see the school, the teacher, the principal as a ray of hope and a way out of slavery and oppression. Because his parents will not accept the fact that it's *possible* that a teacher might be wrong, the child will get very uptight because he says, "Where else can I go—I ask my mother and father to listen to me and trust me and they won't. I can't deal with the school alone." So often the results are a gang or possibly some drugs, or a robbery and eventually a cell in Attica or San Quentin. And whenever the parents have to come to the principal's office, they get a game put on them. The warden always asks them, "What about your child's responsibility? Look at the thing objectively." And when they run that on a parent, what they're really saying is, "Accept my point of view."

How are you dealing with this?

The biggest job is getting adults to look at children as human beings who have rights. We don't have our lawyer running to court every day because we think it's more important to have him explaining the law to parents. Parents respect lawyers, and teachers, and preachers. The lawyer's real job is to give the parents backbone and insight. The parents can say, "We've got our lawyer—he can lay some information on us and then we can deal." So the lawyer's there, backing them up, giving them information.

Remember, a lot of violence occurs in the Black community—folks are scared. So when the Man talks about law and order and responsibilities, Black folks listen and poor folks listen. There is a tendency for people to speak the same words—the words of the oppressor—back to us at the Center and say, when we start talking about the rights of children, "What about their *responsibilities?* Why are you helping the hoodlums?" They have trouble seeing that a child, when he has been in trouble, deserves legal representation.

So we have to remind them first that they don't get upset about a murderer or a rapist having a lawyer. Why should they think that we're protecting criminals when all we're saying is that a child, even though he may be wrong, has a right to be represented? Or even though he may be wrong in terms of his actions, we have to deal with the reason for his actions. Why should they get upset when a child who misunderstands and therefore gets into trouble has someone to represent him? I'm saying you have to develop within the community a new appreciation for the fact that children are oppressed and you have to show the community that if a child does something, he does something for a reason. You have to get the community out of the whole scapegoat syndrome, where they automatically start blaming children for atrocities that adults are responsible for.

So the ombudsmen really have to educate the community in a new way to see how the schools treat children?

The ombudsmen spend most of their time working with individual students and parents. For example, if a child is suspended, the ombudsman calls up the principal, and asks him why the child was suspended. Just the fact that an ombudsman calls up a principal and questions the fact that he has suspended a child changes that principal's behavior. Just the fact that the Student Rights Center exists changes teachers' and administrators' behavior. For example, just before school opened last September we worked with a local newspaper reporter, explaining the negative aspects of corporal punishment. The reporter then wrote a full-page article on corporal punishment. Many teachers told me that they are now apprehensive about paddling children because now they know what the state statute is on corporal punishment. Many parents read the article and said, "The next time my child is mistreated I'm going to do something about it." If we had merely taken it to court, it would have been a legal exercise between two lawyers and a judge.

The fact that students have rights has simply never occurred to many people—and that's rich people and poor people, Black people and white people. We don't even see a child in the context of "rights." We see a child in the context of somebody whom you tell what to do, and somebody who is supposed to do as he or she is told.

When the parents do catch on, it must really help their children.

Yes, it does. Alvin Poussaint, the Black psychiatrist, pointed this out in an article in *Ebony* magazine when he said that the Ocean-Hill-Brownsville incident was one of the best things that had ever happened in education because, oppressed, Black children saw their parents going up against police officers and the system for them to have the right to go to school. A Black child—standing outside one of those schools in Ocean-Hill-Brownsville watching his mother and watching his father confront policemen—started getting things going around in his head about the importance of school and about the need for him to go to school. And he started learning with a new kind of enthusiasm because his mother and his father went in there and fought for him to have that right to go to school. School for those children became an important part of life, not just a prison they were forced into.

The Center's parent ombudsmen include parents who have been on welfare, and parents who have a fair income. There are Black and white ombudsmen who work with Black and white families. When the children see the ombudsmen confronting the system on their behalf, the children show a new desire and have new hope. The ombudsmen help the children develop a positive attitude. The children begin to believe that they are not always wrong and that they have some degree of fate control.

I'm saying that children—like Blacks—like Chicanos—like Puerto Ricans—like Indians—like women—are recognizing that they are human beings as a result of the fact that some of us have been telling them that they are. "You're beautiful, you have a right to this, you have a right to that." If you keep telling somebody that they're good or that they can control what happens to them, then they start believing it and doing it.

While I was assistant principal at MacFarlane School, I used to ask the young Black men to stand up and clap for the young Black women in the school. I still use this method to impress upon young Black men at an early age—like 3 years old—that they should love, trust, and respect Black women. Black men must not fall into the trap set by racist social theorists like Daniel P. Moynihan. Moynihan asserted that Black society is dominated by Black women. He called

Black society a matriarchy, and left the impression that Black men must seek to dominate Black women. Dr. Jacquelyne J. Jackson pointed out in a recent issue of *Ebony* magazine that part of Moynihan's thesis was dead wrong: one of the reasons, she said, that more Black women head households is not that they are domineering, but that there simply have not been enough Black men to go around.

Because they have accepted Moynihan's racist thesis, some Black men have seen strong Black women as a threat to their manhood. This is a tragic waste. Black men should not try to prove their manhood by trying to destroy the strength of Black womanhood. The future of Black people depends, not on Black men dominating Black women, but on cementing their partnership with them. We must revere the courage and brilliance of our women and support and join their actions toward effecting Black liberation.

To get back to the issue of student rights, things like the Students Rights Handbook help too. We've tried to get those books out into the community. The young brothers and sisters walk through the school hall. The teacher says, "Shut up, Johnny." Johnny gets the book out and says, "Hey, man, I can't read this thing. Look in here and see what it says I should do when the teacher hollers at me." So a student who can read reads to him about what he can do about the verbal abuse of a student. Johnny raps to the teacher about Section 2901.20 and 2901.21 of the Ohio Code, and the teacher gets off his back.

But what about the abuse—physical or verbal—of the teacher?

Usually you find that when a child hits a teacher, the teacher has passed the first lick. We're trying to explode the myth about George Washington and teachers and principals never telling a lie. Let me give you another example of how the ombudsmen work. A student came to the Center who had been suspended twelve times. So a student ombudsman worked with him. The student ombudsman's name is James Phillips. James said, "Look, man, what are you going to do when you go back to school?" "I'm going to make sure that the cat doesn't hit me again." "What are you going to do if he hits you?" "I'm going to try to knock his head off." So James said, "Look, man, you've been out of school twelve times for fighting. And you're talking about going back to fighting. Now, isn't it obvious to you that the man, the principal, is running games on you? And what can you do to make sure that you and this cat don't fight but at the same time you can get something out of school, 'cause you're just wasting a lot of time and risking getting yourself ripped off. Do you understand that, man?" One of the reasons the student understood was that James is the same age as he is. So he says, "Yeah, I guess so." So then he and James sat down and they developed a strategy to get five students together so that they could work with each other to protect themselves from the principal and from the teachers of the school.

Have you thought about sending in teams of lawyers?

The one thing that I recognize about a law and order society, about the way we've been trained and programmed, is that we only respond when we become personally involved. Most lawyers analyze the problem. They take the problem through ninety-nine research steps, and they think that they then have all the answers. I'm saying that a mother who has seen her child victimized, a mother who has in fact been victimized herself, feels a lot more compassion. A mother can't go home at five and say, "Well, we'll finish this tomorrow." She stays there until six or seven or eight in the evening until that problem is solved. The other thing is that she's a part of that community. Many of our cases come to our ombudsmen at home, not to the Center. A child with his parent will call up one of the ombudsmen at home, or go knock on the door, and say, "Look, Ms. Wiley, they're doing this to us—what can we do?" And they sit down right there in the home and solve the problem.

Because that ombudsman is in the community, because that ombudsman has come through the whole Civil Rights struggle, because the ombudsman knows and understands the child, because the ombudsman knows the principal and teachers and the kinds of games they run, the ombudsman can relate and deal effectively with the problem. Another important thing is that parents don't feel that they have to speak perfect grammar to be able to talk to the ombudsman about the problem. The ombudsman gets a lot of information, a lot more insight, into the problem, I think, than a so-called professional would. We try to work with the ombudsmen on certain interview techniques. We try to teach the ombudsmen about the importance of confidentiality and follow-up. But I'm saying that the ombudsman is a very emotional, intricate part of that community and the ombudsman responds to clients like human beings rather than like rats running through mazes, which is what most professionals—lawyers, social workers, teachers, administrators, doctors, judges—tend to do.

Is it possible for the legal profession to be deprofessionalized?

Let me answer this way. We are developing a model statute for due process which we will present to the Board of Education and I think that it might work like this: a student is suspended, let's say, for hollering at his teacher. And let's say that we have not necessarily an ombudsman, but maybe one of the women from the League of Women Voters who's hearing the case. Well, the first thing that would be different is that the teacher would have to state why she kicked the student out of school. And then the child would have an opportunity to respond to the teacher's charges. Then the principal would be asked in what kinds of detail he investigated the case prior to the time that he sent the child home. Then the mother would probably be asked, "Has the child had problems with other teachers?" And the child would be asked how he feels about the whole thing. So it's quite possible that in that whole process the child has to take a look at himself or herself, the parent has to take a look at himself or herself, the teacher has to take a look at himself or herself, and the principal has to take a look at himself or herself.

Yes, it is possible for the legal profession to deprofessionalize, but it is also possible for everybody to have access to the strategies used now by the legal profession mainly to protect the rich and the powerful.

But if you want to affect all the children in the country, don't you have to deal with the professionalization in the schools?

Yes. Teacher organizations in my opinion are mainly concerned with making as much money as possible for doing as little work as possible.

One way to deal with the so-called professional is to simply wipe out compulsory attendance. I agree with Edgar Friedenberg that compulsory attendance as it exists today functions as a Bill of Attainder. We have to develop the kind of learning atmosphere where the child learns to love, trust, and respect himself and his peers and others, and to develop skills that will enable him to survive as a human being and to develop to the very maximum of his or her potential. My first inclination is to wipe out compulsory attendance, but at the same time I want to make sure that we develop some kind of mechanisms that will protect children and maximize their life chances.

On the other hand I have very serious problems with deschooling, as Ivan Illich calls it, because it doesn't, in my opinion, adequately deal with the question of institutionalized racism. If you're going to have a de-schooled society run by the racist oppressors who are running this one, then I'm opposed to it. At the same time I see great benefits in developing very special skills in a period of six weeks and not keeping people off the job market by insisting that they go through a number of worthless exercises to be certified. I don't see any magic about going to a building every day, and I believe students learn by doing, not by listening to a teacher who may or may not know what he or she is talking about.

It's hard to decide about programs and changes that look good on the surface. For example, even if Head Start is in many respects a good program, the positive aspects seem to get wiped out anyway. When I consider something like de-schooling, I have to wonder what will happen to the children who are catching hell now. One of the things that I recognize is that, as a result of the whole Civil Rights movement of the 1960's, Black teachers have become a lot more aware. Despite the fact that there's a tremendous amount of pressure being exerted on them to make sure that Black children are not taught properly, Black teachers are beginning to take care of business just the same. As Black children become more aware and start becoming more knowledgeable, all of a sudden we hear talk about reading not being important and arithmetic not being important, and de-emphasizing schooling and de-schooling.

It's the same thing with some white "educators" telling us what is *good* for the Black child. White teachers have developed missionary strategies for slavery 1960–1970 style. When I was directing the Model Cities Education program, I visited a kindergarten class and the children were taking a nap. They got there about eight. They took a nap at 8:45, a nap about 10:30, and another nap at 11:30 and they went home at twelve. I asked the teacher what was going on. She said, "Well, you have to let *these* children develop at their own leisure because you can't psychologically frustrate them." My response to her was, "Well, when these same children get to the third grade and put their heads on the desk and start taking naps because they can't read or because they are in the habit of sleeping all day they will have been taught to sleep and waste time by you. You will be responsible for their being suspended or expelled. Now it seems to me that those who are behind in a race 'must forever remain behind or run faster than the man in front.' So what I want you to do is to get those damn blocks out of the way, stop those half-day naps and siestas and start teaching them to read, write, and do arithmetic. If you push them and they learn, at least they will be able to get a job and afford a psychiatrist. If you go at the rate that you're going and they learn absolutely nothing, then they won't be able to get a job and they won't know anything and at the same time they'll be mixed up and confused because they won't be able to compete in society." The point I'm making is that's another form of racism. Many white teachers assume Black children can't learn and so they let them sleep, play basketball, or not come to class.

As things are now I agree with Mario Fantini and Donald Harris: we have to provide as many alternatives as possible and we have to stop looking for a panacea. The only thing that could be worse than what we have now would be Hitler's concentration camps, and I believe that they are on the way, American style.

Do you have the same kind of mixed feelings about the voucher system or alternative schools?

The voucher system points up another legal point I'd like to deal with—the whole business of school systems functioning as monopolies. One of the reasons the school systems are so ineffective is that they have no competition. One of the things I liked about vouchers is that they have the potential to destroy the monopoly of the public school system. What other alternative does the poor child have? We need competitive models, we need community-controlled schools, we need free schools, university-run schools, welfare-rights-run schools, schools run by militant organizations, voucher schools, etc.

But the critical issue that has to be dealt with is a redistribution of power. Poor folks need power and money to operate different kinds of schools.

As for alternatives to the schools, there are a couple of questions to be dealt with. One is that the big oppressive institution called the school system is responsible for educating our children. So what you're doing if you start a free school, even though *that* free school may have the interest of the children at heart, is relieving the public school of its responsibility. The over-all strategy should be to stay on their cases and make sure they educate the children as they should be educated. But if there were enough alternatives, the school system would be forced either to produce or become obsolete, I would support the alternatives.

Are you saying that if the school system were doing its job right, alternatives wouldn't be necessary?

Schools *are* doing their job though. In fact, the schools in urban communities are doing *precisely* what they're designed to do. They are designed to transmit the cultural heritage. The cultural heritage in this country is one of racism. Urban schools are designed to make sure that you always have busboys, dishwashers, and folks for white people to look down upon psychologically.

The superintendent is paid to be sure that Black children do not learn because the system does not want Black children to be in a position to compete with white children for jobs. It's a perpetuation of the class structure in this country.

Schools are also designed to make sure that banks keep getting money placed into those banks by teachers. You see 85% of the schools' budget goes into salaries. And they're designed for the wax companies to sell wax, for the toilet paper companies to sell toilet paper, and for the food companies to sell food. Schools are a 61 billion dollar a year business. Poor children are used as tools for that business.

Do you think the busing will make any difference to this system?

As Lerone Bennett points out in *The Challenge of Blackness,* integration and separation should be looked upon as strategies for liberation. I am opposed to any strategy that is going to damage children—psychologically or physically. It really amazes me how we have such little regard for the rights of children and how in most instances we have such little regard for the abilities of children and yet on the question of integration we ask *them* to deal effectively with the problem that *we* have not effectively dealt with ourselves.

If we can put them on buses at age seven to deal with institutionalized racism—why can't we put them in voting booths at age seven to vote on whether or not they want to be bused? It's easy for us to say how we feel about it, but then *we* are not being bused. Why can't children be elected to the Board of Education at age seven? Are 7-year-olds or 14-year-olds or 16-year-olds represented by or judged by their peers in our society? I think we should be asking the students how they feel about it.

As I stated at the Conference on Education for Blacks sponsored by the Congressional Black Caucus, I seriously doubt the utility of busing to improve the education of Black students. "Racial balance" and "desegregation" do not ensure that Black children learn; such goals do ensure that Black children will be in the minority in every school. These goals do ensure that Black children will continue to be oppressed by the white-controlled racist school system.

Barbara Sizemore said in her testimony before the Mondale Committee that the first *Brown* decision was racist because it implied that segregation does no harm to white children, segregated schools are seen as good schools for whites. She said, "If an institution supports the folk who give the inference of authority to another folk, how can that institution help the so-called inferior folk?"

Black children today are very different from the Black children of 1954. To tell a Black child today that he will profit by sitting next to a white child in a white-controlled school is to lie to him. And he knows it. The only thing that child will gain is more knowledge of white racism. This is a learning experience for him but it does not help him learn how to read and write.

In light of this, and in light of the student's "rights" which have been shown to exist only in theory, three points can be made about busing children for "racial balance":

First, it appears that busing insures that Black children will always be in the minority, thus providing an ideal climate for racist practices to continue.

Second, the terms "busing," "desegregation," and "racial balance" are used by the power elite in this country to keep poor whites and poor Blacks from joining together to demand a decent life and the right to survive. If the people who are paid to educate children don't do it, what better way to divert attention from their failures than by stirring up the folks, calling poor whites "racists" and forcing both white and Black to go to a school in which no one will ever learn anyway?

Third, "racial balance" is used to curtail the authority of Black teachers and administrators. In Dayton, the community word is that, in balancing the staff of the schools to a 70-30 ratio, the good Black teachers went to the white schools and the incompetent white teachers came to the Black schools.

Because of these effects of "desegregation," it is a denial of a Black student's right to an education to move him to a white school. We are putting the burden on children, both Black and white, to eradicate the mental illness of 300 years in American society. This "racial balance" is easy for the power elite to support because it puts the burden on the children, not on their own racist shoulders where it belongs. True integration, as Sizemore says, would bring about an open society in which segregated housing, economic racism on all levels, and unequal educational and medical services would be eliminated.

I believe in freedom of choice for Black people. If Black parents wish to send their children to white schools, the law should facilitate that wish. If, however, Black parents, having developed a sense of nationalism and racial pride, decide that Black-controlled schools would better educate their children, the law should protect that decision.

As I see it, when we talk about busing we are talking about institutionalized racism. And I believe that urban schools are merely an extension of the slave system. In many respects Black people are still enslaved. In many respects, *poor* people are enslaved. In many respects all oppressed people are enslaved.

Do you think it's possible for Blacks and oppressed white people to join together in a common struggle?

There has to be some kind of cooperation and understanding between poor white and poor Black students. I think that if there is racial violence in this country, initially it would not be between middle-class Black and middle-class white people; it would be between poor white people and poor Black people, and they are both oppressed in many of the same ways.

I have been through an experience where I had to rescue some Black children from a white Appalachian school. One strategy would be to be angry with poor white folks for the rest of my life, but another strategy would be to understand that *they* are oppressed in many of the same ways Black people are oppressed. In many ways they are victims of the news media and victims of the powerful and the rich. I am not saying that poor white people and poor Black people have to love each other, but I am saying they have to get together on things that they agree on to prevent potential genocide of both. I think that that can be done, not by what some expert says, but by giving them power and giving them some money and letting them make their own decision about how they can relate together and how they can live together.

I agree with Lerone Bennett, however, when he talks about the fact that you have to be strong before you go into any coalition. Black folks have been ripped off time and time again in coalition situations. The emphasis has to be on Black folks getting together with Black folks first and poor whites getting themselves together too. The immediate strategy with white folks has to be one of peaceful coexistence.

I think the same thing's happening within the public schools that happened during slavery. For example, during slavery Black people were told that we were dumb, that we were dirty, that we were silly, that we were thieves. That gave us a negative feeling of self. How does the institution called school work? The institution calls students socially disadvantaged, culturally deprived—now don't think that those terms don't have ramifications in terms of how teachers deal with those students, how administrators administrate for those students, how other institutions that are serving those students *view* those students. The institution also stereotypes to cover up its failure, to cover up its inability to produce. Earl Kelly said it very clearly—adults always blame powerless children for their inadequacies. Institutions always find a scapegoat for the fact that they can't produce, or that they are deliberately not producing.

It sounds like there's no way out.

That's what the oppressor wants us to believe. In this country today, Black men who want to be men have few alternatives. We can go to Algiers, we can end up in jail, we can end up destroyed psychologically or physically if we stand up for our rights. In my own case, the Stivers High School incident documented by Dr. Ruth W. Burgin in the book, *An Experiment in Community School Control: An Evaluation of the Dayton Experience,* speaks of a form of genocide, a form that seeks to eliminate Black men from positions of power or potential power. As a result of incidents of this kind, young Black and other oppressed people are forced into despair. Many feel, "Why learn and why study when in a few years I'm going to be destroyed anyway?"

There is a growing concern among Black educators and community leaders that, since there is no more cotton to pick and there are no more ditches to dig, Blacks as a people are no longer necessary to this country, especially in view of the population control themes being developed. Some believe that the billions of dollars being pumped into programs like the Title I Elementary and Secondary Education Act to provide funds for assistance to so-called educationally disadvantaged children are merely being used to prove the racist theory of genetic inferiority of Black children, as espoused by men like Jensen. The argument runs something like this: "You see, we have given billions and look, those children still cannot learn."

How does this oppression actually work itself out in the school?

The school is a certified agent of oppression. There are many similarities between urban schools that I've been associated with and Attica. At Attica they shot people down physically; in the public schools they shoot children down psychologically. The result is the same, death. In fact, as Dr. Martin Luther King stated, psychological death can be even more painful than physical death. Let me give you an example. This nine-year-old brother was watching the Today show. He was Black. A very brilliant Black Ph.D. was on the show. The young brother didn't understand what the Ph.D. was talking about. But he was impressed by his sharp clothes and the fact that he was on television. He ran to school. He was late because he had been watching the Today show. He asked his teacher, "How much money do it cost to be a doctor, so I can be on television and be like that man I saw on television, and be sharp, and be talking like he was talking?" His teacher told him, "Sit down—sit down because you don't have enough money to be thinking about school and you can't read anyway." He was nine years old. He didn't come to school the next day. He started stealing little petty stuff, hub caps, routine stuff. Then he started getting into more serious trouble. Then he started becoming aggressive in social situations. He eventually got into serious trouble—and he is, in fact, doing time now for a very serious crime.

You can multiply that example in one form or another for every child who gets trapped in the general course, or gets pushed out of a college preparatory course, or learns how to sit in class and be a good "boy" or good "girl" and graduates, but can't read. Or gets pushed out of school.

What are the consequences of being in the general course?

Counselors are among the greatest violators of the equal protection granted to all people under the United States Constitution. They can deprive children of this protection with one statement: "You are not smart enough to take the college preparatory course."

When a counselor makes this statement, he often deprives the student of a good job, good housing, good medical treatment, and a happy and healthy life. If the student doesn't drop out, he winds up in another dead end—the general course.

You take a student in an academic course and ask him what he wants to be. He'll say: a doctor, a lawyer, a chemist. You ask a student in the business course what he wants to be and he'll tell you an office manager, a banker, a real estate man, a salesman. Ask a student attending one of the few good vocational schools what he wants to be and he will say a draftsman or machinist.

You ask a student in the general course what he wants to be and he'll say, "I dunno." I look at the classified want ads in the Dayton papers every day and I see ads for all kinds of jobs. But I don't see any ads for "General Jobs."

The general course is a combined concentration camp, babysitting service, and mental graveyard. It is excellent preparation for the future junkies of America, the future jobless of America.

The general course, like the poor conditions of performance and services and supplies and material resources in Black and other oppressed communities, exists not by chance, but by design. I think that those of us who are in constant contact with the people who are suffering in this country must repeat and repeat and repeat the essence of that suffering—institutionalized racism.

I have personal experience with how teachers try to program Black children into failure. The one lesson that I learned well in junior high school only took about two minutes to teach and I have never forgotten it. A math teacher told me that I would never be any good, that I was dumb, and that I would never finish school. I believe today that I made up my mind right then and there to make a damn liar out of him.

Now he told my best friend the same thing, and that friend didn't see that it was the system that was no good—he believed it was him. For shortly after that teacher hit my friend with the same cruel, harsh, and criminal words, my friend started staying away from school, getting in trouble and is, in fact, in trouble today, serious trouble. He is in jail. As far as I am concerned—whatever crime my friend is accused of—the teacher who made that statement to him way back in 1950 is equally guilty and should be serving the same time under the same conditions.

Now, I had a sense of what was happening, but it was still very hard for me. Because of some racist IQ test, when I got to high school, my mother had to spend about three weeks convincing white folks that I should take the college preparatory course. When she finally fought hard enough for me to get into the college preparatory course, they had already psychologically destroyed my will to take algebra and geometry and all college subjects. So when I went into those college preparatory courses I went in there with the feeling—"I can't really do this because the teacher said I couldn't do it, and the counselor said

I couldn't do it, and the principal said I couldn't do it, and the assistant superintendent of the district said I couldn't do it. I must be stupid."

But my main point is that by making sure that most Black children end up in the general course with no belief that they can do or be anything else, the system is committing psychological genocide and perhaps even getting ready for physical genocide. There's hardly a chance that any of *us* are going to be in positions to control the new technologies—those that may mean the difference between survival and death. You have to think seriously about why our children aren't being trained for the future.

Do you want to start educating children for the future or for dealing, first of all, with their present condition?

One without the other is meaningless. Right now we should be teaching children how to make their own worlds more livable. They should learn about legal redress against slum landlords. They should learn about taxes and how they are levied. They should learn consumer law and credit and how to protect themselves in the marketplace. They should learn about due process so that they can protect themselves and their parents from a society that does not look kindly on them.

Besides this, our children must be schooled in the future. We must have architects who can plan low-cost housing. We must have children who can learn oceanography and assure our people a place in submarine communities. We have seen from experience that the white establishment will leave its decaying cities to Black people while fleeing into the suburbs. They will not automatically, out of brotherhood, indulge in integrated submarine communities. Our children must be taught about space flight—so that they will not be left on a pollution-clogged earth while whites hit the moon and beyond. Black children must learn the new medicine so that their children will not be used as spare parts when some white man needs a heart. Our children must learn genetics so that the race is not bred out of existence when the era of test-tube babies becomes a reality. Our children must learn about psychology and the media so that they will not be manipulated back into slavery.

Instead of the general course, why not substitute a curriculum that produces skilled craftsmen in oceanography, genetic research, atomic fusion, chemistry and biology, medicine, computer science, machine design, the media, urban space planning, agronomy, economic planning, and political science as it applies to design models for the survival and liberation of oppressed peoples?

Black people, in the eyes of many people in this country, are no longer necessary. I'm especially pessimistic after reading Sam Yette's brilliant book, *The Choice*. There he deals with *The Issue of Black Survival in America*, the reality that our people are considered obsolete by racists because there is no more cotton to pick, and there are no more ditches to dig. And I see the school as an agency that initiates and perpetuates genocide.

Given the fact that the "sane" Black person must acknowledge the psychological genocide that exists and the physical genocide that is possible, what has to happen now, as you see it?

I have to deal with that question on several different levels. One initial step might be to deal directly with the oppressive school-connected agents of genocide. A group of Black educators suggested just recently that we provide school people with two alternatives: either say (1) our children are genetically inferior, or (2) you do not have the ability to educate them.

Most oppressive educators have trouble dealing with those alternatives because even though they *believe* in the genetic inferiority of Black children, they would be reluctant to admit to others that they do not have the capacity to educate our children because that would mean they would no longer be necessary in our schools or in our communities. They would no longer be able to use our children for the purpose of making a living.

If oppressive educators admit that they cannot educate our children, that would mean that they should no longer have access to Black children and other poor and oppressed children. If they no longer had access to our children they would not be able to deliberately destroy them psychologically for the purpose of protecting the myth of white superiority and the reality of institutionalized racism.

To prevent psychological genocide of Black, Chicano, Puerto Rican, Indian, poor and oppressed children, we must remove them from the physical and psychological control of the oppressor. We must also teach them to protect and defend themselves while at the same time not copying the cruel and vicious tactics of the oppressor.

On another level, some of the most brilliant people alive are Black people who have become political prisoners because of the events of the 1960's and 1970's. They possess the insight and the love for their fellow man to deal effectively with the issue of "bringing us together." I believe that legislation should be introduced to grant amnesty to all those who are currently incarcerated because they have fought for the human and constitutional rights of their fellow man. I suggest that they be employed to work toward making this a truly open, democratic society.

Everett Reimer in *School Is Dead* says that, despite the record, the possibility for democratic institutions remains—men, however, must make up their minds to use institutions for democratic purposes. In order to avoid genocide for some and in order to make democracy a reality for all, we must start practicing what we preach from the womb to the tomb, from the pre-schooler to the Supreme Court justice, to the Congressman.

Everett Reimer contends, of course, that school is dead. He may be right. While it is being buried, however, children are still being destroyed.

We must protect our children by any and all means necessary. For example, the local, state, and federal governments of this country have the responsibility of stopping the psychological and physical genocide that is occurring through the schools, the media, health care, drugs, housing, and law enforcement. We must hold individuals who are responsible for racism within the educational system accountable for their actions by initiating criminal court actions or through para-legal avenues of arbitration. We must institute specific programs to develop positive self-image. The Black, poor, and oppressed must be told repeatedly that they are good, they are beautiful, they can do anything they make up their minds to do. Like Huey P. Newton says, "The will of the People is greater than the Man's technology." We must redistribute money, knowledge, and power, and provide alternatives through community-controlled schools, free schools, welfare rights schools, university-run schools, student-run schools, computer-centered schools, schools without walls, home-based schools, etc. We must reform the decision-making bodies of public education to include students between the ages of seven and seventeen with full rights and responsibilities. We must institute student fact-finding commissions—like the Center's recent models, the Student Boards of Inquiry into discipline and into curriculum—to deal with racial issues, discipline, curriculum, guidance, and all other areas of public education. We must federally fund student groups to initiate their own programs relative to rights and responsibilities and education in general—programs, for example, where students help the blind, the poor, the aged. We must federally fund programs for "Black militants," conservative white, Chicano, Puerto Rican, Indian, poor, and oppressed students, so that they can develop their own strategies for peaceful co-existence and survival.

We must strive to make Oscar Handlin's definition of integration a reality. That definition, as interpreted by Barbara Sizemore, is that condition of society in which any individual has the opportunity to make a multitude of voluntary or involuntary contacts with any other human being based on his own preference, taste, or ability. This definition, rather than racial balance, must be our goal. We must federally fund TV, cable TV, and radio networks throughout this country that can broadcast information to the masses of oppressed people about student rights, welfare rights, and the right to believe in oneself and to love, trust, and respect oneself and others; we must also broadcast the information necessary to eliminate racism, poverty and oppression, and genocide. Although federal grants for compensatory education have failed in the past because money was given to the same racist administrators to help Black children whom they had failed to educate in regular programs, massive expenditures of money could aid Black education—if it were distributed properly, and controlled by the local community, not by the state or the school system.

We must also abolish corporal punishment.

How is it possible to finance these programs?

How is it possible to finance wars? How is it possible to subsidize large corporations? How was it possible to rebuild Germany and Japan?

A number of ideas on how to use such grants have been expressed in Dayton a number of times by myself and others. The ideas were recently re-stated one more time, by the Dayton superintendent who fired me three years ago for developing these same programs.

These ideas include: federal grants used for rent or loan supplements for all poor people—once housing is available to all in all parts of the cities, true integration may be possible. Federal grants for clothing allowances for poor children—the type of clothes a student wears significantly affect teacher attitudes toward the student, and therefore that student's performance. Federal grants for medical and dental service for every poor child—this money could erase some of the outside factors that hinder a poor child's learning. Federal grants to provide part-time jobs for all poor children 12 years and over—if a child can earn his own spending money, he will be less apt to drop out of school. Federal grants for paid transportation either to a special course or a job opportunity for all these children. Federal grants for green space and good playground equipment for all inner-city schools—to alleviate at least the appearance of inner-city schools as prisons. Federal grants for educational travel, camping, and environmental exploration by inner-city pupils.

Then do you feel that such programs could profoundly alter the fate of Black and other oppressed people in this country? Is this the kind of revolution you hope for?

No program for change and liberation can be successful, truly successful, in making equality and democracy a reality unless the people are involved from the beginning. I believe that the only real revolution that can take place in this country, and indeed in this world, is a revolution of peace—love, trust, and respect for each other. There is nothing revolutionary about Black folks and young folks dying in this country. Life is a very precious and dear thing. We have, in this country, made dying as routine as going to the bathroom, and that is a shame. We must somehow emphasize the importance of living and developing strategies to see to it that our young are able to develop to the fullest of their potential. To strive for anything less is to say that all of the Black people who have bled and suffered and died, and all the young people who have bled and suffered and died, have done so for nothing.

In her book, *If They Come in the Morning*, our beautiful, brilliant, and courageous sister Angela Davis states that her life is at stake and that it is not just an individual life but a life that has been given to her people in the struggle against poverty and racism.

James Baldwin, in his letter to Angela Davis, says, "We must fight for your life as though it were our own because if they take you in the morning they will be coming for us that night."

Angela Davis is on trial, Black people are on trial, oppressed people are on trial, and the potential for democracy is on trial. For the sake of our children and for the sake of us all, I hope Angela wins, I hope Black people win, I hope the oppressed win, I hope democracy wins.

We must trust each other. In the end, the oppressed will save themselves and their oppressors. The children, if we allow them to be human, will lead the way.

Notes

1. Tinker v. Des Moines Independent School District, 393 U.S. 503, 89 S. Ct. 733 (1969). This decision is discussed in Richard L. Berkman, "Students in Court: Free Speech and the Functions of Schooling in America," *Harvard Educational Review,* 40 (November, 1970), pp. 567–595.
2. Serrano v. Priest, 5 Cal. 3rd 584 (1971). The text of this decision is published with commentary by William N. Greenbaum, *Harvard Educational Review,* 41 (November, 1971), pp. 501–534.
3. The interview took place in Cambridge, Massachusetts in February, 1972. Interviewers were John Butler, Margaret Marshall, Tom Marx, and Ellen Solomon of *HER.*
4. While the Center has received grants from the Office of Economic Opportunity, Washington, D.C., 20506, the opinions expressed here are those of Arthur E. Thomas and should not be construed as representing the opinions or policy of any agency of the United States Government.
5. All authors and works referred to in the text are cited in the bibliography.

Sources

My mother—who taught me at an early age to always remember that whenever I saw someone who was suffering or oppressed, "there but for the grace of God, go you." She told me that I should always try to help them, because, were it not for oppression, they would be able to help themselves.

My wife—who is brilliant, Black, and beautiful and best described by Isaac Hayes on the record *Black Moses* in the song "Brand New Me."

Ms. Wilhelmina Robinson, Dr. Ames Chapman, Mr. Isaac Sappe Lane, professors Central State University, Wilberforce, Ohio—they taught me and many others that we were not dumb and that we could learn.

Mrs. Margaret Irby, teacher, Dayton Public Schools; my students; the Black community of Dayton—who taught me and many others to always strive to love, trust, respect, and protect our children and our people.

Ms. Jean Camper Cahn and Dr. Edgar S. Cahn—who helped us fight the racist, oppressive school administration of Dayton at the risk of their lives—and who were instrumental in the development of the Student Rights Center.

Dr. Ruth W. Burgin—who helped us fight the racist, oppressive, school administration of Dayton with the courage of Harriet Tubman and the brilliance of Angela Davis.

Black scholar-educator-activists—who have assisted us with ideas, inspiration, co-operation, assistance, protection, and support: Brother Kenneth Haskins, Brother Preston Wilcox, Dr. Donald H. Smith, Dr. Ermon O. Hogan, Dr. Charles H. Smith, Dr. Bernard C. Watson, Sister Barbara Sizemore, Dr. Rhody McCoy, Dr. Oscar Mims, Brother Julius Hobson, Dr. Gloria Joseph, and many, many others.

Organizations and individuals who have played a major role in the development of the Center: the Model Cities Planning Council of Dayton, the Dayton Community School Councils, Dr. Michael Kantor, Mr. Terry Lenzner, Ms. Patricia Clarkson, Mr. Stephen Huber, Mr. Bruce Kirschenbaum, Mr. Elliott Stanley, Ms. Nancy Stanley, Mr. Donnie Moore, Ms. Marcia Brockenborough, Mr. Troy Overby.

The Student Rights Center Staff: Mr. Peter M. Rebold, Ms. Ruthetta Bankston, Ms. Carol Towarnicky, Ms. Maddi Breslin, Ms. Lillian Meeks, Ms. Lori Tannenbaum.

Ombudsmen—Mr. Edward Campbell, Rev. David Gilbert, Ms. Elizabeth Robinson, Ms. Betty Moore, Ms. Corine Tucker, Ms. Mable Wiley, Ms. Judy Mathis, Mr. Robert Turner, Mr. James Phillips, Mr. Ellis Jacobs, Ms. Gail Stewart, Carroll Boswell.

Some of our best friends are white: the late Charles Bridge—our lawyer, who labored unselfishly against racism, oppression, and injustice; Dr. Larry Hillman, Dr. Arthur Eve, Dr. James H. Pelley, Mr. Albert Rosenberg, Mr. Ray Hruschka, Dr. Neal Shedd, Mr. Gregory Favre.

Records—

"Save the Children" as performed by Marvin Gaye, *What's Going On*; "Reach Out and Touch (Somebody's Hand)" as performed by Aretha Franklin, *Live at Fillmore West*; "The Impossible Dream," as performed by Roberta Flack, *Chapter Two*; "Martin Luther King at Zion Hill," "Malcolm X Talks to the Grassroots," "Malcolm X: Ballots or Bullets," "I am Somebody," Rev. Jesse Jackson, *The Country Preacher*; "To Be Young, Gifted, and Black," as sung by Nina Simone, *Black Gold*.

Periodicals—

Ebony Magazine, *Jet* Magazine, *The Black Scholar, Mohammad Speaks*.

Cahn, Edgar S. and Jean Camper, "The Sovereign Immunity," *Harvard Law Review*, 81 (March, 1968).

Cahn, Edgar S. and Jean Camper, "Power to the People or the Profession?—the Public Interest in Public Interest Law," *The Yale Law Journal*, Vol. 79 (May, 1970).

Cahn, Edgar S. and Jean Camper, "The War on Poverty: A Civilian Perspective," *The Yale Law Journal*, 73 (July 1964).

"Mondale Commission Report": *Equal Educational Opportunity Hearings Before the Select Committee on Equal Educational Opportunity of the United States Senate, Ninety-Second Congress*: First Session, Part 13. Washington, D.C.: Government Printing Office, 1971.

Poussaint, Alvin, "A Psychiatrist Looks at Black Power," *Ebony* (March, 1969).

Thomas, Arthur E., and Ruth W. Burgin. *Community School Council, Philosophy and Framework for Urban Educational Change*. Wilberforce, Ohio: Institute for Research and Development in Urban Areas, Central State University, May, 1971.

Thomas, Arthur E. *Delinquency: An Assessment of the Juvenile Delinquency Prevention and Control Act of 1968*, ed. Larry L. Dye, "Love, Trust, and Respect for Each Other, Preconditions of Justice as the Basis for Law and Order." Amherst, Mass.: University of Massachusetts Conference, 1970.

Thomas, Arthur E. and Ruth W. Burgin. *An Experiment in Community School Control: An Evaluation of the Dayton Experience*. Wilberforce, Ohio: Institute for Research and Development in Urban Areas. Central State University, May 1971.

Monographs—

Banks, James A. and Grambs, Jean D. ed. *Black Self-Concept*. New York: McGraw-Hill, 1972.

Bennett, Lerone, Jr. *Before the Mayflower*. Baltimore: Penguin, 1966.

The Challenge of Blackness. Chicago: Johnson Publishing, 1972.

Carmichael, Stokeley and Hamilton, Charles V. *Black Power: The Politics of Liberation in America*. New York: Vintage Books, Alfred A. Knopf, 1967.

Davis, Angela Y. *If They Come in the Morning*. New York: Joseph Okpaku Publishing, 1971.

Fader, Daniel. *The Naked Children*. New York: Macmillan, 1971.

Fanon, Frantz. *The Wretched of the Earth*. New York: Grove Press, 1968.

———. *Toward the African Revolution*. New York: Grove Press, 1967.

Freire, Paulo. *The Pedagogy of the Oppressed*. New York: Herder and Herder, 1971.

Friedenberg, Edgar. *Coming of Age in America.* New York: Random House, 1965.
Green, Robert L. *Racial Crisis in American Education.* Chicago: Follett Educational, 1969.
Hogan, Ermon O., "Racism in Education: A Barrier to Quality Education," Chapter 7 in Green, *Racial Crisis in American Education.*
Illich, Ivan. *Deschooling Society.* New York: Harper and Row, 1971.
Kelley, Earl C. *In Defense of Youth.* Englewood Cliffs, N.J.: Prentice-Hall, 1962.
Lurie, Ellen. *How to Change the Schools.* New York: Random House, 1971.
Malcolm X. "To Mississippi Youth." *Malcolm X Speaks.* Edited by George Breitman. New York: Grove Press, 1965.
McKissick, Floyd. *Three-fifths of a Man.* New York: Macmillan, 1969.
Reich, Charles A. *The Greening of America.* New York: Random House, 1971.
Reimer, Everett. *School is Dead.* Garden City, N.Y: Doubleday and Co., 1970, 1971.
Ryan, William B. *Blaming the Victim.* New York: Pantheon Books, Random House, 1971.
Toffler, Alvin. *Future Shock.* New York: Random House, 1970.
Wright, Nathan, Jr., ed. *What Black Educators Are Saying.* New York: Hawthorne Books, 1970.
Yette, Samuel F. *The Choice: The Issue of Black Survival in America.* New York: G. P. Putnam's Sons, 1971.

Center Publications—
Faust, Ralph and Thomas, Arthur E., *Student Rights Handbook for Dayton, Ohio,* prepared by the Center for the Study of Student Citizenship, Rights, and Responsibilities. Dayton, Ohio and the National Juvenile Law Center, St. Louis, Missouri, September, 1971.
Geringer, Dan, "The Devil Made Me Suspend That Boy," *Rap Magazine,* June, 1971.
Geringer, Dan, ed. "Three Nights in Dayton," a special section of *Rap Magazine,* October, 1971.
Thomas, Arthur E., "Can They Do These Things to Us?," *Rap Magazine,* November, 1971.
Thomas, Arthur E. and Towarnicky, Carol, "Of Scapegoats and Other Healthy Animals," *Rap Magazine,* December, 1971.
Towarnicky, Carol, ed., "Juvenile Rights in Ohio," a special section of *Rap Magazine,* March, 1971.
Towarnicky, Carol, "Respect Each Other, Be Real Nice," *Rap Magazine,* January, 1971.
Towarnicky, Carol, ed., "What We Study and Why," a special section of *Rap Magazine,* April 1972.
Copies may be ordered directly from Student Rights Center, 1145 Germantown St., Dayton, Ohio, 45408.

Violence, Nonviolence, and the Lessons of History

Project HIP-HOP Journeys South

NANCY UHLAR MURRAY

MARCO GARRIDO

> History, despite its wrenching pain,
> Cannot be unlived, but if faced
> With courage, need not be lived again.
> — Maya Angelou, *On the Pulse of Morning*[1]

In July 1994, fourteen students from the Boston area traveled with five educators to the South to visit key sites of the civil rights movement of the 1950s and 1960s, and to learn about the power of nonviolence from people who were often teenagers themselves when they risked their lives and filled the jails on their quest for civil rights.

The students had been chosen to take part in the second summer tour of Project HIP-HOP (Highways into the Past: History, Organizing and Power), a "rolling classroom" devised by the Bill of Rights Education Project, which I direct, and the Massachusetts Student Alliance Against Racism and Violence, directed by Pam Ellis. Project HIP-HOP grew out of a "Youth Against Racism" weekend retreat that the Bill of Rights Education Project held in October 1992 for forty-five high school students from twenty-two schools, half urban, and half suburban and rural.[2] The retreat had been requested by students who were searching for ways to make their voices heard in the aftermath of the acquittal of the police officers who beat Rodney King. It was enormously encouraging in what it revealed about young people's commitment to justice and their willingness to tackle social problems and to listen to each other.

Harvard Educational Review Vol. 65 No. 2 Summer 1995

During that weekend retreat, the staff discovered that they shared an admiration for the philosophy and practice of Myles Horton's Highlander Folk School in eastern Tennessee.[3] For sixty years, people of different races had been gathering at the Highlander to share and draw authority from their own experiences and to find ways to participate together in the creation of a more democratic society. Rosa Parks, while executive secretary of the NAACP in Montgomery, Alabama, was sent to a Highlander workshop by the Alabama NAACP president. Shortly thereafter she made the individual and historic decision not to move from her seat on a Montgomery bus. She later spoke of the strength that first Highlander workshop had given her "to persevere in my work for freedom, not just for blacks, but for all oppressed people."[4]

The Highlander has opened its doors to a range of movement activists, including Dr. Martin Luther King Jr., who was later pictured on Southern billboards attending a "Communist training school."[5] It also has served as the organizing base for the Citizenship Schools that Septima Clark established in several Southern states to train people to read so they could register to vote. Drawing further inspiration from *Eyes on the Prize,* and from the educational vision of movement veteran and theology professor Vincent Harding, we resolved to visit the Highlander as part of an educational tour of the South during the summer of 1993.[6] Seven high school students, including several who participated in the planning process, and four educators participated in this first Project HIP-HOP tour.

Expanding the Dialogue about Violence and Racism

In his lyrical book, *Hope and History: Why We Must Share the Story of the Movement,* Vincent Harding asks what the movement for freedom in the 1950s and 1960s means now "for the gun-filled streets of Dorchester, of Lawndale, of L.A.?"[7]

> Something tells us that one of the deep wounds of the life of the streets . . . is that young people have been separated from both their past and their future, leaving a vast and aching void, often to be filled with nothing more than the most destructive values of society. *Eyes on the Prize* opens a way for such young people to re-enter the humanizing flow of history, to consider the possibility that there is purpose and meaning for their lives far beyond the terror and temptations of their immediate situation.[8]

Students, he contends, can be put in touch with the best in themselves by learning about the lives of those who have created "a powerful heritage, one filled with questions for reflection, discussion, and action. It is a heritage each new generation needs to know, perhaps to claim as a source of power, as a path toward the discovery of its own largest possibilities."[9]

However, it often takes more than showing *Eyes on the Prize* to have the lessons of the series come alive in the classroom. Many young people today, overwhelmed by a sense of being powerless and futureless, may react initially to what Harding calls America's "pro-democracy movement" with anger, cynicism, and even desperation, rather than hope.[10] In schools where the institution of slavery and the resistance to it is "covered" in a lesson or two, and the civil rights movement makes an appearance mainly around the time of Martin Luther King Jr.'s birthday, it is hardly surprising that students feel either incredulous or lied to when they encounter the all-pervasive nature of racism in the United States in the 1950s and 1960s. Many students become enraged when they find out about the level of officially sanctioned violence that sustained an American apartheid. To those adolescents honing their survival skills in today's urban war zones, the techniques of nonviolent civil disobedience depicted in *Eyes on the Prize* seem all but incomprehensible. These young people are often less touched by the movement's triumphs than by a sense of its unfinished business. At a summer institute for teachers on the theme of racism and how to fight it, organized by the Bill of Rights Education Project in August 1993, participants shared with Harding their concerns about the rage that was "a constant undercurrent" when they showed segments of *Eyes on the Prize* to their students.[11] A few teachers said they feared that the series could lead directly to violence, since some of their African American students talked bitterly about the need for "revenge" after viewing one of the episodes.

Young people of color suspect they are not getting the real story in schools, and are well aware that past injustices have not entirely been laid to rest. After a conference on violence held by the Bill of Rights Education Project for 350 students on April 5, 1994, the *Boston Globe* reporter who was present at the event wrote that no one could "stop the teenagers from returning to a bitter, haunting matter the youths say adults try to avoid: the role institutional racism plays in the escalating violence among young people."[12]

This "haunting matter" has been a constant refrain in the dozen conferences and several smaller workshops and retreats the Bill of Rights Education Project has held for students over the past six years. No matter what the theme — be it censorship or teen curfews, "stop and search" policing or dress codes in schools — students inevitably steer the discussion to the issues of racism, intolerance, and violence. African American and Latino students invariably relate these problems to a lack of "respect." They express a deep longing to be treated justly, and to know they count for something in school and in society. Students have frequently said how much they appreciate the opportunity offered by our forums to talk openly about these issues — a chance they rarely get in their daily lives.[13]

Teachers have generally lacked the support, the confidence, the resources, or the incentive to discuss "institutional racism" — a phrase that must be as rare in the classroom as in the *Boston Globe*.[14] School authorities for the most part have preferred the "quick fix" of ready-made violence prevention programs to the long-haul effort of listening to their students on a day-to-day basis, and embarking with them on an exploration of the root causes of the violence engulfing so many young lives. In a nation founded on the extermination and dispossession of the native inhabitants and the brutal enslavement of African peoples, it is remarkable that "violence" is so often talked about today as if it were unique to this generation of urban youth, a product of their defective families and guns-and-drugs culture, and virtually unknown in earlier eras.[15]

This largely ahistorical outlook serves neither students nor the country and its future. Schools seem fearful of controversy, regardless of its educational potential. Young people exposed only to the sanitized history offered by textbooks have little understanding of why things are the way they are. They are seldom exposed to the sort of questions that would help them make sense of the world around them and that could be the subjects of stimulating educational debates.

Did the civil rights movement make the playing field level in racial terms? Where has our society been heading since the Kerner Commission more than a quarter century ago condemned ghetto poverty as the root cause of the burning of the cities?[16] Are growing economic inequalities reversible, or simply part of the natural order? What did Martin Luther King Jr. mean when he reflected during a November 1966 staff retreat on the gains of the civil rights movement, stating: "The changes that came about during this period were at best surface changes; they were not really substantive changes. . . . The roots of racism are very deep in America; our society is still structured on the basis of racism"?[17] What, if any, is the historical basis for his statement? Are there still "substantive changes" to be made before we can say that the battle against racism has been won?

Those who feel that questions like these have no place in the classroom because they could inflame wounds and deepen divisions might agree with members of the Mississippi state textbook committee who rejected a new textbook in 1974 out of fear that it would "cause bad feeling between black and white students."[18] But as Cornel West argues in his book *Race Matters,* "our truncated public discussions of race suppress the best of who and what we are as a people because they fail to confront the complexity of the issue in a candid and critical manner."[19] Tackling these issues head-on in schools and ending the silence or evasiveness that has so often surrounded the issue of race can be an effective means of bringing back into the learning process young people who are currently convinced that school has nothing worthwhile to teach them.[20]

We can only know the best of who we are and what we are capable of as a people if we look at the whole picture. This means examining our society's flaws and tracing their roots back into history. Historian John Hope Franklin has written eloquently of the importance of facing up to history in his book, *The Color Line: Legacy for the Twenty-First Century:*

> Perhaps the very first thing we need to do as a nation and as individual members of society is to confront our past, and see it for what it is. It is a past that is filled

> with some of the ugliest possible examples of racial brutality and degradation in human history. We need to recognize it for what it was and is and not explain it away, excuse it, or justify it. Having done that, we should then make a good-faith effort to turn our history around so that we can see it in front of us, so that we can avoid doing what we have done for so long. . . . Then, we need to do everything possible to emphasize the positive qualities that all of us have, qualities which we have never utilized to the fullest, but which we must utilize if we are to solve the problem of the color line in the twenty-first century.[21]

Turning Our History Around

Many young people today, who have little grasp of where they have come from, where we as a nation have been, and what we have been able to achieve, appear bereft of a vision for the future of our country. Unlike the thousands of children and young adults who, in the 1960s, marched and sat in at lunch counters and spearheaded drives for voter registration, large numbers of students today have little notion of how they can participate in the creation of a United States of America that at last lives up to its democratic promise — or, indeed, of why they should bother.

Vincent Harding believes that the civil rights movement — once the catalyst for the whole "rights revolution" galvanizing women, gays and lesbians, the disabled, and other groups to demand full participation in the body politic — retains its capacity to energize a generation:

> I have seen students of every kind literally moved to tears and to new questions, opened to excitement and new personal resolves, when they have been creatively exposed to this dramatic story of human beings risking all to renew and transform their lives and their communities. Thus the exciting struggle for democracy has come alive for them. They have been able to imagine what it was like not long ago when American citizens, often led by young people, took their rights and responsibilities so seriously that they, like the white Founders of 1776, were prepared to risk their lives, their fortunes, and their sacred honor to create a more just, a more democratic, nation. These were the new founders of the emerging multiracial American nation for the twenty-first century, and they may help our students understand the meaning of the continuing creation of American democracy.[22]

The Bill of Rights Education Project embarked on Project HIP-HOP in anticipation that young people would be opened to the excitement and new personal resolves described by Harding. They would then be in a position to participate in a process that could eventually, in John Hope Franklin's words, begin to "turn our history around." Our 1993 pilot tour generated considerable interest. In the South we were frequently trailed by TV cameras. Producers of programs based in southern African American communities hoped that interviews with young northerners who had come so far to talk with movement veterans would awaken their own youth to a history almost entirely ignored in their schools.[23] We also had enthusiastic audiences in Massachusetts, where participants took slide shows into classrooms and community centers and addressed teachers at workshops and at our 1993 summer institute.

The 1993 tour has certainly had a positive impact on the lives of the participants. Marc Germain, a Randolph, Massachusetts, high school student, said in an interview shortly after his return, "It made me realize that young people can empower themselves to do anything. It gave me hope for the future."[24] Kim Howard, who went on the HIP-HOP trip after completing her final year at Boston Latin School, told the *Boston Globe,* "The trip couldn't have come at a better time for me. I'm about to go off to college, and there is no way I am not going to work my hardest, do my best, after seeing what people went through so I could be where I am today."[25] One fifteen-year-old HIP-HOP participant resolved to break away from his gang, while another, who had always regarded herself as a "non-joiner," subsequently became thoroughly involved in community service activities. Her mother described the trip's impact on her daughter:

> The Project HIP-HOP teens learned lessons that no history book can teach. They came to understand that ordinary people in ordinary places have the power to transform society. For my child, the Project HIP-HOP experience was not simply an intellectual revelation. She has become an activist in her school community on issues relating to racism, sexism and homophobia. Before Project HIP-HOP, this simply would not have been possible.[26]

Part of Project HIP-HOP's power to transform lies in its physical and emotional intensity, attributes it shares with certain Outward Bound programs.[27] The van journeys are long and hard, meals are unpredictable, and sleeping arrangements, often rugged, are sometimes an adventure in themselves. We camped in tents and slept on the floors of homes and community centers. We were permitted to spend the night inside the Lorraine Motel, now the National Civil Rights Museum in Memphis, and we slept in college dormitories and trailers. Some of our students had never been out of New England. Many had never camped before or seen a farm. Most had rarely strayed from an interstate highway. Whether it was going down a coal mine in southern West Virginia, or spending time among the descendants of the original African American inhabitants on an island off the coast of Georgia, students and adults alike were presented every day with new situations, and their horizons were constantly expanded.

Student participants in Project HIP-HOP's pilot year helped interview and select the young people for the 1994 trip. The applicants had already submitted answers in written form or on audiotape to questions such as: What would you like to be doing in ten years' time? How would you describe racism today? What are the similarities and differences between today's racism and that of the 1950s and 1960s? They were also asked to identify the individual(s) whom they admire in public life today, and explain why.

We selected some students who had already seen Henry Hampton's award-winning *Eyes on the Prize* series about the civil rights movement and wanted to learn more, and chose others who were already involved in anti-racism work or showed promise as student organizers. But we were also on the lookout for other forms of motivation. We interviewed one young woman of working-class background who intends to be the first person in her family to graduate from high school. She had read about Project HIP-HOP in a newspaper article and found her way to us without the encouragement of a teacher or other adult. Possessing a strong sense that the world was not the way it should be, and the desire to understand why her family was, as she put it, "so racist," she was among those selected for the 1994 tour. We also decided to offer places to young men who had been immersed in the life of the streets, and were in the process of turning their lives around.

As co-organizers of the program, Pam Ellis and I were seeking to bring together an ethnically diverse group of young people of widely varying backgrounds and experiences who would learn from each other during the grueling five thousand mile trip. All of the students were aged fifteen to seventeen and from the greater Boston area. They were of African American, European American, Latino, Filipino, Haitian, Indian, and Native American heritage, and represented a broad spectrum in economic class. Some of the participants lived in public housing projects; two had no fixed address. Most attended public schools, two went to private schools, one was in the METCO program, and two had dropped out of high school.[28] Four participants were peer leaders in anti-gang violence prevention programs, and one was the student head of her school's conflict resolution program.

Our aim was to connect these students with a history of social transformation brought about not long ago by young people; to bring them into contact with students in the South who are grappling today with issues of racism, violence, and stunted aspirations; and to provide them with the opportunity and skills to reach out to their peers and to share what they learn on the trip in schools and community centers around Boston and the Commonwealth during the 1994–1995 academic year.

Discussion during our seventeen days on the road in July 1994 was framed by the tension between the rhetoric and reality of democracy in the United States. We began our explorations at Philadelphia's Independence Hall, where we viewed the Liberty Bell, and then met with Ramona Africa, the only adult member of the MOVE commune to survive when the Philadelphia police, in a stunning example of state-sponsored violence, dropped a bomb from a helicopter on the commune's house in May 1985.[29] The following day we traveled to Harper's Ferry, where, a year after drawing up plans for a biracial republic and a new Constitution, John Brown resorted to violence to strike what he hoped would be a revolutionary blow against the slave system.

There was no such redemptive purpose behind the violence we confronted as we journeyed into the history of our own century; for example, in the museum built on the site of Martin Luther King Jr.'s assassination in Memphis; or in another Philadelphia, this one in Mississippi, where three civil rights workers were abducted and murdered thirty years ago. Near the site of the memorial erected in their honor, we met under an old oak tree with ninety-eight-year-old Caesar Moore, born in the year of *Plessy v. Ferguson,* who talked to us about his life and about ongoing Klan activity in the area.[30] He challenged us always to be vigorous in the fight against racism. In the Mississippi Delta town of Mound Bayou, founded by African Americans in 1887, we were touched by the spirit of the young people who presented a pageant for us about the creation of their town by former slaves seeking the promise of freedom. We learned about the price young people paid for freedom at the Civil Rights Institute in Birmingham, Alabama, which is adjacent to the Sixteenth Street Baptist Church, where four young girls died in a bombing, and we visited the Kelly Ingram Park, where children were attacked by "Bull" Connor's dogs and fire hoses in 1963 and imprisoned by the thousands.[31] We heard about native people's struggles in Pembroke County, North Carolina, where Lumbees, a Native American tribe that constituted a majority of the population, took it upon themselves to chase away the Ku Klux Klan in the 1950s and 1960s. We literally put ourselves in the footsteps of the demonstrators who crossed the Edmund Pettus Bridge in Selma, Alabama, in March 1965 and were viciously beaten as they tried to march to the state capital of Montgomery to demand the right to vote.

As we learned more about the role that racism has played in our history and continues to play today, the students kept up a dialogue with each other about their own encounters with racism and violence. In the words of *New York Times* journalist Sara Rimer, who accompanied the group for three days, Project HIP-HOP "is a journey not only into the past, but also through their own lives."[32]

The more we talked with young people in the South about the civil rights movement's unfinished business and the problems they are confronting today, the more our group began to find connections between their own situation in Massachusetts and settings as different as rural Mississippi and New Orleans' oldest public housing project, where teenagers working at the Kuji Center met with us after staging a sit-in at the city hall to protest the cutting of funds for their work against violence and teen pregnancy.[33]

The notion of seeking social and political change through nonviolent means did not strike an immediate chord with all Project HIP-HOP participants. At the Highlander Center in eastern Tennessee, we met with students from around the South to talk about violence in communities, discussing, for example, who benefits and who loses by violent actions. We also took part in a workshop on the techniques of nonviolence. Many in our group found it difficult to understand how people could sit passively at lunch counters and endure insults and physical attacks. But as the trip continued, the message driven home by movement veterans was that under the circumstances that prevailed in the 1950s and 1960s, nonviolence was not so much a choice as a necessity. White supremacists, after all, had superior fire power, and if protestors had retaliated in self-defense, they would have attracted neither the mass support nor the national sympathy essential to overcome Jim Crow.[34] And as the members of our group grew closer to each other, we personally glimpsed the kind of unity and shared aspirations that made nonviolent protest possible. Musing about the ethnic and economic barriers that generally separate people today, one young woman commented that nonviolence was not outdated, and could still be an effective tool if we could just get people to work for a common end and respect each other.

But what common end could there be under today's complex conditions, given the absence of a single target as compelling as Jim Crow segregation? This is a question the HIP-HOP youth, now that they have begun to take the measure of their country's problems, will grapple with during our future meetings and in their chosen fields of social activism. We know it will not be easy to nurture their new consciousness under the conditions some of them endure, including all the tensions of inner-city street life and homelessness. But they seem determined to continue the dialogue already begun, and to make sure it includes many different voices. In the words of fifteen-year-old Arnold Chamanlal from Boston, Massachusetts, a sophomore at Jeremiah E. Burke High School, "This trip made a lot of people come together. We were all different races, but on this trip we were one. It worked."[35]

Arnold, a former gang member who now works with the Boston Violence Prevention Program, was the poet of our group. Here is how he sees the challenge facing his generation:

Right now I'm looking at two strange hands
Could be a woman could be a man's
Everybody has something deep in their soul
Their own little story to be told.
Stories about their life and their past
Will come out at last
One man fighting for freedom
Is better than a king's whole kingdom.
We fight for what's right
To put our children's future in sight
The hands fight to be free
One day we all shall see
That hate is destroying the world.
If that happens there will be no more stories to be told.
We must come together and do what's good not what's bad
And our parents will be glad.
My father will say I'm truly his son
I did what's right not what's wrong
And for that I will be a man, my soul will be strong.

And with the blood in my veins
I will defend my home not go insane.
For my hands are strong
and I promise I'll do what's right
And not what's wrong.

The Next Steps

By the end of February 1995, the students of Project HIP-HOP 1994 had shown slides of their trip and made presentations in classes and assemblies to over two thousand suburban and urban high school students, at universities, and to afterschool groups in Boston. They gave the address at the City of Quincy (Massachusetts) Martin Luther King Jr. Day Breakfast on January 16, 1995, and they have a full schedule of commitments throughout the spring, including speaking at the American Civil Liberties Union Biennial Conference and the National Coalition of Education Activists Conference.

Their message is essentially one of hope, of new possibilities. When asked what the trip meant to her personally, a student who was born in Puerto Rico told young people in a largely Latino neighborhood that she used to feel as if she didn't belong in the United States. Now she feels as if the movement was speaking for her, too, and that U.S. history is her history. Another student said that before the trip he never thought he would like or trust a White person, but now the White students from Project HIP-HOP are his close friends, and he realizes how wrong it is to think in simple racial terms. A fifteen-year-old from Boston, who became involved in a voter registration drive before an election, tells her high school and college audiences that people in the movement paid too heavy a price for them to say they can't be bothered registering for the polls. A former member of a Latino gang is spreading the message that Latinos and African Americans, turf rivals in Roxbury, Massachusetts, have far too much in common to be fighting each other.

As they reflect on their experiences, speak publicly, and carry out research for our *Racism, Rights and History* curriculum on the role of young people in the movement, the youth of Project HIP-HOP are continuing to grow in ways that are exciting to witness. Our challenge is to find ways to sustain the excitement and spirit engendered by the trip, and to enable HIP-HOP participants to convey what they learned to their peers in a way that will begin the process of turning our history around.

The evaluations we have received about the impact of Project HIP-HOP presentations indicate that the program can be a powerful motivation to both learning and social involvement. It is perhaps not surprising that Project HIP-HOP has struck a real chord in Boston schools, where the majority of students are African American and Latino. We are now discovering the important role that the program can play in surburban settings, including those where there are very few students of color.

After speaking to classes at a school outside Boston where there had recently been open conflicts between the resident students and students in the METCO program, we have been invited to be part of a school-wide assembly that organizers hope will lead to frank exchanges about inter-racial problems in the school. Beginning this dialogue with a student-led look at this nation's record of positive social change and the "unfinished business" of the movement seems to be a way of getting a discussion going that might otherwise never move beyond the threshold of personal prejudices and painful feelings.

As exciting as many of Project HIP-HOP's school visits have been, we still are aware of how much more needs to be done if the program is to realize its transforming potential. We recognize the need to prepare future HIP-HOP participants more fully for the history they encounter on trips, so that they better understand the significance of what they are hearing and seeing, and are in a position to ask searching questions. We would also like them to have the opportunity for more sustained dialogue with their peers.

These problems could be overcome if we succeed in arranging for Project HIP-HOP to be considered a form of community service, with student participants getting academic credit for the work they do with other schools. We are also laying the groundwork for participants to serve as student teachers who would facilitate a sequence of lessons in particular schools. Eventually, we would like them to be able to teach those parts of our forthcoming curriculum relating to the movement and to the role of young people as agents of social change, which two Project HIP-HOP students are currently helping to create.

Project HIP-HOP needs a consistent source of funding if it is to succeed in putting young people in touch with what Vincent Harding calls the "powerful heritage" of the movement, and to motivate them to work to develop a nation that at last lives up to the promise of its rhetoric and founding ideals. Assuming the resources are available, I am encouraged to imagine a future in which representatives from each year's HIP-HOP tour come together in annual or biennial meetings. These energizing reunions would enable participants to draw strength from each other and give us the opportunity to observe, over a period of several years, what a critical mass of young people who share a common set of potentially transforming experiences can achieve.

We want to continue to build an understanding of the way racism has operated across time and across cultures. We believe the best way to do this is to put students in touch with people who have worked to transform U.S. society. We plan to continue to bring young people together with movement veterans, including those who live locally, and others who have stories to tell about their struggles to make "liberty and justice for all" more than a pious hope. We may in fact find it is not essential to travel five thousand miles to experience what one 1994 HIP-HOP participant described as "the type of 'hands-on' and 'ears-on' learning" that "surpasses anything read in a history book."

Nevertheless, the journey through the South, which is also a journey into history, into our inner beings, and through our own lives, has a very special power. One of the most inspiring dimensions of Project HIP-HOP was that wherever we went we found people who had played a role in the movement, many as teenagers or even younger. We met people on the streets of Mound Bayou, Mississippi, who had marched and sung with Fannie Lou Hamer.[36] We were welcomed into homes and slept on floors. This gave history an immediacy that allowed our young people to feel part of things, and made it seem that the torch was being passed.

Before we turned northward again, we paused at the Civil Rights Memorial in Montgomery, Alabama, to remember the movement's triumphs and those who had died in the struggle. As we leaned our heads against a wall streaming with water, Philippines-born Marco Garrido, now a senior at Boston College High School, summed up the moment for us: "I feel we have just been baptized by the waters of freedom."

Project HIP-HOP Lifts the Spirit and Teaches Lessons

The second part of this article was written by Marco Garrido (the first part was written by Nancy Uhlar Murray). His reflections on the tour are based on his journal. Photographs by James Blackwell.

There is a place in the Lorraine Motel, now the National Civil Rights Museum, that has more than its usual share of ghosts. Not far from where we slept, the left side of the second floor pinches off into an enclosure. A balcony juts out. Martin Luther King Jr., looking out, was shot here. The bullet blew his necktie to pieces and left a bloodstain on the concrete. Just before the balcony, the rooms King had used are on display. The beds are unmade, the breakfast half-eaten, and the coffee seems stale from waiting. A slow lament, sung by Gospel singer Mahalia Jackson, wafts around us. And we stare, noses up to the thin glass divider, out at the still blood-stained balcony.

The Civil Rights Monument in Montgomery, Alabama, has a quiet elegance. The names are carved in the deep, dark granite. The smooth stone slab is circular, and the names are beneath the surface, under a stream of water. The names of the heroes, the martyrs, the leaders, the people, the victims. An upright slab stands adjoining, and beneath a curtain of water the stone's inscription reads, "Until Justice Rolls Down Like Waters and Righteousness Like a Mighty Stream." We wet our fingers, tracing the names in the granite, and we wet our heads as the Alabama sun beats down, letting the flowing water cool us.

Luis Rodriguez and Sarah Wedge look at late-nineteenth-century KKK gear at the National Civil Rights Museum, located in the Lorraine Motel, Memphis, Tennessee. Photo by James Blackwell.

The Highlander Center nestled in the misty Tennessee hills — a place where social activists come to listen, learn, regroup, feel empowered — hosts us as it once did Martin Luther King Jr. and Rosa Parks. We are gathered together, each hand clasped by another; and we sing "We Shall Overcome," and our voices lift our spirits. There is a warm intimacy radiating from the hardwood floor, the subdued light reflected in each of our faces, half shadowed, and in the air pregnant with ideas.

In Mound Bayou, Mississippi, at the Founder's Day Pageant, the children, rich in spirit, very aware of their African heritage, take on the guise of the ghosts of the town founders. The small dark face bobbed a bit. His eyes swept the pews. We, his audience, sat expectant. Then he began. It turned out he was a ghost. Isaiah Montgomery, he said his name was. In 1887, he and his cousin settled this African American-owned town, Mound Bayou. After Isaiah, the other townspeople spoke to us, recounted their history in sweet voices. All were over a hundred years old. Folk of iron determination, they built Mound Bayou shortly after the Civil War. They knew that obstacles lay ahead. But as a community they would overcome. And the ghosts quite clearly expressed to us, through the words of Maya Angelou, Langston Hughes, and N'Kosi Sikelela Africa, a tireless and exuberant spirit.

I can feel the mercilessness of the Selma sun as we walk across the Edmund Pettus Bridge, where only a few decades before civil rights activists were viciously beaten, pummelled by water, sticks, fists, as they tried to march where we now march.

I still see the crack on the back of the Bell of Liberty.

The experiences are vivid, branded into my memory. Project HIP-HOP has furnished us, an interracial group of Boston area students, with intense experiences that continue to enrich us. Our meetings aptly began in Philadelphia, where the hallowed specters of the Founding Fathers, who tried to hammer out a constitution securing liberty, skirted about Independence Hall. Across from the Hall, the Liberty Bell is silent. In the days that followed, as the accent thickened, Boston became a shrinking speck in the rear-view window. Here was a different environment, one ripe with lessons. We had only to open our ears to the voices of the activist, the farmer, the drugstore clerk, the little boy, the corpse, the poetry of the fields, hills, and highway.

The lessons were garnered like pearls for us who were combing the shore.

A Walk Through St. Thomas

The youths of Kujichagulia marched into the Kuji Center. Kujichagulia, "self-determination" in Ki-Swahili, is a youth project based near St. Thomas, one of the oldest federal housing projects in the country, which is located in New Orleans, Louisiana. The youths had marched on the New Orleans City Hall, demanding further funding for youth summer employment programs. We, the HIP-HOPers, watched them stream in. Triumphant smiles bedecked each face.

Ninety-eight-year-old Caesar Moore in Philadelphia, Mississippi, near the site where three civil rights workers were murdered in 1964. Photo by James Blackwell.

The youths spoke in iron tones about their protest: "The political system needs a push now and again. So we push." Kujichagulia celebrated in a joyful uproar. The dancers danced traditional African dances furiously, the rappers rapped the raps of St. Thomas with spirit, and the rest of us talked about life. "So what y'all doin' in Bawhston?" they asked. "Well, tell us what you're doing here," we countered. We, the HIP-HOPers, and they, the youth of Kujichagulia, gathered in a circle. What was life like anyway? Some in our group and all in theirs spoke in angry, sad, determined, tones of similar things: money, drugs, gangs, and guns. I listened and tried to understand the lives they spoke of.

Heedful of the warnings of the Kuji Center youth, I paced on the pavement and looked down at St. Thomas. A block from where I wavered lay the housing project, supposedly infested with drugs, gangs, and guns. To go or not to go. Curiosity compelled me. I went.

As I walked down, I fastened a red bandanna about my head. I slipped on shades and unstrapped my watch, pocketing it. This isn't enough, I thought. I surveyed my clothes: my tan, khaki shorts, grass-green New Orleans "We be jazzin'" tourist t-shirt, my clean white socks snug in black Nike shoes. It wasn't enough.

Heart rages in a palpitating frenzy
Senses on end like a frightened cat
Every engine hum whips my head back.
It is mere silliness, yes?
These phantom images thumbing their noses at me.
Or stupidity?
The headlines lay before me.

A church stood beside St. Thomas. Its steeples stretched high, and saints looked down kindly from elegantly carved niches. This seems out of place, I thought. On the towering doors, ladders leaned. Men stood upon them and installed heavy iron rings. I found myself wondering, was this church full on Sundays?

The boundary was clearly marked. A "No Trespassing" sign stared sternly down from the side of one building. I paused. Here was a chance to turn back. The sign certainly couldn't be disobeyed. Such a rationalization was so transparent that I knew if I didn't continue on, this instance of weakness would linger uncomfortably in my memory. I was also goaded on by pride: I am fearless, adventurous, open to experience. Oh, yes I am. Such an assertion, based on petty experiences, needed to be challenged. If I retreated, my perception of myself would be exposed for the smoke that it was. I knew I had to continue.

I entered St. Thomas. There was a geometry in the arrangement: similar houses stood on square plots; each plot was evenly spaced from the other, and the rows of plots stretched on. Yet a prickly vibrance defied the gray geometry. Life was lived in this place. The houses had red roofs. Green iron railings snaked from a tan wood porch to a balcony overhang. On the balcony lay a mess of discarded furniture; chairs were set for observation and coffee, and little legs hung down. The kids grasped the green bars with little hands, stuck little faces between their hands, and looked at me with big eyes. On a porch, grandmothers rocked in rocking chairs, a periodic creak weaving into the comfortable hum of life. Tired middle-aged women sat on the steps, their heads heavy in their hands. And by their bare feet, little kids played: cards, patty-cake, jacks, tag, hide-and-seek.

As I walked on, those on their porches eyed me warily. I felt sorely out of place. I held my head high. My cheeks pricked with humiliated discomfort. Their eyes stung. An elderly woman rose from her rocking chair, leaned on the porch railing, and timidly asked: "Excuse me, sir. Are you looking for someone?" I, not looking at her, mumbled "Just looking" and walked on. I heard the footsteps of her eyes behind me.

The puddles on the pavement telegraphed the swish of footsteps. Deep in my belly's pit, a big man with a megaphone yelled at me: turn back, turn around, turn away! My senses pricked up. There was significance in everything: a tree's limbs gnarled upward towards the sky; the slap of the jump-rope tapped the time; a Black youth walked past me. As he approached, a climax

A street scene in Jackson, Mississippi. Photo by James Blackwell.

built. When he lined up with me, he gelled with a media image. And when he passed, relief.

There I stood, awash in pretense. I, who had thought myself free of racist stereotypes, succumbed to paranoia each time a Black youth passed. The big man with the megaphone drowned out the tiny voice of sense. Here, in St. Thomas, I was jelly.

In indignation, I walked on.

On that day, I learned this: it takes time to develop a strong and free mind. That small voice of reason needs to be consciously nurtured, so it cannot be so easily obliterated by the man with the megaphone. It'll take plenty of time, and plenty of practice. And so, I walked on.

Some Things Thought About

My lack of direct experience with urban life puts me in somewhat of an observer position. There were a few people on the HIP-HOP tour who lived in an inner city deformed by gang life, drug-trading, guns. The time spent travelling in the vans was long, and the conversations rich. The journey, looked at from a different angle, can be said to have taken place entirely within the vans, within the community, within the individual, and in the sharing of ourselves.

I have been amply exposed to the representations set forth by the media and, as I jarringly learned walking through St. Thomas, representation and reality are often at odds. These images have a sinister way of weaving into the subconscious, and then surfacing when in an environment that has been represented before it has been experienced. Some may profess to enlightenment, but when thrust into a situation challenging this claim, instinct founded on stereotypes, prejudices, often upstages rationality. What then is there to do? Experience everything? (I wish, but not likely.) Profound thought? (A pipe dream.) More likely it is a mix of both: experience, reflection on experience and reflection on ideas, and the experience of others. Then something of a collective experience is gathered, the essence of human wisdom. And so I set to learn.

And as I learned, I had to remind myself that what was being shared with me was real, was lived. I had been so inundated by media images of what life was supposed to be. But life, it seemed, was more elusive than that. My friends spoke of street fights, car break-ins, respect, honor, a drive to rise beyond circumstances, dreams, how to hold a gun to minimize backlash, bullet-wounds, beauty, gang stand-offs, raunchy jokes, perseverance, and love. No, the sense of what I possessed, and what I had taken for granted, did not wash over me as a wave does; instead, I admired these friends, for they seemed to be in the midst of life, a life I had heard about but which for me always seemed to be elsewhere.

It did strike me that my life seemed to progress upon a structure, upward like a leaning ladder: grade school, high school, college, and then . . . life? But with my friends, the "and then . . ." came sooner and the ellipses stretched on, punctuated by a very definite question mark. Should I drop out of high school, sell drugs and strip cars — I need the money, and besides, how will algebra help me get respect, be hip, be feared, be loved? And I'm tired of dodging the kids who have it in for me, uncertain whether I'll limp home, hand over my puffed eye; I need a gun, but only for protection.

I have reflected upon the sense of thick uncertainty, where individual efforts and actions are not judged by some absolute, for everything now seems relative — where killing's fine if you believe you're justified; where nihilism seems to be the life philosophy; where conscience, with a sweeping gesture, may now be proclaimed dead; where, as Kurt Cobain screamed it, "all in all is all we are."[37] But then I think about how wrong I am when my thoughts run like that. The inner city may be seen in such a bleak light, but then the observer will not have seen it all. As I listened to my friends, I also learned about love, tolerance, responsibility, innocence, wonder, kindness, magnanimity . . . humanity. I respect these friends unreservedly, and what I admire them for most is their lovely humanity.

Project HIP-HOP participants. Bottom row (l-r): Nancy Murray, Tanya Daniels, Veronica Valentine, Todd Fry; row 2: Quetzal Mount, James Blackwell, Sarah Wedge, Pam Ellis, Anibal Zayas, Vaughn Simkins; row 3, on bar: Astride Joseph, Marco Garrido, Brenda Velez, Luis Rodriguez, Melody Baker; back row: Mario Taylor, Antoinette Johnson, Marian Hammond, Arnold Chamantal.

Where the Movement Left Off

I remember clearly one morning at an Alabama campsite when, while leaning upon a buzzing washing machine, a middle-aged White woman said, her index finger rising to us, "I pity young people today. They are taught by history to hate." She continued, evidently backed by a feeling of self-righteousness, to say that the movement had unnecessarily angered Black people, stirring them to rail against phantom injustices. Earlier in the morning she had encountered a staff member on our trip, and when told that we comprised a civil rights history tour, she reportedly countered: "Now let me tell you about civil rights." And she did. She said that the movement bred hate; that during pre-movement days, Blacks were content enough. As she spoke to us, she smilingly described her childhood as one filled with a community of Black people with large smiles, people who were happy and untroublesome. And she did not let us leave without calling after us, "Remember what I have said. Remember how it was."

And the words continue to resonate. The purpose of our tour crystallized: remember how it was.

The word "history" relegates what is read in a classroom textbook — no matter how recently it may have occurred — into the cobwebs and dust with the white armless statue. But to actually see history still happening, to see and feel and almost taste without the pages and the classroom walls and windows, then life is breathed into history, and history is no longer history but life.

And life is harder to ignore. I never fully realized the immense significance of the civil rights movement until I could no longer ignore the untied strings where the movement trailed off: the Memphis NAACP youth chapter members speaking to us in the Lorraine Motel alluded quite casually to the schools they attended which remained segregated in practice after the legal barriers had been dismantled, while civil rights veteran Hollis Watkins of the grassroots organization Southern Echo spoke in impassioned tones about the resistance of the "good ole boys" network to any disruption of the status quo, that is, white rule. U.S. Representative Cynthia McKinney of Georgia graciously accommodated us in her Capitol Hill office, despite being in the midst of a redistricting battle begun by her opponent for the seat who, only upon losing, decided that the district boundaries were drawn unfairly. He would rather have it re-drawn in a way that would all but prevent further Black political victories. There is a palpable sense of tension in the stares sometimes received, the ubiquity of the Confederate flag, the pride with which "Dixie" is sung. Injustice and harsh inequality are no myths; if you will dismiss the complaints of the oppressed, look instead at the difference in the quality of things: schools, shelter, streets, life. In the drab city projects, the face within will most likely be Black. The South is not so far from Boston, after all.

A visit in Greenville, Mississippi, with Boston-born Owen Brooks, a movement veteran and continuing activist, made the connection between poverty in the North and South. He surprised us one late Mississippi night when he proclaimed, "The movement has failed!" Slouched bodies, exhausted from a full day, sat up; eyes questioned his face and the seriousness with which he made the statement. The thrust of the movement, he explained, was misdirected; the focus should have been on the economic disparities underlying the intolerance, inequality, injustice. An economic upheaval of such a scale went far beyond the often serene vignettes of Black and White hands clasped in friendship during the civil rights era, but would instead imply a change of revolutionary proportions. The past, with all the human failings and injustices that we might flatter ourselves as a society to have put behind us, still lives. The past is mostly alive, according to Peter Applebome, writing in a special *New York Times* series on the South, "because, for all the sacrifice and triumph of the civil rights era, nothing touched the economic structure that continued to give whites control of the land, the jobs, and the capital, as well as the tax system that revolves around them."[38]

The South and the North are deeply scarred, and although the movement has incompletely stitched the wound, it has not failed, but goes on. The challenge is put to us, the "post"-movement generation that must still contend with all the ugliness that the 1960s activists struggled against. Our challenge, then, is to rise beyond remembering how it was, and to look forward and prepare for how it should be. We must continue the struggle.

And the movement does continue, with an exuberant and tireless spirit. The cool air of the Lorraine Motel is refreshing, providing respite from the searing Memphis sun. Upon entering the National Civil Rights Museum, a gigantic metal mountain stands imposingly before me, yet curves with surprising fluidity. Carved along the mountainside are people bent under immense loads: mothers carrying children, children with parents in their arms, men dragging themselves, women plodding onward — all headed to the top of the mountain, but none has yet reached the summit. But despite their burden, the steepness of the incline and the treachery of the jagged peaks, they march on, with an exuberant and tireless spirit. The robust life that energized the movement is palpable; it refreshes like cool water on tired hair on a hot day. And it energizes us — our spirit, once moved, remembers. And we will go on.

Later Reflections: A Personal Movement

My family emigrated from the Philippines when I was nine. The next few years were awkward. I was old enough to be impacted by the old country, but still too young to be secure in an identity. I wanted to fit in. The sting of racism was of course not a foreign barb to me: I, a Filipino, in a mostly White elementary school. That time, in my insecurity, was painful. I felt the pain of exclusion. At that tender age I learned what injustice was, what it was to be a "non-White" in a White society.

By injustice I mean a weight of oppression. Words oppress. Eyes oppress. History oppresses. What I see — the way people act, the media — is oppressive. I felt discounted because I wasn't White. Everyone was White but me. In the classroom, the teachers were White, we learned U.S. (= White) history, the issues were White, the White students discussed White concerns, the walls were white, my pencil wrote white words. Everything was White but me. The beautiful White people sold white goods, the President was White, the Pope was White, God was White.

The African Americans, the Native Americans, the Latinos, the Asians, we weren't White. We were not part of this White society. Yes, I'd seen the faces, the non-White faces, the faces of those who didn't act White, and I'd see them as outsiders, people who like me didn't fit in because we had the misfortune of being born non-White.

In my exclusion, I felt less human than a White person. White to me was more than skin color. It represented those in power. This society was theirs. I, in my fragile youth, felt inundated by White images. As I grew up, my models were White. I had no Asian role models. My Asian identity for the time was buried. I was, but for that pained voice in the back of my head, White.

I felt the drill of the eleven-year-old eyes of my classmates when issues of race were broached in class. I was uncomfortable. My non-Whiteness, it seemed, was on stage. The fact that people who were not White had to fight to secure rights was testimony to their oppression, to my oppression, to injustice. In my state of "racelessness," this was an all too painful reminder. So, I buried the subject.

I needed time to sort things out: who I was, why race tinted how others saw me, why race seemed part of the inner-city violence, what race really was and why it mattered so much. I still wasn't ready to deal with the movement, its implications, the unfinished business left (for me?). In one fundamental way, my tortured self-reflection did deal with the same issue the movement dealt with: injustice. It wasn't I who was flawed. No. Something else was wrong, and it affected more than simply me.

Then, last summer I had the opportunity to share a van with people of different backgrounds and colors. By the end of seventeen days we would be bound together by an intense experience. Our journey to the heart of the civil rights movement would tie us together as a community. Each of us had a story to tell, and all listened. We learned from one another. Our lives, we found, were lived in many ways. But by our youth we shared a common future, and the shadow of the movement's unfinished business hung over us all. Together we would have to take steps forward to finish what had been begun.

Project HIP-HOP focused what I had been wrestling with into more fluid thoughts. It was a celebration of the movement. The movement had, by the trip's end, come to be symbolically significant to me. I felt the spirit that drove the oppressed into action. Oppressed people who had fought, despite the odds, against injustice. I know how injustice can overwhelm you, and strip you of any sense of efficacy. I could relate to the inertia that kept the oppressed powerless, and the oppressors in power. But with the movement, I had hope.

Rosa Park's toughness, Dr. King's vision, the faith each activist (many of them young) had that their fight would lead to justice — all this gave me strength.

HIP-HOP was also a celebration of diversity. Pick a van and you'd find Black, Latino, Indian, Filipino, Native American, European American. And no oppressors — no one who, because of race, acted in a superior way. Our HIP-HOP group was a model community. I felt at ease with each HIP-HOPer. Being in such an environment, where we of all races communed on a human to human basis, gave me strength in my own identity. I didn't feel as I did in my younger grade school days, that I'd be better off being White. No, in our HIP-HOP community, I was proud to be a Filipino. I saw in our group's chemistry the strength in being not only White, but African American, Latino, Indian, Filipino, Native American.

Talks with my fellow HIP-HOPers, be they from the city or suburbs, ex-gang members or high schoolers, made one thing clear: they have felt the same injustice I have experienced, this feeling of oppression. Some are, of course, weighed down more than I, but it's the same kind of weight. This racism is institutional. Society sustains it. It gnaws at us as youths, as non-Whites. It's at the root of the slurs hurled by the kid: nigger, gook, chink, flip. It sustains those who believe that Blacks are lazy, Asians are good at math. It frequently leads to violence.

My own experience tells me that racism isn't simply a remnant of the Old South. It flourishes up here, an off-shoot of societal injustice. While down south you may see Confederate flags, stereotypical and demeaning Black caricatures, up north racism is as intense, but not as blatant. I've been told that African Americans don't want to work, that they whine about phantom injustice, and that society unjustly favors them — all this prefaced with, "I'm not racist but . . ." "Why do Black people have to act the way they do?" a kid asked me, "Why can't they just act normal?" In other words, White.

Through HIP-HOP, I have felt the spirit that fueled the movement. Our HIP-HOP model community has given me hope that such an environment can exist. One without the oppressive weight of injustice. One where diversity is celebrated. Through this experience, I have grown. HIP-HOP has stirred me to social consciousness. Yes, I saw the good the movement had done, the untiring vigor of its activists, but I have also seen and heard and felt the injustice the movement sought to end. This injustice, which before had overwhelmed me, now angers me. Stronger, I accept my responsibility to continue what the movement began, to finish the unfinished business.

Notes

1. Maya Angelou delivered the poem *On the Pulse of Morning* (copyright © 1993) at the inauguration ceremony of President Clinton. *The Complete Collected Poems of Maya Angelou* (New York: Random House, 1994), p. 272.
2. The Bill of Rights Education Project was founded in November 1987 by the Massachusetts Civil Liberties Union Foundation, in cooperation with the Massachusetts Depart-

ment of Education and the Massachusetts Bar Association. Through its conferences, institutes, workshops, and curricula, the Project encourages teachers and middle school and high school students to think critically about the difficult issues being debated in society and the courts, seeing this as essential to the future well-being of democracy. The Project, which recognizes that racism has been the prime force in undermining constitutional liberties and protections throughout our nation's history and into the present, has placed a particular emphasis on anti-racism education. Providing an opportunity for students to talk with each other across racial lines has become an important part of our anti-racism work.

3. Staff members at the retreat included Pam Ellis, director of the Massachusetts Student Alliance Against Racism and Violence, which is based at the office of the District Attorney for Norfolk County, Massachusetts; William Batson, who at the time was executive director of the Boston-based Teens as Community Resources; and me. Project HIP-HOP owes its name and much of its early impetus to Batson.
4. Myles Horton, *The Long Haul: An Autobiography* (New York: Doubleday/Anchor Books, 1990), pp. 149, 150.
5. See Horton, *The Long Haul,* p. 121, for a picture of the billboard that features King attending the Highlander's twenty-fifth anniversary celebration in 1957.
6. The series *Eyes on the Prize,* which was produced by Boston-based Blackside, Inc., and first broadcast in 1987, is the most comprehensive television documentary on the civil rights movement ever produced. It is the winner of six Emmys and numerous other awards. *Eyes on the Prize, Part I* (America's Civil Rights Years – 1954 to 1965) uses historical film and present-day interviews to bring to life the grassroots struggle for racial equality. *Eyes on the Prize, Part II* (America at the Racial Crossroads – 1964 to 1985) depicts the changing face of the struggle for civil rights and economic equality, beginning with the emergence of the movement for Black Power. It is available from PBS Video by calling (800) 344-3337.
7. Vincent Harding, *Hope and History: Why We Must Share the Story of the Movement* (Maryknoll, NY: Orbis Books, 1991), p. 193.
8. Harding, *Hope and History,* p. 198.
9. Harding, *Hope and History,* p. 71.
10. In his introduction to *Hope and History,* Vincent Harding describes his reaction to seeing "We Shall Overcome" inscribed on banners in Beijing's Tiananmen Square at the peak of China's "pro-democracy movement," and hearing it sung by thousands of citizens who marched for democracy in Leipzig, then East Germany, and elsewhere in Eastern Europe. He writes that "when we look back now from the vantage point of Beijing and Prague, from Berlin and Soweto, we realize that the post-World War II African American freedom movement was our own seminal contribution to the massive pro-democracy struggles that have set the globe spinning in these times. . . . When seen as far more than a contest for legal rights, when understood as a Black-led, multiracial quest for democracy in America, for the healing of the nation, for the freeing of all our spirits, then the story belongs to every one of us in this country —just as the students in Tiananmen Square and the marchers, organizers, and martyrs in Eastern Europe and South Africa realized it belongs to them" (pp. 6–7).
11. Racism, Rights & History: A Summer Institute for Teachers was the third summer institute the Bill of Rights Education Project held for middle school and high school teachers specifically on the theme of racism. Vincent Harding, Jan Carew, and Ron Chisom of the New Orleans-based People's History for Survival and Beyond were among the staff members. Pam Ellis and I used the occasion of this institute to introduce teachers to our work in progress, *Racism, Rights and History: A Curriculum for High School Students.* At the institute, the teachers generally agreed that it was critical to teach about racism in a way that opens up new possibilities for social transformation. That meant digging

deep: "Surface stuff will not do any more," one teacher commented. This was an urgent national priority. "What happens," another mused, "if there is no alternative to rage?"

12. Jordana Hart, writing about "Guns, Drugs, Rap & Rights: A Student Forum on Violence and Social Change" in "Some Say Violence is Skin Deep," *Boston Globe,* April 6, 1994, p. 17.
13. The efforts of the Bill of Rights Education Project to span the gulf dividing students from predominantly White and predominantly Black schools began with a conference for four hundred high school students on March 26, 1990, called Rap about Racism. Follow-up essays, which teachers asked participating students to write, showed considerable confusion about what racism is, or if it even still exists. Many students from largely White schools, some in decayed industrial towns, had felt intimidated by Black students at the conference: they claimed they were "hostile," that they "held a grudge," that they were to blame for an increase in racism since they were now more racist than Whites, and so on. After reading the essays, I visited several schools to talk directly to the students who wrote them. I was surprised at how many students knew the term "reverse discrimination" and seemed to have internalized the view that now the playing field was level, and if "minorities" do not get ahead, they have only themselves to blame. Other White students were more open. One said that "racism is something that just can't be ignored any longer." Another wrote, "What I think we as the White population should do is listen to Black people's experiences and try to get a sense of what's going on. Once we can understand this, we can start to work on it."
14. Schools seem a little more at ease dealing with "prejudice reduction" and the "celebration of differences" than with an examination of the racism embedded in our history. Racism (when it appears at all) is generally used interchangeably with bigotry and prejudice, and is interpreted solely in terms of personal beliefs and attitudes, to be confronted on a purely personal (and not institutional) level. Fighting racism then becomes a personal matter of changing attitudes and feelings — of learning how to get along with someone who may be different from you. Although this may be useful as far as it goes, it does not in fact take us very far. If students believe that this is where the entire struggle against racism lies — in the individual psyche — they may never go on to learn about the way "race" has been manipulated to shape our social, legal, and economic institutions, and is still being manipulated to preserve existing power structures and the status quo. When students realize that there is nothing fixed about racial categories, that categories like "Black" and "White" are social constructions, not biological essences, the students open up to other questions: Where did these categories come from? Whose interests did they serve? What role do they play in society today?
15. I recently had the experience of visiting a school on the perimeter of Boston for an in-service training session with teachers to discuss how the social studies curriculum could be changed to make it more "inclusive." On arrival, I was struck to find all the doors locked. To gain entry, I had to stand in front of a surveillance camera and announce my name and purpose into a microphone. It turned out this kind of security was a preventive measure taken because of the proximity of a largely "minority" part of Boston: there had been no episode precipitating it. In the course of discussion with the teachers, I mentioned the need to go beyond "band-aid" solutions to violence in schools, and to try to engage students in a far-reaching dialogue about violence, which would include a search for the roots of violence in our nation's history. I was immediately cut short by a teacher who insisted that before the last decade or so, violence was practically unknown in this country. He maintained this position, in which he was supported by several other teachers, when I tried to suggest that there was indeed something inherently violent about the process of dispossessing native peoples, upholding the institution of slavery, using the terror of lynch law to regain and retain the upper hand after a Civil War that set a new world record for known casualties, and so on. In his mind, this simply did

not count as "violence." Seldom had I so strongly felt the power of Norman Rockwell's images — and those of the everyday media!

16. The National Advisory Commission on Civil Disorders, chaired by Governor Otto Kerner of Illinois, released its report in 1968 on the causes of the riots that swept U.S. cities in the mid-1960s. The Kerner Commission warned that the nation was becoming permanently divided into two societies: "one, largely Negro and poor, located in the central cities; the other, predominantly white and affluent, located in the suburbs" (p. 22). The report also stated: "What white Americans have never fully understood — but what the Negro can never forget — is that white society is deeply implicated in the ghetto. White institutions created it, white institutions maintain it, and white society condones it." From U.S. Advisory Commission on Civil Disorders, The Kerner Report (New York: Pantheon Books, 1988).
17. Quoted in David J. Garrow, *Bearing the Cross: Martin Luther King and the Southern Christian Leadership Conference* (New York: Vintage Books, 1986), p. 537.
18. Adam Nossiter, *Of Long Memory: Mississippi and the Murder of Medgar Evers* (Reading, MA: Addison-Wesley, 1994), p. 15.
19. Cornel West, *Race Matters* (Boston: Beacon Press, 1993), p. 2.
20. Several teachers who are using parts of our *Racism, Rights and History* curriculum with students deemed hard to reach report a new level of excitement and interest in their high school classes and in their work with G.E.D. students.
21. John Hope Franklin, *The Color Line: Legacy for the Twenty-First Century* (Columbia: University of Missouri Press, 1993), pp. 74 –75.
22. Harding, *Hope and History,* p. 32.
23. Movement veterans told us of their regrets at not having "passed the torch" to the next generation. In *Of Long Memory,* Adam Nossiter writes of the way the movement is ignored in schools in Mississippi: "My own contemporaries in Mississippi, people born around 1960, often seemed shocked to learn of events that had been on the front pages of national newspapers thirty years before. They were dimly aware, from listening to their parents on the subject, that there had been unpleasantness during the 1960s. But the sheer ugliness of the white backlash eluded them" (pp. 14–16). He cites a 1975 revision of the standard textbook by John K. Bettersworthy, *Your Mississippi,* which ignores White violence and passes over the movement of the 1950s and 1960s with these words: "Gradually Mississippians, black and white, found that they could get along together — as they always had."(*Of Long Memory,* pp. 14–16). He then goes on to describe the feelings expressed at a Black History class at the University of Southern Mississippi when African Americans hear what life had been like under Jim Crow. The Black students and the few White students who took the class were, its teacher claimed, "hungry" for the information.
24. Marc Germain in Carol Gerwin, "Visiting the Past: Rights Workers' Graves Bring Reality," *Patriot Ledger,* July 31/August 1, 1993, p. 10.
25. Kim Howard in Constance E. Putnam, "Roots of Civil Rights Movement Open Their Eyes," *Boston Globe,* July 25, 1993, p. 35.
26. Letter of support from Geraldine Hines, March 24, 1994.
27. Outward Bound is an adventure-based program aimed at self-discovery and leadership training through challenging physical activities. It has regional offices around the United States and a national office in Greenwich, Connecticut.
28. The state-funded METCO program (Metropolitan Council for Educational Opportunity) was founded in Massachusetts in the late 1960s to enable "minority" students from Boston's deteriorating city schools to attend elementary and secondary schools in suburban districts. School districts from Massachusetts' North Shore to the Foxboro area west of Boston have adopted the program as a way of introducing diversity into their

own student body. Approximately eight hundred students are currently involved in the METCO program, which has a waiting list of ten thousand.

29. MOVE, which was formed in 1972, is an organization of radical utopians, mostly African American, who follow the teachings of John Africa. Denouncing the U.S. political and economic system for poisoning air, land, and water and destroying life on the planet, they were in turn denounced for many of their allegedly unsanitary "back to nature" practices. Thirteen of the up to 150 MOVE members were inside the house at 6221 Osage Avenue in Philadelphia when it was bombed with C-4 explosives provided by the FBI on May 13, 1985. The resulting firestorm killed six adults and five children and gutted sixty-one row houses, leaving 250 people homeless. Our three-hour conversation with Ramona Africa at the offices of the American Friends Service Committee opened students to the importance of critical thinking, questioning sources, and weighing evidence from all sides, and enlarged our ongoing discussion of the nature and uses of violence. It also provoked a dialogue about the limits of dissent and repression in a country born in revolution — another subject rarely explored in schools.
30. On May 18, 1896, the Supreme Court ruled in *Plessy v. Ferguson* (163 U.S. 537 [1896]) that a Louisiana law mandating "equal but separate accommodations for the white and colored races" on passenger trains was constitutional. The lone dissenter was a former slaveholder, Justice John Marshall Harlan of Kentucky. He wrote: "In my opinion, the judgement this day rendered will, in time, prove to be quite as pernicious as the decision made by this tribunal in the Dred Scott case. . . . The destinies of the two races, in this country, are indissolubly linked together, and the interests of both require that the common government of all shall not permit the seeds of race hate to be planted under the sanction of law." Quoted in Norman Dorsen, Paul Bender, Burt Neuborne, and Sylvia Law, *Political and Civil Rights in the United States*, Vol. II (Boston: Little, Brown, 1979), p. 53.
31. Eugene "Bull" Connor was the police commissioner of Birmingham who became infamous nationally for the brutal methods he used against demonstrations protesting segregation.
32. Sara Rimer, "Trip To History for Boston Teenagers: To the South of the Civil Rights Fight," *New York Times*, July 29, 1994, p. A10.
33. The Kuji Center was organized by the dozen diverse neighborhood groups of the St. Thomas/Irish Channel Consortium in New Orleans in 1990. The Center aims to reduce teen pregnancy by offering young people, ages eleven to eighteen, a holistic program of career development, education, recreation, culture, and classes on family life and sexuality.
34. "Jim Crow" refers to the laws and ordinances passed in the closing decades of the nineteenth century throughout the South that mandated racial segregation in public facilities and deprived African Americans of the right to vote. The U.S. Supreme Court had opened the door to Jim Crow segregation when it ruled in *The Slaughterhouse Cases* (1871) that the Fourteenth Amendment did not place the rights of citizens under federal protection. The Court denied that the national government could interfere with a state's "right" to fail to protect the civil rights of its citizens. If a state chose not to extend the Fourteenth Amendment's "equal protection" and "due process" clauses to all its citizens, that was its business.
35. Excerpt from the evaluation of the tour submitted by Arnold Chamanlal in August 1994.
36. Fannie Lou Hamer, born and buried in Ruleville, Mississippi, was the youngest of twenty children. She worked in the cotton fields with her sharecropper parents from the age of six. Forty years later she attended a SNCC meeting and learned that she had the right to vote. Trying to exercise that right got her imprisoned and viciously beaten. Her cour-

age, powerful singing, and the eloquence of her nationally televised testimony before the Democratic Party Credential Committee that was considering whether the all-White delegation from Mississippi should be replaced by delegates from the multiracial Mississippi Freedom Democratic Party at the 1964 Party Convention in Atlantic City made her an inspiring symbol of the civil rights movement.

37. Kurt Cobain was the lead singer of an alternative music group called Nirvana. This quote is from the song, "All Apologies," on the album *In Utero.*
38. Peter Applebome, "In Selma, Everything and Nothing Changed," *New York Times,* August 2, 1994, p. B6.

Stone Butch Celebration

A Transgender-Inspired Revolution in Academia

WENDY ORMISTON

Leslie Feinberg's fist rose up in exclamation:

> When you are on the front lines fighting for women's equality, and for gay and lesbian rights, *I will be there with you!* When you are fighting for workers' rights, when you are fighting against racism, *I will be there with you!* And in the fight against the oppression of transgender people, *be there with me in the struggle!*

Applause boomed and the audience rose to reach the height of Leslie Feinberg's beckoning hand. All around me I felt my classmates and my professor bursting with enthusiasm. After an hour and a half of uninterrupted speaking, Leslie Feinberg concluded her October 1994 address at Simmons College in Boston, Massachusetts.

When the standing-room-only audience dispersed, I remember wondering what the audience members would do with the content of the lecture. Mulling over this idea, I joined the other students and our professor for our return trip to Beacon College.[1] Our trip to Simmons had been organized in conjunction with a course at our own college. Seniors at Beacon must complete a core requirement by taking a senior seminar in their academic area. "Oppression" was the topic of the 1994–1995 Humanities Senior Seminar. Thirty-two of that year's seventy-four graduating seniors took this course, which examined classism, sexism, racism, fascism, and heterosexism. The course reached its peak when we read *Stone Butch Blues,* Leslie Feinberg's novel about a transgender person growing up in Buffalo in the 1950s.[2]

Until this point, most students in the course were intellectually, if not personally, familiar with issues of oppression surrounding gender and homosexuality. In early October, one week after *Stone Butch Blues* had been assigned, my classmates and I walked into class solemn and disturbed. Leslie Feinberg's narrative told a story so coarse in its passion that it disarmed people emotionally, and so brilliant in its thematic development that it dismantled our comfortable categories of analysis. When examined critically, *Stone Butch Blues* demanded that we move through the narrative personally. For every student in the class, this meant leaving something familiar. Ordinarily, considering the experience of an "other" can be based on notions of "different" from oneself and from one's own identity characteristics. But in our discussion of *Stone Butch Blues,* it was not enough to contemplate the experience of being homosexual if one was heterosexual; it was not sufficient to think about being a female if one was male. Contemplating the life of Leslie Feinberg's protagonist Jess Goldberg, students could not be one or the other. *Stone Butch Blues* breaks down the linear structure of all identity distinctions, and students could neither orient themselves completely inside, nor totally outside, the book's direct meaning. What students had to leave that was familiar was not their identification as male or female, gay or straight; students had to abandon the convention of binary opposition.

The fundamental tenet of binary opposition relates to oppression in the following way: disadvantage cannot exist without ideologically established privilege. Pertaining to the oppression of transgender people in our society, privileged identity characteristics include being heterosexual, and being either female or male.[3] Often, the people benefiting from privilege are the ones who define societal norms, thus creating divisions of difference. Applying language as a tool of domination, the powerful reinforce their own advantage, thus marginalizing the identity of others. To be transgender in our society is to have an underground identity, for there is no ideologically allocated space for transgender people in our culture. If transgender people do emerge into mainstream society from their linguistically assigned space of nonexistence, at best they will be treated as outcasts, freaks, "different." An individual is considered "different" when s/he has been categorically separated from the culturally accepted definition of "normal."[4] In *Stone Butch Blues,* Leslie Feinberg zeros in on this theme as her transgender protagonist, Jess Goldberg, contemplates the limits of expressing her identity:

> It was so hard to be different. The pressure never let up for a minute. I felt all messed up inside and bone weary. That's what I wanted to (say). But the words wouldn't come (p. 140). . . . Who was I . . . — woman or man? That question could never be answered as long as those were the only choices; it could never be answered if it had to be asked. (p. 222)

Female or male? is the question Leslie Feinberg has faced all her life in a society that defines gender according to biology, and misrepresented biology at that. The gender code in our culture maintains that there are two, and only two, genders: based on an infant's genitalia at birth, one is either female or male. From a person's assignment into a gender category, a whole conceptualization of identity, social roles, behavior, sexual expression, and appearance plays out. For the person who encounters Leslie Feinberg, this is a problematic system of gender evaluation. Leslie Feinberg, who is very masculine and can pass as a man; Leslie Feinberg, who was born "female" but is not accepted as a woman; Leslie Feinberg, who loves women.

Leslie Feinberg discusses anthropological research that documents societies in which there are more than two possible gender identifications. The *berdache* — wisdom-healers in certain Native American tribes who embody female and male identity expressions — are a notable example. Throughout history, communal cultures around the world have developed gender identities that fall on different points on the fe/male continuum. Indeed, cultures create their own idiosyncratic gender systems; it is capitalistic, Western culture, Leslie Feinberg asserts, that is unique in insisting that there are two, and only two, diametrically opposed genders.

Conceptualizing "transgender" necessitates thinking of gender as a spectrum rather than as mutually exclusive categories. Transgender refers to individuals who do not comply with the either/or, female/male gender construction in our society. Being transgender usually means living an underground existence. Many transgender individuals are "found out" after they have died: "women" who spent their lives passing as "men," and "men" who spent their lives passing as "women." A common reaction to transgender people is, "Why can't *they* make up their mind?" which implies that there is a choice to be made. If there is such a choice, we all make it all the time — by either reinforcing or resisting a gender system that predetermines the way people can behave and express themselves. Indeed, as Leslie Feinberg proclaimed in her Simmons lecture, "One can only be gender-bent in a gender-rigid society."[5]

Though "normal" implies a code for how one *should be* "naturally," this very definition requires anomalies to verify its existence. Consequently, being "abnormal" is as natural as being "normal"; the viability of each identity depends on the existence of the other. "Others" are those who differ from the "norm." Accordingly, within an ideologically defined code of normalcy, differences are debased in the execution of privilege and disadvantage. The differences that define transgender people represent qualities that are only derogated in comparison to premium values surrounding a norm, and this devaluation preserves a system of inequity. The most abhorrent "difference" about transgender people is that they embody two gender categories, the separation of which is necessary to maintain the current imbalance of power in our society.

Female and male fit into the same binary opposition equation as abnormal and normal, disadvantaged and privileged. In a system of inequity, neither can exist without the other: men's domination is an inverse function of women's oppression. According to cultural codes, we are all either female or male. As we embody this prescription, gender division is categorically perpetuated: privilege is maintained, disadvantage imposed. Heterosexism, a derivative of sexism, is the consequence of this diametric gender system's effect on sexuality. Understood as polar opposites, heterosexuality and homosexuality are products of an oppositional gender system. Heterosexuality is the societally approved extreme wherein gender distinction is reinforced; on the other end of the spectrum, same-sex unions challenge oppositional gender structure. Transgender deconstructs these normative divisions of gender and sexuality. A person who embodies female and male qualities is not simply gay or straight; s/he is somewhere in the middle of both, manifesting a unique sensibility of gender expression.

The oppressions of homosexuals and women in our society are structural mechanisms essential to maintaining a system of gender inequity. Perverse as it is, homosexuals and women are valued for being objects, in aversion to which the dominant culture defines itself. This is one explanation for double messages that many oppressed groups receive, such as praise bestowed upon women for exhibiting the very qualities for which they are objectified.

Unlike women and homosexuals, transgender individuals do not possess an assigned space of degradation in which to exist. They live in a psychic void, outside of society's diametrically defined gender structure. Transgender individuals face violent rejection from privileged and disadvantaged groups alike, for their existence challenges the viability of an entire society's identification system. Though they are objects of prejudice, homosexuals and women are not necessarily sympathetic to the oppression of transgender people: binary opposition fosters aggression between oppressed groups, preventing a unified strength that could work to eliminate the basic structure of inequity. Transgender, for the very reason it is perceived as a threat to the normative structure of society, contains conceptual potential for ideological change. The manner in which transgender challenges gender and sexuality oppression can be applied theoretically to other forms of oppression in our society. The concept of transgender resists the very ideology of inequity by reconciling individuals and groups split by the definitions imposed upon them.

Transgender is a theoretically unifying concept: it can provoke individuals to consider personally the ideological arbitrariness of their gender/sexual identity; politically, it challenges the binary structure of our society that teeters toward inequality. This imbalanced sociopolitical agenda perseveres as transgender and other human rights issues are excluded from the curricula of most elementary and high schools, and are unaddressed in many of our country's institutions of higher learning. In this article, I chronicle an episode in which transgender issues were brought to the center of the collective awareness of a small college, wherein personal alliances grew from political analysis and education became a medium for activism.

Our classroom discussion of *Stone Butch Blues* encouraged students to question their own gender definitions, intensifying their identification with Leslie Feinberg's first-person protagonist. In ongoing conversations, my classmates and I considered aspects of our own gender/sexual identity that had never before been allowed expression, and reflected on ways that our own behavior contributes to the systematic oppression of transgender people. And so, when

Leslie Feinberg personally appealed to the audience at Simmons College to join in the common struggle, we were ready. As narrative became reality, we transformed our education into action.

Leslie Feinberg spoke so deeply to us in her writing and in her lecture that our senior class considered her an ideal candidate to speak at our graduation. We imagined that her words would bridge the gap between what we cherished most about our education and what we imagined we would face when we applied these values against "real world" opposition. But opposition flared inside academia before we ever had a chance to fight it in the real world: the president of our college vetoed Leslie Feinberg as our nominee for commencement speaker. Protesting this decision became the practical application of our education; it was the connection we would have had Leslie Feinberg speak to us about. When Leslie Feinberg finally did speak at our graduation, s/he voiced victory and congratulations. The bridge had already been built; on it we met and won together.

In the middle of March 1995, shortly before spring break, our college president, John Anderson, informed the officers of our senior class that he had one more commencement speaker candidate he wanted to pursue, and he assured them that if this person declined, he would extend an invitation to Leslie Feinberg to speak at graduation. His words encouraged the senior class officers, for up to this point, President Anderson had been opposed to Leslie Feinberg as a prospective commencement speaker. But on the Friday the campus closed for spring break, President Anderson sent a letter to the senior class officers noting that his other choice had declined and that he had again decided against inviting the students' choice, Leslie Feinberg. Recognizing that time was running out to invite any outside speaker to give the commencement address, President Anderson presented a final option: the senior class could select a faculty member to speak at graduation. Facing limited alternatives and relieved that the senior class would at least have a say in choosing the commencement speaker, the senior class officers agreed to President Anderson's proposal.

At the first senior class meeting following spring break, the class officers detailed President Anderson's re-rejection of Leslie Feinberg as our nominee for commencement speaker. While the officers began advancing plans to organize an election for a faculty commencement speaker, unrest over President Anderson's veto of Leslie Feinberg persisted. Following our class meeting, three seniors, Colleen Cruz, Eric Muniz, and I, convened to plan a protest of the veto.

From the outset, our protest of President Anderson's rejection of Leslie Feinberg concerned not his authority to make a decision regarding the commencement speaker, but rather the reasons upon which he based his decision. President Anderson established four criteria that a prospective candidate must meet to be considered an "appropriate and viable" commencement speaker: 1) the candidate must have made a meaningful contribution to some field;

2) the candidate should be an excellent speaker in addition to her/his other accomplishments; 3) the candidate should be reasonably accessible to the College; and 4) a speaker's fee needed to be one that Beacon could afford. Though they changed and evolved throughout the course of our protest, President Anderson's reasons for vetoing Leslie Feinberg never reflected a conflict with his own established criteria.

Leslie Feinberg's professional contributions and speaking ability were no cause for question; President Anderson was so impressed by a video of her speech at Simmons that he suggested inviting her to campus as a Whittermore Fellow guest lecturer in the future. Living in New Jersey, Leslie Feinberg also fit the accessibility requirement. Regarding the issue of a speaking fee, President Anderson's rejection of Leslie Feinberg preceded any attempt to ascertain whether Beacon could afford her services. Initially, President Anderson defended his veto with the following rationale:

> [Feinberg's] message is extremely important and . . . the commencement speech is not the easiest format to put over complex and controversial ideas . . . Normally, we want people to speak for no more than fifteen minutes. (*Beacon Voice,* 3/31/95)

Leslie Feinberg proved herself quite eloquent in response:

> I don't buy that at all. I speak very inspirationally in 15 minutes, thank you. . . . I don't know what [President Anderson] is more afraid of, me or appearing to be intolerant. (*Tribune,* 4/6/95)

Most disturbing about President Anderson's veto of Leslie Feinberg was his protection and perpetuation of the very dominant, oppressive ideology we had been critically dissecting in our courses: the president of our college was violating the values of our education. As a class, we had been studying complex and controversial ideas for four years, so inviting a commencement speaker who would address such issues would have validated our education and would have offered us guidance on how to apply such ideas in the "real world." On the other hand, to deny the vocalization of these ideas by a clearly qualified speaker would only demonstrate the limits of their appropriateness, as defined by protectors of the status quo. In denying Leslie Feinberg the right to speak at our commencement, President Anderson was symbolically rendering our education meaningless.

Colleen, Eric, and I began to meet regularly. Our first objective was to contact Leslie Feinberg, inform her of our protest, and invite her to graduation as a special guest of the students. In the event that we would not be successful in persuading President Anderson to retract his veto of Leslie Feinberg as our nominee for commencement speaker, we planned to protest graduation, and strategized alternative ways s/he could speak. Even if s/he were unable to attend the ceremony, we hoped s/he might write something we could read aloud.

While Colleen, Eric, and I worked on the commencement speaker controversy in late-night meetings in the faculty lounge, other students were organizing around other high-tension issues on campus. In April, two hundred students (of the 521 in the student body) staged a sit-in in the lobby of the main building on campus to demonstrate against the administration's handling of multiple issues, ranging from a lack of full-time minority professors, to the alcohol policy, to changes for Latin honors requirements. The dismissal of the seniors' nominee for commencement speaker was included among the demonstrators' grievances. Following the sit-in, students met with the academic dean and the dean of students, who successfully addressed many concerns. However, neither of the deans was able to offer recourse for President Anderson's veto of Leslie Feinberg as commencement speaker. Since President Anderson was out of town, this issue remained unresolved.

The commencement speaker controversy persisted on campus and soon exploded into the outside world. When reporters covering the student demonstration learned of President Anderson's veto of a transgender activist for the College's commencement speaker, they set off waves of media attention. On the day of the student demonstration, before Colleen, Eric, and I were able reach Leslie Feinberg, s/he called us, having obtained our number from a reporter who already had contacted her. Connecting with Leslie Feinberg affirmed the meaning of our struggle and instantly energized our protest efforts. S/he was moved and amazed, and offered to do everything possible to foster the protest and attend commencement. As a political activist, Leslie Feinberg knew the value of instantaneous response. S/he generated information about the protest over the Internet and made contact with special interest media groups, such as GLAAD (Gay and Lesbian Alliance Against Defamation). Leslie Feinberg became our strongest supporter, eventually calling our effort the first sustained protest (of non-transgender people) against the oppression of transgender individuals in modern history. After that first call, Colleen, Eric, and I spoke regularly with Leslie Feinberg to coordinate our resistance actions. One night when we could not reach her, we were treated to Leslie Feinberg's answering machine message: "If this is the heroic Beacon students, I'll be back at 10:00. If not, please support the heroic Beacon students in their struggle!"

Two local newspapers, the *Gazette* and the *Tribune,* printed front-page coverage of the student demonstration. The following day, the opinion section of the *Gazette* sported an article by the editor, Bert Stake, commending President Anderson on the strong moral leadership he exhibited in vetoing Leslie Feinberg as our nominee for commencement speaker. Stake's piece, entitled "A tip of the cap to President Anderson," never named the "object" of his attack, but ranted at length, comparing Leslie Feinberg's status as a transgender individual to hate-expounding homosexuals, neo-Nazis, KKK spokespersons, bigots, racists, and off-beat radicals. Stake praised President Anderson for maintaining executive strength to discern moral right from moral wrong in the face of a mere "political/social fad" that had seized the students at Beacon College. When President Anderson realized the kind of support his rejection of Leslie Feinberg was receiving, he hastily pleaded that Stake "keep his cap on." Responding to the *Gazette*'s editor, President Anderson wrote:

> In the editorial you congratulate me for having the moral courage to veto a "recommendation to have an avowed transgendered lesbian to be the school's commencement speaker." You suggest then that lesbians are "off-beat radicals" whom most of us would not want to welcome to our homes, or by extension, to our commencements.
>
> If the *Gazette* had talked with me before going to press with the editorial, you would have had some facts upon which to base your opinion. . . . You would know that I deplore ugly and ignorant harassment and discrimination against gays. (Letter distributed to the Beacon College community, 4/7/95)

But this reply did not silence Stake or others who shared his views; coverage of the commencement speaker controversy by both the *Gazette* and the *Tribune* escalated. The media's slanderous attacks continued, reaching an inhumane peak in a Sunday edition of the *Tribune.* On the front page, a sound-off read, "Is being a transgendered lesbian the highest ideal to which a Beacon College student can aspire?" In his own opinion piece, "We know the truth; it's living it that's hard," *Tribune* editor Steve Host fed the sensationalism:

> Academia has weighed in with the tabloid talk-show mentality as students at Beacon College in Centerville toss a tantrum because they aren't allowed to pick their favorite freak, a "transgendered" lesbian as commencement speaker. (*Tribune,* 4/9/95)

If President Anderson was unsuccessful in converting the local press to critical enlightenment, the only effect his response to the media had on us as students was to confirm our suspicion of his own hypocritical stance on the issue.

Two days after the sit-in, Colleen, Eric, and I, joined by the senior class officers, met with President Anderson, asking again that he reconsider his veto in light of press coverage of the demonstration. Instead, we found that the press attention had made President Anderson intransigent. It appeared to us that President's Anderson's logic had devolved from faulty to indefensible. He responded that, precisely because of the press coverage, he found it even more difficult to rescind his veto of Leslie Feinberg. Explaining a point he addressed in his letter to the editor of the *Gazette,* President Anderson reasoned

> that if Leslie Feinberg spoke at commencement, her humane, intellectual and inspiring presentations of self and views . . . could easily be drowned out or even exploited by those who are anti-gay, want to defeat her views and values, or even sell newspapers by sensationalism.

We responded, stating that

> Leslie Feinberg does not need your protection. S/he is a professional speaker and activist, and given her identity, plenty experienced at negotiating opposition. What's more, if in fact Beacon's commencement audience is to contain homophobic, ignorant people, then a speech from Leslie Feinberg is just what they need.

We insisted that instead of protection, Leslie Feinberg deserved President Anderson's support — support in the form of freedom to speak openly in defiance against marginalization. In refusing to allow her to speak at commencement, President Anderson was keeping Leslie Feinberg locked "safely" behind the very walls of her oppression; he was teaching us that the way to fight injustice is to be sympathetic in the shadows.

People in positions of privilege merely reinforce their dominance when they presume to define the lines of others' oppression; it is only through listening to the truth of how oppressed groups define their realities that the privileged can realize the bias of their own power. As committed to critical thinking as he claimed to be, it appeared to us that President Anderson was not yet strong enough to risk this learning. This suspicion was cemented in our meeting's devastating conclusion. In a last-ditch attempt, we put to President Anderson a hypothetical question:

> Were this 50 years ago, with the same press coverage, the same student support, and the desired speaker was a person of color, would you come to the same conclusion?

Our conversation came to a shocking end when President Anderson responded that he would indeed pursue the same line of reasoning and arrive at the same conclusion. In grappling with the fact that in a similar situation President Anderson would have prohibited several of us, who are persons of color, from speaking at our own graduation, we realized we were protesting in an historical vacuum.

Our meeting with President Anderson generated painful questions concerning our education — questions about its inherent bias that needed to be deconstructed with the same critical analysis we had been taught to apply to the world. The bigotry we interpreted in President Anderson's actions demanded that we examine our own roles as members of the Beacon College community. We concluded that as much as it was President Anderson's job to ensure a long and stable life for Beacon College, it was our job to critically examine and speak out against oppression.

Our protest in support of Leslie Feinberg as our commencement speaker became a practical application of our liberal arts education. Colleen, Eric, and I worked in accordance with four principal tactics. We established an equal arrangement of authority among ourselves by sharing all protest information and internally refining our goals and plans. Aware of the possibility of corruption by division, Colleen, Eric, and I participated equally in all parts of the organization of our protest: we wrote letters, held interviews, and presented meetings together. We strove to represent, inform, and engage our class by holding open meetings regularly to compare our actions with their ideas and sentiments. Finally, we sought to respond to antagonistic backlashes calmly and with clarity, refusing our opposition the power to pull us down to their level of fragmented and contradicting prejudices.[6]

Hours after our meeting with President Anderson, we held our first emergency senior class meeting to rouse our classmates. More than 40 percent of the graduating seniors were Humanities majors familiar with Leslie Feinberg's work from the Humanities Senior Seminar. They resented the irony that they had been required to read Leslie Feinberg's book to graduate, yet they were prohibited from hearing her speak at graduation; these students immediately rose to support our protest. Conveying our cause to the other seniors was also easy. When all biases were laid out analytically, President Anderson's use of his authority to silence an oppressed voice became obvious. When we played a video of Leslie Feinberg's speech at Simmons College, her call for common cause action became the conviction of our class.

Our class' response to the cause was deeply heartening. Any reservations we and our classmates had about advancing resistance tactics were discussed openly as the basic fears they were, and did not fester as unresolved issues. Real fears did exist, such as disapproval of unsympathetic family members and the effect on graduation if we continued our protest and President Anderson refused to back down. But these fears were overwhelmed by the potential and much larger horror of having only complacency to celebrate at our commencement. Our class confirmed collectively its goal to bring Leslie Feinberg to Beacon to speak at our graduation. As a result of this first emergency meeting with our classmates, several individuals and student organizations wrote to President Anderson to condemn his veto of Leslie Feinberg as our choice for commencement speaker. Petitions were passed, and students took on the media with pointed letters to editors. One student, outraged at the *Gazette*'s homophobic propaganda, wrote to the editor:

> Your editorial is especially reprehensible for what it says to young gays and lesbians who might make the mistake of reading your newspaper. You are effectively declaring that they are immoral, unnatural, abnormal, and even a threat to society. There is a direct connection between this kind of prejudice and the fact that 30% of all teenage suicides are those of gays and lesbians. Shame on you! (*Gazette,* 4/15/95)

Students concerned about the relevant application of their education found friends in professors concerned about what they perceived as unchecked administrative control undermining academic freedom. Disturbed that President Anderson's veto of Leslie Feinberg as commencement speaker insinuated that what was important to teach in the classroom was inappropriate to apply outside the classroom, the faculty passed a unanimous resolution to support the students' choice. Unknown to us at the time, this faculty vote took place concurrently with the first emergency senior class meeting. Elizabeth West, the Humanities Senior Seminar professor whom the senior class had elected to be the faculty commencement speaker, approached Colleen, Eric, and me in the dining hall bearing this news of faculty support. Professors who had previously been our academic advisors now became our resistance mentors. In the face of fast-approaching academic deadlines, Professor West and two other faculty members encouraged our all-consuming devotion to the protest. We were learning more than ever before: we were actualizing our education.

In the days to come, the Beacon College staff assumed its own position in our protest. The Student Affairs Division distributed a statement to the college community indicating their support of Leslie Feinberg and their plans to meet with President Anderson to express their views. College staff members, from the grounds crew, to secretaries, to mail room workers, to the deans, to the kitchen staff, were consistent in encouraging our struggle. As we raced from meeting to meeting they hollered praise and offered hope. And as our resistance gained momentum, it seemed that the entire Beacon College community aligned with us against President Anderson's veto of Leslie Feinberg as commencement speaker.

Augmenting our campus-based resistance, Beacon alumni/ae began a barrage of dissent against President Anderson's decision, and disgruntled parents faxed and phoned President Anderson's office. Galvanized by Leslie Feinberg's messages over the Internet and statements we faxed to the press, activists, human rights workers, and academics from all over the country besieged President Anderson with their outrage. The Associated Press picked up the story of our protest, and it was mentioned in major periodicals all over the country, including the Boston *Globe, Mother Jones, Bay Windows,* the *Chronicle of Higher Education, USA Today,* and *Workers World.* The external responses were so numerous that, according to some persistent activists, President Anderson was ultimately forced to turn off his fax machine to incoming calls. The protest so effectively isolated President Anderson that we could not reach his office with an in-campus call connected by the College operator.

In spite of it all, President Anderson remained unmoved. The next week, Colleen, Eric, and I met with Professor West to brainstorm the next tactic of our struggle. Aside from President Anderson's intransigence, the greatest obstacle we faced at this point was Beacon's speaker policy. Our class was already collecting funds to cover Leslie Feinberg's travel expenses to attend commencement, when we discovered a clause in the Student Handbook stating that written approval from the dean of students must be obtained before inviting any speaker to campus. Ironically, this condition violates the spirit of Beacon's speaker policy, which reads from its first paragraph:

> Beacon College has long recognized that academic freedom for its faculty and students is not a privilege granted by administration and trustees, but an abso-

> lutely necessary atmosphere without which excellence in education cannot be attained. . . . The sole purpose of inviting a speaker is to contribute to the aims of the College as a center of free inquiry and sound learning. (*Beacon College 1994–1995 Student Handbook*)

At the same time President Anderson persisted in refusing to rescind his decision, we were making plans for Leslie Feinberg to speak at commencement as a special guest of the students. However, the speaker policy threatened to obstruct our plan. Though the dean of students supported our protest, we could not expect him to authorize an approval contrary to President Anderson's stance.

Relaying an idea of a friend, Professor West suggested that we present an honor to Leslie Feinberg; s/he would not have to be an officially invited speaker to receive an award, but could speak as an award recipient. This idea inspired a plan that would cement the meaning of our protest's victory in Beacon's history. We remembered that our class had voted to create a fund for faculty and staff diversity training as its parting gift to Beacon. We reasoned that Leslie Feinberg's work speaks to the very values we would want emphasized in diversity training; why not invite her to receive an honorarium in conjunction with the presentation of the class gift? The point of Leslie Feinberg's presence would not be lost, and President Anderson could not prevent her from coming any more than he could refuse our class gift. Thus, the Feinberg Fund for Diversity Training was created.

In this same conversation, Professor West read to us her respectful declination of our class's nomination for her to be the faculty speaker at commencement. After much discussion, we all concluded that no matter what Professor West could say in a commencement address to advocate for equal rights, her speaking in a position that had been denied to Leslie Feinberg reinforced divisionary tactics of oppression. With this decision made, our protest plan became even more comprehensive: we would support no commencement speaker other than Leslie Feinberg, we would protest anyone else, and if Leslie Feinberg were not invited as the official commencement speaker, s/he could speak in receiving an honor we would present with the Feinberg Fund for Diversity Training. Leslie Feinberg laughed when we shared our plan with her over the telephone: "So either I am the commencement speaker, or I am the commencement speaker!"

At an emergency senior class meeting the next day, we distributed copies of Professor West's formal declination to speak at commencement. We voted unanimously to approve the dedication of our class gift to Leslie Feinberg, and to support no commencement speaker other than s/he. Coinciding with the organization of our protest on campus, GLAAD released an urgent press release:

> [President] Anderson says that Feinberg was rejected because he "wasn't convinced that she was the most appropriate commencement speaker . . . that her

> topic, or the perspective from which she would come would not be easily presented in a ten or fifteen minute format.". . . "It is always an appropriate time for an oppressed voice to be heard," said . . . a group that organized . . . to protest Anderson's decision. (GLAAD Press Release, 4/11/95)

United as a class, we stepped up our networking inside and outside the Beacon College community.

Following our emergency senior class meeting, the faculty arranged an emergency session of their own, to which they invited Colleen, Eric, and me to present our protest plan for their possible endorsement. Up to this point, the faculty had verbally supported us, and some of them had written letters to President Anderson. Now we wanted them to participate with us in direct action resistance. While we passed out petitions demonstrating that an overwhelming majority of the senior class supported our goals, we explained the background of our struggle and detailed our Feinberg Fund for Diversity Training plan. In conclusion, we requested that two faculty members, the dean of academic affairs and the dean of students, join the three of us in a coalition to approach President Anderson again about reversing his veto. The faculty approved our request without delay. President Anderson agreed to meet with our coalition the next morning.

For two hours Friday morning, the deans, faculty representatives, and Colleen, Eric, and I met with President Anderson. By this time he had received Professor West's declination of his invitation to speak at commencement, the faculty resolution to support the seniors' choice of Leslie Feinberg as commencement speaker, an onslaught of faxed outrage from all over the country, and more media coverage both condemning and praising his rejection of Leslie Feinberg as commencement speaker. The discussion in this meeting closely reflected our first conference with President Anderson: we argued for our right to apply and celebrate the skills we had developed through our education, and for our responsibility to resist systematic oppression. Again we hauled out our petitions, informing President Anderson that Leslie Feinberg had pledged her name at the top of our list of protesters. The professors and deans affirmed our points, indicating that to invite Leslie Feinberg to speak at commencement would symbolically demonstrate the meaning and value of a Beacon education; likewise, to continue to reject her would indicate a stance of intolerance, violating the integrity of Beacon's academic mission and reputation. President Anderson remained reluctant, being concerned about offending others in the Beacon College community who shared the views of Bert Stake. We countered President Anderson's reservation by taking inventory of Beacon's constituencies one by one: the students, the faculty, the staff, parents, and alumni/ae had all demonstrated their support for our choice of Leslie Feinberg as our commencement speaker; we had not, however, been able to ascertain the views of the Trustees. In response to those who were not persuaded by the supportive sentiment of the college community, we insisted that accommodating the fears of such people is not the way to overcome oppression. Our meeting ended with President Anderson still undecided; he asked to have the weekend to think everything over and to have time to consult with the Board of Trustees. This period of consideration got off to a good start in our eyes when, on Saturday morning, a College librarian called us trying to track down a copy of *Stone Butch Blues*, which, the librarian indicated, President Anderson had requested.

We called Leslie Feinberg Friday night to update her and to check in on her end of the protest. After our report that the emergency senior class and faculty meetings had culminated in another conference with President Anderson, s/he was convinced we were going to win. S/he had been receiving loads of e-mail and expected an international fax flood to kick in during the next week. S/he encouraged us, "It's getting bigger and bigger. If he still says no, we'll just intensify the next wave. You're going to win this one."

Tuesday morning our coalition reconvened with President Anderson. In a brief meeting, he informed us that he had changed his mind and would invite Leslie Feinberg to be our commencement speaker. As soon as we left his office, Colleen, Eric, and I called Leslie Feinberg to leave a victory message on her answering machine. We passed the phone among the three of us: "We have some marvelous news — President Anderson will be calling to invite you to speak at commencement!"

Beacon settled into a state of victorious enthusiasm. Within a few days, President Anderson released a statement to the Associated Press:

> The hallmark of Beacon College has been international and cultural education that fosters values of tolerance, civility and diversity. My decision [to invite Leslie Feinberg to speak at commencement]is a reflection of the progressive spirit of Beacon College.
>
> I was impressed by students' conviction and commitment to human rights for all people. . . . A good leader learns from students, faculty, and staff. My decision to invite Leslie Feinberg was a natural outgrowth of that learning process. (*Beacon Voice*, 5/3/95)

Colleen, Eric, and I drafted a victory statement. In order for our resistance to be meaningful to other protests, we explained our guiding philosophy:

> In raising our voices in protest, we were not assuming a cause, only resisting a norm. A norm, that every day denies voice to someone, because of who or what they are. President Anderson's rejection of Leslie Feinberg as our commencement speaker reinforced this bigotry. We did not expect to change President Anderson's mind, but we could not validate his decision by remaining silent ourselves.
>
> We united our own voices for a common goal of having Leslie Feinberg speak at commencement. Our constant concern was to create and maintain consensus. Consensus grew from the establishment of a common ground, first with fellow students, then with Faculty and Staff, and finally with President Anderson. In uncovering similar values, we were able to pursue a path of action joining efforts rather than polarizing interests.

> The sustaining lesson of our [victory] is that critical thinking is the ultimate tool of resistance. Through critical resistance space can be made for more voices to be heard. (*Students Daring for Diversity,* 4/23/95)

The deep relevance of common cause resistance astounded even Colleen, Eric, and me. Just as we were celebrating President Anderson's rescinding his veto, a representative of the National People's Campaign contacted us to request that we attend and speak at a rally in Boston organized to defeat the "Contract with America."[7] We spoke at the rally, one of forty held simultaneously across the country for the same cause. As people from all segments of society rose to speak in defense of workers' rights, women's rights, gay, lesbian, and transgender rights, rights of disabled individuals, and affirmative action programs, we learned as much as we shared. If we needed proof that our education was applicable outside of academia, this was it.

The day before commencement, Leslie Feinberg, accompanied by Minnie Bruce Pratt, arrived at Beacon College to receive the plaque Colleen, Eric, and I presented at baccalaureate in conjunction with the announcement of the Feinberg Fund for Diversity Training. When we introduced Leslie Feinberg, the audience of Beacon students, faculty, staff, alumni/ae, and family and friends rose in a wave of ovation. As a token of the Feinberg Fund for Diversity Training, we presented President Anderson with his own copy of *Stone Butch Blues,* which he asked Leslie Feinberg to autograph on the spot.

The next morning at breakfast, before graduation, Leslie Feinberg mingled with people from all parts of the college community in the dining hall. S/he wanted to meet personally every Beacon College employee who had supported the protest, and spoke with janitors, parents, secretaries, and deans. Her commencement address later that day built upon these exchanges. Before the speech, President Anderson introduced Leslie Feinberg as one who "[has] much to say to [Beacon's] graduating seniors and to us all . . . about oppression, about courage, about compassion, and about love." The senior class greeted Leslie Feinberg's rise to the podium with an instant standing ovation — s/he beamed victory back at us, and for a few long moments we just clapped for each other. And then s/he spoke:

> Thank you so much. What an honor it is to be able to deliver this commencement address to you. I'm so proud of you. . . .
>
> I hope you all get to pick up a copy of the *Gazette* this morning. I made it on the front page. It was not quite what I had envisioned when I was a child looking forward to adulthood. But you know, I read some of these editorials attacking me and attacking your decision, saying I was a freak, saying "well, this is a lesbian." And you said, "Yeah, so what?" And they said s/he is very masculine and cross-dresses and you said, yeah? And when all those hollow, empty slurs didn't work, they brought out their big guns this morning. They brought out the ultra right-wing organization that goes under the misnomer of Fairness in Academia. And they brought out a tactic that I grew up with in the 1950s under the McCarthy era. They used red baiting, they said this is a Communist. . . . Yes, I am a

Socialist and I believe that inequality and injustice need to be fought — so? . . . We've been brought up to think that in all societies like this one it is dog eat dog. But if all human history were shrunk to one year, over 360 days of human history would belong to societies that were cooperative, in which people work together in equality and share the fruits of their labor. And believe it or not, those societies on every continent, including on the North Pole, allowed much more room for people's sex and gender expression than society does today. We just come to think the way we see it is an immutable fact of history when, in fact, it is a relatively recent historical development. . . . The difference is that one time people were able to express themselves as part of a group; diversity meant the individuals who all came together made up the whole and were respected and honored for their expression. And it was really only in the last few thousand years with the division of society into the haves and have-nots that the economic system necessitated division and resulted in laws partitioning the sexes, and mandating what form of human love would be legal, and degrading the status that women had enjoyed for millennia. And it is only in societies in which the human fabric has been rendered into classes that we find men executed for effeminacy or women hounded and punished for being masculine. But with the division of society into classes and with the rise of oppression, there has always been resistance. And transgendered people have always been a part of those struggles against oppression and in some cases even led the charge.

Like Joan of Arc, an illiterate peasant teenager and brilliant military strategist who led an army of 10,000 peasants in battles that were victorious and ended up instituting the nation state of France. Joan of Arc, a cross-dressing masculine woman, not unlike myself, Joan of Arc who was burned alive at the stake by the Inquisition for the crime of transgender. . . .

I guarantee you that the combatants at Stonewall did not know they were making history. Sometimes in the crucible of struggle we are all drawn together to fight for justice just because we know it is the right thing to do in our hearts. But we don't know we are changing the world when we do it. And I think similarly that you, the senior class at Beacon, do not fully realize that you have helped to change the world. You have set a precedent which has already created significant social change. You may not fully realize it yet, but those of us who are transgendered do. Each of us knows who have stood up against centuries of condemnation and ridicule, each of us whose parents were not proud of our struggles, but who were ashamed of our differences. Each of us who yearned in our hearts to change the world but couldn't do it alone and didn't know how to do it, we know what you have done. So if there is a single one of you here at graduation who is feeling anxious because you are afraid you will never again experience the kind of community you have experienced here, let me reassure you that the moment you joined the struggle here against oppression, you joined a larger community that affects all our lives. You joined a movement for social change, and we welcome you to our community. . . .

Perhaps twenty years ago your commencement speaker would have told you the world is your oyster, you can go out and take any job you want because you have a good education. But of course that was not true for many African Americans, Latinos, for many Jews. It wasn't true for women, or people who refused to hide the simple fact that they loved someone of the same sex. And it's not true

> now. This lean and mean corporate restructuring means there's not a whole lot of jobs out there. . . . We live under the crushing weight of the boom and bust economic cycles. It's a system in which I didn't make up the saying "the rich get richer and the poor get poorer." . . . And even the *New York Times* sometimes admits it. Like a couple of weeks ago when they ran a front page article reporting that in this, the richest country in the world, there is the greatest polarization of wealth. The *Times* article reported that one percent of the people in this family enjoy 40 percent of the wealth that we've all created from our collective labor. And so you ask yourself how could a system that is unjust for the majority remain in place unless we were all pitted against each other. Unless we were meant to fight each other instead of getting together to fight for real change. . . .
>
> You know, I invite each one of you, and I don't mean just the seniors, I mean every parent, every groundskeeper, every faculty member, and alum, and trustee to join in an organizing conference on June 3rd and 4th in New York City; see me afterwards and I'll give you directions on how to get there. Because we're going to plan a very organized long hot summer of protests to say "Newt Gingrich doesn't speak for mainstream America. We are mainstream America, all of us and our families and our co-workers". . . and all the people we can gather, are going to converge on Washington in October. . . .
>
> You, the seniors at Beacon, have taught us what can be won through unity. Now let's put every muscle and every breath into continuing the fight against injustice. Let's not stop until we've really won some genuine change. And there is a place in this struggle for every single person here whether you are a working person, an unemployed person, a single parent, whether you are a librarian or a janitor, whether you are a student or about to become unemployed and out in the world, and I have a word that there is a place for every single one of you in the struggle. And so I leave you with this question: are you ready? (yes!) are you ready? (yes!) are you ready (yes!) Then let us commence! (Transcribed from the community cable access television station videotape recording, August 1995)

We began by leaping to our feet, applauding. Leslie Feinberg truly did welcome us to her community, hugging many of the graduates as they crossed the stage to receive their diplomas.

The first lesson of the "real world" is that the struggle never stops. A barrage of sensationalized media coverage directly followed Leslie Feinberg's appearance at our commencement. The backlash, which lasted for weeks, made its first attack the morning after commencement in the Sunday *Tribune*'s front-page headline: "Grads Told to Become Communists." One professor remarked of Leslie Feinberg's graduation speech: "One has to be either paranoid or very guilty to have been offended by anything Leslie Feinberg said." As discomfiting as it is, the media raving reflects the success of our resistance.

However, President Anderson's response to the negative publicity was to revert to his policy of protectionism by imposing a ban on the videotapes Beacon College had recorded of its 1995 baccalaureate and commencement ceremonies. His video censure was unilateral, extending beyond the media to include Leslie Feinberg and the graduated seniors. Unlike other graduation videos made by Beacon College, which are generally considered common property of the Beacon College community, we could not view the tape of our commencement.

For months after our graduation, Colleen, Eric, and I corresponded with one another transcontinentally, and networked among our dispersed classmates to petition that President Anderson release our commencement tapes, which he did by the end of the summer. However, before freedom of speech was restored, we had again faced serious questions about President Anderson's, and consequently Beacon College's, commitment to advancing politically the principles it teaches in its classrooms. The media backlash from Leslie Feinberg's commencement address would have been an opportune moment to shed light on disparate power structures in contemporary U.S. society. Those who attended Beacon's 1995 commencement could assess the ideas illuminated in Leslie Feinberg's address for themselves, but those who did not attend were susceptible to media bias. Beacon College could have established itself as a vanguard of political analysis if President Anderson had disseminated copies and transcriptions of the commencement tapes for the public to see what Leslie Feinberg really said. People could then have considered for themselves the discrepancy between Leslie Feinberg's criticism of capitalist superpower inequities and the *Tribune*'s comparison between education at Beacon College and a tabloid talk-show.

In spite of restrictive college policies, many people persevere to sustain the meaning of what we accomplished by securing Leslie Feinberg's right to speak at our commencement. The struggle never ends: our professors are still teaching what so inspired our senior class; Leslie Feinberg continues to write about common cause connections in the oppression of transgender people;[8] Colleen is presently studying at Columbia Teachers College to become a teacher herself; Eric is working on film projects in San Francisco; I am also in California, writing more about our protest. Our seventy-four classmates went seventy-four different directions after graduation, but, inspired by our education, we share a value of building common causes that actively resist our culture's ideology of binary opposition: in this space we can meet people like Leslie Feinberg; in this space all people can make love in any form, in any color. Our activism to bring Leslie Feinberg to Beacon as our commencement speaker is inseparable from our education as a whole. We did not revolutionize the world through our episode of activism; we did revolutionize our minds with the realization that we can make change. Our victory and Leslie Feinberg's voice sent us off into the world to continue this work for the rest of our lives.

Notes

1. Beacon College is a pseudonym, as are the names of college faculty and administrators and various community identifiers, such as names of towns and local newspapers. Student names are not pseudonyms.
2. Leslie Feinberg, *Stone Butch Blues* (Ithaca, NY: Firebrand Books, 1993).

3. Heterosexuality inherently demands orientation within a binary gender structure: in order to relate heterosexually with a man, one must by definition be female; in order to relate heterosexually with a woman, one must by definition be male.
4. In this article, I will use the pronoun s/he to refer to Leslie Feinberg. As the symbolic function of ideology, language promotes specific identity categories and divisions that are critical to "normal" cultural assimilation. "Transgender" is a concept that is neither contained nor accounted for in dominant ideology. Consequently, there are not adequate pronouns to refer to transgender individuals in the third person. Minnie Bruce Pratt responds to this lack in our language in her recently published book *S/HE* (Ithaca, NY: Firebrand Books, 1995). Through her work, which contains anecdotal reflections on her relationship with Leslie Feinberg, Pratt honors both the masculine and the feminine elements of Leslie Feinberg's identity by offering a new pronoun, "s/he." This pronoun represents distinct qualities of female and male that have not been divided. "S/he" is a person who cannot be defined as only he or only she; "s/he" is one who blends qualities of both masculine and feminine. With this construction, Pratt challenges linguistic convention that promotes a "reality" that does not include transgender individuals.

   However, conventional possessive pronouns (his and her) have yet to be reconciled on the gender continuum. In this article, when referring to something of Leslie Feinberg's, I will use the pronoun "her." Please note that this is an arbitrary choice made necessary by the inadequacies of conventional language, and does not accurately reflect Leslie Feinberg's full identity.
5. For a more comprehensive discussion of transgender theory and history, see Leslie Feinberg's recently published book, *Transgender Warriors: Making History from Joan of Arc to RuPaul* (Boston: Beacon Press, 1996).
6. In our leadership roles, Colleen, Eric, and I consistently strove to meet people at any place of doubt, and then bridge gaps with analysis and sincerity. However, we recognize that the more formidable we felt, the less able we were to relate to people outside our definition of "right." It may be that as Colleen, Eric, and I rose to define our resistance, we unintentionally silenced dissenting voices of students or others in the college community.
7. The National People's Campaign (NPC) is a nonprofit organization that has organized a united resistance among oppressed groups in the United States. Endorsed by human rights leaders and activists, NPC was formed with the primary goal of working to defeat the "Contract with America."
8. See Feinberg, *Transgender Warriors,* and articles Leslie Feinberg writes as a contributing editor to *Workers World.* Selected articles can be accessed on the Internet: ww_info@wwpublish.com.

I would like to dedicate this article to the Professor of Oz, who, from the outside, worked deeply in this struggle and guided my inspiration.

PART II

Participatory Democracy

"Education for the People, by the People"

PART II

Participatory Democracy

"Education for the People, by the People"

Efforts at educational reform are often led by policy makers and researchers removed from the particular needs, experiences, and realities of local communities. The "what works" model—often a top-down, one-size-fits-all approach to school change in which uniform strategies are transplanted from one educational site to another—misses the opportunity to utilize the strengths, resources, and expertise of the local people. By contrast, this section showcases examples of participatory education: community-organized sites of learning that prepare people to transform their own lives and to engage openly in public spaces. In these sites communities demonstrate their ability to define what works based on their own values and vision of education, creating and transforming their own spaces of teaching and learning.

Setting the frame, Bill Ayers's 2009 essay argues, "We should focus our collective efforts on schooling for a participatory democracy, on the production of fully developed human beings who are capable of controlling and transforming their own lives." Drawing inspiration from the democratic fervor of Obama's election, Ayers asserts that it is time to reform our educational traditions to more genuinely value, recognize, and develop the humanity of all students.

In the first example, from 1999, Montse Sánchez Aroca presents a case study of the founding, structure, and ethos of La Vernada-Sant Martí, a school for adults in Barcelona, Spain. Originating from within the community to meet the community's needs, the school utilizes egalitarian dialogue to maintain shared power and responsibility.

The next piece, first published in 1993, further illustrates community-based education, as historian Vanessa Siddle-Walker presents the Caswell County Training School, a segregated rural school for Black students in North Carolina. Through this tale of successful pre-integration education, Siddle-Walker highlights the importance of recognizing local knowledge and validating the expertise of parents and practitioners. In another 1993 article, Kathy Boudin, an inmate working as a teacher's assistant in a prison literacy class, describes moving into the teacher's role and transforming the course curriculum. Drawing on a humanizing pedagogy, Boudin describes how learning about AIDS and building academic work around this relevant issue empowered the students to take education into their own hands and feel ownership over their developing literacy skills.

The final piece in this section, an example of community-based education from 1998, demonstrates the power of nationalist ideals for members of three Puerto Rican neighborhoods in Chicago. Ana Ramos-Zayas tells the story of the Puerto Rican Community Center, which integrates Puerto Rican nationalism into activities at the center, a center-based alternative school, and the local comprehensive high school. Throughout Ramos-Zayas's telling, she reveals that these educational spaces foster students' passion and commitment to their community and their native Puerto Rico.

These articles capture grassroots efforts in which participatory education emerged from within communities and collectively exemplify Ayers's call for "education for the people, by the people."

Barack Obama and the Fight for Public Education

WILLIAM AYERS

Grant Park, Chicago, November 4, 2008

It was a human river in full flood, people flowing into the gathering stream, moving, churning, surging happily forward, spilling over the shifting banks without incident, and then effortlessly remaking the shore. There were children of all ages in hand or tucked into strollers and backpacks, buoyant parents delighted to let them stay up late, just this one night, in order to witness this precious and perhaps fragile moment. "Eighty years from now I want her to tell her grandchildren she was here," a young man said to me as he posed for a picture with his infant daughter. "She's a part of history, even if she doesn't know it yet."

What had been unimaginable a year, a month, even a day before had become inevitable and, on this special night and in this specific place, unforgettable—an African American president, a community organizer in the White House, a generational shift at last. We sang and we danced, and the enchanted night sparkled in reply. We felt ourselves to be a brand-new shimmering galaxy, a little bit of heaven on earth.

The crowd was diverse in a thousand ways. I saw a newborn wrapped tight on his mother's chest pushed up next to a small old woman smiling broadly from her wheelchair, waving an American flag in wide arcs above her head. I saw a young black police officer with a gold earring joined in a circle dance with two gray-haired white women.

We had stopped by my brother's to watch the early returns. He and his partner are lifelong Democratic Party stalwarts, and, with their friends, they had spent the weekends of the past year phone-banking and canvassing for Barack Obama in Michigan, Wisconsin, and Indiana. We were tied to multiple screens:

Harvard Educational Review Vol. 79 No. 2 Summer 2009

every precinct in those three battlegrounds was taken personally, every vote a distinct and intimate victory or defeat. We were a little ecstatic.

We moved on to a gathering at the home of longtime peace and justice activists just as the outcome was becoming clear. There was joy here, too, and a sense that this was not the end of anything, but a new beginning, an opening of sorts—rising expectations and expanding imaginations, but with lots of work to do tomorrow and the next day and the next. The mood here was more a sigh of relief, less an inclination to dance in the streets.

But we couldn't resist. And before John McCain conceded, we decided that dancing in the streets was exactly what was needed, so we headed for the door with friends in tow: a young historian from the Netherlands visiting for a few days of jaw-dropping Chicago experiences, a brilliant twenty-six-year-old cartoonist collaborating with me on a graphic novel about teaching, and an accomplished Zimbabwean scholar whose irrepressible excitement poured steadily into his cell phone, connecting Grant Park to the world.

I'd been a part of large crowds before this—demonstrations and rallies, sporting events, and the fabulously extravagant Taste of Chicago, also held in Grant Park—but every one of them had been edged with tension or anger or demand or performance, characterized by fighting or drunkenness or gluttony or narcissism. Grant Park 2008 was different. This was a huge mobilization sharing a deep sense of unity and satisfaction and relief—closing a door on eight years of fear and loathing, war and divisiveness. It was oddly serene and sober, and, while there was rejoicing, there was no crowing. The dominant tone was a soft purring as folks felt themselves going gently over the moon.

We saw more friends every step of the way, and we stopped for kisses and hugs and group cell phone photos, the spirit spilling seamlessly over to strangers, with more hugs, more photos. I surprised myself each time I burst into tears: first, just seeing the animated convergence grow and keep on growing; second, when I ran into two African American high school kids I knew, their videocams in hand, filming a curriculum project called "Searching for Democracy"; finally, standing on the exact spot where forty years ago, at the infamous 1968 Democratic Convention, I was beaten bloody by Chicago's finest and hauled off to jail. I corralled two young police officers—a black woman and a Latino man—to pose with me while a friend took photos. We all had tears in our eyes.

For the People, by the People

When President-elect Barack Obama stepped onto the Grant Park stage at the south edge of the park, the exultation rose up anew, as if for the first time. This was the moment; this was our time.

> If there is anyone out there who still doubts that America is a place where all things are possible . . . tonight is your answer. . . . It's the answer that led those who have been told for so long by so many to be cynical, and fearful, and doubt-

> ful of what we can achieve to put their hands on the arc of history and bend it once more toward the hope of a better day. (Obama, 2008)

There was a simple straightforwardness to his talk, an authenticity even in his acknowledgments and thank-yous that felt somehow new. And there was a deep bow to the reality that every community organizer knows well.

> For even as we celebrate tonight, we know the challenges that tomorrow will bring are the greatest of our lifetime—two wars, a planet in peril, the worst financial crisis in a century. . . . The road ahead will be long. Our climb will be steep. We may not get there in one year or even one term, but America—I have never been more hopeful than I am tonight that we will get there. I promise you—we as a people will get there. (Obama, 2008)

There were echoes here of Amilcar Cabral, the anticolonial African leader, insisting that the movement tells no lies and claims no easy victories, and reverberations of Martin Luther King Jr.'s hopeful insistence that the arc of history bends toward justice and that with effort and sacrifice we can achieve our dreams of righteousness and freedom. Everyone there also heard the echoes of the legacy of slavery and the struggle for abolition and equality. Everyone saw a new symbol of change. And everyone felt that our imaginations, our initiatives, our creative juices would flow more freely now and that future accomplishments were newly possible. That night we remembered King's insistent evocation of "the fierce urgency of now" (King, 1967) and his final question: "Where do we go from here: chaos or community?" (King, 1968)

During the heat of the primary battle, when Senator Obama was asked which candidate he thought Martin Luther King Jr. would support, he responded without hesitation—Reverend King would not likely endorse any of them, because he'd be in the streets building a movement for justice. That's a community organizer's answer and a good place to begin again.

Barack Obama looked positively Lincolnesque that night standing tall in front of our starry sky and our vast blue-black lake, but I'm an entirely untrustworthy witness: after all, I was in the park breathing all that rarified air. It's wonderful to breathe in the good air, to breathe out the bad air, and then just to keep on breathing—wonderful and refreshing. It's great to feel the energy of rising expectations, to hear the sounds of heavy chains dropping from our minds, to see the shining faces of hope everywhere. It's a moment to embrace, a moment to hold onto in tough times. But it's up to all of us now to get busy transforming ourselves, linking up to change the world.

Here we enter the necessary if unglamorous world of organizing, of reframing debates and dialogues at every level, of challenging the insistent dogma of common sense, of beginning political education, of enacting self-change and making a movement from the bottom up. Through what may be the most participatory national campaign in the country's history, a new generation has learned the tools of campaigning, community organizing, political discourse, and civic debate. Their experiences can now be turned; now they can mobilize others to insist on the changes they had hoped for and imagined. There is something stirring.

But we must remind ourselves that Lyndon Johnson, the most effective politician of his generation, the leader who passed the most far-reaching civil rights legislation in history, was never involved in the Black Freedom Movement. Franklin Delano Roosevelt was never a labor leader. Abraham Lincoln didn't belong to an abolitionist political party, and yet reality forced on him the opportunity to free an enslaved people. Each of these famous and effective presidents, in fact, responded to grassroots movements—and to reality itself—to do the right thing when it mattered.

It's to movements on the ground that we turn as we think beyond this election or the next and consider the problems and possibilities of building a future dramatically and decisively different from today. We must agitate for democracy and egalitarianism, press harder for human rights and a sustainable world, link the demands that animate us—for peace and education and universal health care and lifetime guarantees of income, against war and incarceration and surveillance—and learn to build a new society through our collective self-transformations and everyday struggles. We must seek ways to become real actors and authentic subjects in our own history. Every demand we are inclined to press on government should be matched by an equally forceful demand pressed on ourselves. If we want a foreign policy based on justice, for example, we ought to get busy organizing a robust anti-imperialist peace movement. We are not allowed to sit quietly in a democracy awaiting salvation from above. We are equal, and we all need to speak out and act up, for the truth is that Barack Obama cannot save us—though, with hard work and some luck, we just might save Barack Obama.

Organizing and Changing the Education Framework

The power of rising expectations, of imagination unleashed, of hope for something better than the politics of division and war and fear—all of it is in the air and on the move. Combined with serious and abiding crises—economic, financial, military—it announces a unique moment to reimagine and reignite a push toward fundamental change. It's a moment to shed some of the burdens and baggage of the past, a time to reach beyond the walls and entanglements we know too well, a time to restore the basic propositions and values of a more authentic, vibrant, and participatory democracy.

On that magical Grant Park evening, Obama intoned, "This is our moment. This is our time. . . . Yes we can" (Obama, 2008).

But, of course—and everyone says it—we need to ask, yes, we can . . . *what?*

For me, the answer involves returning to my roots as an antiwar organizer and civil rights activist, my roots as a teacher who believes that schools and classrooms, at their best, are powered by the engines of enlightenment and freedom. The promise of education is always tied up with the radical proposition that we can change our lives right now, today. It is a promise with particular resonance and urgency in a democratic society, for democracy assumes the necessity of continual and dynamic revitalization, and it demands regeneration as its lifeblood.

The dominant frames, controlling discourses, and common metaphors that have powerfully shaped our choices and set the terms and limits of our discussion about schools and reform for so long are narrowing and constraining. During the presidential debates, when John McCain repeatedly said that we need to get the lazy and incompetent teachers out of the classroom, almost everyone nodded dully—after all, who will stand up and defend the incompetent or demand that our children deserve the lazy? He won the point by framing the issue, setting the terms, limiting the options. If I had gotten to the podium first, I'd have said, "Every student in a public school deserves an intellectually engaged, morally grounded, thoughtful, caring, and compassionate teacher who is both well-compensated and well-rested," and I would have gotten support, too. Setting the frame is a powerful piece of work—who names the world and who frames the issue matters.

In area after area, issue after issue, we might productively open space for debate as we question the wisdom of the dominant frame: Why is our foreign policy based on military might rather than the principle of living together as a nation among nations? Why does every newspaper have a business section but not a labor section? Why are workers who cross borders in search of jobs considered "illegal immigrants," while the conditions that give rise to their movement—collapsing prices and massive unemployment caused by the unchecked flow of capital and environmental degradation—are rarely a part of the story? Why is the so-called achievement gap accepted as an empirical reality decontextualized from the "education debt" (Ladson-Billings, 1996) and "savage inequalities" (Kozol, 1991), or absent a sustained critique of the testing industry?

In the contested space of schools and education reform, and in this particular moment, educators, parents, theorists, citizens, and teachers should press to change the dominant discourse of education—a controlling metaphor that posits education as a commodity rather than a right and a journey and imagines schools as little factories cranking out products. This is a nineteenth-century image for twenty-first-century schools, and even the language of production dominates the discourse—assembly lines, management and supervision, quality control, productivity, and outputs. Within this metaphor, students are the raw materials moving dumbly down the assembly line as value is added by the workers/teachers; or, if the metaphor shifts its angle slightly, students are the workers themselves—workers-in-training, of course.

In this metaphoric straightjacket, school learning then becomes a commodity traded at the market like boots or hammers. Unlike boots or hammers, the values of which are inherently satisfying and understood directly, the value and use of school learning is elusive and indirect—hence, students are asked to accept its unspecified worth on faith and must always be motivated and rewarded externally. The value of school learning, we're assured, has been calculated precisely by wise and accomplished people, and these masters know better than anyone what's best for the kids and for the world. The payoff is way down the line, but it's surely there, somewhere, over the rainbow. "Take this medicine," students are told repeatedly, day after tedious day. "It's good for you." Refuse the bitter pill and go stand in the corner—where all the other losers are assembled.

Our schools too often teach indifference, emotional and intellectual dependency, provisional self-esteem, and the need to submit to certified authority. What, after all, are the lessons of report cards, grades, and the endless batteries of tests that play the part of autopsies rather than diagnostics? Don't trust yourself; seek approval from your betters. And what is the point of the established schedule and the set fifty-minute periods, the uniform desks all in a row, the exhaustive use of time with no room to breathe and certainly no space to dream or wonder or wander or drift or reflect or imagine or just be bored? You are not important and unique; be only malleable and productive in terms established by a higher authority.

The school-as-factory metaphor is more than an offensive image; worse, it is a model that betrays the demands of democracy. Those of us who want to work for a more robust and participatory democracy must change this metaphor and reaffirm the basic proposition that we share a common faith—every human being is of incalculable value. A democracy, theoretically at least, would build schools to fit children, not the other way around. We would not bend and break children or hammer them until they fit as cogs in a mindlessly menacing machine, automatons without the ability to think clearly or feel deeply. We would resist—because we do not want the schools to train a nation of sheep—the forceful imposition of standardized ways of seeing and knowing. In a robust and functional democracy, we would expect schools to reflect the principle that the fullest development of all is the necessary condition for the full development of each, and, conversely, the fullest development of each is necessary for the full development of all.

This expectation has huge implications for educational policy: racial segregation is wrong, class separation unjust, disparate funding immoral. There is no justification in a democracy for casting students out of school, none for categorical thinking in terms of potential or performance. There is no rationale for the existence of a well-funded school for wealthy white kids and a dilapidated, poorly resourced school for poor immigrant kids or the descendants of an enslaved people. That reality—this savage inequality—offends the foundational idea that each person is equal and reflects instead the reactionary idea that some of us are more deserving and more valuable than others. It expresses a simple but cruel message we send to children through our social policy and priorities: Choose the Right Parents! If you choose parents with money, access, social connection, and privilege, your choices and your chances will expand; if not, sorry, you're on your own.

A foundational belief in the value of every human is also belied by current "reform"—closing schools, privatizing the public space, testing children relentlessly. Michelle Rhee, CEO of the Washington, DC, schools and one of the four failed urban superintendents President Obama was considering for the top post in education, warranted a cover story in *Time* called "How to Fix America's Schools" (Ripley, 2008, p. 39). In a pivotal paragraph, the author praised Rhee for making more changes in a year and a half on the job than other school leaders—"even reform-minded ones"—make in five: closing 21 schools (15% of schools in the district), firing 100 central office personnel, 270 teachers, and 36 principals. These are policy moves held on faith to stand for improvement; they only make sense if education is a product. This is nothing more than downsizing and cost-cutting; the article included not one word on kids' learning or engagement with school, not a nod to any evidence that might connect these moves with any measure of student progress, not a mention of getting greater resources into this starving system.

Schools serve their larger societies in direct and indirect ways—the schoolhouse is both a window and a mirror into any social order. If, for example, you had wanted insight into the workings of apartheid in the old South Africa, you could simply have peeked into the schools. There you would have noticed white kids attending small classes with up-to-date equipment and well-trained teachers dispensing a curriculum consistent with white supremacist assumptions. You would have also seen black kids in overcrowded, collapsing buildings being fed a steady diet of obedience. Clearly one set of youngsters was destined for the mines and the mills, the fields and the prisons, while the other was being tutored to administer and profit from the injustice.

Our schools show us exactly who we are—the good, the bad, and the ugly—beneath the rhetoric and the self-congratulatory platitudes. If some of what we see is not as we would like it, well, we can search for all kinds of explanations and justifications. Or we can, in our defense, retreat to our good intentions. Or we just might conclude that some things *need* to be changed—and we might even decide to join hands with others in order to create those changes.

Returning to Education for the People, by the People

We should focus our collective efforts on schooling for a participatory democracy, on the production of fully developed human beings who are capable of controlling and transforming their own lives, the development of citizens who can participate fully in our shared public life. Such a democracy requires that people must actually make the decisions that affect their lives; such a democracy requires dialogue—each one speaking with the hope of being heard and each one listening with the possibility of being changed. Such a democracy requires a democratic school that would be generously supported, abundant with resources and materials of all kinds; it would be small, numbering no more than a few hundred students. In this school, participatory democracy could be enacted, practiced, and embodied; it would be a workshop for discovery and surprise, a laboratory for inquiry and experimentation. And the curriculum would unfold in endless pursuit of an inexhaustible question: what knowledge and experience is of most value?

Democracies require students to think for themselves, to make judgments based on evidence and argument, to develop minds of their own. Democratic classrooms are places where teachers encourage students to ask those fundamental questions—Who in the world am I? How did I get here, and where am I going? What are my choices? How shall I proceed?—and to pursue the answers wherever they might take them. We must refuse obedience in favor of teaching initiative, courage, imagination, creativity, and more. These are the qualities to be modeled and nourished, encouraged and defended.

We must invite students to ask serious questions: What's the evidence? How do we know? Whose viewpoint is privileged, and whose is left out? What are the alternatives, the connections, the resistance, the patterns, the causes? Where are things headed? Why? Who cares?

Teaching and organizing—at their best—are each powered by a common faith: when I knock on the door of a stranger in a public housing project, when I look out at my students, I assume the full humanity of each. I see hopes and dreams, aspirations and needs, experiences and intentions that must somehow be accounted for and valued. I encounter citizens, not consumers—unruly sparks of meaning-making energy, not a mess of deficits. This is the evidence of things not seen, the starting point for teachers and organizers in any democratic society.

* * * * *

On September 23, 2008, the right-wing theorist Stanley Kurtz (2008) wrote a widely circulated op-ed in the *Wall Street Journal* entitled "Obama and Ayers Pushed Radicalism on Schools." The piece was putatively about a reform initiative in Chicago called the Annenberg Challenge; I cofounded the initiative, and Barack Obama served as the vice chair of its board. However, the larger point of the editorial was the dishonest guilt-by-association gambit Obama's rivals spun in a new direction: The "domestic terrorist" [me] is not so much a danger because of his despicable past, but because of his Trojan Horse strategy to turn America's youth into little revolutionaries" (p. A29). Then, a few weeks later, Sol Stern (2008), a "senior fellow at the Manhattan Institute" currently "writing a book . . . on William Ayers and social justice teaching," weighed in with a *Wall Street Journal* op-ed of his own: "Ayers is no Education 'Reformer'" (p. A15). Stern, who claims to have studied my writings for years, concluded that my "hatred of America is as virulent" (p. A15) as ever and that an Obama victory would ensure that "Mr. Ayers's social-justice movement in the schools" (p. A15) has greater freedom to grow and spread.

I have written about social justice and its link to education in a free society, it's true; but it's not *mine*, and I've never thought of social justice as something arcane and alien in a democracy. I do not consider social justice an add-on or a separate event—chess club, cheerleading, driver's ed, *social justice*? It's important to reaffirm that education in a democracy—at least theoretically—is distinct from education under an authoritarian regime, a dictatorship, or a monarchy. In a democracy, life is geared toward and powered by a particularly precious and fragile ideal: every human being is of infinite and incalculable value, each a unique intellectual, emotional, physical, spiritual, moral, and creative force; each born free and equal in dignity and rights; each endowed with reason and conscience; each deserving a community of solidarity, a sense of brotherhood and sisterhood, recognition, and respect. This core value is the heart of the matter, and it must express itself explicitly and implicitly in education just as in every other aspect of democratic living. In a democracy, we have a responsibility to organize society to reflect these ideas; education must be concerned with social justice.

Much of schooling forecloses or shuts down or walls off meaningful choice-making. Much of it is based on obedience and conformity, the hallmarks of every authoritarian regime throughout history. Much of it banishes the unpopular, squirms in the presence of the unorthodox, hides the unpleasant. There's little space for skepticism, irreverence, questioning, or doubt. While many of us long for teaching as something transcendent and powerful, we find ourselves too often locked in situations that reduce teaching to a kind of glorified clerking, passing along a curriculum of received wisdom and predigested and often false bits of information. This is a recipe for disaster in the long run.

Education in a democracy challenges and reframes all of that: there is space for a curriculum of questioning, for a curriculum of doing and making, for a curriculum of learning from the world, not simply about the world. In classrooms, students would learn—through inquiry, experimentation, invention, and play—the value of empathy, of openness, of dialogue and conversation, of documentation. Classrooms would become galleries and exhibition halls, stages and studios, laboratories and libraries and performance spaces.

The most fundamental purpose of public schooling in a democracy—rather than loyalty to the state or fealty to job training—is teaching citizens to think about the issues that affect their lives and how they might be otherwise. Pressure from government to make schools little outposts of patriotism or from business to align the goals of education with the needs of corporations jeopardizes the democratic foundations of education. We must ask ourselves whether schools geared to preparing loyal subjects or obedient workers also create thinking, literate, active, and morally sensitive citizens capable of carrying out their democratic responsibilities to one another, to their communities, to the earth.

Education is an arena of struggle as well as hope—struggle because it stirs in us the need to look at the world anew, to question what we have created, to wonder what is worthwhile for human beings to know and experience; and hope because we gesture toward the future, toward the impending, toward the coming of the new. Education is where we ask how we might engage, enlarge, and change our lives; it is, then, where we confront our dreams and fight out notions of the good life, where we try to comprehend, apprehend, or possibly even change the world. Education is contested space, a natural site of conflict—sometimes restrained, other times in full eruption—over questions of justice. Through education we are called to resist dogma, to expand inquiry, to raise queer questions. Participatory democracy at its heart requires dialogue—each one speaking with the hope of being heard, and each one listening with the possibility of being changed.

The Inauguration of Hope

On a bright, transcendent January morning—one day after honoring Martin Luther King Jr. on the eightieth anniversary of his birth—the once unthinkable was, suddenly and inevitably, done. The forty-fourth president of the United States was sworn in, and who could resist the embracing magic of that moment?

Poet Elizabeth Alexander (2009) called for common people "repairing the things in need of repair" (p. 3). In a bleeding world marked by so much unnecessary pain, a world so precariously out of balance, we must find ways to come together in vast missions of repair: "A teacher says, 'Take out your pencils. Begin.'"

And so it begins.

Years from now, the magic of November and January will survive, or not—and that judgment will rest largely on questions of war and poverty. Martin Luther King Jr.'s (1967) conscious and courageous connection of racial justice to economic justice and peace is a legacy to embrace in "the fierce urgency of now." Will this moment be ruined in the furnaces of war, or can we hammer swords into plowshares and become a nation among nations? Can we learn to really live by the principle that anyone's suffering diminishes us all? Can we turn away from war and surveillance and incarceration long enough to invest in education and health and productive work for all?

The president's speech looked in both directions: a return to past imperial "glory" and a new awakening of peace and justice. A page was turned, but it's up to all of us to write the next chapter.

This is the moment, this is our time—yes, we can. But the question lingers: yes we can *what*? Education is a way out of no way, the special intersection of desire and transformation, of possibility and reality. Education, knowledge, and learning are unique. No matter how much knowledge you give away, you never lose a bit; it's yours forever.

Goodbye to schooling that's arid, dry, self-referencing, and self-satisfied. Goodbye to teaching as a theory of the mundane, a trivial pursuit of the obvious. Goodbye to deference, didacticism, ego, and complacency in a heartless world. Goodbye to prisons and border guards and walls—whether in Palestine or in Texas—and goodbye to quarantines, deletions, and closures. Goodbye to all that.

Welcome to the unknown, to jumping off the edge, to the dance of the dialectic. Welcome to an approach that is overflowing with life, crackling with the surprising and contradictory harmonies of love, stunning in its hope for a better world. Welcome to endlessly learning how to live again and how to love anew. Embrace relentless curiosity, simple acts of kindness, the complexity of humanity, the wonder of it all. Embrace struggle and the poetics of resistance, history, and agency. Embrace world peace and inner peace. Each day in every way, vote for love—all kinds of love for all kinds of people in all kinds of circumstances and situations. Embrace a new world in the making, and then dare to taste it with a kiss.

References

Alexander, E. (2009). *Praise song for the day.* St. Paul, MN: Graywolf Press.

King, M. L., Jr. (1967). *Beyond Vietnam: A time to break silence.* Retrieved March 23, 2009, from http://icujp.org/king.shtml

King, M. L., Jr. (1968). *Where do we go from here: Chaos or community?* Boston: Beacon Press.

Kozol, J. (1991). *Savage inequalities: Children in America's schools.* New York: Crown Publishers.

Kurtz, S. (2008, September 23). Obama and Ayers pushed radicalism on schools. *The Wall Street Journal.* Retrieved March 23, 2009, from http://online.wsj.com/article/SB122212856075765367.html

Ladson-Billings, G. (1996). From the achievement gap to the education debt: Understanding achievement in U.S. schools. *Education Researcher, 35*(7), 3–12.

Obama, B. (2008). *"Democracy, liberty, opportunity & unyielding hope"—The victory speech.* Retrieved March 23, 2009, from http://www.nbcwashington.com/news/elections/national/text_barack_obama_victory_speech.html

Ripley, A. (2008, December 8). How to fix America's schools. *Time, 172*(23), 36–44.

Stern, S. (2008, October 16). Ayers is no education "reformer." *Wall Street Journal.* Retrieved March 23, 2009, from http://online.wsj.com/article/SB122411943821339043.html

La Verneda-Sant Martí

A School Where People Dare to Dream

MONTSE SÁNCHEZ AROCA

Ahora soy feliz. La gente me ha dado mucho apoyo, estoy muy contenta. Antes no conocía a nadie, pero ahora todo el mundo me anima y pienso que de esta forma lograré llegar a la universidad. La escuela es como si fuera de todos, y cada persona es importante.

—*Fátima*[1]

[I am happy now. People have supported me a lot, I am really happy. I didn't know anybody before, but now everybody encourages me and I think that in this way I'll be able to get to the university. It is as if the school belonged to all of us, and every person is important.]

Ten years ago, I started teaching at La Verneda-Sant Martí School for Adults in Barcelona, Spain. Since then, many participants at the school have shared their positive feelings about the school with me, as did Fátima, above.[2] Our school has close to sixteen hundred participants and about one hundred teachers and volunteer collaborators, all of whom work hand-in-hand to expand their knowledge, create new learning opportunities, and improve the school and their community, a working-class neighborhood in Barcelona. What surprised me when I first came to La Verneda School, and continues to amaze me today, is the participants' and educators' high level of involvement, as well as the various activities they generate. Fátima, for instance, is a member of one of the school's participants' associations. Like other participants, she always takes part in the coordination meetings and is active on several committees. While her experience with learning differs from the teachers', it is equally valued in a school that is, as Fátima said, a place that belongs to all of us.

What moved me to write down Fátima's words that night is also driving me today to write this piece. I believe it is important to bear witness to what the

Harvard Educational Review Vol. 69 No. 3 Fall 1999

school is about and to share it with others, whether they live nearby or far away. La Verneda is a school at which people dare to dream because we know that dreams can become reality. For example, Fátima's dream is to go to the university. Other people's dreams have been to learn how to read and to participate in diverse conversations in their daily lives. For many people in the community, the dream is to overcome difficulties through education. Here, many people overcome the social exclusion that they might suffer elsewhere. We know the process is not easy and that we must work hard and fight for what we need and want, but the teachers and participants at La Verneda know that we can transform our reality together. We also know that the dream is worth the struggle.

In this article, I describe how La Verneda developed and how it functions today. I describe the community's participation in the school, the democratic way decisions are made, and the ways ideas are generated and responsibilities shared. By narrating various experiences and events that I have witnessed, I portray a project grounded in egalitarian dialogue and its outcomes — both the growing participation and range of possibilities within the school and the generation of solidarity beyond it.

As I start to write, I look around the staff room at La Verneda and see a crowd of people coming and going, greeting me, smiling. They are many kinds of people: young and old, men and women, fathers and mothers, graduates or not, but all of them are devoted to their community and its improvement. They have in common their participation in the school, a school that, thanks to their work, can host various activities. Everyone is working on something different: some are working on BASIC, a pilot project on basic literacy and employment that we share with educational centers in the Netherlands, Belgium, and Germany; others are organizing events for the Fiesta Mayor, the annual local festival; others are planning an exchange program with a school in Galdakano, a town in Spain's Basque region, to help them create a participants' association; and others are studying for the access-to-university comprehensive exam.[3] Still others are preparing a literary gathering to discuss the poet Federico García Lorca. I sit here, thinking of how to capture on paper how that dream was created and what I see and feel in this school.

Creating a Dream

When I first arrived at La Verneda in 1988, it had just celebrated its tenth anniversary with a big party. In Spain, the 1970s were years of grand debates, demands, changes, and many political and social hopes. Our neighborhood, La Verneda-Sant Martí, took part in these changes. In the aftermath of Franco's dictatorship, the doors to democracy were beginning to open, and people felt they could contribute to the ideal of creating a better society through civil and cultural participation. The neighbors of La Verneda-Sant Martí formed local groups and associations to analyze their needs and discuss ways to improve their neighborhood. One of the needs considered then was a school for adult education that would provide a public space in which people could share knowledge and learning in order to participate in what was then an incipient transition to democracy. This was also seen as necessary to defend the idea that education should be a public good available to everybody. Thus, in 1978, a group of people began to build this dream called La Verneda-Sant Martí School for Adults.

A group of seventeen people from the local residents' association engaged in a shared community-based learning process.[4] During the first year, people were so enthusiastic that they started to reflect on what they were doing and how interesting it was. They would talk about the school at the workplace, when they went shopping, and when they were with their children at the park. As a result, the initiative became increasingly well-known. The following year there was a sense of great expectancy, and the number of participants increased dramatically beyond the one hundred already involved. The many informal interactions of participants with people in the neighborhood contributed to the ease with which information about the school circulated by word of mouth.

When a group of university professors of education visited the project a few years ago, Carmen, one of the early participants, explained to them how the school started. As she spoke, her enthusiasm showed not only in her words, but also in her facial expression:

> The building in which you are now is a Community Center. It used to be a facility used by Franco's dictatorial administration. Therefore, it became vacant in the late 1970s with the advent of democracy, with no specific function assigned to it. . . . In 1978, we decided to take over the building and set up a cultural center with all the services we demanded: the childcare center, the school for adults, the youth club, etc. We, the neighbors, decided what we wanted it to be like and what to do to achieve it. Afterwards, once we managed to get the center started, our struggle turned in part to demanding the different public administrations to take on their share of responsibility with funding. What still remains from all that is the way in which everybody gets involved and participates. . . . What we achieved is an extensive cultural project for the community, housed in our center. This center brings together most of the community's cultural life, and that is why here, on its fifth floor, the School for Adults is located.

During the late 1970s, the changes at La Verneda were part of the transformation taking place in adult education throughout Spain. At the time, adult education followed a compensatory education model designed for those who had not been able to attend school earlier in their lives. Educators and participants at La Verneda challenged the assumption that childhood and adolescence were the appropriate periods of life for learning. Using research from the fields of psychology and pedagogy that focused on adult learners, they showed that people of all ages could learn and argued that education is a basic right throughout life.[5]

Creating Opportunities

La Verneda's doors open at 9 A.M. and close at 10 P.M., which provides opportunities for extensive community participation. The school offers a wide range of activities to respond to community members who are involved in the school, who have diverse interests, expertise, and cultural backgrounds. Courses and activities available to students include basic literacy, certification courses (equivalent to the secondary school level), literature gatherings, computer science, painting, pottery, health, sociology, psychology, Spanish as a second language, and English for hotel business and tourism. Participants also attend seminars, such as "Where is science heading?" "Art and society," "The world of plants," "Ecology," "The Euro," or "What is happening in the world?" This diverse selection helps students discover or create what they need and care about.

The activities that elicit the greatest interest and the highest participation are those related to reading. Literature has opened previously unimaginable paths for action, created new attitudes, and contributed to sharing values and feelings. For example, Heura, the women's association, holds a literary contest every year in March, around International Women's Day. The contest is open to all, and the association receives numerous narratives and poems about women, many of exceptional quality. Last year one submission beautifully highlighted a woman's personal experience, relevant to all domains of women's lives. The poem was about her life as a woman — being a mother, a wife, and working in extreme conditions. It also referred to other women who, through very hard work, now also had control over their lives. The author expressed the thrill she feels when she realizes how women's expectations have been transformed so dramatically in recent years. The text was signed with a pseudonym and an epigraph that said, "86 years and 200 days." She was also overcoming the ageist participation concept. She was a transformative woman.[6]

The school community pays a great deal of attention to life stories, to literature, and to dialogue. A few years ago, a team of people from the library, the school, the community center, and other people who lived in the neighborhood created a project called *Vuit menys Set: Un Escriptor, Un Món* (Seven to Eight: A Writer, A World) to promote reading in the neighborhood. For four years, a writer has been invited every month to speak at our center, and between two hundred and four hundred people crowd the room in anticipation of hearing such noted speakers as José Luis L. Aranguren, one of the most acclaimed Spanish philosophers of our century.[7] After his participation in *Vuit menys Set,* he told us it would have been impossible to host such an activity without the community participation and support we had in the center. He said, *"Venir al centro me da más vida porque aquí se habla de la vida. Ustedes hacen que sienta vida y no teatro"* ("Coming over to the center gives me more life because here you talk about life. You make me feel life, rather than fiction"). In the *Vuit menys Set* events, we do not discuss literature as some "experts" do. Instead, people offer their impressions about the author's work, or comment on something they watched on TV about the guest writer. People ask questions based on what really interests them from the readings, rather than what is "proper" to ask, such as the influence of reading in our everyday lives, and whether writers have any responsibility to society.

In a sense, *Vuit menys Set* is a space where education and learning happen in a way similar to the way that people of La Verneda interact in their community. It has become, as Jürgen Habermas puts it, a space where system and lifeworld meet.[8] Visitors often ask us why the room is always packed for these events, while similar gatherings elsewhere are not so successful. We believe it is because the people of La Verneda have participated in the creation of each event. Nobody had a preconceived plan of what was going to happen; it was a creative act in which everyone participated in the way that suited them best.

Egalitarian Dialogue

Different kinds of knowledge can be considered equally valuable in a lifelong learning process. Interacting with others on equal footing is a way to learn from those with whom we debate and share our doubts and our experiences. At La Verneda we have learned that the key to learning is egalitarian dialogue. Egalitarian dialogue can occur if teachers have no preconceived strategy they want to impose on learners, and if participants know at all times what is going on in the classrooms, why things are done in a certain way, and what the goals of each pedagogical intervention are. In addition, participants must have the option to change, debate, or discuss all that goes on in the school. The collaborative environment that this creates makes knowledge multiply because it is intermingled with other people's knowledge; this sharing allows people to search with others for the best arguments and solutions to problems they may face. Today, such dialogue generates a comfortable atmosphere of familiarity and belonging at the school.

People share equal potential when they are given the same opportunities. When people can assume that their opinion or idea will be defended or criticized only in open arguments, and that all arguments will be listened to equally, they can let their creativity flow and not be afraid to contribute their thoughts. For example, in class, students freely contribute their own ideas and questions. I remember a course organized by three groups of four people each that decided to carry out small pieces of research. One of the groups included Alonso, a paraplegic person, and for this reason they decided to conduct research on the nervous system with a part of their research focused on paraplegia. The day they presented their work to the rest of the class, Alonso presented the portion of the study on paraplegia, drawing from his own life as an example. At the end of their presentation, the other groups suggested that they focus on the human body in the following semester. By paying greater attention to participants' own interests, it is possible to increase their motivation to learn and to increase their knowledge. Furthermore, when their contributions relate to their own life experience, they move closer to understanding the reality of other people's lives and further away from relying on stereotypes.

Typical examples of such dialogue take place at the literary gatherings. This activity was created eighteen years ago by participants at the basic and new-reader literacy levels who chose to read classics by authors such as Federico García Lorca, Antonio Machado, James Joyce, Franz Kafka, and many others. In 1998, the participants in the literary gathering created a new adventure: they found a way to merge two of the authors they knew and admired most — poet Federico García Lorca and educator Paulo Freire. They decided to devote the year to remembering these two men who struggled so for equality.[9] While reading the work of these intellectuals, the group talked about literature, ideas, society, and *flamenco.* One of the participants was a young Gypsy musician, and sometimes they listened to his music and let their creativity soar. They used this creativity to put together a presentation for the Freire Year events at the university. These people, who had not been able to read a book when they had started school but who had poetry in their lives, moved an audience of five hundred with their emotional presentation. Students, professors, university representatives, colleagues from La Verneda, and others who had come to remember Paulo Freire were moved by every verse of Lorca's poetry, by every image from the lives of the presenters, and by the educational experiences the writers conveyed in their words. Some even said the presentation created a kind of catharsis. I think it provided a perfect fusion between reality and dreams, between literature and life, thus breaking down the wall between academic and community cultures.

In the literary gatherings, people's dreams of reading literature become a reality through egalitarian dialogue. In such gatherings, their opinions are valued without any stigma, regardless of their status or their educational background, and they are free to speak in a language in which they can freely express themselves. The whole group selects the classic books they read. After reading the book at home, participants meet and discuss what made an impression on them. The project is based on group solidarity: all members must be ready to share their feelings and reactions with the rest of the group. After all the ideas are expressed, participants discuss and come to a collective interpretation of the reading, rather than a "correct" interpretation provided by the teacher. It is in this way that dialogic learning, the learning that emerges from egalitarian dialogue, becomes possible.

Democratic Participation

The dialogic dynamics generated at the class and activity levels are representative of the school's dialogic organization. La Verneda School is managed collaboratively by educators and participants who work together within an organizational structure that allows everyone to express their needs, interests, and ideas.

For instance, participants at the school have organized two associations, Ágora and Heura, to develop their initiatives. Ágora represents participants in the school's decisionmaking process. Recently, Ágora has been important in creating new guidelines for an adult education curriculum that is broader and more consensual than the national curriculum proposed by the Spanish government, which did not take adults into account. Through Ágora, participants have been able to get involved in designing specific curricula for adult secondary education.

Heura is a participants' association of women struggling to overcome the barriers they encounter as adults and as women, since women face more cultural barriers than men. This association tries to make women's voices heard. For example, Heura collaborated in the 1999 Women's Conference held in Barcelona.[10] It developed a paper about women's social participation, and also contributed to the debate by talking about women's representation in public spheres. Heura argued that even in today's environment, with the dramatic increase in the number of female representatives in public decisionmaking bodies, there is still much to do in order to make *all* women's voices heard. It stressed the need to consider the difference in the economic and cultural status of these female representatives, who tend to belong to higher social ranks, and that of the female population as a whole. Heura works through committees, and all participants contribute their personal experiences to the association. Heura's presence has helped introduce topics related to the world of women to the school.

Another example of La Verneda's democratic participation is the school's management. The management is organized into three open-discussion panels that function as the school's decisionmaking bodies: the Assembly, the School Council, and the Monthly Coordination Meeting. All of them are made up of teachers, volunteers, and participants.

The Assembly, which meets once a year, is open to all teachers, participants, and volunteers, as well as to representatives from the neighborhood and the Community Center. It also may be called as needed between these annual meetings. Direct democracy is practiced in these assemblies. This decisionmaking process, which has also been promoted in many other community movements, allows everybody to present problems in order to solve them together. The School Council meets every one-and-a-half months and is the forum where the school's operation and guidelines are discussed. The Council is comprised of one participant representative from each class, representatives from among educators, school committees, participants' associations, the Community Center, and VERN.[11] Participants can raise all types of questions and concerns, propose and discuss new activities, and create committees. Furthermore, the management of resources (human, material, or economic) is discussed publicly. Decisions on the use of public resources are made in different ways, but they always take into account the school's general principles. When a need is detected, it is presented at the Monthly Coordination Meetings. A commission is then formed, which works according to the priorities and criteria established at the larger meeting. The final decision is always the Council's. Public resources can be provided by local, regional, national, or European Union governmental bodies, or by some foundations. Resources are then applied to specific actions to produce results. In this way, we seek consensus on every question. Sometimes, however, such agreement is not reached easily, and further discussion on a question is continued in the different groups in order to devise new solutions. Thus, we achieve consensus through the dynamics of dialogue and seeking understanding.

An example of this consensus at work is related to an issue widely discussed in Spain in recent years: immigration. This debate is most significant in Spain, a port of entry for many North Africans into Europe, given the construction of a collective European identity. The issue of immigration also affected the debate about our school guidelines, as people took different positions on it. Right in front of the school, for instance, there is a police station that is in charge of controlling "illegal" immigration, and participants have different opinions about this type of control. However, we all agreed that, in spite of differences of opinion regarding immigration and related issues, the school would be committed to admitting everybody because education should know no frontiers. Consequently, we never ask about the residency status of any applicant, leaving the doors to education open to everyone.

This working procedure requires that everybody involved in the everyday operation of the school attend the Monthly Coordination Meeting (COME), at which participants and educators coordinate different activities, announce important information, and reflect on our teaching-learning practice and educational innovations. A different committee is appointed every month at the meeting to prepare the following COME. As part of its duties, the committee creates an agenda for the meeting, provides handouts with information to be disseminated in the classes, and prepares a discussion activity. Discussion is usually prompted through a variety of techniques — such as use of a sketch, a text, or a videotaped scene from real life at the school — and is carried on in small groups. At the end of each meeting, each group reports to the plenary and formulates conclusions, comments, and recommendations that will help to shape the school's philosophy, guidelines, and methodologies. On the first Tuesday of every month, about one hundred people gather in the COME — a level of commitment and collaboration that I have not seen in any other school I have visited.

For example, in January 1999, when a commission of women was working on their presentation for the Women's Conference, some proposed to focus the March COME on women's issues. At the beginning of the meeting, a member of the committee introduced the importance of adult education for women to the audience and three different ways it could be approached (equality, difference, and equality of difference). Some specific cases from the school were given as examples. We then worked in small groups to seek solutions to the problems presented. Then, each group explained what they had discussed. As a result of our discussions, we agreed that the school would follow the equality of differences perspective.[12] Since then, all our actions have been guided by the criteria developed at that meeting.

Throughout the year, participants and educators also take part in professional development activities, evaluation of the school's programs, and generation of new ideas. It is understood that fostering the learning process is the responsibility of both participants and staff. By extending the opportunity of professional development to all of us, the school emphasizes the fact that everybody is able to participate in the decisionmaking process. This is the key to being successful as a school, as well as to attracting new participants.

The most important professional development activities are three intensive workshops devoted to reflection and learning:

- The first one, early in the academic year, is primarily devoted to educators' professional development — full-time teachers and part-time collaborators. One of the workshop's goals is to share our current knowledge and expertise with the new volunteers, as well as to improve ourselves through training.
- The second one, which takes place around February, is devoted to the continuing assessment of the project, as well as to the generation of new ideas. Educators and members of the participants' associations spend a weekend working in a house off campus. This workshop includes presentations, reflection activities, and discussions of different topics.
- The last of these workshops, which deals with the final evaluation of the academic year, is held during three full days in July. Working in small groups, we discuss how the past school year went and delineate prospective guidelines for the next year through a process of dialogue, making sure that participants express their needs and make proposals. The workshop ends with a plenary discussion, at which all the groups assess how the school's curriculum matched the participants' interests over the previous year.

Overcoming Strategies of Power

In our school, solidarity and equality are more than mere concepts; we put them into practice through our democratic procedures. When democratic practices increase, however, multiple pressures and threats arise.

We have frequently faced people who wanted to impose their way of doing things. Those who use pressure to push what is often their hidden agenda tend to describe all groups as self-interested and to then use this assessment to justify their own egocentric aims. This approach causes confrontation and leaves no room for dialogue, mutual criticism, or deliberation about the best options for both the school and its participants. Those who use pressure to achieve their goals often try to put themselves above the rest by emphasizing the differences between participants and teachers, and to dominate and control everything according to their own interests.

For example, in September 1994, before the start of the new academic year, a group of teachers started to devise a "strategy for change," with a focus on the class schedule. Schedules had always been made collectively and with the diverse needs of local people in mind. During summer break, these teachers, who represented a majority of the full-time staff, met to lay out a new schedule. They did not submit it for discussion, and they tried to impose it on the rest of the teachers at the beginning of the fall semester. The new schedule expanded class hours for the higher level courses, which failed to take into account people's working and parental schedules. Many classes were scheduled for 9 A.M., a time when parents are taking their children to school, or 5 P.M., when they pick them up after school. The plan also reduced night classes. In other words, the schedule did not serve those who were to take the classes, but those who were to teach them. The teachers' idea of change did not emerge from the school's usual decisionmaking process, but from their own interest. Soon it led to a separation between the teachers' place and that of the students.

This could not change our project, however. Opposition to the new schedule grew quickly: many participants, teachers, and volunteers, with the support of various neighborhood organizations, fought the goals and procedures of these few teachers. Eventually VERN called a special School Council in order to discuss the issue, to hear the arguments of all parties involved, and to solve the schedule conflict. More importantly, this hearing was to take place within the school's discussion and decisionmaking bodies. As expected, the teachers' group did not want to explore alternative solutions; instead, they criticized the process and disregarded anything the Council decided. The rest of us remained committed to our democratic procedures. Those teachers were moved to another school where their interests were better represented.

I have an emotional memory of the first COME we held after this conflict. One of the most senior participants stood up at the plenary and explained the new scenario. Now we had fewer people who worked full-time at the school, but the goal was to at least provide what we usually offered. After hearing her words, every person who was at the meeting — the remaining teachers and volunteers, current and former participants, members of local organizations, and local neighborhood residents — stood up and said what he or she could do. The reigning sentiment was, "This is everybody's project and we must go ahead; we will do whatever is needed!" It was an emotional moment.

Many of us at La Verneda School have read or attended a performance of the play *Fuenteovejuna*, a classic of Spain's literary Golden Age. Playwright Lope de Vega presents the struggle against authoritarianism and injustice. Villagers fight against a rapist, a king's subject taking advantage of his *droit de seigneur.* In the denouement, the whole village rises and fights as if they constituted a single voice under the lemma, *"Fuenteovejuna, todos a una!"* ("Fuenteovejuna, all together!"). This was the key in our struggle at the school: all our voices became as one in naming what was fair. The people in our neighborhood knew what they wanted, knew how to fight for it, and knew that their strength lay in solidarity.

We are now about a hundred people collaborating at the school. Among us are eight full-time teachers — four hired by the public administration and four by the Ágora and Heura associations. Most of those who volunteer are former participants and members of the community who live in the neighborhood; some come from the university environment to the school as part of a field experience. The very nature of the project generates involvement in it. The nature of participation would not be the same if the school had not been born as a result of people's debates and actions in the local associations and their struggle to improve living conditions in their neighborhood. Emerging from a grassroots tradition and being shaped continuously by the community, our project is committed to maintaining its participatory orientation.

For this reason, La Verneda is embedded within a network of local organizations, each with different and complementary social roles, all committed to community development. Ágora and Heura, the school's participants' associations, together with thirty other associations, groups, and collectives, form the VERN Coordinating Committee. This umbrella organization analyzes and provides solutions to the neighborhood's social needs, whether they relate to urban development, public health, culture, sports, or related social values, such as the fight against xenophobia and other types of discrimination. Only through dialogue is it possible to know the abilities, interests, and needs of others. It follows that the best way to overcome discrimination is through intercultural dialogue. VERN's work is organized through committees, which coordinate neighborhood demands, information sessions, workshops, seminars, and local celebrations. In this way, all of the agencies participate in community development. Among the projects La Verneda-Sant Martí community promotes through VERN are the preservation of the neighborhood's old town, which had been targeted for demolition due to urban development plans; the construction of a new underground line and the improvement of public transportation in the neighborhood; a plan to eliminate architectural barriers in the neighborhood; and the creation of a committee for local youth groups.

Opening Doors

The democratic organization and opportunities that La Verneda provides have opened the door for many people. Throughout my ten years of involvement in the school, I have met many people, but there is one I want to single out. He came to La Verneda to obtain the *graduado escolar* degree he was not able to earn as a teenager.[13] He was one of those kids referred to as a "dropout," who is not expected to go further with his studies. When I first met him, he was teaching Catalan language courses at La Verneda as a volunteer collaborator. He had already obtained the graduado escolar degree, passed the access-to-university exam, and was studying pedagogy at the university. At La Verneda

School, he had found the human and material support he was unable to find in the educational system before. He is now a professor at the university and soon will receive his Ph.D. He continues to collaborate with the school, teaching adults as he did fifteen years ago. He decided he had many resources to help others who, like himself, could build on their own abilities and go a long way. When he teaches at the university, he never tells the soon-to-be educators in his classes about people's *failure,* but about the capabilities inherent in every person, as well as how cultural intelligence opens new perspectives to many learning forms. We often refer to him as a role model, but he says that his was not an individual accomplishment, that he would never have gotten there alone. There was, he says, a bigger project backing him, and working together made it easier to open doors for all.

Working from a perspective of community also means working from one of solidarity to promote dialogue and increase people's opportunities, focusing especially on those who have more obstacles in their way. When they are perceived as participants, people become cultural creators, rather than cultural consumers. At La Verneda School we struggle to bring down the barriers that impede equality by promoting participation at all levels, from activities to improve basic living standards to intellectual and political debates.

We saw vividly how participants are breaking down cultural barriers in a collective effort that took place in April 1997, when Jürgen Habermas came to Barcelona to lecture on *The Intercultural Discourse on Human Rights.* A group of participants from La Verneda School attended along with an audience made up primarily of university students and professors. When Habermas finished his talk, Mariana, one of the participants at La Verneda, dared to raise her hand and ask a question about the working rights of women.[14] She phrased her question in a way that revealed her unfamiliarity with the academic discourse usually spoken in the university's lecture hall. Some of the professors felt a little uncomfortable; some even giggled. I became indignant and restless, but Mariana spoke for herself, *"No hablo como una intelectual, pero sé lo que me digo"* ("I do not speak like an intellectual, but I know what I am saying"). Responding to Mariana, Habermas applied the proposal of universal dialogue he argues for in his work — that everyone has the right to argue in her/his tone and language. He began his reply by saying, "This is a brilliant and critical question." Many in the lecture hall changed their expression; their grins froze on their faces and a general atmosphere of approval suddenly began to spread throughout the room.

In October 1998, Ulrich Beck visited the University of Barcelona. At the end of his talk, I met Mariana, and she told me, *"Si Habermas no me hubiera tratado de esa forma, hoy no hubiera venido a escuchar a Beck, aunque haya leído cosas de él"* ("If Habermas had not treated me the way he did, I would not have come today to listen to Beck, although I have read things by him"). We shared this anecdote with Beck that evening, and his face revealed his satisfaction and emotion. He said, "Jürgen must know about this, I will explain it to him!"

A Wealth of Possibilities

At La Verneda-Sant Martí School, it is important that everyone involved be able to express their opinions. It is also important that the school have enough flexibility to pursue new projects and ideas. Our community is trying to prevent the school from becoming the private domain of a minority of people with technocratic and corporative goals, rather than democratic perspectives. That is why the school promotes grassroots groups and movements in which individuals are advocates of their own ideas and actions. One of last year's initiatives was therefore the creation of an organized national movement of participants in adult education.

A few years ago, the participants' associations began meeting to organize discussions about the effects of the new Spanish educational reform in the field of adult education. They met with other participants' associations in the region, and together created the Federation of Adults' Cultural and Educational Associations (FACEPA), which set out to make the voices of *all* the people involved in adult education heard. This Federation is organized into working committees, and a few people work full-time to take care of everyday issues. Funding comes from specific activities or intervention projects at the local, national, and European levels.

Many times we, the education "professionals," take over all possible fields of action in the belief that we are the only ones who know how to develop educational initiatives or, even worse, that we are the only ones who can be in charge of such initiatives because it is "our field." As a result, education policies in general and adult education policies in particular are practically colonized by education professionals, thus barring participants, who supposedly are the main characters in education, from taking part in the game. For example, in the case of Spain's Adult Education Act of March 1991, it became evident that when all the people involved can take part in the decisionmaking process, all views are collected, as all agents involved were part of an open discussion throughout the process until the Act was approved. Otherwise, the view of the "technical experts" on the issue will be only one, partial perspective. FACEPA counters such assumptions by coordinating efforts of participants who have much to say about their education and by working to make these voices heard.

One of the most important projects FACEPA initiated is the drafting of the Declaration of Adult Education Participants' Rights. The draft began in Catalonia, Spain's Autonomous Community where Barcelona is located, and its goal was to create a text that echoed the claims and needs voiced by *all* adult participants regarding their education and to establish common standards of action.[15] Many schools for adults in Catalonia sent drafts to FACEPA's headquarters, where participants drafted the organization's first proposal. Other Spanish Autonomous Communities followed the same process. Later, a nationwide symposium took place to discuss the proposal, work on the different sections, and ensure that all the important questions were addressed in the final version. The symposium ended with a Declaration of Adult Education Participants' Rights.

In the summer of 1997, representatives of Spain's participants presented the Declaration to UNESCO's Fifth International Conference on Adult Education. Since then, it has also been presented to different Spanish governmental bodies. This year, the European Union funded a project by which FACEPA will extend the Declaration to adult education associations in other European countries, following the same consensus-based method they used in Spain. FACEPA's goal is to be able to draft an International Declaration agreed upon by consensus, by all adult education participants worldwide.

Conclusion

La Verneda-Sant Martí School for Adults started as a grassroots project and continues with the same orientation, supporting the voice of new movements like FACEPA. Such forums are open to everyone's worries, interests, and dreams, regardless of age, ethnic origin, gender, religion, or social status. To be part of such projects makes me feel more alive, more supportive, and more able to create.

People's dreams *can* become reality. Writing these reflections after ten years of involvement with La Verneda School makes me realize that nothing is impossible if, through inclusiveness and tolerance, we strive for common goals. I do not believe those who say that nothing can be done to change the world. I know that things can change, because people in my community dared to dream of this school twenty years ago. It became my reality through my participation in their dream. Since then, many more have joined in our struggles and today the reality of thousands of people is the result of that dream.

A few days ago a journalist was interviewing a young Maghrebi woman who has participated in a basic literacy class at La Verneda for six months. When he asked her what she thought she had achieved, her eyes opened wide, and with a special spark in them, she replied:

> *Ahora que ya he empezado, soy feliz. Nadie va a detenerme.*
>
> [Now that I have begun, I am happy. No one will stop me.]

Notes

1. Fátima, a participant at La Verneda-Sant Martí School, said these words to me after a meeting. Her name, like those of others mentioned in this article, is fictional. Behind each name, however, there is a real human being.
2. By participants we mean the people who are involved in an educational process as students in their adulthood (adult education).
3. Adults older than twenty-five who did not go to high school can gain access to the university by passing a difficult and selective exam popularly called *"Mayores de 25"* ("Beyond 25").

4. In Spain, people associate in order to discuss and address their community needs. Residents' associations represent communities before the different governmental agencies. They are a type of association typical of areas that primarily have problems related to poor public services and the like. These associations are concerned with education, health care, urban planning, and similar issues in their district. They are constituted from the bottom up, mostly by people of working-class background.
5. Sylvia Scribner and Michael Cole, *The Psychology of Literacy* (Cambridge, MA: Harvard University Press, 1981).
6. Henry Giroux, *Border Crossings: Cultural Workers and the Politics of Education* (London: Routledge, 1992).
7. Aranguren wrote on ideas, on ethics in politics, and on women's liberation, all under Franco's regime. As a result of this, he went into exile in the United States, where he taught at the University of California in the late 1960s.
8. Jürgen Habermas, *The Theory of Communicative Action: Reason and the Rationalization of Society* (Boston: Beacon Press, 1984).
9. During 1998, many events took place in Spain in commemoration of the centennial of Federico García Lorca's birth and in memory of Paulo Freire, who had just died.
10. *Congrés de les Dones de Barcelona* [Barcelona's Women's Conference] was held January 15–17, 1999, in Barcelona, Spain. It was organized by the Local Council of Women.
11. VERN, the Coordinating Committee of La Verneda-Sant Martí neighborhood organizations, works as an umbrella under which different types of organizations can be found: residents' associations, sports clubs, children's and youth clubs, cultural associations, mountaineering groups, etc. It was created to coordinate improvement initiatives for the community.
12. Alain Touraine, *Comment Sortir du Liberalisme?* (Paris: Fayard, 1999).
13. *Graduado escolar* was a degree that certified a student for successful completion of compulsory primary education (1st–8th grade) and was required to go to high school (9th–12th grade). Today, a new educational reform is being implemented in Spain. Compulsory education is now K–10th grade, and the graduado escolar degree disappeared, and *graduado en educación secundaria obligatoria* appears. However, there are new ways of selecting which students will go to high school (now 11th–12th) and which ones will go to vocational education — that is, who will go to college and who will go straight to work (or unemployment).
14. Mariana is a member of Heura and regularly participates in the literary gatherings.
15. With the advent of democracy, Spain's historic regions were given the status of Autonomous Communities. These regional political units were granted legislative and administrative powers by the Constitution.

Caswell County Training School, 1933–1969

Relationships Between Community and School

VANESSA SIDDLE WALKER

When court-ordered school desegregation plans were announced in 1969 for rural Caswell County, North Carolina, the local newspaper recorded the reaction of one White parent:*

> We have no animosity toward the Board. They have done all they can to stall. However, we now feel that this reorganization of our public schools will destroy our high standard of education, depriving our children of the quality of education they deserve and what we all want.

What they wanted, the parent continued, "was the highest standard of education in [the] county" ("Eighteen-Member Board," 1969, p. 1).

That parent's implicit denigration of the county's one Negro school was ironic.[1] The county high school for Negro children, the Caswell County Training School (CCTS), was a three-story, immaculately kept brick structure that included a gymnasium and a 722-person-capacity auditorium with a balcony.[2] The principal, Nicholas Longworth Dillard, who held a master's degree from the University of Michigan, was esteemed locally by both Black and White educational leaders for his knowledge of national educational issues. By 1954, 64 percent of the school's teachers had graduate training beyond state recertification requirements, and during Dillard's thirty-six-year tenure from 1933 to 1969, the school offered more than fifty-three extracurricular clubs and activities to enhance student leadership and development. Moreover, the school's educational programs had been on the approved list of the Southern Association of Colleges and Schools since 1934, and were formally accredited in 1955

* This article was originally published under the name Emilie V. Siddle Walker.

Harvard Educational Review Vol. 63 No. 2 Summer 1993

after that agency began accrediting Negro schools. In contrast, the area high school for White children was smaller, older, had fewer facilities, and was not accredited.

Yet this White parent's belief that White educational systems were superior to Black, and that Negro educators could have nothing to offer White children, is an accurate reflection of many White Americans' perception, both during that era and into the present. Indeed, the history of U.S. education documents so well the inequities African American children experienced during the pre-integration era — specifically the lack of resources, the substandard facilities, and the poor response of school boards to the needs of schools (see Anderson, 1988; Brown, 1960; Clark, 1963; Clift, Anderson, & Hullfish, 1962; Kluger, 1977; Newbold, 1935) — that these images of uniform deprivation have become the dominant picture at the center of most thinking about the segregated schooling of African American children.

This perception of inequality, while not totally inaccurate, is, however, one-sided. It highlights the need and struggle for equality, but overlooks any suggestion that not all education for African American children during segregation was inferior. Sowell (1976), for example, in his description of six "excellent" historically Black high schools and two elementary schools, lists some traits common to these good schools. These traits include, but are not limited to, the commitment and educational levels of the teachers and principals, and the support, encouragement, and rigid standards that characterize the schools' atmospheres. Similarly, in Jones's *A Traditional Model of Educational Excellence* (1981), the segregated school environment is described as "one's home away from home, where students were taught, nurtured, supported, corrected, encouraged, and punished" (p. 2). These and other studies (Adair, 1984; Foster, 1990; Irvine & Irvine, 1984) suggest the presence of a positive sociocultural system in which "uniquely stylized characteristics" reflective of the student population developed independently of White control (Irvine & Irvine, 1984, p. 416), and in which African American youth were successful because of the school environment in which they were taught.

The degree to which such descriptions of segregated Black schooling might also apply to other undocumented cases is further suggested by the numerous voices in southern African American communities, which today speak forcefully of the "goodness" of their pre-integration schools. These voices do not speak of test scores and/or any measured success of school graduates in defining "goodness." Rather, they fondly recall a time when, in the words of one eighty-year-old grandmother, "colored children learnt something in school." Cecelski (1991) has captured some of this appreciation as he chronicles a little-known political struggle in which Negro parents and students boycotted their school system for a year, rather than sacrifice their schools in a locally proposed desegregation plan. Though other voices remain undocumented, the fact that they are heard so frequently in many small-town communities suggests that schooling that was valued by parents, students, and school personnel may have been more common than has been realized.

However, little is known about these unidentified good community schools. Even the paucity of literature that exists on pre-integration Black schooling focuses almost exclusively on good urban high schools, so defined because of their success with standardized test scores, the number of doctoral degrees earned by graduates, or some other easily measured outcome variables. Educators understand little of the emic perspective — that is, how and why communities considered their schools to be good. Educators also do not understand the nature of the schooling in those community-defined good schools. This lack of knowledge not only denies that there are valuable lessons to be learned from principals and teachers who successfully schooled African American children in the past (Foster, 1990), but it also ignores the fact that the communities were pleased with that education. Perhaps more significantly, this lack of knowledge also results in ahistorical approaches to school reform that deprive reformers of important contextual information that could directly impact the success or failure of select school programs. Such oversight could well decrease opportunities for African American children to succeed in today's schools.

I premise this article on the idea that segregated schools that were valued by their communities did exist, and that understanding more about the nature of those schools is important for historical accuracy and for educational reform. As I discuss below, I believe that understanding the history of education in these schools, as well as the types of parent and community participation that were present, will facilitate our ability to ask the right questions as we tackle current reform issues. This is preferable to focusing on questions that are premised on negative assumptions about African American communities.

With this in mind, I present the case of CCTS, the segregated Negro school described earlier. Situated in North Carolina's rural Caswell County, CCTS was a self- and community-defined "good" school. The belief that their school provided a good environment for learning was shared by its graduates, parents, and teachers. This belief is documented in the school's written and oral history, and remains generally consistent throughout most of its existence. In this article, I accept the community's evaluation of CCTS as a good school. I make no effort to argue that by traditional criteria, such as test scores or college attendance rates, CCTS represents the best in segregated schools in the South, or even in its region. Importantly, my description of why CCTS was perceived as a good school is not meant to validate the inequities or minimize the discrimination that existed in this and other segregated schools, where parents were overly burdened to create for themselves the educational facilities and opportunities school boards often denied them (Anderson, 1988; Bullock, 1967). Rather, I offer this case as representative of the many other southern African American schools whose communities were also pleased with their schools, but whose histories have been lost and whose value is understood now only by former teachers, principals, parents, and students.

This case, ethnographically approached, uses eighty open-ended interviews with former teachers, students, parents, and administrators, to uncover the themes of the school's goodness, and also to explore the nature of the relationships within the school environment that explain that goodness.[3] To reduce the influence of interviewee nostalgia, school documents such as yearbooks, school newspapers, handbooks, and so forth, as well as newspaper accounts, minutes of school board meetings, Southern Association reports, and other archival materials are used to corroborate emerging themes. The knowledge base derived from a triangulation of documents with interviews is used in this article to analyze one area little explored in segregated schooling — that is, the nature of the relationship between community and school. Within the context of this discussion, "community" refers to all of the African American adults who lived within the forty-square-mile county and who shared a real or imagined bond with CCTS. While some of the adults lived within the town in which the school was located, and thereby had more than the usual informal contact with the principal and teachers at the churches, stores, and other incidental meeting places, this discussion is not confined to their relationship with the school. It also incorporates the feeling of relationship and perspective of those adults who lived outside the town. Thus, the community was not defined by physical proximity. In this article, I focus specifically on the ways in which this community and CCTS supported each other. I further explore the significance of these activities, both in their historical context and in their implications vis-à-vis current advocacy for more involvement of African American parents in their children's education.

The Case in Historical Context: African Americans in Traditional Modes of Support

CCTS did not always boast the facilities or programs it enjoyed in 1969, the year it ceased to operate as a high school. Indeed, like most other segregated schools, its history was one of financial struggle, broken promises, delayed response from White school authorities, and financial burdens on its students and parents. It began as a small elementary school in a two-story house purchased by several prominent Negro citizens in 1906.[4] In the 1924–1925 school year, it expanded to a four-room "Rosenwald" structure, which teachers and community patrons had contributed $800 to complete.[5] Having previously been denied permission to expand the school beyond the seventh grade, community patrons, under the leadership of newly arrived Principal Dillard, were able in 1934 to add a high school attended by seventy-seven students, many of whom had to travel twenty miles to school on an open-air truck. The truck was donated by a parent, Ulysses Jones, who operated it at a loss for two years, before finally donating it to the state as collateral for the new truck the PTA promised to supply. Meanwhile, another parent, T. S. Lea, paid the electric bill, and others who had dug an unauthorized well were not reimbursed by the school board for their expenses.

Although by 1938 the over-crowded school housed six hundred children in fewer than ten rooms, and a "colored citizen [had] offered to donate to the county nine-and-a-half acres of land as a site for a new school" (Newbold, 1935), the community was forced to wait thirteen years before the new facility was completed.[6] This delay can be attributed in part to the school board's self-description of being "hindered in the making and completing of their plans by lack of sufficient funds" (School Board Minutes, November 3, 1941). However, the minutes also suggest that the county was initially unwilling to use local resources for the building of a Negro school. Further, even after local resources were appropriated, the building needs of the Negro children were merged with those of two other schools for White children.

In the meantime, while the school board passed four resolutions affirming its commitment to build a new school, Negro parents continued to provide resources for the twenty-two teachers and 735 pupils who were part of the school by the 1948–1949 school year. The 1949 yearbook notes that "while the building does not yet satisfy our patrons, they are proud of its equipment." This equipment included modern tablet arm chairs; instructional supplies, including audio-visual aids such as radios, a movie projector, a 35-mm projector, and a wire recorder; and other items they considered important for education, but which the school board refused to supply. The academically oriented school curriculum was complemented by an award-winning debate team, a band (the first in any Caswell County high school), a newspaper, and other student organizations (Caswell County, 1949).

In March of 1951, when the students and teachers finally moved into the twenty-seven-room facility described by the local paper as "modern in every respect," the new building reflected the tremendous community support that was part of its history. While the county contributed $80,000 toward the cost of the $325,000 state-funded project, the Negro citizens themselves added close to $8,000 in equipment, almost a tenth of the cost the county expended, to create the kind of facility they had envisioned in 1949 — "a physical plant second to none in the state" (Caswell County, 1949). Among the items added were an $1,800 stage curtain and colored footlights, $3,000 worth of venetian blinds for the windows, a $400 time clock to regulate classes automatically, and a $2,000 public-address system ("Dedication," 1951). The money for these items was contributed by students, parents, and other community supporters.

Between 1951 and 1969, parents continued to support the financial needs of CCTS, supplying such items as band uniforms and instruments, science equipment, a piano, and workbooks. While they engaged in many fundraising activities during those years, the most consistent and most remembered was the Popularity Contest. In this annual event, each high school class nominated a king and queen; members of the class, with the participation of parents and other community leaders, then raised money to support their nominees. In the heyday of this event, records indicate that the winning class alone contributed as much as $1,410.35 to support the school. In February of 1969, however, things began to change: Principal Dillard died unexpectedly in the midst of planning desegregation, and that fall the school was reorganized as a fully integrated junior high. After these two events, Negro parents ceased all such financial assistance to the school.

Considering a rural community where, in 1953, 58 percent of the parents were farmers, 23 percent homemakers, 6 percent laborers, and 8 percent service and domestic workers, there is a temptation to view the CCTS community's financial contributions to the school as exceptional. Their self-reliance, sacrifice, and sense of community responsibility not only created ongoing support for the school, but also provided their children with a model for the role interested parents should play. Their commitment insured that continuous resources would be provided for the education of Black children, despite the lack of adequate support from the all-White school board. Yet, the sacrifices, self-help, and support of these CCTS patrons were typical of Negroes in many communities in the South during this era. This story of self-help for segregated schools has been most notably described and analyzed by Anderson (1988), who emphasizes the fact that, although such help was helpful in improving school conditions, it also was oppressive in that it imposed a "double taxation" on Negro citizens. According to Anderson, "rural Blacks in particular were victims of [this] taxation without representation" (p. 156). They were often forced to "take from their meager annual incomes and contribute money to the construction and maintenance of public schools for the Black child because southern state and local governments refused to accept responsibility for Black public education" (p. 176). In other words, Black parents paid taxes for services they did not receive. The history of CCTS lends additional evidence to Anderson's thesis.

What has been less often discussed, however, are the other avenues of parental support that existed in segregated school environments. Although CCTS grew significantly between 1933 and 1969, the nature of the relationship between school and community remained consistent. In addition to providing financial support, parents at CCTS 1) maintained a physical presence in the school, primarily through the Parent Teachers Association (PTA) and other events to which they were invited; 2) played an "advocacy" role for the school in soliciting funds from the school board; and 3) provided invisible home-based support for the principal and teachers.

Parents in the School: Other Avenues of Community Support

In the CCTS environment, the PTA functioned as an umbrella organization that took the lead in providing financial contributions to the school, and also provided other opportunities for parental involvement in school activities. Perhaps the most obvious facet of this involvement was parents' attendance at PTA meetings. While exact attendance figures are not available, former teacher Helen Beasley remembers:

> I don't know how many folks we *didn't* have at PTA! Good gracious. If the auditorium wasn't filled up, it was maybe like three-fourths. That great big auditorium would be three-fourths full with the mamas and daddies and the brothers and the sisters and the grandmamas and the aunts, and the uncles and whoever.

Though not all informants are as enthusiastic in their memories of the number of people attending and often focus instead on whether there should have been even more, they do report that the auditorium was frequently filled to capacity as Beasley relates. In absolute numbers, PTA attendance was less in earlier years, when parents were more likely to sit around a pot-bellied stove rather than gather in a formal setting; nevertheless, participation was reportedly high, especially given the distance parents had to travel and the lack of automobiles. When parents did not attend, it was usually because of transportation problems or conflicting work schedules. Lack of interest in the school or a feeling of alienation were seldom the reasons given for their absence.

Several activities were consistently part of the business portion of the PTA meeting. First, parents received reports about the school's financial and educational status. Since one of the PTA's primary missions was to help supply the school's needs, the financial report often involved the president or the principal outlining the most pressing needs. Based on these reports, parents organized collaborative plans of action with teachers and the principal, and actively engaged in completing the projects. These activities typically included overseeing a teacher's homeroom activities and reporting on that class's participation, or joining in a parent-teacher basketball game. Parents who were not active in planning often provided support by attending an event, and supplying or buying items on sale there.

The principal also regularly used a portion of the meeting to report to the parents about education, what was going on in the school such as problems drivers were having on buses, or ways in which parents could help their children succeed academically. He also reviewed his expectations for the children, the school policies, and the events planned for the year. Parents who recall Dillard's PTA reports remember how interested he was in the children. Says one parent: "[Having every child succeed] — that was his main priority."

Dillard also shared with parents his experiences at any national or regional meetings he had attended. His teachers, who were required to join their professional organization and urged to attend non-local meetings, were also expected to report to parents during this segment of PTA meetings. Today CCTS parents describe little about the educational trends that were discussed during those times, but they still remember the jokes Dillard was famous for collecting and sharing with them.

In addition to the PTA business reports and discussions, parents could also expect entertainment and refreshments. This entertainment came from various high school groups or elementary classes, who were assigned a time in the school year to make a presentation to the PTA. Teachers often repeated for the PTA the assembly programs they were periodically scheduled to have in Chapel.[7] Since few parents saw these programs during Chapel, they usually played to a new audience. The refreshments that were served afterward to cast, teachers, and parents were supplied by the PTA.

When the formal portion of the PTA meetings ended, the informal talk between teachers and parents began. According to parent Dorothy Graves, these informal talks, during which the parents could find out how their children were doing in school, were one of the primary reasons they went to PTA. She explains:

> You didn't go to the schools during the day or after school to talk about your children. You didn't go in unless there was a problem and the principal called you in. The time during the school day was allotted for the teaching of the student. Parents just didn't go in to school and disturb a teacher. [The teachers would say], tell your parents to come to PTA.

These informal conversations between teachers and parents sometimes took place in the classrooms, at other times in different areas of the auditorium. Most conversations began with the parent's single question: "How is my child doing?" If the teacher responded "fine," little else would be said, other than the parent perhaps saying, "Now you let me know if there's a problem." Or if there was a problem, the teacher might consult her rollbook and say, "Jeff is doing fine in English; however, he needs to work on his math." Such informal conversations continued until each parent had the opportunity to speak to every teacher he or she wished to see. Since teachers were required to attend PTA meetings, said one parent, "there was never any worry that [your child's teacher] wouldn't be there."

Besides attending the regular monthly meetings, some PTA members implemented planned tasks, such as preparing appreciation dinners for the teachers or continuing their ongoing fundraising activities. They referred to this as "working along with the teachers," and valued the time as an opportunity to get to know each other. Parents also attended major school functions, filling the auditorium for the concerts held by the high school choir and band every Christmas and spring, and the annual "operettas" held by the primary and upper elementary schools. A few parents were also involved in some classroom functions, such as providing food and setting up for a class Christmas or end-of-year party, supervising the Maypole dances in preparation for field day, or, in the case of at least one teacher, assisting in classroom instruction by playing educational games with the children. Reports indicate that parents on all socioeconomic levels were likely to participate in the events, if they were asked.

What is central to the nature of this parental presence at CCTS is the key phrase, "if asked." For example, Nellie Williamson, the teacher who had parents play educational games with the children, emphasizes that "not many did this"; those who did, she says, did so "because she had a conversation with them individually." Thus, parents who helped in the classroom or assisted with other events were responding to teachers' notes or oral invitations. PTA meetings and student performances were other events to which parents had invitations. Says Janie Richmond, a former student and later an elementary school teacher, "the parents supported the school" and came whenever you asked them, but they didn't schedule parent-teacher conferences, or volunteer to assist with tutoring, or concern themselves with other areas of classroom instruction. Long-time English teacher Chattie Boston concurs that "parents left curricula concerns to the teachers." The data suggest both are correct, as parents never describe themselves as having initiated visits to the school to observe or to discuss any curricular concerns. Some parents, however, did assume a political role that might be termed "working for the school." This role of advocate was historically associated with the PTA leaders. These advocates positioned themselves between the school's needs and the oversight of the school board, and on numerous occasions lobbied for additional funding for the school. No records indicate that the White school board was hostile to the Negro patrons who sought their assistance; they were generally polite, even as they postponed and denied repeated requests for funding.[8]

The leadership role these parent advocates took in going before the board to lobby for the school is termed "working" for the school because the teachers and principal seldom appeared before the board. In the political climate of the era, those employed by the school system could expect to lose their jobs if they involved themselves in questions of equity. As one parent advocate recalls, "Dillard himself couldn't afford to come out. He was a very smart leader who knew how far they would let him go." A second parent recalls, "Mr. Dillard provided prompting on preparation, who to speak to. He would give you an idea. Usually [men] would go. They would go as a group and usually have one spokesman." This behind-the-scenes prompting most often occurred with farmers who owned their own land, preachers, or private business owners. While in the earlier years these were primarily men, documents and interviews from later periods indicate that women also assumed an advocacy role. What all advocates generally had in common was that they relied on other Negroes for their income, and thus did not need to fear repercussions from the White school board.

The role of parent advocates also extended beyond the county level. Records indicate that these citizens, like Dillard, made numerous trips to the state capital to seek assistance when their requests were denied on the local level. This was particularly true of their efforts in the early years of CCTS to see that a high school be established, and later, that a new one be built. In response to these visits, and as a part of his push to get the county to build a new school, the Director of the Division of Negro Education wrote the Caswell County school board requesting that an "adequate brick building be supplied" for the Negroes. He freely admitted that his urging was the result of having been "approached by a group of very intelligent colored citizens from [Caswell] County."[9]

The importance of this advocacy role over the years was recognized and appreciated not only by other parents, but also by the students. Consider their commendation of three parents in the opening pages of the 1960 yearbook:

> The annual certainly would be incomplete if the seniors failed to salute the successful efforts of these three patrons in obtaining a modern physical education building for the school. Over a three year period they continuously appeared before the Board of Education in behalf of a new physical education building. Time and time again they made appeals and, needless to say, at times they were disappointed, but not enough to ever cease their efforts. Soon, thanks to them, this facility will be available. The students and patrons of C.C.T.S. shall ever remember with gratitude their untiring efforts. Again we salute you, Mrs. Bigelow, Mrs. Saylor, and Mrs. Little. Words will never express our appreciation.

The passage is accompanied by a portrait of the three women. While other CCTS yearbooks do not contain such elaborate expressions of appreciation, special thank you's to parents for their assistance frequently appeared in dedications and in class histories.

Perhaps the most consistent way parents supported the school — even those who never participated in PTA or related activities or assumed the role of advocate — was accomplished without the parents ever leaving home. They instilled in their children a respect for teachers, which carried with it an expectation of obedience. Says parent Nannie Evans, "I would always tell my child, 'when you go to school, remember you are supposed to obey your teachers just like you obey me at home.'"

These attitudes about obedience led students to believe that if they were punished at school for an offense, they could expect additional punishment at home. In the words of one student: "I knew not to get sent home for anything. If I did, I knew my daddy was going to whoop me good — not spank — but whoop me. I knew not to try to get into trouble." And if a child did get into trouble at school, the parent's likely response to the teacher was, "Well, if he doesn't do well, you just let me know again."

This "home training," as southern African Americans are likely to call their parents' expectations of them, reinforced school policies and provided a solid mechanism of invisible support. While the disciplinary skills of the CCTS principal and teachers will not be discussed in this article, I will point out that demands on their disciplinary skills were lessened by this seldom-articulated, yet forceful parental support. Thus, parent and school were united in their expectations of the students. As one student described the relationship: "My mommy and daddy are pushing me and my teachers are pushing me . . . oh well, I got to do good."

School Supports Community

CCTS parents provided financial and physical support, advocacy, and home-front support. From the vantage point of current advocates of parental involvement (see, for example, Henderson 1987, 1988; Rich, 1987), the parents' degree of activity might not be considered unusual. However, given the current lack of involvement of many African American parents in schools (Henderson, 1987), the degree of their support is exceptional. To what might their level of involvement be attributed?

Several explanations are possible. As Lightfoot (1978, 1981) has noted, African Americans have traditionally believed in the importance of education, and have made sacrifices to be certain that their children had opportunities to achieve in school. That parents valued education and therefore contributed to the support of CCTS is corroborated by records from other elementary schools scattered throughout Caswell County, where parents were also active in PTA and other school events. Thus, the parental response at CCTS might well have been the public manifestation of the parents' private beliefs about the importance of education. Another equally compelling reason for the relationship between CCTS and parents in later years might relate to existing community ties. As many parents point out, they had known Principal Dillard themselves as children, when they attended school under his leadership; they had also gone to school with some of the teachers. Therefore, school personnel were not strangers, but rather people with whom they already had a relationship.

Though parents' belief in education and the existence of community ties are both important factors in understanding the parents' relationship to the school, they offer an insufficient explanation for the levels of support provided by parents. Teachers who had not grown up in the county, for example, were equally accepted, supported, and welcomed by parents, as was Dillard, even in his early years. According to Inez Blackwell, a parent and former student, this was because new teachers quickly made themselves known to the community. "They were never stuck up," she says. "Within months," Blackwell notes, "it seemed like they had been here all the time." Thus, teachers who had previous ties with the community had little advantage over those who came into the county. Moreover, though African American parents today still believe in the power of education, their belief does not evoke the responses described at CCTS. Perhaps a more compelling explanation for the consistency of support from parents at CCTS lies in the manner in which the school reached out to and supported the parents.

For example, in his weekly Chapel talks with the students, Principal Dillard was heard to say on more than one occasion: "I'm not going to let you come up here and wear your mama and daddy's clothes out and they're out there working hard for you and you're up here doing nothing." The band director, Leonard Tillman, recalls the admonishments students received in the classroom:

> I used to tell my kids — Miss Ann doesn't need anyone to cook for them anymore. ["Miss Ann" was a term used by Negroes to describe White women who had servants.] They got frozen foods. All they got to do is throw them in the oven. Don't you think you need to stay here and get this education?

In their talks with students, the principal and teachers assumed the posture of protectors of the parents' sacrifices, and their frequent reminders of the need to get an education echoed parents' aspirations for their children.

The school also actively assisted parents. For students who wanted to go on to college, this assistance included helping them fill out forms, providing financial aid, traveling with students to campuses, and in some cases giving advice on what would be expected in college. As Aleane Rush, a former student and later president of the state teachers' association, remembers:

> [Mr. Dillard] would try to help students. . . . He would refer them personally to college contacts, friends; he was very helpful in trying to see that they would leave Caswell County with the appropriate kind of clothing. Remember I said he knew his students. So, he would not feel intimidated, nor would the student if he said, "Now Vanessa, you can not go to Shaw with those kind of shoes on. . . . You will be in college and you are coming from CCTS, remember that. And you've got to represent yourself, your family, and your community." And when he spoke of community, he was speaking of Caswell County. And parents of those students were very, very appreciative.

In some cases, as in that of teacher and former student Deborah Fuller, the principal actually accompanied the student and parents on their first trip to a campus, functioning as mediator between the family's aspirations and the unknown expectations of college admissions. Teachers also engaged in these sorts of supportive activities, providing financial assistance through their teachers' clubs and, more frequently, offering the encouragement a student needed to go to college. Irvine and Irvine (1984) have characterized this behavior most succinctly:

> Black schools served as the instrument through which professional educators discharged their responsibility to their community. Black educators labored to help students realize their achievement goals. In this role both principals and teachers were mere but profound extensions of the interests of the Black community. (p. 417)

In effect, the authors note, parents and school had a "collective stake in the educational process of the youth in the community" (p. 419).

But the school's support was not only available for college-bound students. The principal and teachers also assumed responsibility for students who were having difficulty in school by working with the child and contacting parents about any problems. One parent remembers Principal Dillard telling her about her son's school behavior: "Well, he just loves to sometimes stand out in the hall and have a chance to go uptown." ("Uptown" is a local slang term used to refer to the town's small business district, which was located approximately one mile from the school.) Of Dillard's disciplinary approach and contact with her, this parent says, "I felt good because I felt like he was there with him and he was paying attention [to my child]." After describing the events of mischievousness that accompanied her son through his school years, she concludes, "But anyway, he finally finished . . . and I felt like Mr. Dillard had a great hand in that."

The school's protectiveness toward the children — going the extra mile to see that students succeeded — instilled in parents an adamant conviction that the teachers and principal really "cared about those children." In the words of Rachel Long, a farming parent who sent nine children through high school and college, "I think all those teachers were really close to those students. I know they were to my children." Her conviction echoes the sentiments of many. A former student, the Reverend Cephaus Lea, remembers Principal Dillard:

> He was never too busy to talk with you about your problems. Not only was he interested in you in school, he was interested when you left school. He knew all the children by name. He wasn't like some other people I've known. He loved people and he was concerned about you. And that's the kind of principal Mr. Dillard was.

While the influence of the school's ethic of caring is a story that I cannot explore fully in this discussion, I must note that parents' belief that the school cared about the success of their children might help explain the "respect" and "trust" that parents had toward CCTS and their support of it. In essence, in supporting the institution, the parents were directly supporting those responsible for the success of their children.

Principal Dillard's particular style of interacting with parents is another way that parents were drawn to CCTS. In effect, Dillard created a sense of "us" that helped to forge the collaboration between school and community. Though he was clearly the visionary, "he did not boast [about] what he did," says one parent. "He used to always say, 'we're working together. See what we can do if we work together.' But he never did say what *he* did." This style of interaction was probably carefully chosen. In the traditional African American community, the "educated" are often viewed with suspicion if they are perceived as "above" the other members of the community; thus Dillard's approach represented an important way of reaching out, and conveyed to community members his respect for their contributions.

Perhaps the most striking way in which the school reached out was in its willingness to meet the parents on their own turf. Dillard, for example, was an avid member of community organizations and would often walk to town after school was out and take the time to talk with farmers gathered on the corner. He sang in the local choir, attended both the Methodist and Baptist churches, and frequently visited the rural churches and the homes of parents who lived out in the country. Says one parent:

> He visited my home a lot of times. He would get around. Then another thing he would do — if his children's [relatives] or somebody passed, he would try to make it to the churches to the funerals. He had a closeness to people.

Valuing community members apparently was an important part of Dillard's philosophy. Even "from the beginning, he worked with the community," reports teacher and former student Janie Richmond, whose mother worked actively in the creation of the first PTA. "Whatever project they put on, he was very diligent in working with them — picnics, fishing trips, etc. His being present helped to draw other people."

It is important to note that Dillard also used his visits in the community as opportunities to communicate. Often when invited to speak in area churches, he would speak about his belief in the value of education. Thus, parents were apprised of the goals of the school and the needs of the children in their own communities, churches, and homes. These visits and talks were supplemented by frequent notes that children brought home with information about school events or classroom needs.

Dillard expected no less community involvement from his teachers. "I would hope you would be broad enough to attend some of the area churches," he was known to tell new faculty members. In essence, he expected that if they worked in the community, they should make themselves known and become part of it. He wanted teachers who were accessible to the average parent. He also expected teachers to visit the students' parents in their homes, whether or not a disciplinary problem had arisen. "If you could see the circumstances out of which the children have come," many teachers remember him saying, "you would understand better how to teach them."

And the teachers did go — both to the churches and the homes. Fifth-grade teacher Betty Royal remembers telling parents who opened the door to her knock, "I just happened to have been in the area and I thought I would just stop by and say hello." The parents generally responded positively to these unannounced visits, having been told to expect them at PTA meetings.

Reaching out to support parents occurred in other ways, too. The school offered adults classes in agriculture, typing, and sewing, and provided guidance and counseling for adults. The school also ranked itself highly on "providing community use of the school and facilities" (CCTS Faculty, 1950). From the parents' perspective, however, the school's interest in their children's development and the teachers' community visits are the ways of reaching out that are most remembered and most valued.

Significance of School and Community Interactions in the Historical Context

Long-time residents of this Caswell County community who participated in the CCTS culture remember the interaction between school and community as a collaborative relationship, a kind of mutual ownership in which the community and school looked out for each others' needs — the parents depended on the school's expertise, guidance, and academic vision, and the school depended on the parents' financial contributions, advocacy, and home-front support. They were united in a common mission to provide a quality education for their children.

This relationship provides several important ideas to consider. While school and community members moved easily in and out of each other's domain, the participants were clear about the boundaries of their relationships. The parents' role was to attend school events, to reinforce discipline at home, and to get their children to school. They also made economic sacrifices to allow their able-bodied offspring to go to school rather than keeping them home to help "take in the crop." When the students went home in the afternoon, parents made sure the children had time to do their lessons. As one student remembers, "[Our] parents didn't have any education, but after you finished your work and chores, they knew to tell you to sit down and get your lesson." The teachers' and principal's reciprocal role was to exercise authority in the school environment and address issues of curriculum and instruction.

The strength of the respect for these boundaries was reinforced by its presence across economic and class lines. For example, even teachers who had children in the classrooms of other teachers did not discuss curriculum or help their children with homework. In fact, the attitude that the teacher was completely in charge of the child once in the classroom was reflected in private conversations with their coworkers. Said one teacher, "I've got my classroom to see to. If anything happens, you do the punishing. I don't have anything to do with it." Like other parents, these teachers did support the punishment given by their child's teacher by reinforcing discipline at home. However, they did not interfere with the teacher or class activities within the school.

Unlike current situations in which parents and schools disagree about how they should support one another (Henderson, 1987), in the CCTS environment, participants shared common expectations. The distinct roles minimized conflict between school and community, as all interaction was defined by mutually accepted boundaries of authority.

Also significant are the opportunities for, and the positive nature of, the communication that was possible in the CCTS environment — unlike interaction today, in which talk between teachers and parents is almost uniformly negative, and parents indicate that they only hear from the school when there is a problem (Lightfoot, 1978; Swap, 1987). The school's fund-raising activities, for example, created opportunities for parents, the principal, and teachers to discuss how to achieve their common goals. Moreover, during some fund-raising activities, opportunities existed for role-reversal between administration and members of the school community. For example, if parents were assigned to oversee participation in a particular classroom, it meant that the teacher looked to the parents for assistance. This created a sense of teamwork and reinforced the idea that parents and teachers could both be authorities — even if they exercised power in different domains. Thus, the creation of teamwork between teacher and parent was a direct outcome of the fund-raising activity.

Also important to the school-community relationship were the informal interactions maintained outside of school. When teachers visited the churches, parents were likely to invite them to other services, such as a revival or church homecoming, and teachers in turn used these opportunities to invite parents to particular activities at the school. Students' work was not necessarily discussed in these incidental interactions.

The opportunity to engage in dialogue both in the school environment and in the community was important to the community-school relationship, but it would not have succeeded had not the principal and teachers known how to talk to the parents. Parent Marie Richmond confirms this:

> I heard [Mr. Dillard] say it so many times. He would say, "When you are in a situation, you don't go in there using a lot of big words and you know the people can't understand you.". . . He wasn't one of these people that kept so high up that he couldn't get in where a person was and understand him. I think that's why people loved him so. You could relate to him. But when you go into a place . . . and are so high and mighty, parents would stay away from you, because they feel like you think you are better than they are because maybe they didn't get any schooling. But if you know how to mix, and they feel comfortable with you, they will work with you.

The ability to adapt his language to the demands of a situation is a talent for which Dillard is consistently credited; he told his son he learned it in his job as an insurance salesman after graduating from college. Of the teachers, parents also said, "They knew how to talk to you, and that made a big difference."

The "difference" was that, when parents had the opportunity to talk with teachers and the principal, both in and out of school, they were positive exchanges in which teachers and principal communicated with language parents could appreciate and respect. That is, they used the language of the parent, adopting informal forms of language and styles of communication that created an atmosphere in which parents did not feel intimidated to speak.

This atmosphere of respect also created a positive environment for handling more sensitive problems. Teachers or the principal could begin a difficult discussion with positive comments about a child, because they knew the children so well, understood their family circumstances, and likely had some interaction with someone in the family. Moreover, because of the opportunities for positive informal talk and the school's proactive role in its relationship with parents, the parents did not view the teacher or principal as always being the bearer of bad news about their child, which diminished the potential for hostility or animosity.

The nature of the community-school relationship, strengthened by the principal's personal characteristics, eased tensions when differences did occur. English teacher Chattie Boston recalls that, if a parent came in upset over a perceived injustice done to his or her child, "Mr. Dillard didn't get excited. If the parent was excited, Mr. Dillard listened and let them talk. He let them get it off their chest." Then, she says, "he would explain the situation and when [the parent] left, everybody would be buddy-buddy."

This personal style of settling conflicts was impossible when the disagreement involved larger concerns, such as choosing a location for the new school. Such differences were resolved through an open meeting where both sides had opportunities to air their concerns, and the final decision was made by voting. But even when the community-school relationship was not completely tranquil, the dissonance did not destroy their working relationship or the individual respect between parents, the teachers, and the principal.

Segregation in Retrospect: Issues and Challenges for Today

The nature of the relationship I have described between CCTS and its community suggests some valuable lessons for education today. One suggestion is a possible change in the definition of parental involvement. Although parental involvement has been defined by researchers in a number of ways (Henderson, 1987, 1988; Rich, 1987; Swap, 1987), for purposes of this discussion, consider a definition offered by Hoover-Dempsey, Bassler, and Brissie (1987), who define parent involvement in their child's school as including: 1) parent-teacher conferences; 2) parent involvement in classroom volunteer work; 3) parent involvement in tutoring at home, such as assisting with homework; and 4) parent involvement in carrying out home-instruction programs designed or suggested by teachers to supplement regular classroom instruction (p. 423). In each of these cases, parents initiate and/or are involved in complementing the curriculum and instruction provided by the teacher.

Current definitions of parent involvement, however, do not explain the kind of support the CCTS parents demonstrated. They did not have formal parent-teacher conferences as they are now defined; they did not volunteer unless they were specifically asked; and they did not tutor at home or carry out home-instruction programs.

By current definitions, these parents could be deemed failures. One wonders, then, if African American parents and White teachers and school leaders are operating out of different frameworks for parental involvement. Perhaps schools apply dominant cultural definitions of good parental involvement, such as those described by Hoover-Dempsey, Bassler, and Brissie (1987), while African American parents lean towards more traditional perceptions and modes of interaction, such as those practiced at CCTS.

To explore this possibility, consider the comment of Dorothy Graves, a Black parent who observed the CCTS parents when they first attended PTA meetings after court-ordered integration began in Caswell County in the fall of 1969:

> You just didn't see any teachers hardly. What few teachers came said, "you don't walk up to teachers and ask how your child is doing; you have a conference."

> They said we were not supposed to ask about any [concerns] about our children [in the presence of] anyone else. We were used to when we were there at the PTA meeting, we could just talk.

This parent further explains that PTA meetings after integration seemed to focus more on bringing in resource people than dealing with the problems of the students. She notes that before integration, the students were the primary focus for PTA meetings — either discussing their needs and jointly devising plans of action, and/or watching their performances before the PTA. After integration, she remembers that less attention was paid to students and that there was more of a focus on procedures. She sums up the differences by adding, "I guess this was their method. [It seems] when we integrated we went into using their pattern and not our pattern."

This difference in handling the PTA meetings suggests that after integration a cultural mismatch occurred between school personnel and parents on at least two levels. First, for parents accustomed to using the PTA to talk informally with teachers, the absence of many teachers and the directives by those present to schedule a conference represented a system for interacting with teachers that was not familiar to Black parents. While the data are not available to document the response of Black parents to this new system, it is worth noting that Dorothy Graves, the parent quoted above, recalls scheduling only one conference after integration, as compared to monthly meetings with teachers before integration.

In addition to creating new expectations of the appropriate way to relate to teachers, the focus of the PTA in the integrated system also was perceived by Black parents to change. At the segregated PTA meetings, parents expected to discuss the needs of the school and to see their children perform — both activities that contributed to the importance of attending PTA meetings. In the integrated system, they describe a system where "your part was already outlined and you just went through the procedure." PTA was thus transformed from a parent-school gathering where meaningful input was expected, to meetings that became the "contrived occasions" that Lightfoot (1978) describes.

The data are not available to argue that the failure of African American parents today to volunteer, to schedule parent/teacher conferences, and so forth is the result of historical differences in definitions of involvement. However, the forms of support demonstrated at CCTS suggest that it is at least possible that historical models of parental involvement may differ from current definitions, and that this may be one area to consider in efforts to understand African American parents' failure to conform to expectations about school involvement. The failure to consider the possible influence of conflicting expectations about roles may result in parents, especially African American parents, being labeled deficient and uncaring.

Consider further the current literature on parental involvement, which emphasizes the parents' desire to be involved in school decisionmaking. According to Henderson (1987), "Educators tend to relegate parents to insubstantial bake sale roles, leaving parents feeling frustrated, belittled, and left out" (p. 2). Yet the CCTS parents did not express a desire to have input in the school's curriculum decisionmaking. The same is true in Sowell's (1976) descriptions of other historically Black schools:

> The interest of the teachers in the students was reciprocated by the interest of the parents in supporting the teachers and the school. . . . Parental involvement was of this supportive nature rather than an actual involvement in school decision making. (p. 36)

Sowell's finding is consistent with the type of support CCTS parents offered, and their parallel lack of discussion of curricular matters. This is not to say that parents should not now be involved in such decisionmaking. However, making decisions on curricular matters may not be a traditional parental role valued within the African American community, where community and school shared similar values and where parents trusted the teachers and principal to create the best learning environments for their children.

Moreover, while the current literature on parental involvement denigrates the bake sale and the ritualistic PTAs (Henderson, 1987, 1988), CCTS parents found comfortable avenues of support through such activities. Perhaps the value of these activities, especially their ability to create ownership and pride in the school, should be explored before they are unilaterally dismissed as trivial functions. Swap (1987) has advocated having refreshments at PTA meetings and using children in the program as examples of incentives that schools might use to help initiate parental involvement in school functions. Both of these activities made useful contributions to the CCTS PTA meetings, so perhaps the CCTS examples suggest extending the parent-school relationship beyond some current practices.

Two other ideas should also be briefly considered. The data suggest that the community-school relationship is a two-way process, that involvement should not be defined simply as how to bring the parents into the school, but also how the school can be "in" the community. It was CCTS's outreach to the community that prompted the parents to "reach in" to the school. While some studies have considered the positive results of home visits (Olmstead, 1983, cited in Tangri & Moles, 1987), too little has been done to create schools with positive attitudes toward the community, both in terms of the schools' general outreach and the attitude of individual teachers. School reform leaders might do well to remember the CCTS example, and to consider ways that teachers and principal can become advocates for, rather than adversaries in, their students' communities.

Schools might also consider the benefits of implementing activities that communicate to parents a sense of caring about their children. The response of CCTS parents to their school should not be considered atypical; people generally respond well to those they believe are concerned about their loved ones. When people, or communities, perceive that this caring is no longer present, they respond with mistrust. Thus, it should not be surprising that many African American parents are now distrustful of schools in which their offspring are the ones most often punished, most frequently on the lower tracks (Braddock, 1995), most likely to have the least successful teachers (Darling-Hammond, 1995), and most likely to feel alienated and drop out of school. This care ethic would seem to be as crucial to conversations about how to induce parental involvement as is advocacy for parental voice on curricular matters.

Can all ideas applied at CCTS transfer simply and easily to today's schools? Indeed they cannot. CCTS functioned in a uniquely closed society in which the school for the Black community was one of the two major social, cultural, and educational centers, the church being the other. Together these centers served to counteract the effects of racism in a segregated society. Since that era, the nature of problems confronting children has changed, as has the structure of families. The 1990 U.S. Census Bureau, for example, indicates that Black children are less likely to live with two parents today than they were in 1967, and that families are now more likely to be polarized between the well-educated and the poor. Moreover, crack, AIDS, and guns are the serious issues confronting school personnel, as compared with alcohol, smoking, and truancy during the era of CCTS.

What we can gain from the case of CCTS is a deeper understanding of what African Americans valued in their schools during legal segregation, an understanding of the community-school relationships that allowed for the schools' successful operation, and a series of ideas about school-community interaction that might spur thinking on how to achieve similar ends in new contexts. Moreover, the CCTS case provides an important framework within which to consider current problems of school reform. For example, understanding the various possibilities for parental involvement may lead to more appropriate questions when considering how to link schools and communities. A question asked frequently about African American parents in reform meetings I have attended is, "How can we get them to become involved with the school?" a question that suggests that parents have never been involved and are generally uninterested. Yet, as the evidence demonstrates, these poor, rural parents were very much involved, when one applies their definition of involvement. They only ceased to be so when the schools integrated. Thus, perhaps a more appropriate question is, "Why did they stop supporting schools and what can be done to eliminate the barriers so they will come back?" These different questions suggest a variety of different answers and strategies. Only by asking the right questions, however, are we likely to find answers that will result in meaningful and lasting solutions.

The CCTS case also suggests an agenda for new research questions: for example, how do African American parents currently view the schools? Are there still "invisible" ways they support the school that are generally unknown and unappreciated? Are African American parents and schools operating from the same expectations about appropriate community-school interactions? To what extent has the advocacy role ceased, or is it operative in other ways? For example, at the school level, do African American parents have a mode of advocacy that creates dissonance, rather than collaboration, between parents and administrators? Is it possible that the level at which they protest treatment of their children has moved from the school board to the teachers and principal in the school itself?

Serious consideration of these and other questions about the relationship between African American parents and their children's schools is important for enlightened educational policy and agendas. Seeking answers to these questions is also important in restoring voice to African American educators and parents, whose knowledge has been devalued and whose opinions have been silenced since the onset of integration (Foster, 1990; Irvine & Irvine, 1984). Most importantly, documenting the nature of community-school relationships in the segregated school is important because it begins to correct the commonly held misperception that those schools were without any merit, and that educators have nothing to learn from them. The correction of this misperception is long overdue.

Notes

1. The terms "Negro," "colored," "Black," and "African American" are used interchangeably in this article. In general, the term used reflects the appropriate label given to those of African descent during the particular era being discussed.
2. During the last decade of segregation, the name of the school was changed to Caswell County High School, even though it continued to maintain an elementary department for the local township until 1967. In the early years, it was referred to as the Yanceyville School and, after integration, the name was changed to Dillard Junior High School. For purposes of consistency, this article consistently refers to the facility as Caswell County Training School, the name by which it was known for the longest period of time.
3. "Open-ended interviews" is a term used to describe a questioning format that allows the researcher to ask for facts about the matter under discussion, as well as to ask the interviewee's opinion about the facts. This method was used in conjunction with Spradley's (1979) suggestions for the "ethnographic interview," which describes specific procedures to tap the knowledge base of a participant in a culture scene. Interviews lasted usually from 60 to 90 minutes; participants represented varying regions of the community and varying degrees of involvement in the school.
4. Under a fund set up by Julius Rosenwald in 1917, Negro patrons received matching funds for any monetary or other contributions they could make towards the building of schools for Negro children. Records indicate that Caswell County school patrons participated in this program, and that their school, like the 5,000 others built in the South before 1948, was known as a "Rosenwald" school. This name, of course, detracts attention from the numerous contributions made by Negro parents and educators. This emphasis on the program rather than the parents is more fully discussed by Anderson (1988).
5. Although I refer here to the first known building, the education of Negro children in the area precedes the purchase of a school building in Yanceyville in 1906. The North Carolina Session of 1897, for example, notes the incorporation of the "Yanceyville Col-

ored Graded School" for the education of the colored children. Moreover, the oral history records the existence of church schools throughout the area in the late 1800s.

6. This information is based upon a letter recorded in the school board minutes from N. C. Newbold, director of the Negro Division of Education, to Holland McSwain, Superintendent of Caswell County Schools. The letter itself is dated August 29, 1938; the letter is recorded in the school board minutes under the meeting for September 5, 1938.
7. Chapel was a weekly gathering of the principal, teachers, and students, where student talent was showcased and where the principal used the time to talk to the students about pressing issues, such as life, discipline, or any other topic he felt compelled to address. While religious services were not the focus of the gathering, talk often emphasized moral values that were consistent with the values held by the community.
8. The board's receptivity did, as may be expected, increase in the 1950s and 1960s. This may be attributed in part to the aftermath of the *Brown* decision, when the county sought to be certain that all its Negro schools were "equal." However, the parents also credit the efforts of a new superintendent, Thomas Whitley, who they characterized as a "fair" man who was willing to go "as far as he could go" to promote equity.
9. In 1921, the Negro Division of Education was established by legislative act in the state of North Carolina. Although headed by a White agent, the director, N. C. Newbold, has been credited with helping to "set in motion the development and standardization of secondary schools" in North Carolina (Brown, 1960, p. 49). The school board minutes in Caswell County indicate that through both letters and meetings with the board, Newbold was instrumental in pressuring the county to address the needs of the Negro community.

References

Adair, A. A. (1984). *Desegregation: The illusion of black progress.* Lanham, MD: University Press of America.

Anderson, J. D. (1988). *The education of blacks in the south.* Chapel Hill: University of North Carolina Press.

Brown, H. V. (1960). *A history of the education of Negroes in North Carolina.* Raleigh, NC: Irving Swain Press.

Braddock, J. H. (1995). Tracking, literacy, and minority status. In V. Gadsden & D. Wagner (Eds.), *Literacy among African-American youth: Issues in learning, teaching, and schooling.* Norwood, NJ: Ablex.

Bullock, H. A. (1967). *A history of Negro education in the south.* Cambridge, MA: Harvard University Press.

Caswell County Training School PTA: 1924–1948. (1949). In *Caswell County Training School Yearbook, 1949.*

CCTS Faculty. (1950). *Evaluative criteria* (Washington Cooperative Study of Secondary School Standards).

Cecelski, D. (1991). *The Hyde County School boycott: School desegregation and the fate of black schools in rural south, 1954–1969.* Unpublished doctoral dissertation, Harvard University, Cambridge, MA.

Clark, K. B. (1963). *Prejudice and your child.* Boston: Beacon Press.

Clift, V., Anderson, A., & Hullfish, H. (1962). *Negro education in America.* New York: Harper.

Darling-Hammond, L. (1995). Teacher quality and equality: Implications for literacy among black youth. In V. Gadsden & D. Wagner (Eds.), *Literacy among African-American youth: Issues in learning, teaching, and schooling.* Norwood, NJ: Ablex.

Dedication of new Caswell County school will take place tomorrow. (1951, March). *Caswell Messenger,* p. 5.

Eighteen-member board of trustees named to direct private schools. (1969, February). *Caswell Messenger,* p. 1.

Foster, M. (1990). The politics of race: Through African-American teachers' eyes. *Journal of Education, 172*(3), 123–141.

Henderson, A. T. (1987). *The evidence continues to grow: Parent involvement improves student achievement.* Columbia, MD: National Committee for Citizens in Education.

Henderson, A. T. (1988). Parents are a school's best friends. *Phi Delta Kappan, 70,* 148–153.

Hoover-Dempsey, O., Bassler, J., & Brissie, J. (1987). Parent involvement: Contributions of teacher efficacy, school socioeconomic status, and other school characteristics. *American Educational Research Journal, 24,* 417–435.

Irvine, R., & Irvine, J. (1984). The impact of the desegregation process on the education of black students: Key variables. *Journal of Negro Education, 52,* 410–422.

Jones, F. (1981). *A traditional model of educational excellence.* Washington, DC: Howard University Press.

Kluger, R. (1977). *Simple justice.* New York: Random House.

Lightfoot, S. L. (1978). *Worlds apart.* New York: Basic Books.

Lightfoot, S. L. (1981, Spring). Toward conflict and resolution: Relationships between families and schools. *Theory into Practice, 20,* 97–104.

Newbold, N. (1935). *Report of the governor's commission for the study of problems in the education of the Negro in North Carolina* (Publication No. 183). Raleigh, NC: State Superintendent of Public Instruction.

Rich, D. (1987). *Teachers and parents: An adult to adult approach.* Washington, DC: National Education Association.

Sowell, T. (1976). Patterns of black excellence. *The Public Interest, 43,* 26–58.

Spradley, T. P. (1979). *The ethnographic interview.* New York: Holt, Rinehart & Winston.

Swap, S. M. (1987). *Enhancing parent involvement in schools: A manual for parents and teachers.* New York: Teachers College Press.

Tangri, S., & Moles, O. (1987). Parents and the community. In V. Richardson-Kolher (Ed.), *Educator's handbook: A research perspective* (pp. 519–550). New York: Longman.

This research was supported through a Spencer Post-Doctoral Fellowship from the National Academy of Education. The author also acknowledges early research support provided by the Graduate School of Education at the University of Pennsylvania and continuing support provided by the University Research Committee at Emory University. Research assistants Trudy Blackwell and Evelyn Lavizzo aided in the data collection and processing.

Participatory Literacy Education Behind Bars

AIDS Opens the Door

KATHY BOUDIN

> I started hanging out and not taking school seriously when I was a teenager. At seventeen I met my first baby's father, and he had a lot of control over me. After he went to jail, I started using drugs. I had a job for one or two years on and off in a grocery store, running a cash register. But I left that job to sell drugs, because I could earn more money that way. I always wanted to be a bookkeeper, but you have to know how to read, filing, math. Now I think about a porter job in a hospital. Nothing I have to use reading for. I would like to think of nice things: nice clothes, an investigator, a secretary, nice jobs. I see ladies all dressed up, legs crossed. I like things like that, bubble baths, but I can't be thinking too many dreams cause I got five kids. I hope I can make it when I go home.
>
> — *Anna, Adult Basic Education student, Bedford Hills Correctional Facility*[1]

Prison lies at the end of a road taken. Although women arrive for many reasons, we have one thing in common: we share a deep desire to leave prison and not return. Many of us are looking for alternatives to the actions that brought us here. We are working to imagine new choices, to widen options, and to figure out how to make these real.

When Anna spoke, she was in an Adult Basic Education (ABE) literacy class, hoping it would open doors for her. She was not alone with her literacy problem. In Bedford Hills Correctional Facility, New York State's maximum security prison for 750 women, 63 percent of the incoming women do not have a high school diploma and almost 20 percent do not read at a fifth-grade level (Nuttall, 1988).

Although having limited literacy proficiency is a serious problem, it is only one of many that women in Bedford Hills face.[2] Prior to their imprisonment, most were confronting more pressing problems: poverty, drugs, domestic abuse, neighborhood violence, single-mother parenting, and immigration issues. Many, feeling permanently locked out of the economic mainstream, were trying to make fast money illegally, usually through involvement with drugs. Basic literacy education meant a time commitment, a slow, long-term investment in a life moving fast, so fast that it got out of control, and ended up with imprisonment. In prison, life slows down enough for these women to take time for such things as a literacy class, yet the women know that when they leave here, most will return to the same broad problems, problems that loom as permanent and intractable. Improved literacy will not be the miracle that will change their lives, especially since the average stay in prison is less than three years (Division of Program Services, 1992) and literacy growth is a slow process. It is rare for a woman to leave Bedford with a goal of changing social conditions, even if she believes those very conditions contributed to her ending up in prison. "You can't change the world" is a commonly held attitude. Trying to deal with immediate issues such as housing, jobs, and child raising are foremost in most women's minds when they leave. The urgent need many of us from a diversity of backgrounds feel is to change the things inside ourselves that landed us here, to be more able to negotiate the system and to cope with the problems we will face when we leave. Improved literacy is part of something bigger, part of their whole struggle to grow. As one woman said, "The only way out . . . is in."

What kind of literacy education would best meet the needs of the women in prison who face these issues? This is the question I grappled with some years ago, when I came to prison, as I became involved in studying and teaching adult literacy. I am an insider, a prisoner myself, a woman and a mother, serving a twenty-to-life sentence. I am also something of an outsider — White, from a middle-class background, college educated, and a participant in the social movements of the 1960s. I had not shared some of the most common realities of the women in the ABE class, realities including racism, drugs, family violence, immigration, or poverty. Nevertheless, twelve years of prison life has broken down barriers: living through the daily experiences such as lock-ins or cell searches, cooking or gossiping; deep friendships; working on AIDS, foster care, and literacy; and sharing the life events such as mothering, deaths, and graduations. All of this has created for me windows into the lives, past and present, of women from different backgrounds and has also led to a new commonality among us.

Early in my master's degree work in adult education (which I undertook when I first entered prison), I learned about Paulo Freire's problem-solving approach to literacy education, an approach that places literacy acquisition in the context of learners' daily concerns and social reality (Freire, 1970, 1974). I hypothesized that it would be effective at Bedford because it could offer an education in which women could think and act around urgently felt needs while developing their literacy ability.

I, like many other prisoners, wanted to be productive and to do something meaningful with my time in prison, and I looked to teaching literacy as one way to do this. Yet prison administrators usually limit the amount of responsibility and independence a prisoner can have, and teachers who have inmate teacher aides usually use them only in very limited roles. Would I, a prisoner, as a teacher's aide to a civilian teacher, be able to create the space to do meaningful work?

Would it be possible in a prison classroom to create conditions for self-awareness, a space where people felt safe to identify and address their own problems and then struggle toward solutions, to imagine the world as it could be otherwise? Prisons are founded on assumptions of control, obedience, and security. Thus, independent thinking and individual and collective initiative create sharp tensions around these assumptions.

Prison is a metaphor for failure, the failure of those who end up there, while a sense of self-worth is a foundation for active learning, for being willing to take risks. Would it be possible, in the prison atmosphere, to break through the prevailing ideology about prisoners as failures, an ideology that had been internalized to varying degrees by the women themselves, and to release their psychological energy for creative learning? These were among the questions I faced as I began to think about becoming a literacy educator in prison.

In this article, I tell the story of what happened between 1986 and 1990 at Bedford Hills Correctional Facility as I struggled to develop a literacy program that was meaning-based, problem-posing, and relevant to learners' lives. Written from my perspective and observations as both a teacher and a prisoner, with quotes drawn from my detailed journal entries over a five-year period, I start by examining the prison environment, and then relate my experience of teaching while evaluating which educational approach best met the needs of incarcerated women at Bedford. Finally, I discuss the possibilities and constraints that the prison context creates for establishing participatory education.

The Prison Context

The primary missions of prison — control, punishment, and deterrence through social isolation (Sullivan, 1990) — serve to intensify the powerlessness and dependency that many women prisoners have already experienced outside of prison. The loss of the ability to make decisions permeates every aspect of prison life cumulatively in the way it increases powerlessness. The authorities move women freely among the nine female prisons in New York State; thus, within a moment, a woman's entire world may shift. Lack of control over where one lives means lack of control over all the pieces of a life — friends, work, education, routine, possessions, environment, and, of central importance to women, contact with children and family. If a woman is in prison near her children, she can maintain an active relationship with them; when she is moved, the ties are ruptured.

Prison policies dictate what clothing to wear and what colors are permitted. When the telephone rings, a prisoner cannot pick it up. Only guards can open doors. Intimate relationships are illegal and must be hidden. This lack of control extends to life outside prison as well. For example, a woman may learn that her child is in the hospital, but cannot be present to comfort her or him. When a child runs away from home, the mother is helpless to work on the problem. We as prisoners must rely on people outside to help with the details of daily living — from buying clothes, food, and presents for children, to phoning lawyers who don't accept collect calls.

While women's prisons can be brutalizing, they are often infantilizing.[3] The social conditioning in a women's prison encourages a childlike dependency (Burkhart, 1976). For example, at Bedford Hills we constantly have to ask permission to do some of the most basic things: when at work or at school we must ask an officer for toilet paper, and she or he will then tear off a few pieces and hand them to us; we must wait for an officer to turn the lights off or on in our cells, since cell lights are controlled by a key that the officer has; we may stand by a gate or a door for five minutes or more until an officer feels we are quiet enough, and only then will she or he open it. Women operate within the confines of power and control, reward and punishment; women typically express their overall sense of having no control when they refer to authorities and say, "This is *Their* jail."

Although prison intensifies powerlessness, for many women it paradoxically also offers a space for growth. There is a release from the pressures of everyday survival, abusive relationships, family responsibilities, and drug addiction; some women have their first drug-free pregnancy while in prison. Incarceration can be a time for women to reevaluate and reflect on their lives, to get an education and acquire skills they never had a chance or didn't want to get, and to think about issues they may never have thought about.

There are numerous educational and social programs that women can make use of in prison.[4] These programs are shaped by the conflicting goals of security, control, and punishment on the one hand, and rehabilitation or self-development on the other (Bellorado, 1986; Sullivan, 1990). The various basic education programs at Bedford Hills — ABE, pre-GED, GED, ESL, Bilingual Literacy — can serve either as a means of control (primarily used to keep prisoners occupied and having limited educational goals) or as a fruitful context for deep growth. It was in this environment of constraints and possibilities that I set out to teach.

Entering the Classroom: Education for Control

I started to work as a teacher's aide in the ABE class in February 1986. I requested to work in this class because the teacher had expressed support for my teaching ideas and, from my observation, seemed to have a strong rapport with the students. By this time, I had spent a year-and-a-half in both graduate study and individual tutoring of ABE, GED, ESL, and college students. This range of experience led me to define three goals for my work in the ABE classroom: first, to teach reading and writing; second, to foster participants' intellectual and emotional strengths (e.g., analytical ability, imagination, and self-esteem); and third, to create a context for exploring and possibly acting on personal and social issues faced by women in the prison. When I entered the classroom, I was in for a rude awakening.

On an average day, the women in the ABE class ranged in age from seventeen to seventy, with the vast majority in their mid-twenties. They were primarily African-American or Hispanic, coming from a variety of cultures and places: New York City, the South, Puerto Rico, Jamaica, Colombia, and the Dominican Republic. A few were working-class White women from upstate New York, and some came from other countries (Hong Kong, Yugoslavia, and Israel).

Typically, women arrived in class and took their individual folders and workbooks from a shelf. Their work consisted of reading paragraphs or short passages on various unrelated themes (e.g., popcorn, insects, and newspapers), and then answering multiple-choice questions that focused on skills (e.g., finding the main idea, understanding a particular word, or locating a detail). When a student finished a designated amount of work, the teacher or aide checked the answers against the answer key. The student then tried to correct her wrong responses.

The class was silent, except when the teacher spoke to individual students or when friends exchanged a few words. There was no instruction to the whole class by the teacher. What mattered most was whether the students answered workbook questions correctly. The answer key and the teacher were the only sources of knowledge. The learning process was entirely defined by the teacher, and it was narrowly confined to a limited body of information.

Occasionally, group discussion followed a movie; the teacher might encourage writing a few times a year, for example, during Black History month. Once in a while there was a lesson on a life skill relating to the state-mandated functional competency program or computer work, but these activities were not the norm. Day after day, year after year, women came to class and silently read workbooks in which they repeated discrete skills in preparation for periodic tests.

My first reaction to the classroom was physical. My eyes strained from trying to match up answer sheets with hundreds of tiny boxes, and my mind went dull. I found myself de-skilled and transformed into a clerk. I was neither expected nor able to use any intellectual or emotional aspects of myself. I found no room for choice, judgment, or authentic interaction. The experience of almost two years in this role contributed to passivity, conformity, and a feeling of uselessness, which, as a prisoner, I was constantly struggling against anyway.

For the women in the literacy class, reading paragraphs day after day and taking tests with similar paragraphs resulted in incremental improvement on test scores over time, and, therefore, in some sense of progress and satisfaction. Yet communication and meaning, the essential core of reading, were not the point of the classroom experience. There was no writing, no explicit development of strategies to enhance construction of meaning from texts, no exposure to various literary genres such as poetry, stories, or drama, and no building on interaction between the different language processes of reading, writing, listening, and speaking.

I asked myself what we were telling women about the importance of literacy, when there was no link between literacy and self, no development of literacy as a powerful means to construct a world. What message were we giving the women about themselves and their lives in this classroom, where their thinking and all their experience were irrelevant? The women I taught brought into the classroom a rich tapestry of knowledge, experience, and cultures. They knew first-hand about the social problems of crack, homelessness, the crisis of being mothers behind bars, the immigrant experience; they shared basic human conditions of love and friendship, betrayal, death, community, work. If learning materials did not portray a life that was familiar, did not reflect their reality, did not contain their voices or their languages, what did that tell them about their cultures? If the teacher and the workbooks were the only sources of knowledge and authority, what did that say about their capacity to know and to create?

I believe that this approach, with its excessive emphasis on obedience and limited possibility for initiative or constructive learning, with its lack of attention to self and its undervaluing of affect in learning, was detrimental to basic mental health. This kind of instruction could not foster self-esteem or self-confidence. And, in denying the possibility of making choices, solving problems, looking at different options, or figuring out one's own opinion, it thwarted the possibility of helping women to change their lives.

Educational policy and curriculum for all New York State prisons is set by the Department of Education of the New York State Department of Correctional Services (Nuttall, 1988). The approach used in the prison literacy classes, like that used in many adult literacy programs throughout the country (Fingeret, 1984; Hunter & Harman, 1979), is a decontextualized, subskill model of reading in which content, real life issues, creativity, and imagination are all irrelevant. It is individualized and programmed, precluding interaction or social action (Nuttall, 1983). The reading process is conceptualized as a bottom-up process in which comprehension of the message of the text is slowly built up by accumulating small pieces, sound by sound, word by word, moving from lower to higher levels of complexity (LaBerge & Samuels, 1985). An adult who has failed to learn to read adequately is presumed to be lacking in particular subskills. Initial testing identifies those particular weaknesses, remediates for them and then retests in this diagnostic prescriptive model (Nuttall, 1983). The concept of literacy that guides the curriculum in the ABE class is based on grade level: a literate inmate is defined as one who scores at or above the

5.0 reading level on the standardized achievement tests used throughout the system (Nuttall, 1983).[5]

As in any other teaching context, the rationale for the choice of approach to prison literacy education is informed, in part, by assumptions about learners. A report from the Education Department of the New York State Department of Correctional Services states:

> The most serious obstacle to a successful program and "habilitation" or "rehabilitation" is the make-up of the population itself. For the most part, commitments to the Department represent individuals who have little education, who have no viable occupational skill, who have a history of substance abuse, and who often have a long history of criminal activity (Nuttall, 1988, p. 2)

This policy statement characterizes prisoners themselves as the main obstacle to their own rehabilitation. Although it identifies objective problems, it fails to recognize strengths that prisoners bring to the learning process. From my observation, viewing prisoners primarily as a problem meant that correctional services' education personnel were unlikely to involve prisoners in their own education, let alone to think they might make a contribution to society. I knew from my years in prison that this perception of women exclusively as "problems" was inaccurate, and that this prevailing view would never lead to a process of meaningful educational growth.

Women who have committed serious crimes may well have survived serious pressures. Many women have not just survived, but have actively refused to accept a passive or victimized role. While women may have acted in a destructive and/or self-destructive way, assertiveness can be a lever that opens options for new action. The ability to survive and fight back may be a strength on which to build. It is crucial to discover and work with this and other strengths because, however deeply hidden, they are, in the end, women's greatest allies. And so a question began to form and to follow me: Could I create a process whereby the potential and strengths of the women could be expressed and developed, becoming part of the literacy process and fueling it with energy?

An Alternative Vision

I developed an alternative vision through a combination of my past history as a community organizer, my experience in the individual tutoring and ABE class, and the theory and methods that I learned through my graduate studies. In the 1960s, I had been involved in teaching about welfare rights, housing, and health issues. I had worked with women who had little formal education and who were regarded by society as inadequate, or as "victims" to be helped by those who were more educated by formal academic standards. Yet these women and people like them throughout the United States were learning together, acting on their own problems, and, at the same time, providing social insights that affected the entire society. I brought to my classes a certain optimism from my experience as an educator outside the classroom. I believed that, even in the controlled prison environment and in a different historical period, it might be possible to create a participatory learning process in which people felt a relative sense of empowerment.

My studies confirmed that, when literacy was taught as a collection of skills outside of any meaningful context and divorced from any importance in the learners' lives, the work would not fully tap their intellectual capacity. Neither would it draw on their prior knowledge, which, as schema theory had taught me, is so critical in the development of reading proficiency (Anderson, 1985; Bransford, 1985). Taken together, my community organizing experiences, my graduate studies, and my observations of prison classrooms led me to hypothesize that a meaning-driven, whole-language orientation might be more effective in the prison context (Altwerger, Edelsky, & Flores, 1987; Goodman, 1973, 1985; Smith, 1973).

I believed that such an approach would be stronger not only cognitively, but affectively as well. The women whom I taught were once the children who had failed in school or, more accurately for many of them, whose schools had failed them. From my interaction with the women in and out of class, I learned that they brought with them negative feelings about education and about themselves as learners. Attitudes about race, class, and gender undermined their confidence to learn academically, compounding the insecurities about school. I knew from conversations that many were only in the ABE class because it would look good for the parole board or because they had been assigned to be there. It was critical to use an approach that built on the women's intelligence, experience, and culture in order to counter these forces.

The existing classroom process, depending as it did on passivity and the rote learning of isolated skills, did not link literacy learning with the daily needs of the women, nor did it equip them to take an active role in their own education. As such, it ran counter to what we know about adult learning in general: a) the complexity of adult social roles and related responsibilities (spouse, worker, parent, community member) means that adults want learning to be applicable to their needs; b) the broad knowledge and life experience that adults have acquired mean that they have a great deal of prior knowledge that can be used as a strength in developing literacy ability; and c) the independence and self- direction that characterize adults mean that learning — both in content and in process — should be participatory (Ellowitch, 1983; Knowles, 1984).

For the women with whom I worked, the general needs of all adult learners were magnified by the multitude of urgent issues they faced; thus, the need to overcome powerlessness and to create new choices was essential. Freire's approach to literacy education was particularly relevant, as it is rooted in work with marginalized and oppressed groups. His ideas influenced my work in several ways. First, his approach begins with students developing the ability to analyze their experiences and their social reality, as they explore the meanings of this reality in the words and the sentences they are learning to read and write. The literacy class can, at times, become a place where students may even act on issues, using and further developing their literacy ability. Second, his work raises issues about teachers, their methods, and their relationships with their students. I had been frustrated with the one-way street of teaching that left the ABE students in a passive situation. Freire argues that this passivity comes, in part, from the tendency of many middle-class teachers to feel superior to their students from poorer backgrounds. He proposes a "dialogic" method, in which students and teachers together explore a shared set of issues. This dialogue, while not removing the teacher's responsibility to teach a body of knowledge, can unleash an active role for the learners, enhancing not only their present learning, but also their lives beyond the classroom (Freire, 1970, 1974).

These views resonated with my community work with African-American and poor White women, largely from Appalachia, prior to my incarceration. As I had come to know these women and their life stories, I became acutely aware that my formal education represented only one kind of knowledge; in fact, my own background, while having given me certain advantages, also had left me with certain blinders. My work with these women had been a two-way street — we learned from and taught one another. I wanted now to build on both the reality we shared as women prisoners and the differences in our backgrounds and experiences.

The Struggle for Change

For almost two years as a teacher's aide, I struggled to implement this alternative vision. Sometimes I worked with small groups of women, reading a particular text of interest, striving always to keep meaning in front of us. We read plays, did interviews, and read stories. Although each project engaged women and taught them a wider range of literacy skills, nothing altered the overall routine. The women frequently did not want to work with other women, feeling either embarrassed and ashamed of themselves or contemptuous of the others.

In many cases, they did not want to attempt any writing, which was rarely required by the teacher. The classroom context was still set by the teacher and the sub-skill approach; the approach I was using was simply not considered "real work." Moreover, I found myself experiencing the same frustration as other teachers with the "call-out" system (in which students could be pulled from class at any time for appointments). This system, along with transfers to other prisons, pushed the curriculum toward individualized work and away from a content focus, since it was difficult to develop a cohesive unit of study with a constantly changing group of people.

Slowly, the sub-skill model began to seduce me. Although I never lost my aversion to this limited sense of education, I began to become preoccupied with how women were doing in their workbooks and on the tests, measuring my worth as a teacher in these terms. I lost a strong sense of initiative. The structure and machinery of school were undermining my vision of education. I was turning into the teacher I did not want to be. I understood what had happened to other teachers, many of whom encouraged me and seemed to identify with my vision, but didn't have the energy to implement it.

The existing curriculum materials, testing apparatus, and overall conception of literacy set terms for success and failure that brought all of us — teachers and students alike — into its orbit. From my observations in class, and from conversations with the students, it appeared that the students had internalized years of failure in school, and without the confidence in themselves as thinkers they were very open to the safe routine of workbooks. In addition, prison, with its system of rewards and punishments (the ultimate of which was meted out by the parole board), contributed to students' willingness to accept a rote method of learning. By the fall of 1987, after almost two years of trying, I wanted to quit.

While I was wrestling with whether or not to leave teaching, the ABE teacher resigned; the Educational Supervisor then asked me to teach the class for four months until a new teacher could be hired. This offer was unexpected and unprecedented, since prisoners are permitted only to be aides to civilian teachers. I saw the opportunity to try to implement my vision of education, and I took it, as I felt it would allow me to define the approach to literacy education for the class as a whole, rather than as a side project.

The Education Supervisor, as an educator, was supportive of a problem-posing approach. He knew of my graduate work and was willing to take a risk with me. In allowing me to teach the class, the prison authorities had to balance their personal interest in my ideas about education with the system's policy of limiting an inmate's level of responsibility and influence over other inmates, along with concern not to threaten the civilian teachers' job security and status.[6] According to prison authorities, the decision was possible because it was limited in time, and I would officially remain in the position of teacher's aide to the other ABE teacher who worked with students at a tested reading level of K–3.[7]

The Issue of AIDS Enters the Classroom

The most important challenge facing me was to create a reading class in which concerns that had meaning to the women would "drive" the learning process. The issue of AIDS opened this possibility. In September 1987, the ABE reading class watched a television show on the National AIDS Awareness Test. At that time, AIDS was still largely an issue prisoners did not discuss, although it was deeply affecting their lives. Close to 20 percent of incoming women inmates tested positive for the HIV virus (New York State Commission on Correction, 1988). Women lived in a state of anxiety over whether they might be

HIV positive and whether to take the test. Many women had used intravenous (IV) drugs, and many had lovers or spouses who still did. Women were sisters, mothers, daughters, and homemakers for people with AIDS. Here, women shared cooking areas, showers and toilets, and a life together. People were scared — scared of each other, scared for their lives. The stigma that AIDS carried reenforced a sense of guilt and shame that the women already felt as prisoners pronounced "guilty" by the courts and society. There was a fear of just being associated with AIDS. This fear created both a collective silence and a desperate need to talk.

During the television show, I noticed that the women were riveted to the screen, trying to write down information, their voices sounding out rapidly staccato, one after another: "How do you spell 'pneumonia'?" "How about 'disease'?" "And 'infection'?" "What's an antibody?" "What do they mean, 'immune system'?" "Spell 'protection,' 'hemophiliac.'" While they tried to hold on to the meaning of new terms, I went to the blackboard to write down all the words they were calling out. AIDS was a powerfully emotional issue; a new sense of urgency entered the classroom.

That night I focused on everything I had learned but, until then, been unable to implement. I prepared a vocabulary worksheet, an activity that was familiar to the women. While the words were typically drawn from a textbook list for children at different grade levels, the words on this list came from the AIDS show. The women studied avidly, learning words far above their difficulty level in their workbook lists. Some words were conceptually familiar but difficult to spell, such as *transmit, doctor, disease, patient,* and *pneumonia*; some led to learning new concepts, such as *immune system, antibody,* and *hemophiliac.*

In addition to the vocabulary, I asked three questions that were on all of our minds: *What are the pros and cons of taking the AIDS test and how do you feel about it? If you tested positive would/should you tell somebody and who would you tell? What do you think would be a good program for AIDS here at Bedford Hills?* These questions created an environment in which the students related to real life emotional and social issues; they began addressing problems that they faced both individually and communally. I asked the women what they thought.

"I don't want to take the test. I'm scared to find out. I used needles."

"You have to tell your lover, otherwise you might hurt her."

"I don't even know what the test tells you, do you?"

"I'm not worried now, but what about when I go home? My man, he's been with women while I'm here. Even though he says he hasn't, he's like any other man. I know the real deal."

"I shot up with some people and now they're dead. I don't want to know and then again I do."

Everyone participated. The women speaking to one another turned their orderly rows into an informal circle. I also talked, feeling my commonality with the women because I too had feelings about testing, safe sex, and fears of rejection. I also felt our differences as women spoke about IV drugs in their lives and decided to speak to these differences, making explicit the fact that I didn't know about IV drugs and wanted to know more. This was the first of many times that I would try to make the differences in our backgrounds a point for exchange. In that first discussion, I began to change my role as teacher: I was a prisoner, exploring shared problems; a facilitator, guiding learning and discussion; and a person with specific information I wanted to learn and impart.

Soon, women began to write about personal experiences with AIDS, and even brought unsolicited writings to class. For example, Lucia wrote:

> My friend died from AIDS last year. . . . Since then I've been scared. This is a disease that they haven't found the medicine for. I would like to be one of those persons from the big laboratory to help find the medicine for those people who have AIDS. I'm trying not to think about the disease, but I have a brother and a sister and they are into drugs. They say they don't use anybody's syringe, but still I'm afraid.

Lucia had never written anything in class and had difficulty writing in her native Spanish, as well as in English. When she presented her piece, she was sharing a hidden secret about her family, her fears and her dreams, as well as asking for help in English and writing. The drive to express her intense feelings had led her to take real risks in her writing and use of English.

With reading centered on AIDS-related materials, the women contributed to the curriculum, something that had not happened previously. They brought in newspaper articles and pamphlets to share with the class, which I developed into reading lessons. One day Juana, who was about to transfer to the GED class, came to me holding pages of paper tightly in her hand. She said, "I've written something; it's a story, maybe the class would like it." She had a look of triumph on her face, and a triumph it was! Juana's story, called "Chocolate and Me," was about a relationship between two women in jail, one of whom had AIDS.[8] When she read it, the women listened intently as they felt their own lives being described by one of their class members, and clapped enthusiastically when it was over. Juana worked on it, learning the concept of paragraphs, struggling with sentence structure and spelling. Then I typed it, made copies, and developed a reading lesson from it. The class felt proud that one of their members had written something that they were studying. This was the first of many times that the women's own writings became the reading materials for our class.

Writing a Play: Building on the Strengths of an Oral Tradition

During this time, I proposed to the class that we write our own play.[9] I had several goals: to develop literacy through the process of creating a play in which women would be communicating important thoughts and feelings; to broaden literacy ability through studying the genre of a play and integrating the language forms of reading, writing, talking, and listening; and to develop the strengths of working in cooperation with others.

We began by talking about what a play is, learning about the elements of plot, character, conflict, dialogue, and setting. I gave out vocabulary worksheets with words related to theater. We read plays from a literacy program facing issues similar to those in our own community.[10] This encouraged us: if another basic literacy class could write a play about issues of housing, health, and drugs, then we, too, could write such a play. When one woman asked, "What should the play be about?", another responded, "It should be something about us, our lives." This was one more step by participants in gaining confidence that their own life experiences were significant. When it came time to decide on a focus, the women chose AIDS, because we were increasingly involved with it in class.

During the next weeks, the conflicts around which to base the plot emerged from our real questions and anxieties about AIDS: Should a person take the HIV test or not? If she tests positive, should she tell her parents? Her lover? The work on the play allowed women to reflect on their day-to-day experiences, and the play changed along with their reflections. One day Elena said, "A friend of mine told me last night that she just tested positive. She's supposed to go home in four months. She had so many dreams — traveling, having kids — now those dreams have all gone down the drain. Maybe I shouldn't push so hard for testing."

Jackie added, "Yeah, I agree, here I am in the play, pushing Anna to take the test, but I'm scared. I'm not ready to deal with it; I know I'm not, and I bet I'm not the only one." From this discussion, the group decided to make the dialogue in the play less pressured toward taking the test.

As we improvised dialogue around each conflict, plot and characters slowly developed. When it was time to create a script, two or three people followed each person's spoken words and wrote down whatever they could. We then pieced the entire dialogue into a whole. Finally we put all the scenarios on the blackboard and made choices as to the sequence of action.

The theater framework allowed participants to try out different resolutions to conflict, to experience the emotions they most feared, and to learn from the process. During one rehearsal, we focused on the woman who was the counselor in the play. "Try to get into it more, try to really put yourself into it," the women coached and pushed. Suddenly Teresa burst into tears. "I think I'm afraid," she said, "afraid to put myself in it completely because then it makes it real, and I guess no matter how calm I seem to all of you, really I'm afraid to think about AIDS." Women went to her and hugged her. After that moment, she did put herself more into the acting and was more open about her experiences and fears.

Work on the play further molded my changing role as teacher. The women urged me to take a part in the play. For a moment I hesitated, wondering if it was appropriate for a teacher to do that. Then I laughed at myself, realizing I was feeling afraid I might lose my authority. Taking the part strengthened my teaching, as I identified with the women in working on a shared problem.

Theater gave the Hispanic and African-American women an opportunity to build on a strong oral tradition. They were able to use their own language, dialects, informal speech, and body language. Some of the women who had the greatest problems developing their reading and writing were outstanding in the development of dialogues and acting. The theater process accentuated the strengths of some women, while valuing the strengths of each as language, communication, reading, and writing all developed.

A Community Develops in the Classroom

The students' growing consciousness of themselves as part of a community, first in the classroom and then in the prison, became a positive factor in literacy development. The classroom had been a place in which each person individually felt locked into her own sense of failure. "I hate being in this class, people think it's for dummies. Maybe it is," Anna had said. No one wanted to be identified with being in the ABE class, "the lowest spot on the totem pole," just as no one wanted to feel like they were part of the prison.

But as people began to talk about their fears and questions concerning AIDS, something changed in the classroom. A sense of community, an awareness of common experiences, and a feeling of support began to grow. The most emotional moment reflecting this came when Lucia shared with the class that she had just found out that her brother was hospitalized with AIDS. I wrote in my journal:

> When Lucia came back into the classroom, people said they were sorry and wanted to be there for her. Elena suggested that Lucia write about her feelings. So Lucia spent the rest of the class writing about what is happening with her brother.

When people arrived at class in the morning, they now spoke with each other differently, with an openness, a sense of identification, and growing trust. As one woman wrote, "In our class we talk about a lot of things and learn a lot of reading. Sometimes we talk about real things that make our tears come out. . . ."

The support for one another expressed itself in the classroom in many ways. For example, when a woman got sick, everyone made a card for her; when a woman made parole, people had a celebration for her. The class organized a Christmas party, something that had never before happened in an ABE class. The most significant articulation of community occurred when we were picking a title for the play. When someone said, "Let's call it *Our Play* because it is about us," there was enthusiastic agreement. That sense of there being an "us" had never existed before, and the title expressed a pride in the "us" that had emerged.

ABE class members carried this ethos of support beyond the class and into the prison population. Word began to get out that the ABE class was talking about AIDS in a supportive way; other prisoners now sought out women in the ABE class as confidantes on their living units. One day Ching came to class and said to me, "A woman on my floor found out she has AIDS and tried to kill herself. I'm the one person she told. I know why she tried. She came to me, I'm the person she talks to." Ching's eyes filled with tears. I saw then that the knowledge that the ABE class was accumulating was also bringing with it awesome responsibilities.

The feeling of community influenced literacy ability, as well as intellectual and emotional growth. People took risks in reading and writing because they were no longer afraid. They felt less ashamed of themselves and were willing to express their thoughts more freely. As they brought increasingly complex reading materials to class and began to teach one another, recognizing that each one could teach as well as learn, a tentative grouping of learners and teachers emerged. One of many examples of this occurred when the women were preparing for a spelling test. "I'll help Jamie," said Ms. Edna, who was seventy years old. They worked for a while, and then Ms. Edna brought the test over to me. They had gotten 100 percent on it. They were beaming at their mutual success.

A growing social awareness laid the basis for the next critical leap: the desire to change the conditions that were causing problems. "What can we do with everything we're learning?" Jackie asked. "People are coming to me, asking me things," Alicia added. Instead of seeing AIDS as an individual problem, people began to see it as a common one, and one they could work on together. First the women worked on an article for the school journal, hoping to share what they had learned. I took the class through the process of writing a composition, focusing on what they wanted to say about AIDS. After five hard-working sessions, the article, *Alert to Aids*, was done, and was published not long after with all the class members' names on it. Although the feeling of community had first grown inside the class, it now extended beyond the class into the prison as a whole. The women continued to use their developing literacy skills to make a difference. *Our Play* became the means of accomplishing this.

Are We Really Learning to Read and Write?

The transformation that was taking place in the classroom challenged participants' notions about what counts as education. In place of filling out multiple choice questions from workbooks, the women were learning from their own experiences and reading materials that did not have "yes" or "no" answers. The range of literacy activities was far beyond those normally carried out in the ABE class. Yet, it was not an easy transformation, and not everyone was comfortable with the process. The students had questions, and so did I. Randy said, "I feel I've learned a lot about AIDS, I'm learning to write a composition, I'm reading lots of articles, and I'm actually writing a play, but I'm just not sure I'm really learning." Many women wanted a clear sense of right and wrong answers. The workbooks had provided this, as well as a sense of progress because of the movement through the book and from one level to the next. Some women did not like working in groups. Others wanted to know whether their progress would show up on the test scores.

During the work on the play, one woman playing a major role did not do as well on the quarterly TABE test as she had hoped. She announced that she was quitting the play to go back to the workbooks. Everyone wanted her to come back to the play and eventually she did, with renewed commitment. However, I knew that I had to take her concerns seriously, and that they were shared by others. I, too, was worried about whether this work would give them the needed test preparation.

During this period, when I encountered both a variety of student resistance and my own insecurities as a relatively new teacher of literacy, I asked myself whether I was imposing on the women an educational approach that I thought was best for them, but that they didn't want. Perhaps my views were linked to the differences in my background. Would it give them adequate test preparation? With time, the range of reading materials, the explosion of writing, and the students' engagement and personal growth all made me more confident about my approach. And now, having established a meaning-driven context within the classroom, I was able to begin focusing on problem areas. I took readings and developed lessons similar to those in the workbooks. This, I felt, would allow the women to feel a relationship between the past and the new learning experiences. I tried to develop a better balance between group and individual work, spending time with each person on specific areas of need. Many of the women needed work on both the sound symbol relations and the basic structure of English language. Finally, I developed lessons on test-taking skills.

Performing the Play: Empowerment within a Prison

By mid-December of 1987, we were ready to put on the play. We were all nervous. AIDS was still a subject associated with fear and stigma. Those who were taking the risk to open up a hidden subject were not seen by either themselves or other inmates as potential educators, because they were in the lowest level academic class.

The play was performed six times, and each time the audience reacted beyond all dreams. It brought into the open fears, questions, and issues in a safe social setting, breaking the silence so that people could together begin to deal with the epidemic. Women cried as a father rejected his daughter, moving his chair away from her after she told him she had tested positive. Yet the tears were mixed with embarrassed laughter, because they knew that they, too, might move away from someone whom they thought to have AIDS. When a woman told her lover she had tested positive, there was a dead silence as people waited for the lover's reaction. Everyone was able to identify with one of the women or the other; they were living through what they themselves might face. When the support group in the play came together for the last scene and told each other of the good and of the difficult reactions they had gotten from family and friends, the audience stood up and cheered, feeling the strength that came from people supporting each other.

After several performances, we held discussions with the audiences about what could be done to deal with the crisis of AIDS here at Bedford Hills. The audience asked for support groups and a program to be built like the one depicted in the play. Members of the prison administration came to watch one of the performances. The superintendent requested that the class put on the play for the civilian counselors in the prison, and the class made a video of it.

Several months later, a group of women separate from the ABE class, including myself, formed an organization for peer education and counseling called AIDS Counseling and Education (ACE). The ACE Program has created a major difference in attitudes, medical care, mental health, knowledge, and support in the prison around AIDS-related issues[11]. It uses the video of *Our Play* to help women deal with the emotional issues that AIDS raises.

After the play, the ABE class did its first evaluation of their learning experience, another step in the women's self-consciously helping to mold their own education. The Education Supervisor, who facilitated the evaluation, asked, "What did the work in the AIDS unit accomplish for you?" The answers included, "Writing skills, vocabulary, recognizing words, spelling, how to write a play, learning about conflicts and resolutions."

"Learning about AIDS."

"How to put on a play and how to act."

"How to respect people's feelings, how to speak louder, and how to express our feelings."

"I liked the counseling group because it involved counseling each other."

"We gave people a message, we helped people."

"The play brought a level of emotions, awareness to help learn."

"I feel wise, learning how other people feel."

"The play gave me a mirror to look at my own life."

I believe that these quotes reflect how the women in the ABE class felt empowered in different ways, both as individuals and as a group. The classroom experience allowed individuals to understand their own lives more clearly. Their self-concept changed from being poor learners to people who could teach others. Although the process had begun with one peer educator, myself, the participatory problem-posing approach generated many others, as women taught one another in the classroom, and as the ABE class educated the population through informal discussions and writing the play. A sense of efficacy and agency developed for all of us — myself as teacher, the women in the class as students, and all of us as prisoners. As a group, the class knew that they had made a major contribution to the entire prison population by breaking the silence about AIDS, using their growing literacy ability to do so. The play had helped to create conditions whereby an ongoing program developed. Three years later, I asked one of the ABE class participants in *Our Play*, who is presently a member of ACE teaching others about AIDS, how she felt about her experience in the ABE class and the play. She said to me:

> The play made people more aware. Some people didn't want to face it, some people went around judging people that have AIDS. The play helped change that. I felt good about myself. I didn't know what AIDS was before I came to Bedford. It made me feel good that I'm educated and how I can help educate others. I grew in the process, that was a step, and a step makes for progress.

The Model Repeats: A Multicultural Community Expresses Itself

Was the intense student involvement during the unit on AIDS tied only to the issue of AIDS, or was it linked to the new way of teaching? Clearly AIDS was an issue of great emotional urgency, and it did provide the initial energy to transform the educational approach. Once the ABE class openly embraced the issue of AIDS and owned it as a shared human problem instead of as a badge of guilt, then, paradoxically, the very issue that led to oppressing and denying people their humanity became a vehicle of transformation and hope. As women freed themselves from the dehumanization of stigma and prejudice, proclaiming their own self-worth and humanity, an energy was created that drove the learning process, the desire for knowledge, the confidence to create.

Once the women had experienced a literacy education that focused on issues of importance, they wanted it to continue. Fundamentally, it was the educational approach that had provided the glue to overcome the fragmented reality that is debilitating to prisoners and teachers alike. Fragmentation was overcome when the learning process tapped into the whole person, and when a sense of community was created so that people felt committed to each other, as well as to broader goals.

An indication of the power of such an educational approach occurred when the new teacher was hired and reestablished the individualized, basic skills model, sending all of us — students and myself — back to the workbooks and multiple-choice questions. I felt a sadness, almost as if there had been a death of a fragile new life. The students evidently felt the same way and, as the weeks went by, many of them complained to the teacher and to administrators, asking for a return to teaching in which their ideas and issues mattered. This active role of ABE students requesting a certain type of education was unprecedented at Bedford Hills.

The AIDS unit had generated enough support for a participatory approach that not only the education supervisor, but also higher prison authorities were interested in seeing it continue in some form. The new teacher, who was troubled by declining attendance, and was also open to the problem-posing approach, agreed to let me teach the class two out of five days, during which time he would be present in the classroom. This arrangement left him in authority, yet gave credence to my work.

The model repeated itself as the ABE class explored other thematic units over the next year. In one called "Mothers and Daughters," we explored our mothers' lives, our relationship to them as daughters, and our own role as mothers. In another, we explored issues of personal experiences and values with money. Finally, for a six-month period, we took on a major project — writing a handbook for incoming inmates, entitled *Experiences of Life: Surviving at Bedford Hills.*

For two days a week, the class became a writers' workshop. It began with the women, myself included, sharing what was on our minds the first night we arrived in prison. Then we brainstormed about what we had known, feared, and wondered about prison life in Bedford Hills before arriving here. I found writings by other prisoners about these concerns and used them as the basis for structured reading lessons. They triggered intense writing, from several sentences to several pages, until enough material was created for the book. The chapters included, "Advice for How to Survive in Prison," "Coming from Another Country," "Being Pregnant in Bedford Hills," and "Mothers and Children."

The exploration of each new issue deepened participants' sense of themselves and of shared realities. Out of the cumulative experience of feeling our commonality as prisoners and women, a trust developed that made it possible for us to explore our cultural, racial, ethnic, and linguistic differences. Literacy acquisition interacted with the exploration of cultural identity. One among many examples of this occurred when it came time to edit the handbook. We looked at the different forms of language that were found in the writings of the women in the handbook: Standard American English, informal speech, Black English, and slang. For the first time, many women heard that the Black English, which always had been corrected as "wrong," was a dialect reflecting a culture.

The class had a long discussion about what style of language to use for the handbook. Some wanted it to be in Standard American English because they felt that new women coming in should see that the ABE students knew the standards of accepted grammar. Other women wanted to leave some of the informal language or slang and Black English dialect in order to facilitate communication with the new women. A Chinese woman proposed a solution: to leave it in the style that the particular woman had written if she wanted, but to explain in the beginning of the book that the decisions about language had been a conscious, educated choice. Thus, the readers would know that the ABE students knew enough to distinguish between and to choose different types of language. This was how it was done.

Prisoners as Educators

As a prisoner teaching, I experienced a shifting of roles and identities. I was an inmate, reminded of that reality by a twenty-to-life sentence and the day-to-day experiences of being strip-searched after a visit, separated from my son, and locked down; yet, at times I felt myself to be a teacher in training, headed for an identity as an educator, occasionally asked by another inmate, "Are you a teacher or a prisoner?", until they noticed my green pants and gave me a knowing nod. In my role as educator, teachers would sometimes speak to me with respect, almost as a peer; some were genuinely excited about the work and supported my educational growth. Yet there was an ambivalence about me as an educator. One example can be seen in the words of a teacher who was familiar with the quality of the AIDS work, yet who introduced me as her "inmate clerk." At times I would be a translator, negotiating between two worlds. Then the reality of control and limits would bring everything back into focus. Although there was a shifting of roles, I found that the primary tendency of the system was to define me as prisoner. It was always a struggle to transcend the limitations of that role.

To what extent was the participatory approach tied to a prisoner being the one teaching? In the class evaluation, the women addressed this issue, responding to the Education Supervisor's question, "How was Kathy's teaching like past teachers or different from them?" The women responded, "In the past a teacher was always just a teacher, but she (Kathy) was both part of it and also a teacher."

"She was learning also. She was also like a counselor."

"Teachers never participated in learning, past teachers taught 'what to do,' not 'how to'." The Education Supervisor asked, "Could a civilian do it, not just a prisoner?" One woman said, "Yes, but they would have to be sympathetic to the group and have to pick up on the vibes. It wouldn't happen as fast, have to build rapport, that takes time." To the question, "How do you build rapport?", someone responded, "Show care, speak what you're about, you open up to us, we'll open up to you, forget that you're a civilian."

There was a strength in the peer education process, of a prisoner teaching prisoners. It allowed for a shared exploration of issues that became the basis of literacy curriculum development. Additionally, as a prisoner I shared the powerlessness felt by the students and had a deep stake in creating a participatory learning process, in which we as prisoners were ourselves making decisions, taking on problem-posing and problem-solving.

Yet the very strength of the peer education process was also its weakness in the prison context. Although most of the prison administrators with whom I dealt expressed personal enthusiasm toward the educational approach I was using, they also expressed a dilemma when the question of whether I could actually teach arose: how could they permit me real responsibility as an educator without giving me too much responsibility as a prisoner? How could such an empowering group process be initiated by prisoners without it becoming a threat to security?

Future Prospects

> The paradox of education is precisely this — that as one begins to become conscious, one begins to examine the society in which one is being educated. The purpose of education, finally, is to create in a person the ability to look at the world for oneself, to make one's own decisions, to say to oneself this is black or is white, to decide for oneself whether there is a God in heaven, or not. To ask questions of the universe, and then to learn to live with those questions, is the way one achieves one's own identity. But no society is really anxious to have that kind of person around. What societies really ideally want is a citizenry which will simply obey the rules of society. (Baldwin, 1988, p. 4)

If creating a liberating education is difficult and paradoxical within the society at large, as James Baldwin writes, then it is all the more so within a prison, an institution of authoritarian control. Yet, after a year-and-a-half of utilizing a problem-posing approach in the classroom, there was change. The experience was so positive that it moved not just inmates, but also some teachers, educational administrators, and some prison officials towards supporting more of this kind of teaching.[12] This support led me to ask: could a problem-posing approach to literacy become an ongoing part of the educational programs in the prison? Was the experience simply a chance occurrence, or was it consonant enough with the prison goal of rehabilitation to imagine extending it to involve more classes and more inmates as peer educators?

Three education supervisors agreed to work with me on a proposal to implement a problem-posing curriculum more widely. We addressed the question: Who were the most appropriate people to do the teaching? We agreed that inmates would bring particular strengths to the process, namely that of identification with the learners. Moreover, a program using peer educators meant extending the rehabilitative process beyond the students in the literacy classes to those women with higher educational backgrounds. In this prison alone, more than one hundred women are either in college or have bachelor degrees; therefore the potential number of literacy peer educators was large, and developing teaching skills, carrying out work that required self-reliance, and contributing to the broader community was clearly within the concept of penal rehabilitation.

The final proposal involved training peer educators from among prisoners to work four hours per week in every basic education class, using a problem-posing curriculum developed in cooperation with the students. The Superintendent approved the program and productive meetings began with education administrators, teachers, and interested peer educators. Then, midway through the planning period, the prison Administration disapproved it.

Both the support and the withdrawal of support for the peer education program can only be understood as aspects of the broad contradictions among the primary prison goals of control, punishment, and deterrence, and that of rehabilitation. These conflicting goals manifest themselves in many ways, including what type of behaviors are rewarded or sanctioned, the perspective towards inmates, and different education models. How this contradiction is resolved at any moment in time depends on specific conditions. In this case, a number of conditions as diverse as personnel and social climate changed between the time of approval and disapproval: 1) The key education supervisor, who was the critical link between the teachers and our group of inmate peer educators and who supported the program, left the prison for another job; 2) The New York State financial crisis led to education cutbacks, and teachers were laid off. I knew from conversations with teachers and administrators that this increased anxiety among remaining teachers about their jobs made them more resistant to, and threatened by, inmates teaching or even inmates playing an active role in their own learning; 3) There was an increasing tendency towards law and order policies and attitudes within the society with concomitant social-service cutbacks. The general political climate was more antagonistic towards prisoners, inmate initiative, and program innovation. The prison administration reacted to all these factors by canceling a program involving inmates' critical thinking and initiative.

The current education crisis facing most prisons illustrates the impact of these conflicting goals. Prison populations are swelling due to drug-related crimes — in New York State, they have grown from 35,000 to 55,000 since 1985, when crack became a driving force in crime, and prison officials estimate that 75 percent of the inmates are incarcerated for drug-related offenses (Browne, 1991). The need for basic education programs has grown with the population increase.

Conversely, the budget cutbacks in education mean elimination of classes taught by civilian teachers. The first layoffs at Bedford Hills, in January 1991, led to the elimination of the ABE class for those inmates reading at the K–3 level and also of the ESL class; the GED class has also suffered significant cutbacks. Between 1989 and 1993 the number of academic and vocational teachers was cut from 25 to 9. The crying need for educational services could be alleviated by allowing inmates to be peer educators and by using participatory methods in which learners actively work on problems they face. Yet prison authorities are reluctant to allow such a problem-posing curriculum to develop or to allow inmates to teach classes. In short, while prison administrators may talk about providing an education for rehabilitation, they rarely do what is necessary to make it happen.

These contradictory needs and goals are integral to the structure of the prison system and, as such, cannot be transcended. At the same time, however, they frame the conditions under which struggle can occur; the very existence of these contradictions offers possibilities for change.[13]

Prisons, like other societal institutions, contain cracks and openings for change — conflicting goals and policies, a diversity of people, changing historical directions. At Bedford Hills, due to a particular combination of these variables, it became possible to create a liberating form of education that lasted for several years. This experience is now an immutable part of the educational history at Bedford Hills, a basis upon which to build.

The enormous expansion of prison populations suggests that prisons mirror and are part of a larger social crisis. This connection is reflected in the words of one New York State Department of Corrections spokesperson who said that prisons "probably give out more high school equivalency diplomas than ninety percent of the high schools in the state. Why do people have to come to prison to learn to read and write and get drug treatment?" (Browne, 1991). Human potential, which will be wasted or encouraged, is crowding into prisons. The challenge that problem-posing education raises in prison is part of a larger challenge facing the entire society: will social problems be dealt with by measures of control from above or through mobilization and education from below?

Conclusion

One never knows what improved literacy ability in itself will do for women in prison. One person may gain in self-esteem, while another will make practical improvements in letter writing, filling out forms, or reading to her child. For some, the ability to compete in the job market may increase, but indications are that for most it will not. For the adults with whom I work, the kinds of improvements necessary to increase job opportunities involve great effort over an extended period of time.

What if one embeds literacy acquisition in a broader education that has at its heart problem-posing, critical thinking and acting on shared problems? How might that affect people's personal growth, family relationships, jobs, and their ability to create the lives they want? Although the answer to this clearly depends on many unknowns, these are questions I have asked myself as I have thought about the struggle to build a problem-posing approach and about the women with whom I work and live.

One story in particular illustrates the complexity of this issue. When Anna was here, she participated fully in the AIDS unit, in the play, and in every successive unit during the year-and-a-half that the educational program existed. She, as much as anyone, felt empowered by the entire experience. When Anna went home, she started by getting a job in a flower shop. When the father of her children came out of prison, she made a decision to go back to him in spite of their problems with drugs, because he offered economic and emotional security. Soon afterward she became pregnant and, during her pregnancy, her husband began seeing another woman. Anna went back to drugs.

She was rearrested on a parole violation and came back to Bedford Hills for eight months before going home again.

When Anna was in the play and learning to read and write, while also learning about AIDS, this approach to education seemed like the answer. There were moments when I felt that the human potential and creativity that were emerging in the classroom would allow the women to take on the world, or at least in their own lives, and remake them to fit their dreams. Then, when Anna came back and told me her story, I felt the crushing limitations of even the most positive educational experience in light of what Anna and other women face, including personal scars and the need for social and economic changes.

As educators, we are often forced to accept more limited results than we envision in our hopes and dreams. The success of a short-term literacy program, one that meets our best vision, cannot be measured by one set of tangible standards; the social forces are too complex. Thus, despite Anna's return to prison, I believe that her learning experience and that of the others in the ABE class affirms an approach to teaching literacy based on the lives and experiences of the women themselves. Anna and the others so often have spoken with great pride of what they read and wrote, of the things they learned and taught to others. The participatory approach encouraged a feeling of their own worth and capacity. Although it contains no guarantees, it does offer a powerful hope, because it involves the full potential of participants. Lucia, who is among the many who have not returned to prison, said before she left, "I never thought I would be doing this. I never even did it on the street. I never thought I would act in a play and here I am reading everything. I can go home to my kids and say, 'I've done something!'"

Notes

1. This quote is a verbatim statement taken from an interview with an ABE student with whom I worked. Some of the quotes in the article come from similar interviews, while others come from my own journal entries. Although this article was written when almost all of the women quoted had already left prison on parole, or had transferred to a different prison, I was able to get in touch with the majority of them to tell them that I was doing public writing and to get their permission to use material about or by them. Because some of the women consented to have their real names used and others preferred to remain anonymous, I used fictitious names throughout. The one exception is Juana Lopez, who previously had material written for the ABE class that was published using her real name.
2. The prisoners in Bedford Hills Correctional Facility are overwhelmingly Black and Hispanic women, mothers, undereducated in a formal sense, frequently poor, and usually single heads of households. The ethnicity of the general prison population in New York State prisons is 50 percent Black, 31 percent Hispanic, and 19 percent White. (The United States population as a whole is 12 percent Black and 7 percent Hispanic.) The ethnicity of those prisoners with serious reading problems, that is, those under the 5.0 reading level, is 54 percent Black, 37 percent Hispanic, 9 percent White, and 5 percent other. In terms of the education levels of the women who enter the New York

State prison system, 18 percent read below a fifth-grade level; 16 percent have math skills below a fifth-grade level; 77 percent dropped out while in high school; and 63 percent do not possess a high school diploma (Nuttall, 1988). Seventy-three percent of the women in Bedford Hills are mothers (Division of Program Services, 1992), and the majority were single heads of households (Humphrey, 1988). One study showed that over half the women in prisons have received welfare payments during their adult lives (Craig, 1981); in a National Institute of Corrections study of men and women, 80 percent of those who were employed before arrest made less than a poverty-level salary (Bellorado, 1986). Forty-four percent of the women in Bedford Hills Correctional Facility were convicted of a drug offense; however, the warden at Riker's Island, which is the largest feeder jail to Bedford Hills, estimates that drugs underlie the incarceration of 95 percent of the female inmates there (Church, 1990). Lastly, in a study done at Bedford Hills in 1985, 60 percent of respondents said they had been victims of abuse (sexual, physical, or emotional) (Grossman, 1985).

3. Recent examples of women's prisons in which repressive measures such as extreme isolation or sexual abuse have been documented include the underground prison in Lexington, Kentucky, and the Shawnee Unit in Maryanna, Florida.
4. In addition to the basic education programs, some of these programs include: The Parenting and Foster Care Programs of the Children's Center, where women learn about issues related to being mothers; the Family Violence program, where women examine violence in their personal lives and some of the social values and roles that permit or even encourage such violence; the AIDS Counseling and Education (ACE) program, where women have struggled to build a community of support around AIDS-related issues and have trained themselves to become peer educators and counselors; and the four-year college program run by Mercy College, where women can earn bachelor degrees.
5. The Department of Education of the New York State Department of Correctional Services defines literacy by using a combination of grade level and functional competency definitions. The functional competency definition was crystallized into a Life Skills curriculum (Nuttall, 1983). However, in the three-and-a-half years during which I was involved in the ABE class, the Life Skills curriculum was not put into practice except in an occasional lesson.
6. A recent policy statement of the New York State Department of Correctional Services states, "Although the Department has been reluctant to place inmates in positions where they might possibly acquire influence or authority over other inmates, we have used inmates as teacher's aides and vocational aides and in recent years have begun to employ them as pre-release peer counselors and ASAT aides (Division of Program Services, 1991, p. 3). This statement is comparable with the long-standing practice of not permitting inmates to teach academic classes, but of encouraging them to do one-on-one tutoring, either as a teacher's aide or volunteer tutor.
7. In the summer of 1987, the ABE class was divided into two classes defined by level K–3 and level 3–6. I was working with the 3–6 level, and it was this class that I was offered to teach. Beginning with the winter of 1991–1992, the K–3 teacher was laid off, and once again there is one ABE class, level K–6.
8. Juana's story, "Chocolate and Me," was published by the PWA Coalition in *Surviving and Thriving with AIDS: Collective Wisdom*, vol. I (1988).
9. The sources of the suggestion and the guidance in using theater with literacy instruction were Dr. Ruth Meyers, my graduate study mentor, who worked with the Creative Arts Team (CAT), a professional educational theater company in residence at New York University, and Klaudia Rivera, who at the time was Director of the Community Language Services Project of the Adult Learning Center at LaGuardia Community College, where literacy and theater work was developed.

10. The plays were written by different classes of the Community Language Services project (CLS) of the Adult Learning Center at LaGuardia Community College in 1986, under the coordination of Klaudia Rivera, coordinator of the program.
11. For more information about the ACE Program see J. Clark and K. Boudin (1990), "A Community of Women Organize Themselves to Cope With the AIDS Crisis: A Case Study From Bedford Hills Correctional Facility," and K. Boudin and J. Clark (1991), "A Community of Women Organize Themselves to Cope with the AIDS Crisis: A Case Study from Bedford Hills Correctional Facility."
12. In December 1987, Educational Supervisor Rob Hinz wrote about my teaching after the completion of the AIDS unit: "Her use of Dr. Freire's theoretical work on praxis combining thought and action in a dialectical approach to the teaching of reading to adults has had remarkable results. The women with whom she was working are technically classified as technically illiterate, yet she was able in three months time to provide classroom instruction on AIDS . . . and to, using the vehicle of a play, have these women writing and reading while at the same time boosting their self-image and confidence." In the spring of 1988, the prison authorities gave permission for the ABE class video to be shown at an ABE conference of educators in New York City, with a presentation of the teaching methods done by Klaudia Rivera. In the winter of 1988–1989, the Bedford Hills Correctional Facility Education Department sent a copy of the ABE class handbook to Albany as an example of an education product.
13. An example of how the contradictory needs and goals present opportunities for change is reflected in a recent development in the New York State Department of Correctional Services. The enormous increase in the prison population has created the need for a greatly increased work force inside the prison. Looking toward inmates to partially meet this need has led to a reformulation of a philosophy about inmates: "In keeping with our new emphasis on training inmates to meet the needs of the Department and encouraging and recognizing individual inmate responsibility, it is now our intention to make even greater use of properly trained and qualified inmates. We plan to establish new job titles of 'Inmate Program Associates.' The Program Associates will work in such areas as classrooms, orientation, pre-release, libraries, and counseling" (Division of Program Services, 1991, p. 3). It is too soon to know how this new philosophy will actually manifest itself.

References

Altwerger, B., Edelsky, C., & Flores, B. M. (1987). Whole language: What's new? *The Reading Teacher, 41,* 144–145.

Anderson, R. C. (1985). Role of the readers' schema in comprehension, learning and memory. In H. Singer & R. B. Ruddell (Eds.), *Theoretical models and processes of reading* (3rd. ed., pp. 372–384). Newark, DE: I.R.A.

Baldwin, J. (1988). A talk to teachers. In R. Simonson & S. Walker (Eds.), *The Graywolf Annual Five: Multi-cultural literacy.* St. Paul, MN: Graywolf Press.

Bellorado, D. (1986). *Making literacy programs work: Vol. I. A practical guide for correctional educators* (Grant No. FZ-7). Washington, DC: U.S. Government Printing Office (Stock No. 027-000–1293-1).

Boudin, K., & Clark, J. (1991). A community of women organize themselves to cope with the AIDS crisis: A case study from Bedford Hills Correctional Facility. *Columbia Journal of Gender and Law, 1,* 47–56.

Bransford, J. D. (1985). Schema activation and schema acquisition: Comments on Richard Anderson's remarks. In H. Singer & R. B. Ruddell (Eds.), *Theoretical models and processes of reading* (3rd. ed., pp. 385–397). Newark, DE: I.R.A.

Browne, A. (1991, February 10). Cuomo: Release nonviolent cons. *The Daily News,* pp. 3, 24.

Burkhart, K. W. (1976). *Women in prison.* New York: Popular Library.
Church, G. J. (1990). The view from behind bars [Special Issue: Women: The road ahead]. *Time,* pp. 20–22.
Clark, J., & Boudin, K. (1990). A community of women organize themselves to cope with the AIDS crisis: A case study from Bedford Hills Correctional Facility. *Social Justice, 17* (2), 90–109.
Craig, G. M. (1981, July). The development of literacy/conscientization program for low-literate women in prison. *Dissertation Abstracts International, 42,* p. 68. *(University Microfilms No. 81-12, 793)*
Division of Program Services. (1991). *Division of Program Services action plan.* New York: New York State Department of Correctional Services.
Division of Program Services. (1992). *Female cluster program services action plan.* New York: New York State Department of Correctional Services.
Ellowitch, A. (1983). *Women and the world of work.* Philadelphia: Lutheran Settlement House Women's Program.
Fingeret, A. (1984). *Adult literacy education: Current and future directions.* Columbus: Ohio State University, National Center for Research in Vocational Education.
Freire, P. (1970). *Pedagogy of the oppressed.* New York: Seabury Press.
Freire, P. (1974). *Cultural action for freedom.* Cambridge, MA: Harvard Educational Review (Monograph Series No. 1).
Goodman, K. (1973). Psycholinguistic universals in the reading process. In F. Smith (Ed.), *Psycholinguistics and reading.* New York: Holt, Rinehart & Winston.
Goodman, K. (1985). Unity in reading. In H. Singer & R. B. Ruddell (Eds.), *Theoretical models and processes of reading* (3rd. ed, pp. 813–840). Newark, DE: I.R.A.
Grossman, J. (1985). *Domestic violence and incarcerated women: Survey results* (Prepared by New York State Department of Correctional Services; administered in July 1985 to female inmate population at Bedford Hills Correctional Facility). New York: Department of Correctional Services.
Humphrey, C. (1988). *Female, new court commitments (1976–1987).* New York: Department of Correctional Services.
Hunter, C., & Harman, D. (1979). *Adult illiteracy in the United States: A report to the Ford Foundation.* New York: McGraw Hill.
Knowles, M. (1984). *Androgeny in action.* San Francisco: Jossey-Bass.
LaBerge, D., & Samuels, S. J. (1985). Towards a theory of automatic information processing in reading. In H. Singer & R. B. Ruddell (Eds.), *Theoretical models and processing of reading* (3rd ed., pp. 689–718). Newark, DE: I.R.A.
Lopez, J. (1988). Chocolate and me. In *Surviving and thriving with AIDS: Collective wisdom* (vol. 1). New York: PWA Coalition.
New York State Commission on Correction. (1988). *Acquired immune deficiency syndrome: A demographic profile of New York State inmate mortalities 1981–1987.* New York: Author.
Nuttall, J. H. (1983). *Reducing inmate illiteracy in New York State.* New York: Department of Correctional Services.
Nuttall, J. H. (1988). *An update of illiteracy in New York's correctional system.* New York: Department of Correctional Services.
Smith, F. (1973). *Psycholinguistics and reading.* New York: Holt, Rinehart & Winston.
Sullivan, L. E. (1990). *The prison reform movement: Forlorn hope.* Boston: Twayne.

I would like to acknowledge the invaluable role of Ruth Meyers who, as my mentor during my graduate program, helped shape the thinking, practice, and interpretation of experience described in this article. I am grateful to Klaudia Rivera, who shared with me her own experience in adult literacy education and also played an important role in the use of theater in literacy work. I owe a special debt to Elsa Auerbach and Bill Ayers, who took considerable time and effort editing the many drafts of this article and who helped inform its content and style. I wish to acknowledge the contributions of Susan Kessler, Paul Mattick, Rose Paladino, Margaret Randall, Ruth Rodriguez, Ann Seidman, and Ruth Wald, each of whom raised critical questions of content and organization. I want to thank the numerous women from Bedford Hills Correctional Facility, both prisoners and civilian employees, who took the time to read the article and who brought the particular perspective of people who were living and/or working inside a prison. Finally, I owe a special debt to the women in the ABE class and to the group of twelve prospective peer educators, without whom the educational process would not have been possible.

Nationalist Ideologies, Neighborhood-Based Activism, and Educational Spaces in Puerto Rican Chicago

ANA Y. RAMOS-ZAYAS

[Pedro] Albizu Campos [High School] is a school where the students want an education, without the gang violence, without racism; [it's] a place where you can find out about your background. This is good, because if you don't know where you come from, then you don't know where you're headed. My first impressions of this school were many, but what stood out the most was the different types of murals about people who had committed their lives and their hearts to give us, the next generation, the opportunities that they did not have. This school has changed me in many different ways. This school taught me to be me, and not what other people want me to be. This school helped me look at my community and say, "I can make a difference." I can be anything that I want to be, only if I put my mind to it, only if I want it. This school taught me about something that I'd never been taught before, and I realized that I needed to learn about my culture. I learned about how hard it was to come from the island of Puerto Rico or from Mexico and find a well-paying job to maintain a home, and to support children, in the land of opportunities, so to speak. (David Villalobos, 16)[1]

[Pedro Albizu Campos High School] is about keeping us away from the gangs in the community and getting into the activities of the community. It is a comfortable place to come to, where everyone takes the time to listen to your problems and tries to help you out. The teachers understand when you are having trouble with a certain question or problem. They would actually go over it until you finally got the hang of it. I was really messed up at Clemente [the other high school in the community]. I never really knew how an A would look on my report card until I came here. This school is a real good experience for me. There is a lot of activities to join, like [the march against the] *Sun-Times,* which I participated in. The Washington trip [to advocate on behalf of Puerto Ricans impris-

> oned for political reasons] was a lot of fun. This school is the best thing that has happened to me since I first started high school. (Lydia Vélez, 15)

In this article, I focus on the role of grassroots, pro-Puerto Rican independence activists in community-based educational projects in Chicago. Through this focus, I attempt to understand Puerto Rican education at the intersections of conflictive political narrative, notions of "community building," and nationalist identities, as I believe that schooling cannot be divorced from the political and socioeconomic forces governing neighborhood development. In the case of Chicago's Puerto Rican barrio, there is a powerful irony in the fact that a pro-independence ideology, which encourages critical appraisal of U.S. policies toward Puerto Rico and of the myth of the "American Dream," actually encourages high school students to pursue mainstream mobility routes, such as abandoning gangs, finishing high school, and enrolling in college. One would think that such nationalist ideologies and identity politics would instead create resentment and anger, and encourage program participants to reject mainstream U.S. institutions. However, the opposite seems to be the case: high-risk Puerto Rican youths — including gang members and teenage mothers — are being drawn into the alternative high school, peer counseling initiatives, and the community-building process sponsored by the pro-independence activists. I argue that it is precisely the identity politics behind the oppositional education programs that explains why these students defy the odds and remain interested in schooling.

This article is based on field research in northwestern Chicago, including a series of follow-up visits to the area. The sampling frame for this research consisted of employees and clients of not-for-profit and grassroots multiservice agencies, most of whom live in Humboldt Park, West Town, or Logan Square, all neighborhoods in this part of Chicago. These multiservice organizations included a continuing education program for adults and teen mothers; GED and ESL programs; a parental involvement project at the main local high school; and a local chapter of a national not-for-profit youth education agency. The ethnographic methodology was eclectic, including participant observation; informal and semistructured interviews; life history interviews; focus groups including youths and young adults; and textual analysis of journals, murals, and area markers, personal letters, grassroots publications and newsletters, and autobiographical writings by students at various educational and informal sites. Archival research was also done at the Chicago Historical Society.

First I present the historical background of militant Puerto Rican politics in Chicago, as well as the urban patterns that define the largest Puerto Rican community in the Midwest. Second, I examine the Pedro Albizu Campos High School (PACHS) and its umbrella organization, the Juan Antonio Corretjer Puerto Rican Cultural Center (PRCC). In particular, I look at how students, teachers, and staff conceptualize "struggle," nationalist identities, and community building. Finally, I explore the political and class dynamics involved in the interaction between pro-independence grassroots activists and barrio residents on the one hand, and white-collar Puerto Rican city officials, professionals, and the mainstream media on the other. I argue that an oppositional education (an education that centers on promoting social criticism) premised on political ideologies — including developing an understanding of struggle, nationalist pride, inequality/oppression in the United States, and community involvement — is a potentially powerful, yet largely untapped, philosophical resource for ethnoracial youth education and popular education programs.

Historical Background: Puerto Rican Political Militancy in Chicago

Social and political awareness triggered by the civil rights movement in Chicago, coupled with early Alinsky-style community development efforts in Humboldt Park in the 1970s (Cruz, 1997), partly explains the distinctive politicization of Puerto Rican identity in Chicago.[2] The nationalist political militancy that has characterized the Chicago Puerto Rican community ever since resulted in part from the simultaneous arrival of Puerto Ricans in Chicago in the 1960s and community strategies developed during that time, as well as the continued neighborhood activism of the 1970s and 1980s.

The civic organizations of the early 1960s — particularly the "hometown clubs," made up of people from the same hometowns in Puerto Rico — had provided recreational and social structure to recently arrived Puerto Rican families (Padilla, 1987). After the Humboldt Park Riots of 1966 and 1977, both triggered by confrontations between the police and residents after the Puerto Rican Day parades, and the implementation of community action programs, more militant efforts emerged. The Young Lords Organization, among the most renowned embodiments of Puerto Rican political militancy in the United States, was founded in Chicago at this time, when a group of Puerto Rican high school dropouts and former gang members launched neighborhood-based programs by occupying and taking over local institutions.

In the early 1980s, the Chicago Puerto Rican community was at the center of political controversy in the United States and Puerto Rico. The Fuerzas Armadas para la Liberación Nacional (Armed Forces for National Liberation, or FALN), a clandestine group advocating political independence for Puerto Rico "by any means necessary," publicly admitted responsibility for a series of bombings in military facilities in both the U.S. and Puerto Rico in the late 1970s (Fernández, 1994). The fifteen Puerto Rican group members of the FALN, thirteen of whom were born or raised in Chicago, were eventually arrested and given lengthy sentences on charges of "seditious conspiracy to overthrow the U.S. government."[3] Reporters from Puerto Rico and all parts of the United States arrived in Chicago's Humboldt Park to interview the relatives of the youngsters involved in the FALN; some were hoping to resurrect a waning nationalist tradition, while others were curious to see who these "terrorists" were (Bruno, 1981).

The FALN redefined Puerto Rican politics and social networks in Chicago in several ways. Deep divisions developed between the prisoners' supporters and opponents and today remain a source of intragroup conflict among barrio activists in Chicago. Since the prisoners, prior to their incarceration, had developed grassroots programs that tended to the Puerto Rican poor (examined below) and were working poor themselves, many barrio residents and activists associated grassroots activism and militant nationalism with antipoverty programs in Humboldt Park. In some cases, these political divisions were understood along class lines. Most informants claimed that the militant activists were working-poor barrio residents; their opponents were perceived to be more white collar. However, there were exceptions in both camps.

In the 1980s, at the peak of FALN activity and FBI persecution, when most group members were still "underground," Puerto Rican residents of Humboldt Park/West Town appeared divided. "Signs of 'FALN Welcomed Here' appeared on people's houses and cars," commented Lola Rivera, a Puerto Rican woman in her early thirties, whose uncle is an FALN prisoner (Rivera was named an "outstanding teacher of the year" at both the local high school and the Pedro Albizu Campos High School). Jaime García, an active statehood advocate, said he agreed with the FBI and other government agents that the FALN members were "terrorists" who "gave all Puerto Ricans a bad name."[4]

Puerto Rican *independentista* (advocating for independence), nationalist, and communist militancy has been traditionally marginalized from "official" narratives — that is, those conveyed by mainstream sources, such as media reports, textbooks, legal discourse, and so on — in "an attempt to create a unifying, non-conflictive history of 'the Puerto Rican people' . . . [in which] violence was the missing aspect of historical discourse" (Díaz-Quiñones, 1993, pp. 26–27). The marginalization of these events contributes to *la memoria rota* (the broken memory), which Díaz-Quiñones defines as "the rupture of the continuity in the Puerto Rican community, the memory deliberately negated by political power, or broken by official repression and cultural exclusion" (1993, pp. 11–12). However, in Humboldt Park, Puerto Rican nationalist history has been resurrected, modified, and incorporated into all aspects of barrio life. In fact, Puerto Rican nationalism and a militant history that view violence and armed struggle as sometimes necessary serve as ideological foundations for neighborhood development and educational projects. Nationalist narratives have been adopted as ideological foundations of alternative and/or oppositional social service programs in Humboldt Park. Barrio activists and residents see their socioeconomic condition as Puerto Ricans in the United States as analogous to the political relations between Puerto Rico and the United States; in both cases, narratives of colonialism and struggle are evoked. Hence, a Puerto Rican youth "struggles" with the consequences of poverty, just as Puerto Rican nationalists have historically "struggled" against U.S. political control of Puerto Rico. These analogies bridge community-building projects (such as the urban renewal project of Humboldt Park's commercial area, community health clinics, alternative education programs, and cultural events) with metanarratives of heroism and sacrifice drawn from Puerto Rican nationalist movements of the past.

Ethnographic Context: Urban Patterns and Threats to the Puerto Rican Community

Chicago's neighborhood-based urban pattern contributes to the strong associations between cultural groups and specific city areas.[5] In Chicago, the "Puerto Rican community" is coterminous with the Humboldt Park/West Town/Logan Square area, while the heart of the "Mexican community" is on the South Side (especially Pilsen, or "la Villita"), and African Americans are largely concentrated in the west and southwest sides of the city.[6] Awareness of this neighborhood-based ethnic distribution is essential to understanding the interethnic relations, territoriality, and nationalist manifestations among Puerto Ricans in Chicago.

Of the three adjacent neighborhoods that border the Puerto Rican community, West Town is the closest one to downtown Chicago and, hence, is a very desirable real estate area. Within West Town itself, structural differences are dramatic. Sections of West Town are considered "historic landmarks," with gray stone mansions similar to those in the most exclusive Chicago neighborhoods. These mansions are less than a couple of blocks away from abandoned factories, car repair garages and dealers, unpaved streets, and run-down houses that appear abandoned, but often are not.

Racial and social differences between Puerto Rican residents and non-Puerto Rican newcomers exacerbate group misperceptions. While many interviewees referred to the newly arrived residents of West Town as "yuppies," the White twenty-somethings moving into Wicker Park, the easternmost section of West Town, are far from being the clean-cut, high-paid professionals one associates with this label. More typical of Wicker Park residents is a style of numerous body piercings, tattooing, spiked and dyed hair, and worn-out clothes — what one informant wittily described as "the Harley Davidson meets Morticia Adams look." The area is advertised as perfect for artists, and, indeed, many aspiring young White artists have moved there. A proliferation of trendy coffee shops, art supplies stores, and New Age music clubs cater to the expanding Wicker Park artist population.[7]

"They are . . . they are like hippies or something," commented Alma Juncos, a middle-aged Puerto Rican woman who is a parent-volunteer at the local high school. "That looks so disgusting. Look at those tattoos, the tongue and nose earrings. That's self-mutilation!" "These White kids think that living in poverty is 'cool.' They wanna be friends with Blacks and Latinos and pretend they are homeboys and homegirls themselves," explained Tamika Miranda, a stylish Puerto Rican woman in her mid-twenties who works at a local Latino agency and attends law school at night. The general feeling is that these gentrifiers are privileged people who mock the evils of actual poverty by appropriating the discourse of the poor as their own. Because most of the young Latino agency workers and grassroots activists themselves grew up in poverty, they are particularly condemning of the romanticized version of a very painful reality of barrio life.

The influx of non-Puerto Ricans — particularly White artists, African American families, and Central American immigrants — into West Town, Humboldt Park, and Logan Square, respectively, has strengthened nationalist sentiments among Puerto Rican barrio residents and activists. The growing importance of making it known that "Humboldt Park is Puerto Rican" is partially evidenced by the symbols used to mark key sections of the neighborhood. The most recent addition to the numerous nationalist murals, statues, and streets named for Puerto Rican heroes consists of two fifty-ton Puerto Rican flags of steel erected on Division Street to mark both ends of Paseo Boricua, Humboldt Park's main commercial area. Neighborhood flyers explaining concepts like "gentrification," "ethnic cleansing," and "urban renewal" are frequently distributed to barrio residents, as activists encourage Puerto Ricans to "sell to other Puerto Ricans" and to "support Puerto Rican businesses."

Barrio residents know that their chances of moving to a "better area" are bleak, and that the threat of displacement into even more run-down areas looms on the horizon. Some residents see Humboldt Park, West Town, and Logan Square as leading venues for employment among Puerto Ricans of all socioeconomic and occupational levels, but these employment opportunities will vanish if the community disperses. Social service agencies are already contemplating relocation as their clients are displaced by other groups. Owners of small businesses that rely on the community for survival are threatened with extinction as well. Similarly, ambulatory businesses, like the unionized fritters cooks (*los fritoleros*) in Humboldt Park or the sellers of miscellaneous area souvenirs (e.g., Paseo Boricua T-shirts, stickers, Puerto Rican flags) on Division Street are also threatened by the changing composition of the neighborhood. These small and ambulatory businesses target a very specific, Puerto Rican population, and are unlikely to survive the changing ethnic composition of the area. Thus, new symbols, urban plans, and agendas to "Puerto Ricannize" Humboldt Park have been promoted by neighborhood residents and grassroots activists.

When the two steel Puerto Rican flags were unveiled on Division Street, many nationalist activists commented on how "these flags are the only monuments to the Puerto Rican flag there are in the world." Presumably, prominently displaying Puerto Rican nationalist symbols would prevent further gentrification and protect small Puerto Rican businesses in Chicago. "This is the use of nationalism to reclaim space . . . away from gentrifiers," argued a leading neighborhood activist and administrator of the Puerto Rican Cultural Center, one of the main grassroots organizations in the area, also founded by FALN members.

"Los Nacionalistas" in Humboldt Park: The Puerto Rican Cultural Center, Militant Narratives, and Nationalist Identities

One cannot pass by the Juan Antonio Corretjer Puerto Rican Cultural Center (PRCC) without noticing the building. The bright colors of Puerto Rican revolutionary flags and quotations of "Viva Puerto Rico Libre," "Freedom to Puerto Rican POWs," and "No to Colonialism" written on the building walls are in sharp contrast with the underutilized gray factories and small walk-up houses surrounding the Center. The faces of several men and women — the FALN prisoners who founded the Center — hang on colorful poster boards on the walls of the building. The Juan Antonio Corretjer Puerto Rican Cultural Center is named after a celebrated Puerto Rican poet, activist, and member of Puerto Rico's Nationalist Party from the 1930s through the 1950s. The Cultural Center building was a Walgreen's photo lab before being rehabilitated in 1976 by a group of community activists who were advocates of Puerto Rico's independence from the United States. The hard work that transformed a deteriorated building into a comfortable, welcoming place is a source of great pride to the community.

The atmosphere of the Cultural Center is one of constant motion; people of all ages walking up and down the stairs, answering phones, calling each other out. The feeling that everybody knows each other well, combined with a sense of purposefulness in the building, evokes the need to be "doing something" or "working on something" at all times, as if a sign were hanging by the entrance door stating, "no lounging allowed beyond this point." In fact, most members of the Cultural Center spend long evenings and most weekends in this building — planning activities, printing flyers, designing projects, writing grants, cleaning and repairing, and even doing "overnight security" shifts to make sure the Center is always attended.

Approximately fifty or sixty staff and twice as many project participants — not including the residents who receive occasional services or attend specific activities (e.g., a museum exhibit, health clinic orientations, a City Hall demonstration) — constitute the regular members of the Cultural Center. Most members, barrio residents, and youth who participate in the Center's projects live the daily torments of poverty, which serve as an unfortunate common bond among them.

The projects sponsored by the Cultural Center have emerged as specific needs have arisen in the community, rather than according to a planned strategy. For instance, the National Committee to Free the Puerto Rican Political Prisoners (NC) was founded to guide the campaign to liberate five nationalists, who were granted amnesty in 1979. Most recently, the NC has continued its efforts to gain amnesty for the fifteen Puerto Rican men and women — including the founders of the Cultural Center — still being held in U.S. federal penitentiaries.

The high incidence of HIV and AIDS in the Puerto Rican community, and the funding available for AIDS education, research, and treatment, led to the creation of the Center's Vida/SIDA health education program. Similarly, the need for safe child care prompted the development of the Consuelo Lee Corretjer Child Care Center. The Family Learning Center (FLC) represents a grassroots effort to involve parents in their children's education, and to advance their own educational development by pursuing high school degrees and job training. When the Chicago Park District refused to place a statue of nationalist leader Pedro Albizu Campos in Humboldt Park, the Center founded the Pedro Albizu Campos Museum of Puerto Rican History and Culture to house the statue. In an effort to "Puerto Ricanize" Division Street and deter further displacement of Puerto Ricans out of Humboldt Park, the Cultural Center created the BOHIO housing cooperative and bought three buildings in the Division Street area, one of which houses the Borikén Bakery and Café. These buildings are increasingly desirable real estate areas.

Awareness of nationalist Puerto Rican history and notions of "community building" are transmitted through popular education and social service programs aimed at high-risk students in Humboldt Park. One of the oldest and best-established projects of the Cultural Center is the Pedro Albizu Campos High School (PACHS), an alternative Puerto Rican high school. PACHS illustrates the intersection of popular education and community building in a nationalist context, and how learning among at-risk Puerto Rican youth takes place in controversial political settings.

Founded a year before the Cultural Center, PACHS — or "la Escuelita," as it is affectionately known — was created by a group of teachers and eleven Puerto Rican students who had been expelled from Murphy Tulley High School (now called Roberto Clemente High School). As Cultural Center activists and students proudly narrate, these students were expelled after organizing several strikes demanding a more culturally sensitive curriculum for the predominantly Puerto Rican student body, and refusing to salute the American flag, a pro-independence act of political defiance.

When their petitions for educational reform — including bilingual education and Puerto Rican history classes — went unheard, the eleven student leaders and other community activists, most of whom advocated Puerto Rican independence and belonged to pro-independence groups in the 1970s, rented the basement of a Presbyterian church in West Town and held Puerto Rican history and Spanish classes there. Once the Cultural Center was rehabilitated by some of the same students and community members in 1976, the high school moved to its present location on the second floor of that building.

Most of the students who come to PACHS are escaping gang activity or have been expelled from public schools because of too many absences, poor grades, or disciplinary problems.[8] When they arrive at PACHS, these students are one step away from dropping out of school altogether, if they have not already done so. "These kids have had lots of discouraging experiences with schools in general, [and with] racist teachers. [They have] been put down a lot. . . . Some others just come here because they want a school that teaches Puerto Rican history and culture," said Elena Colón, who teaches a Women's Studies and Health class, does individual counseling, and is in charge of most administrative work at PACHS.

Through its affiliation with the Cultural Center's other programs and with other community organizations, PACHS provides resources and information on a variety of issues outside the academic curriculum, such as health-related, legal, psychological, and financial problems. The school's long waiting list indicates that it has become a desirable option for many young people and their families. Director Melvin Rodríguez explains the increasing popularity of PACHS: "Students who fill out applications learn about us through friends or because they've had family members who have come here. Parents talk to parents, students talk to other students. They are all saying positive things about what we do here. Also, people know more about us through the work we do in the community."

"If even one, just one, student stops coming to the school, drops out, we have all failed," Rodríguez once said in a teachers' meeting, when frustration with one particular student had escalated. "Mondays are the worst days because we haven't seen students in two days and a lot happens in their lives, especially over weekends," one of the teachers explained. On this day, one student had just found out she was pregnant and needed guidance, another one had been raped, and yet another one had been arrested for writing gang signs on a wall and his mother did not speak enough English to get him out of detention. Like most Cultural Center members, the PACHS teachers are second-generation Puerto Ricans born in Chicago or brought to the Midwest as children; some are the sons and daughters of early steel mill workers (Bensman & Lynch, 1988). They have strong ties to Chicago's Puerto Rican barrio, where they grew up and still live, and have longstanding social and kinship networks. Fifteen-year-old Mark Anthony Rodríguez, a PACHS student, powerfully articulates the physical safety, cultural awareness, and emotional sustenance la Escuelita provides:

> This escuelita is a family that cares and supports you and will always be there to give you advice when you need it. They care so much about our education. Teachers and students treat each other like a big family. We can feel safe coming to this school because no one will shoot or shank you because they assume you are gang related.

Students' stories are poignant. Isis, a senior attending the Family Learning Center, a program for teen mothers and middle-aged students, recalls the support she received: "Melvin [PACHS's director] took food, clothes, everything to us when our house burnt down. We had lost everything. People from here helped us a lot." Whenever attendance drops below 85 percent, teachers commit themselves to making sure that the missing students show up to school, even if that involves giving students wake-up calls, rides to school, or literally dragging them out of bed.

Early in the school's admissions process, potential students realize that la Escuelita, besides being an alternative to gang violence, also supports explicit political stands and has its own philosophy, as student José Vega describes:

> During the [entrance] interview, the teachers told me that Pedro Albizu Campos is a different school from other high schools. The reason was because the Escuelita had its own philosophy and a whole different environment from other schools. They also mentioned that the reason why this school exists is for the purpose of teaching and showing the youth about their culture, their past, their ancestors, and where we stand as Puerto Ricans in the world. Students attend here because they want to get away from the gang conflicts and want a better education where they feel safe.

Nationalist Narratives and Conceptualizations of "Struggle"

A wooden sign at the school's entrance reads, "Dr. Pedro Albizu Campos High School, Excellence in Teaching Award, 1986." The sign is a souvenir of an incident frequently remembered at the Cultural Center as part of "the struggle," an occasion when the school's academic excellence award was rescinded because of its political history. In 1985, the Council for American Private Education (CAPE) and the U.S. Department of Education selected Pedro Albizu Campos High School as one of the exemplary private schools of the year. Shortly after the high school was notified of its award, a local television station aired a news series interspersing shots of the school with those of the trials of FALN members, suggesting that the school was a poor choice for the award. In response, the award was temporarily withheld, and a second team of observers was sent to assess whether the high school actually deserved the award. The award was reinstated, but suddenly rescinded again just five hours before the school's graduation ceremony, where the award was to be celebrated. "Eventually, after having it taken back the second time, they said they did want to give it to us. That's when we said we didn't want it anymore," explained a PACHS teacher. Feeling that they nevertheless did deserve an award for educational excellence, teachers and students at PACHS inscribed their own award on the plaque that now stands at the entrance to the school.

"Some people refer to us as 'Those communists down the street,'" joked Armando Medina, a Cultural Center activist, "but when they come to us for services and get to know us, see what we do in the community, they understand what we're about." Many neighborhood residents recognize that the Center is one of the few places that offers viable and affordable alternatives in adult education, high school and infant programs, and health and housing counseling. Yet, they are also aware of the Center's political history, including its clashes with the FBI and support of the FALN.

At PACHS, activists and students tell about the day in 1983 when the FBI raided the Center and apprehended its founders. At 5 A.M., over fifty FBI agents wearing black jumpsuits and raid gear marked "FBI" entered the Puerto Rican Cultural Center, alongside Chicago police officers and members of the Illinois Law Enforcement division. Astonished neighbors and students working in summer programs stood outside the building while the FBI searched for evidence that linked other Cultural Center activists to the FALN members. None was found, but substantial damage was done to the computer equipment and the Center's archives. As one informant recalls:

> [When] the FBI raided the building they caused a lot of damage. We thought we'd have to close down, but the community helped out in rebuilding the place. In the first day alone, we collected $3,000 through fundraising. Eventually we raised $15,000 among the people of West Town.

This has become one of the most repeated stories about the Center's history, and Cultural Center activists still recall the impact of the incarceration of the FALN members on neighborhood life. Although no evidence was found, the school and the Cultural Center were listed as sites searched for terrorist activity, which colored the community's perception of the Center for a long time thereafter.

The controversy around these political prisoners — were they heroes of the Puerto Rican independence movement or terrorists unappreciative of the United States' generosity toward Puerto Rico? — is central to militant politics and social activism in Chicago's Puerto Rican community. While the Center avidly portrays the political prisoners as heroes, this image is contested by the prisoners' opponents. Yet other residents advocate for the prisoners, stating that "they have been in prison too long." Their statements offer humanitarian rather than political reasons for their support; still others perceive this campaign and the activists as "dated," leftovers from the 1960s (Fernández, 1994).

Perceptions of the political prisoners are mixed, conflictive, and provocative. Opponents of the prisoners perceived them as terrorists who brought unwelcome violence to the community and created a bad reputation for all Puerto Ricans, who were considered "trouble" by surveillance agents. In contrast, the prisoners' supporters and barrio residents, who remember the prisoners as "one of us" and as cherished community activists, perceive the prisioners' actions as heroism, nationalism, and authenticity.

One of the most telling narratives about the prisoners was articulated by Doña Luz, the grandmother and legal guardian of Zaida, a troubled and impoverished PACHS student. Doña Luz and Zaida's house is on the street that marks the gang warfare zone between the Cobras and the rival Latin Kings gang. The bare cement floor of Doña Luz's house oddly contrasts with the ornate religious images on the walls. The pungent smell of the uncollected dumpster near the house infiltrates the tiny living room on a humid summer afternoon.

"I've had to raise this kid all alone," said Doña Luz, a tired, dark-skinned Puerto Rican woman in her late fifties, pointing to Zaida, who sits quietly listening. Then, in a voice impregnated with contained emotion, Doña Luz added:

> That's why I wanted her to go to la Escuelita [PACHS], because my own sons went there, and I'm always grateful for that opportunity. I remember how I used to cook for school activities back then [1970s and 1980s]. But, it's not the same . . . since Alejandrina [Torres, one of the prisoners] has been gone [to prison]. It's not the same. She used to come here all the time, helped my sons. She helped us so much. . . . She helped everyone so much.

Doña Luz sees Alejandrina as a "savior" of sorts, similar to those on her house's walls, a woman who acted as a sacred mediator for the poor. Doña Luz remembers Alejandrina for her efforts in community building and her humanitarian commitment to barrio residents.

In Humboldt Park, narratives and myths around the FALN members abound and are at the center of both barrio mobilization and conflict. As Lancaster (1988) argues, "Once told, these tales are nothing; recited a thousand times, they become folklore, myth, collective representation . . . they ultimately pass into mnemonic devices of class consciousness, the guideposts and blueprints of future praxis" (p. 133).

The teaching award incident and FBI raid serve as narratives that illustrate, as one teacher commented, "the significance of terms like 'struggle,' 'resistance,' and the 'sacrifices' of standing by one's beliefs." These narratives, along with the numerous public demonstrations on behalf of the FALN prisoners, against educational budget cuts and media misrepresentations of Puerto Ricans, create unique definitions of struggle. As Carmencita Martínez, an eighteen-year-old PACHS student, recalls:

> In my second year [at PACHS], all I did was experience things that were related to school. My first experience was when I went to protest with the school. We were protesting for the Puerto Rican POWs. We want them free! It was good. These protests have taught me that no matter what you want, you should always stand up for your rights. It showed me that if you want something you have to go out there and get it. It ain't going to be easy, but you will get it.

Hence, the politics behind education and community projects becomes explicit, implicitly encouraging students and parents to adopt these politics in their involvement with community projects.

While the Cultural Center values ideas of struggle and community building as signs of strength and resilience, for many students struggle implies daily dangers, poverty, and sacrifices that create conflictive attitudes toward the community-building process. For instance, Vanessa Acosta, a bright young woman who has struggled with poverty, gang activity, and sexual abuse, wrote in a class paper that she hoped to "get an education so that I can get my parents a house outside this community."

Nonetheless, notions of "giving back" are also solidified at PACHS and other projects of the Center. As Diana Sánchez, an upbeat seventeen-year-old PACHS student, powerfully conveys:

> I came [to PACHS] with very little knowledge about my people, my community, and my history. But I came out with enough to give people a good argument, and to know what I am talking about. I chose to pursue my college education and major in criminal justice. I would like to come back someday and help my people, and of course my Escuelita. In the four years that I have been here, we have struggled as a family to keep this school open, and we have luckily succeeded. If I had a wish, I would wish that the students, teachers, and staff would never have to struggle again.

Like Vanessa and Diana, students appreciate the process of community building in addressing some of their immediate social needs. However, in the long term, these younger Puerto Ricans hope to pursue mainstream mobility routes, such as higher education, to improve their socioeconomic condition and be able to move out of or give back to Humboldt Park.

For many Cultural Center members of all ages, joining the PRCC marked a personal transformation or a raised political awareness — a *concientización,* as PACHS director Rodríguez describes the process — that also contributed to a heightened sense of their Puerto Ricanness and ethno-nationalist pride. PRCC activists associate involvement at the Center with an enhanced sense of Puerto Ricanness through the forging of an ideological identity grounded on a knowledge of nationalist Puerto Rican history, literature, symbols, and neighborhood activism. Juan González, a sixteen-year-old PACHS student, explains:

> What I really liked [my freshman year at PACHS] was when the school took a trip to Colorado. On that very same day we marched for the Puerto Rican Prisoners of War. We marched for Oscar López; he was going to be transferred to a maximum[security] prison called Florence, where if you get locked up you can't associate with any prisoners. I thought that was messed up.
>
> I know if I would have gone to another school, I wouldn't have made it this far [to graduation]. . . . I like this school because they teach you about your heritage, and when you learn about yourself and where you come from, you would be so amazed that you'd like to learn more. The only thing I can say now is I'm proud to be a Puertorriqueño, not to mention, I feel very good knowing two languages.
>
> I'm going to miss this school a whole lot. . . . You will not find another school like this one. I like this school because it helps teenagers realize that gangs aren't the only option there is in this world. Some of the students that come to this school work with Vida/SIDA; they become peer educators. They go out into the community, and sometimes they give out condoms to people. The Latinos in the Humboldt Park community have the highest rate of having AIDS. That's why we go out into our community to help Latinos and prevent them from getting the disease.

Students learn firsthand that they have skills valuable to their community by participating in numerous community-wide activities — from producing flyers announcing community events, to creating floats or artwork, to recruiting sponsors for particular events and conceptualizing projects. Some of the events, like the Boricua Festival, "el Desfile del Pueblo," and the Pedro Albizu Campos Puerto Rican Week, take place once a year, while others (e.g., Vida/SIDA peer counseling and workshops) are ongoing throughout the school year. Like Juan González, other PACHS youth perceive schooling as a conglomerate of interconnected activities, which encourage community building, sociohistoric awareness, and enhanced ethno-political identity. These provide a more immediate stage on which to enact their notions of struggle.

Puertorriqueñidad and Boundaries: The "Unity" Class

At PACHS, like in other nationalist projects sponsored by the Cultural Center, Puerto Ricanness is the leading factor in determining the level of access a participant is allowed. Support for (or at least sympathy with) the Center's political visions is perhaps a close second. Asked to become director of the school after just one year of teaching, Melvin Rodríguez recalls: "There were people better qualified than I was, but they were not Puerto Rican. I had the most important qualification: being Puerto Rican." For many of the Center's activists, the Puerto Rican independence movement and the community work at the Center legitimizes Puerto Ricanness as an ideological identity premised on nationality-based alliances, even when this requires the avoidance of more inclusive multicultural or pan-ethnic identities such as "Latinos," "Hispanos," or "minorities."

"I would like to have more Puerto Rican teachers, but some people don't want to work here. The pay is too low or they don't believe in the political work," commented an activist, who stressed the need to create a "unified all-Puerto Rican front" among teachers in the school to make sure that "Whites don't follow on their natural tendency to take over." Elena, another PACHS teacher and administrator, echoes this sentiment: "As colonized people, we have a tendency to go to the White faces for guidance. And the White faces have a tendency to want to take over. In this school, White people are challenged with a different power structure, which places Puerto Ricans in charge."

The White teachers who have been at the high school the longest accept, and even understand, the boundaries they are not supposed to transgress by virtue of their not being Puerto Rican. The recent arrivals, however, wrestle with the fact that they are expected to remain at the margin of the school and the neighborhood issues discussed in all-Puerto Rican spaces, like the Unity for Social Analysis class.

The Unity for Social Analysis class, or "Unity," as this town meeting-style class is commonly known, is one of the most obvious "Puerto Rican spaces" at PACHS. This is a class in which Puerto Rican students and teachers talk about issues affecting the school and neighborhood, resolve conflicts, and plan activities. The fifty Puerto Rican students and five teachers sit in a circle in the basement cafeteria. White Americans, even those who have been teaching at PACHS for years, do not attend Unity unless invited in advance. During the academic year of my fieldwork, none of the White teachers was invited and a Mexican female teacher was invited once.

Many Unity gatherings aim to address the social conditions affecting all Humboldt Park youth. When Miguelito, a sixteen-year-old boy with severe learning disabilities and incredible mechanical skills, pulled a knife on Michelle, a first-year student, the question of whether Miguelito should remain at PACHS was discussed in Unity. In a particularly moving Unity session, students expressed their concern for Miguelito's behavior. Daniel Pérez, a senior whose broad smile shatters his tough-guy appearance, analyzed the situation: "Miguelito, I know you have a lot of anger in you, but we're like a family here. We're here to help you. In this school. With Melvin and the teachers. Not out there in the streets." A general nod indicated other students' agreement with Daniel's words, which echoed one of the phrases the school adopted from Consuelo Lee Corretjer — "Live and Help to Live." The students themselves decided that Miguelito should stay in the school, seek counseling, apologize to Michelle, and, by Michelle's request, not even go near her for a while. Melissa Lebrón, a fifteen-year-old PACHS student, comments on this unique aspect of the Unity class:

> One thing that I found very weird was "Unity" class. I had never heard about a class like this before. Unity is a class where you could bring up issues or problems that you have with a student or teacher. I will never forget this school. This school means a lot to me. If it wasn't for this school on this planet, I think I would've been a dropout and doing nothing with my life.

Unity also serves to engage Puerto Rican students and teachers in the political life of the Puerto Rican community. Political and social discussions in Unity transcend the limits of Humboldt Park; they revolve around demonstrations against federal cuts in education, letter-writing campaigns to free the Puerto Rican political prisoners, and planning neighborhood festivals and fundraisers. Abstract ideas such as struggle, liberation, sacrifice, and Puerto Rican culture often shape the discourse of the Unity class. This is demonstrated by the comments of PACHS students Haydée Ramos and Guillermo Morales. Haydée states:

> Leaving this school [after graduating] will leave me with memories like Unity, a class where everyone sat in a circle and discussed the problems affecting the school, community, teachers, and students. One of the biggest struggles in and out of Unity is the release of the prisoners of war, POW. Activities like Paseo Boricua, Fiesta Boricua, Puerto Rican Parade were also planned in and out of the Unity class. As I graduate from my Escuelita, I will proceed with my education by attending Northeastern [Illinois] University and study[ing] for my social work

> degree. I chose social work because as a Puerto Rican woman I want to help my Latino community [lead] a successful life.

Guillermo comments similarly:

> I see that [at PACHS] we do a lot of things with the few resources we have. I learned about Puerto Rican history. I see our prisoners of war as Puerto Rican heroes, and I thank them for having the courage to give up their own freedom for la Patria. I will never forget Unity class. The times we used to just sit together in a circle and joke around will never go away.

Understandings of Puerto Ricanness among Cultural Center activists are complex. The Center implicitly connects Puerto Rican "authenticity" to political ideology. Thus, a pro-independence Puerto Rican is somehow perceived as "more Puerto Rican" than a pro-statehood Puerto Rican. Other aspects that designate a "real Puerto Rican" are even more rigid, based on Spanish-language mastery and place of birth, similar to those constructions of "Otherness" harbored by Puerto Rico's elite (Díaz-Quinoñes, 1993).

The same essentialism that Chatterjee (1993), Said (1978), and many authors of autobiographical Puerto Rican literature (e.g., Esteves, 1980, 1984; Laviera, 1981, 1985; Piñero, 1980; Thomas, 1967) magnificently articulate is described by Díaz-Quiñones:

> It is very easy to fall into the same essentialism and orientalism of the imperial gaze, in the name of "national" identity. . . . Nationalist discourse negates the cultural superiority of the imperial power, but often appropriates the pretended occidental rationality and turns it into discourse of power. The essentialist, exclusionary thought persists. The judges continue to be the judges, impeccable. (1993, p. 80; translated by author)

Old and young activists alike draw strong connections between ethnic identity and political militancy. For many second- and third-generation Chicago Puerto Ricans, knowledge of Puerto Rican history, mythology, and literature is associated with "being a real Puerto Rican."[9] For these activists, the Center is a catalyst for personal and political transformations, as well as a vehicle to earn cultural authenticity. Many authors (Klor de Alva, 1988; Oboler, 1995; Safa, 1988; Sánchez-Korrol, 1988) have argued that the Latino label homogenizes the histories, migrations, and socioeconomic characteristics of the individual Latino groups. These internal distinctions are essential to assess the specific needs and challenges each nationality-based group, like the grassroots activists in Humboldt Park, faces. As Oboler argues,

> Yet, it was precisely at this point [in the Mexican American/Chicano and Puerto Rican movements of the civil rights era] that the term "Hispanic" began to be heard. Once again, the racial, class, and gender heterogeneity and the very real ideological differences within their respective communities were to be deemphasized. At the same time, it served to obscure the specific historical roots of each group's respective experiences in the United States. In other words, both

> in a sense were once again thrown into invisibility, although this time under an umbrella term ostensibly aimed at strengthening awareness of "ethnic diversity" within the "national community."(1995, pp. 78–79)

In Chicago, white-collar Puerto Ricans ally as "Hispanics" or "Latinos" through their occupational affiliations, while barrio groups reject pan-ethnic labels and direct their services to specific local needs. In fact, many barrio activists point to "the problem of multiculturalism" and, in the case of Puerto Rican nationalist activists, tailor their social services to Puerto Ricans by resurrecting images of a Puerto Rican militant past. While the techniques embraced in Unity — developing conflict resolution skills, encouraging self-criticism, opening communication channels, defining a support system, etc. — are perhaps not unique to PACHS, one of the main goals of these biweekly gatherings consists of "creating a Puerto Rican space," grounded on notions of Puerto Ricanness as the main binding force. Unity is premised on nationalist understandings of Puerto Ricanness as the primary bond between the Cultural Center members, including PACHS teachers and students and the surrounding Puerto Rican neighbors.

Clemente High School: Educational Reform, Political Conflicts, and "Los Profesionales"

Cultural Center activists do not limit their community involvement and notions of struggle to the multiple projects the Center sponsors in Humboldt Park/ West Town. While primarily pro-independence, supporters of the Center — many of whom have extensive insight into areas of popular education, gang activity, housing issues, and other social services — are also involved in mainstream local institutions. Because these activists understand their sociopolitical commitment in light of youth and neighborhood development, many of them have actually become involved in other key (predominantly Puerto Rican) spaces, such as Clemente High School. In fact, some of the best Clemente High School teachers (those evaluated by students and coworkers as "superior") are sympathizers, volunteers, or core members of the Center. These teachers are familiar with successful educational alternatives through their connection with Center-sponsored programs like PACHS and its adult equivalent, the Family Learning Center.

Clemente High School, the third-largest high school in Chicago, is located at the easternmost end of the main commercial Puerto Rican area on Division Street. Most Puerto Ricans who grew up in West Town and Humboldt Park attended Clemente High School, and a large percentage of the student body is still Puerto Rican (1,281 of its 2,373 students and 29 of its 153 teachers are Latino), despite a changing population in recent years. A discussion of Clemente High School is significant here because the building marks a physical space in which Puerto Rican concentration is high, and because Clemente

High School is a space in which intergenerational and interorganizational barrio concerns are articulated (Cruz, 1997; Padilla, 1987).

The polemic at Clemente High School can best be understood as a conflict between two broad groups: the Cultural Center's pro-independence activists, who are largely from working-class or working-poor backgrounds, on the one hand, and a small group of powerful white-collar Latinos, including pro-statehood and conservative commonwealth Puerto Ricans, on the other. At the neighborhood level, these political affiliations are embodied in the specific ward aldermen and congressmen each group supports.[10] Each group perceives Humboldt Park and the urban development projects in a different light. Many of the white-collar professionals are involved in real estate and would like to capitalize on the recent interest White artists and yuppies have demonstrated in the area. The grassroots activists, by contrast, have drawn up concrete agendas to rehabilitate buildings, prevent further Puerto Rican displacement, and to mark the barrio as Puerto Rican.

Hence, divergent political ideologies vis-à-vis the status of Puerto Rico and local politicians in Humboldt Park, coupled with the posture toward urban barrio development agendas, partially account for the antagonism between grassroots activists and some white-collar professionals. The white-collar professionals distinguish themselves from pro-independence activists, whom they consider "terrorists," by focusing on their more mainstream political ideologies as "law-abiding citizens." The grassroots activists, by contrast, draw upon their class-based identity as *la gente pobre* (the poor people) — rather than the white-collar, suburban identity of *los profesionales*, as these activists refer to their opponents — to create solidarity among Humboldt Park residents.

As many grassroots activists explained in their interviews, los profesionales are the tiny minority of lawyers, city officials, real estate agents, and other corporate professionals who advocate traditional mobility routes, like the ones they themselves followed. For many of them, the American Dream worked. They lived through the process of earning professional degrees, attaining upwardly mobile corporate jobs, and moving to the suburbs to avoid their painful associations with barrio life. Many of these people do not live in the barrio, though they grew up in Humboldt Park. Some of these Puerto Rican professionals fail to address the different socioeconomic contexts faced by younger generations, or the employment venues provided by nationality-based barrio institutions (Cruz, 1997). Moreover, a desire to raise real estate prices and appropriate PRCC-owned buildings located in increasingly desirable areas have also been cited as reasons to attack the Cultural Center (Cruz, 1997; Geovannis, 1998).

Los profesionales are not an abstract contingency, as the emergence of *El Pito* ("the whistle") shows. *El Pito*, a clandestine newsletter published by Cultural Center opponents and distributed throughout the neighborhood, aims to discredit nationalist activists. The newsletter consists of personal attacks on barrio activists who are openly pro-independence and on supporters of Congressman Gutiérrez and Alderman Billy Ocasio (both considered *macheteros*— a historical term for militant nationalists — by their opponents).

These political postures become concrete in the debates around Clemente High School reform, which partially shifted school governance away from the centralized Downtown Board of Education and into the hands of neighborhood activists, parents, and students. In the 1980s, Chicago underwent a citywide reform that aimed to decentralize the control of schools, passing it to local decisionmaking councils. Discretionary funds were allocated to participating public schools, which were encouraged to develop local school councils to administer these funds. Clemente's local school council, called the School Reform Council, was composed of parents, students, barrio residents, and activists in Humboldt Park. Clemente's local school council outlined the special services to parents, students, and the community at large on which it would spend the discretionary funds. The elements of the reform were summarized in four main categories: 1) awareness of Puerto Rican history; 2) socioeconomic development strategies for the school community and neighborhood (e.g., promoting notions of "self-sufficiency," institutional autonomy, grassroots-driven urban renewal projects); 3) emphasis on individual commitment to the community and activism through hands-on involvement (e.g., parents' involvement in the school); and 4) enhancing cultural pride through artistic presentations, conferences, museum exhibits, and so on. The Clemente School Reform Council undoubtedly shared community development values harbored by grassroots activists, since many of these activists were involved in the conceptual and implementational aspects of the reform. This pro-independence presence is noticed (and even praised) by the parents of many Clemente High School students.

Alma Juncos is the mother of three adolescent sons and a parent aide at Clemente High School. Alma learned of the Cultural Center through her son's involvement in Son Del Barrio, a popular student Salsa band, which is led by Pedro Vidal, a Puerto Rican man in his early thirties and a core member of the Center. Having moved from Puerto Rico to Chicago in the mid-1980s, Alma mentioned that she noticed a much higher independentista presence in Chicago than in her hometown in Puerto Rico. When asked to explain further, Alma replied:

> Well, quite frankly, I don't know [why there are so many independentistas]. But, I know there are a lot of them. I'll tell you one thing. For what I've seen, I've seen that independentista people help . . . and work. They are hard workers. And they create projects for the community. For instance, somebody told me, "Uff, Clemente . . . that's bad in there, because all the teachers are independentistas." And I tell them, "Well, if they are independentistas . . . they still are good people." Because I have no complaints about the teachers. And, if they are, that's their right. But I've seen that they strive, struggle. They are hard working. . . . I've noticed something. Let me tell you. The people whom I think are independentistas care for the wellbeing of Puerto Ricans. I've seen that. They want the

well-being of Puerto Ricans. And they help their own. If a community exists here, it's because of them.

Like other Clemente High School parents, Alma Juncos is not directly involved in the Cultural Center, other than through the work she does as a parent participant in the Clemente school reform. Nonetheless, like many other Humboldt Park residents, Alma has friends or relatives who have participated in programs sponsored by the Center, and she recognizes that the nationalist activists advocate for barrio Puerto Ricans. This echoes Justino Ramírez, an ASPIRA worker,[11] "who points to his ironic predicament as a pro-statehooder who finds himself working alongside nationalists because they [the nationalists] are the ones involved in community work here . . . the ones who have a vision and an actual understanding of the community's needs."

Many Humboldt Park residents and social service agencies consider the Clemente reform a pivotal point in the Center's history, since "the cause of Puerto Rican independence" acquired grounding on the local issues affecting the community. Since Center members have unsurpassed levels of neighborhood activism and are experienced in the educational field — having designed and implemented highly successful youth and adult education programs — their participation is especially noticeable in the ideological bases of the Clemente school reform. Under the banner of "Live and Help to Live," a variety of community projects have been developed at Clemente High School.

The Clemente High School houses satellite programs for several Puerto Rican community agencies, such as ASPIRA's Parents Institute,[12] Vida/ SIDA's AIDS education clinic, etc. These programs, aimed at serving its students and their parents in the neighborhood, bring together white-collar workers at not-for-profit organizations, barrio residents, nationalist activists, local politicians, and Puerto Rican high school students.

In addition to opening Clemente High School to the community through cultural events and emphasizing parental autonomy through the Parents Institute, the reform included programs to raise sociohistorical awareness among the students. Among the projects the PRCC activists have helped create are painting murals of Puerto Rican historical figures; recording a CD of music with social messages by the Son Del Barrio salsa band; a proliferation of self-reflective classes based on autobiographical writing by students; and a trip to Madre Isla, a coffee plantation in a small mountain town of Puerto Rico run by a grassroots cooperative.

Since Clemente is one of the few local institutions that receives significant state funds, the ways in which the local school council used the funds were closely monitored by white-collar professionals, some of whom disapproved of how the council used the monies. White-collar real estate professionals, city officials, and the media became the active outside critics of school reform and the School Reform Council.

On a misty June morning, Roberto Clemente High School's administrators called a press conference to respond to a cover-page article that had appeared the previous day in the *Chicago Sun-Times*, entitled "Public School's 'Pathetic' Use of Poverty Funds" (1995). The article condemned the Clemente School Reform Council's use of Chapter I funds to give parents part-time jobs (through the Parents Institute); to finance student trips outside the country (to Puerto Rico and Mexico); to open a legal clinic to advise students and parents on migration-related issues, and drug and gang cases; and to hire two out-of-state consultants to develop a "culturally sensitive" curriculum. "Funds earmarked for the education of poor children had, on this account, been thwarted," the article claimed. Then it pointed out that the two consultants hired "have close links to the Puerto Rican pro-Independence Movement" and that "the funds also were used to establish satellites for Clemente [High School] at the Pedro Albizu Campos School and Cultural Center — two Chicago pro-Puerto Rican Independence institutions." The article ends by noting that "the FBI would not say whether it is investigating the local school council's spending" (p. 6).

Several issues, recurrent in most social reform efforts in Humboldt Park, are illuminated in the heated disagreements over Clemente High School reform as played out in subsequent press conferences, articles, and community meetings. First, the reform made Clemente High School into an important community space, where essential sociopolitical networks develop and ideas of "community building" are forged. Given its strategic location at the heart of the Puerto Rican commercial strip on Division Street and being one of the few significant connections between the local neighborhood and the city government, Clemente High School is perceived as "a Puerto Rican space" that is key to the educational and occupational advancement of barrio youths and residents in general. Efforts aimed at "creating a better Puerto Rican community" directly place Clemente High School at its center. Because of this, the possibility of turning Clemente into an elite magnet school (in light of the changing ethnic composition and gentrification in Humboldt Park/West Town) is resisted and regarded with suspicion by the community (Cruz, 1997).

Second, the Clemente High School reform conflict points to the class and occupational dimensions of political conflict among Puerto Rican leaders in the Chicago barrio. Attacks on Clemente High are perceived by neighborhood residents and activists as attacks on the Puerto Rican community, as well as on the community-building efforts of la gente pobre.

Distinctions between los profesionales and la gente pobre highlight class and occupational divisions. These distinctions are also based on a sense of commitment to Humboldt Park, which is associated with particular political stands vis-à-vis the status of Puerto Rico (i.e., the notion that independentista activists are more committed to the community). Because of its involvement in the Clemente High School reform, the Center became more visible, and heated attacks came from corporate Puerto Rican pro-statehood and pro-commonwealth professionals. Right after the press conference in June 1995, discussions occurred about who the author of the article was and who the people quoted in it were. "That [article] was initiated by los profesionales again!" expressed a furious Esteban López, a controversial nationalist leader and director of the Center. Whenever he mentions los profesionales, López never names names, yet other activists, parents, and students seem to know who he means.

Third, the Clemente High School conflict raises issues of "interventionism" around the question of whom the barrio residents and activists perceive as "legitimately" able to criticize the efforts of la gente pobre. As an informant commented, "It's not so much what is said about us, but who is saying it." Humboldt Park activists challenged those outsiders who criticized efforts without actively engaging in neighborhood projects, with the idea that "if you're not part of the solution, you're part of the problem." The sensitivity to negative media reactions and to comments by nonbarrio residents — particularly non–Puerto Ricans or Puerto Ricans perceived as lacking community commitment — is enormous in Humboldt Park.

In an essay entitled "They're at It Again!" Josslyn Laracuente, a sixteen-year-old PACHS student, echoes the sentiment of Puerto Rican youth whose lives have been transformed by the very activists under attack:

> I can't believe the school is still being attacked. People fear what they don't understand, people are afraid of change. People are just blinded by the money they have, they think they could buy everything they see. But you know what, they could take our homes, push us out, but they will never, never break our spirits, or change the reason that we are Puerto Ricans, so as much as they try we will never lose and they will never win.

Media representations of Humboldt Park activism overlook the achievement at Clemente High School in both standardized test scores and the dropout rate. The theme of a Son Del Barrio song — "los profesionales come from the outside to talk about our school; looking at the negative but never at the positive" — echoes Puerto Rican youths' attitudes toward these media depictions (Integrity, 1997). The polemic on Clemente High School and on the reform is seen as an attack on the efforts of la gente pobre, as well as on Puerto Ricanness. However, as distinctions between Puerto Ricans based on class, activism, place of residence, and political stand are compounded with local struggles over positions and resources, intragroup boundaries become more complex. Puerto Ricanness among activists is not the same when one looks into Puerto Ricanness in the corporate or real estate sectors. Among activists, nationalist ideologies create the space for community building, but this space is constantly being ideologically and financially challenged.

Conclusion

Some of the key philosophical components of the Center are a politicized cultural identity grounded in an awareness of alternative/militant Puerto Rican history, and a positioning of the self in a global sociohistorical context. Recognizing the obstacles, this requires a constant struggle for survival (resistance, unity, autonomy, and agency). These philosophical components also permeate other community forums in which the Center activists are involved, such as the Clemente School Reform Council. These politics and their potentially positive effects on disengaged Puerto Rican students merit further ethnographic and theoretical examinations. By becoming acquainted with political protest strategies and neighborhood politics, and by developing a critical appraisal of socioeconomic opportunity structures, these students gain new insights into their own predicaments and generate a unique sense of possibility.

Education research has overlooked the strong underlying currents that shape ethnoracial educational settings. Politics and local neighborhood contexts are inseparable from schooling. When these political undercurrents are used to heal students' sense of powerlessness and despair, they deserve attention. Regardless of one's political stand, the accomplishments of nationalist activists, precisely because of the explicitly political visions that ground their commitment, are undeniable.

Pedro Albizu Campos's words, *La patria es valor y sacrificio* ("The fatherland is valor and sacrifice"), appear on a framed poster at the PACHS as a reminder of the intersections of community activism and Puerto Rican nationalism. For Chicago's Puerto Rican activists, nationalist history is not a "history of defeat" (Díaz-Quiñones, 1993), but a history of continuous struggle, community building, and educational alternatives. In addition to recognizing the process by which an abandoned discourse regains pertinence, as well as the discursive transformations of a "migrant" Puerto Rican nationalism, it is essential to examine the concrete social, economic, and political shapes that these forms of politicization and historicization take in U.S. Puerto Rican barrios.

Nationalism is indiscriminately considered a negative term in much Western literature, since many violent acts have been committed in the name of nationalist integration. Grassroots activists in Humboldt Park hesitate to embrace a nationalist label, not because they feel the label does not apply to them, but because they are aware of the negative connotations nationalism has in contemporary literature.[13]

In Puerto Rico, debates over nationalism are often associated with the university intellectual elite. In Chicago, however, these debates take place at the grassroots level. Nationalism is not only an intellectual ideology, but also a concrete vehicle for social reform among some barrio activists. As Sánchez (1994) comments, "to be a nationalist in the island involves secret prestige, but to be a nationalist in New York involves public hostility" (p. 15). And, while the meaning attributed to being a nationalist in Puerto Rico and being one in the United States is different, being a nationalist in the U.S. Puerto Rican community of Chicago is also perceived as the ultimate "proof" of cultural authenticity — in particular, when measures such as place of birth and Spanish language aim to challenge one's nationalist identity.[14]

As illustrated by the Clemente High School conflicts, nationalist projects experience heated opposition, mostly from nonbarrio Puerto Rican residents, city officials, white-collar professionals, and business or real estate people. However, to the many community residents who receive social services provided by nationalist activists, and for the thousands of Puerto Rican youth who learn firsthand their impact on the community-building process, *los nacionalistas son los únicos que de verdad se preocupan por los suyos* ["the nationalists are the only ones who truly care about their own people"].

Nearly two years after the end of my fieldwork, the Cultural Center activists were once again the source of heated conflict among mainstream media and opponents of pro-independence Puerto Rican politics. As seen in this article, this is not the first time that Clemente High School has been challenged for its administration of Chapter I funds. However, questions around Clemente High School's funding become secondary to the anti-independentista overtones of the articles. Continual reference to the political ideologies and kinship networks of several Clemente High School teachers and administrators — in particular, the connection between these teachers and FALN prisoners — occupy center stage.

"The manufactured crimes at Clemente High School are being used by the School Reform Board to say, 'Look, we need to have all the authority downtown,'" warned Sheila Castillo, director of the Chicago Association of Local Schools Council (Cruz, 1997, p. 5). Grassroots groups like the Center have withstood criticism by the mainstream media and anti-independentista factions. Opponents of the nationalist activists have traditionally focused on the group's controversial politics and critical view of history, while ignoring its outstanding educational and community achievements.

Carmencita Martínez, a charismatic seventeen-year-old student at Pedro Albizu Campos High School, describes the impact of the nationalist alternative education program on her life. In a poignant autobiographical essay, like many others published in local publications, Carmencita narrates her life trajectory, from a six-year-old living in the dumpsters (quite literally) to a hopeful high school graduate. She points to PACHS's role in her life:

> The porch [where Carmencita and her family slept during their early years in Chicago] was filthy. It had dirty diapers everywhere. Some rats and the garbage were right next to us. There were times when one of my brothers or I had to stay up all night and watch, making sure the rats wouldn't bite any of us. . . . In the morning when we got up, we would have nothing to eat. My older brother and I had to go around the neighborhood and see what we could find. Sometimes we got lucky. There was a lady who would give my brother and I food. My mom couldn't see us live like that anymore, so she had to give my older brother and I away. She stayed with the two younger kids. But she couldn't live without us. One day she got up and decided to apply for public aid. As soon as she got her money, she found an apartment and got us back together. Our apartment didn't have any light, gas, food, or windows, but we lived there. We ate peanut butter

> all day and drank powder milk that the church would give us. All we had in the apartment was a chair and a curtain. . . . The school I attend now [PACHS] is helping me get where I want to go, and they're giving me all the hope and support I need.

In a community considered among the poorest of the poor, where Puerto Rican youth and barrio residents continue to drop out of high school, join gangs, and experience the most inhuman consequences of poverty, any successful social initiative must be considered carefully. The powerful presence of nationalist or pro-independence activism in Humboldt Park is undeniable. Equally undeniable is the sense of hope and possibility that students and barrio residents, like the ones who appear in this article, experience at Pedro Albizu Campos High School and other community development programs sponsored by nationalist activists in Humboldt Park.

Notes

1. Elsewhere in this article, pseudonyms are used in compliance with informants' wishes as expressed at the time of the interviews. The names of the young people quoted here are their real names. Many of them wanted to be recognized for their participation and some actually published the autobiographical writing that appears in this article in school yearbooks and local newsletters.
2. Saul Alinsky was a Chicago community organizer who later created the Urban Institute for Community Organizations. In the 1960s, he and his followers aimed to teach organizing skills/techniques to residents of marginalized Chicago neighborhoods so that they could become grassroots organizers.
3. Like Black militants and other sectors of the New Left (Anderson & George, 1986; Evans, 1979), many Puerto Rican activists in Chicago suffered the surveillance and harassment of FBI, CIA, and Defense Department agents and infiltrators. Personal files recorded Puerto Rican barrio residents' activism and "communist tendencies" in the most meticulous ways (see Padilla, 1987). This charge insinuates that those charged were active in the planning and execution of these bombings.
4. The impact of the FALN on the lives of barrio residents has been neglected in studies that focus on the structure, history, and motives behind these groups (Fernández, 1994; Zwerman, 1995). Yet, attitudes toward FALN members and the barrio activists who support them continue to be a source of heated conflict attached to community resources and activism among Puerto Rican activists and residents in Chicago.
5. The proliferation of smaller Puerto Rican communities outside of New York City has been noticed since the 1950s (Jones, 1955; O'Brien, 1954; Siegal, Orlans, & Greer, 1954; Vivas, 1951), when Puerto Ricans developed heterogeneous migration patterns. However, little scholarly attention has been given to these communities, or even to significantly sized urban Puerto Rican areas outside the Northeast. As Backstrand and Schensul (1982) and Enchautegui (1992) emphasize, variations in geographical context and community size must be considered in order to adequately address the special needs prompted by shifting demographic characteristics of the Puerto Rican population in the United States. In their study of Puerto Ricans in Hartford, Connecticut, Backstrand and Schensul conclude that any study of Puerto Rican communities must examine the total environment, "not around the ethnic group, but around the interactive relationships relevant to the group's achievement of its goals" (1982, p. 29). This model advocates an understanding of the area's "carrying capacity" (i.e., the availability

of resources in the environment), the skills, characteristics, and resources brought into the adaptation area, the cultural and community strategies used by the residents, the characteristics of other groups sharing the area, and "the shifting relationships between competition/cooperation as Puerto Rican strategies overlap or conflict with the strategies of other sectors" (p. 30).

6. Chicago has the fifth-largest and most diverse Latino population of any city in the United States. According to the 1990 U.S. Census, Mexicans in Chicago, representing 65 percent of the city's Latinos, are the largest Latino group of the twelve nationalities with a significant presence (more than 1,000 people in each group) in the city. Puerto Ricans are the second-largest Latino group, with over 120,000 people (22.6%), followed by Guatemalans (2.4%) and Cubans (2%). All these Latino nationalities combine to make up 20 percent of the city's total population (includes only the Chicago Standard Metropolitan Area) (Fornek, 1992).
7. In 1990, Puerto Rican concentration in West Town ranged from 10 percent to 29.9 percent, while Puerto Rican concentration in Humboldt Park ranged from 40 percent to 69.99 percent (based on 1990 Census Tract of the Humboldt Park area). Important literature has been published on the subject of race and class relations in the context of gentrification (Anderson, 1990), urban renewal and homesteading (Von Hassell, 1996), and community dissolution as a consequence of residential desegregation (Molotch, 1972). The actual impact of these processes on the lives and identity of residents — who naturally view displacement as undesirable — fuels suspicion toward incoming Whites.
8. Most PACHS students live below poverty level in the Humboldt Park sections hit hardest by gang warfare, drugs, unemployment, and a plethora of severe social problems. Their families receive some form of government assistance, primarily through AFDC and Social Security. Although the school's 1994–1995 annual tuition was only $500, only 20 percent of the students were able to pay it in full; most students participate in school fundraising activities, work-study, or hold an afterschool job to pay their tuition. No student has ever been turned down or expelled for being unable to pay, despite the school's precarious financial situation.
9. In her groundbreaking literary critique of Nuyorican literature, Acosta-Belén (1992) argues that Puerto Rican identity is configured, articulated, and mediated through the literature of the Puerto Rican migrant community in New York City. Acosta-Belén emphasizes that such literary expressions must be examined in regard to "the Puerto Rican national question and the subordinate socioeconomic position occupied by Puerto Ricans within U.S. society" (p. 980). She continues: "This literature provided to Puerto Ricans born or raised in the United States a means of cultural validation and affirmation of a collective sense of identity that served to counteract the detrimental effects of the socioeconomic and racial marginalization that Puerto Ricans have experienced in the metropolis" (p. 980).
10. In the case of the grassroots activists, the support is ideological, but not electoral; Center activists do not believe in the process of voting because of their nationalist stance.
11. ASPIRA is a national not-for-profit agency focused on educational issues affecting Latino/Puerto Rican youth. Local branches of the organization exist in the larger U.S. cities (e.g., New York, Philadelphia, Hartford, Miami, and Chicago).
12. The Parents Institute is a concrete effort to bring more Puerto Rican parents (especially single mothers living in poverty) into the work force by providing work space in their children's schools. The act of giving jobs to parents, perceived by barrio activists as an effort toward self-determination, self-actualization, and self-reliance, was criticized by the more conservative white-collar professionals and news reporters, who thought the reform's main aim should have been to raise standardized test scores and encourage students to move out of the community.

13. While nationalist movements have been examined in light of state fragmentation, collapse, and repression, internal group dynamics have been overlooked. Warren concludes that "much less attention is directed to the internal dynamics of these [new social] movements: to the particular ways participants create and consume culture through their activism, to the ways social relations (not just individual choice) mediate involvements, or to the ironies of identity politics in movements that foreground one of many identities relevant to activists" (1996, p. 25).
14. As Díaz-Quiñones explains, the "need to preserve identities" and maintain "real and symbolic places" gains strength precisely by being away from the Island, and in perceptions of "the past and the present reconciled in the construction of a new version of history" (1993, p. 49). When nationalist identity is essentialized so that only Island Puerto Ricans who can speak "proper Spanish" belong, nationalist agendas in U.S. Puerto Rican communities are challenged to seek new forms of self-identification that will reincorporate individuals into the Puerto Rican history from which they have been excluded.

References

Acosta-Belén, E. (1992). Beyond island boundaries: Ethnicity, gender, and cultural revitalization in Nuyorican literature. *Callaloo, 15,* 979–998.

Anderson, A. B., & George, W. P. (1986). *Confronting the color line: The broken promise of the civil rights movement in Chicago.* Athens: University of Georgia Press.

Anderson, E. (1990). *Streetwise: Race, class, and change in an urban community.* Chicago: University of Chicago Press.

Backstrand, J. R., & Schensul, S. L. (1982). Co-evolution in an outlying ethnic community: The Puerto Ricans of Hartford, Connecticut. *Urban Anthropology, 11*(1), 9–37.

Bensman, D., & Lynch, R. (1988). *Rusted dreams: Hard times in a steel community.* Berkeley: University of California Press.

Chatterjee, P. (1993). *The nation and its fragments: Colonial and postcolonial histories.* Princeton, NJ: Princeton University Press.

Cruz, W. (1997). Witch hunt at Clemente High: Puerto Rican nationalism and Chicago politics. *Crítica (34/35),* 11–18.

Díaz-Quiñones, A. (1993). *La memoria rota.* Rio Piedras, PR: Ediciones Huracán.

Enchautegui, M. (1992). Geographical differentials in the socioeconomic status of Puerto Ricans: Human capital variations and labor market characteristics. *International Migration Review, 26,* 1267–1290.

Esteves, S. M. (1980). *Yerba Buena.* New York: Greenfield Press.

Esteves, S. M. (1984). *Tropical rains.* New York: African Caribbean Poetry Theater.

Evans, S. (1979). *Personal politics: The roots of women's liberation in the civil rights movement and the new left.* New York: Random House.

Fernández, R. (1994). *Prisoners of colonialism: The struggle for justice in Puerto Rico.* Monroe, ME: Common Courage Press.

Fornek, S. (1992, September 16). Latinos here are epitome of diversity. *Chicago Sun-Times,* p. 16.

Geovannis, C. (1998). *The charges against Clemente High School.* Chicago: Chicago Ink.

Jones, I. (1955). *The Puerto Rican in New Jersey: His present status.* New Brunswick, NJ: Department of Education, Division against Discrimination.

Klor de Alva, J. (1988). Latino sociocultural diversity in the United States. In E. Acosta-Belen (Ed.), *The Hispanic experience in the United States* (pp. 107–136). New York: Praeger.

Lancaster, R. (1988). *Thanks to God and the revolution: Popular religion and class consciousness in the new Nicaragua.* New York: Columbia University Press.

Laviera, T. (1981). *La carreta made a u-turn.* Houston: Arte Público Press.
Laviera, T. (1985). *American.* Houston: Arte Público Press.
Maldonado, E. (1979). Contract labor and the origins of Puerto Rican communities in the United States. *International Migration Review, 13*(1), 15–32.
Molotch, H. (1972). *Managed integration: Dilemmas of doing good in the city.* Berkeley: University of California Press.
Oboler, S. (1995). *Ethnic labels, Latino lives: Identity and the politics of (re)presentation in the United States.* Minneapolis: University of Minnesota Press.
O'Brien, R. (1954). *A survey of the Puerto Ricans in Lorain, Ohio.* Lorain, OH: Neighborhood House Association of Lorain.
Padilla, F. M. (1987). *Puerto Rican Chicago.* South Bend, IN: University of Notre Dame Press.
Piñero, M. (1980). *La bodega sold dreams.* Houston: Arte Público Press.
Public school's "pathetic" use of poverty funds. (1995, June 4). *Chicago Sun Times,* p. 1.
Said, E. (1978). *Orientalism.* New York: Pantheon.
Safa, H. (1988). Migration and identity: A comparison of Puerto Rican and Cuban migrants in the United States. In E. Acosta-Belén (Ed.), *The Hispanic experience in the United States* (pp. 137–150). New York: Praeger.
Sánchez, L. R. (1994). *La guagua aerea.* Rio Piedras, PR: Editorial Cultural.
Sánchez-Korrol, V. (1988). Latinismo among early Puerto Rican migrants in New York City: A sociohistoric interpretation. In E. Acosta-Belén (Ed.), *The Hispanic experiences in the United States* (pp. 151–161) New York: Praeger.
Seijo-Bruno, M. (1981). Son pobres y Puertorriqueños. *Claridad,* "En rojo" section.
Siegel, A., Orlans, H., & Greer, L. (1954). *Puerto Ricans in Philadephia: A study of their demographic characteristics, problems, and attitudes.* Philadelphia: Commission on Human Relations.
Son Del Bario. (1994). *Echando Pa'lante.*
Thomas, P. (1967). *Down these mean streets.* New York: Alfred A. Knopf.
Vivas, J. (1951). *The Puerto Ricans of Cleveland: A challenge to community organization.* Unpublished masters thesis, Western Reserve University.
Von Hassell, M. (1996). *Homesteading in New York City, 1978–1993: The divided heart of Loisaida.* Westport, CT: Bergin & Garvey.
Warren, K. (1996). Reading history as resistance: Mayan public intellectuals in Guatemala. In E. F. Fischer & R. McKenna Brown (Eds.), *Mayan cultural activism in Guatemala* (pp. 121–145). Austin: University of Texas Press.
Zwerman, G. (1995, September). *The identity vulnerable activist and the emergence of post-new left armed, underground organizations in the United States* (Working Paper Series, No. 218). New York: New School for Social Research, Center for Studies of Social Change.

PART III

Critical Hope

"The Courage to Pursue the Painful Path"

PART III

Critical Hope

"The Courage to Pursue the Painful Path"

If communities can and do organize themselves to change their own schools and realities, then what is the role of educators and policy makers in bringing about reform? In the collection of articles that close this book, we learn to envision a stance in which the problems of education do not belong to any particular individual or group but, rather, to our collective humanity. As such, each article highlights an example of the radical empathy required for a truly shared, common struggle against dehumanizing educational conditions. The thread that binds this final section together is that of educators in solidarity with students, realizing what Jeffrey Duncan-Andrade describes as "the courage to pursue the painful path" through working to "reconnect to the collective by struggling alongside one another, sharing in the victories and the pain."

Building on the centrality of "hope" in the Obama campaign, Duncan-Andrade's 2009 essay frames this section by explaining the notion of critical hope, which is comprised of *material, Socratic*, and *audacious* hope. The articles that follow demonstrate these three components of critical hope as they are reflected in classrooms and communities. To begin, Kathe Jervis's 1986 article illustrates material hope: the fundamental resources of a quality education. In this instance, material hope emerges from the relationship between third-grader Daryl and his teacher Karen. Despite Daryl's seemingly "oppositional" orientation toward school, Karen gives him the academic freedom and safety that become the pathways for his journey toward self-discovery. In a 2007 piece, Travis Wright exemplifies Socratic hope—which requires us to examine our role in creating injustice—by exploring his work as a counselor. Wright confronts his own assumptions about gender and masculinity through a portrait of his relationship with Jorge, a three-year-old Latino boy whose struggles in preschool reflect his family's struggles at home. Finally, Fernando Cardenal and Valerie Miller provide an inside account of the 1980 National Literacy Crusade in Nicaragua, which embodies audacious hope by boldly demonstrating solidarity with disenfranchised communities. Detailing the work of organizing and implementing the crusade to provide basic literacy skills to more than 400,000 Nicaraguans, this piece includes moving reflections from the young *brigadistas,* the teachers who journeyed into remote, rural villages and homes to bring dignity and empowerment to the people of Nicaragua.

As a whole, this section elucidates the power of hope to support educators undertaking difficult and bold risks that challenge the oppressive nature of traditional approaches to teaching and learning.

Note to Educators

Hope Required When Growing Roses in Concrete

JEFFREY M. R. DUNCAN-ANDRADE

> The idea that hope alone will transform the world, and action undertaken in that kind of naïveté, is an excellent route to hopelessness, pessimism, and fatalism. But the attempt to do without hope, in the struggle to improve the world, as if that struggle could be reduced to calculated acts alone, or a purely scientific approach, is a frivolous illusion. (Freire, 1997, p. 8)

Barack Obama's presidential campaign positioned him as the leader who could help restore hope to the nation. Drawing heavily from his widely read memoir *The Audacity of Hope* (2006), the campaign used hope as a core principle around which Obama laid out his vision for "reclaiming the American dream." However, Obama was not the first to use a framework of hope to generate social movement. Historically, hope has been a theme in the lives and movements of the poor and dispossessed in the United States. During the civil rights era, as well as other key historical moments of social change, the nation's hope connected moral outrage to action aimed at resolving undeserved suffering.

In the past three decades, however, there has been an assault on hope, particularly in our nation's urban centers. This attack has taken place on numerous fronts, including disinvestment in schools and overinvestment in a prison industrial complex. Such policies have eroded true hope and given rise to false hope, a reactionary distortion of the radical premise of hope. Therefore, this essay begins by cautioning educators against three types of false hope often promulgated in urban schools: hokey hope, mythical hope, and hope deferred.

The second half of this essay attends to the work of educators in rebuilding the critical hope that has been worn down in our communities. Such educators deliver us from false hope by teaching in ways that connect the moral outrage of young people to actions that relieve the undeserved suffering in their communities. The spread of this kind of educational practice in our schools adds to hopefulness because it develops a transgenerational capacity for long-term, sustainable, critical hope in communities. Brazilian critical educator Paulo Freire (1997) described this kind of hope as an "ontological need," especially in the lives and the pedagogy of educators working in communities where forms of social misery seem to have taken up permanent residence. And so, on the heels of a hope-filled, history-making election that comes sixteen years into my calling as an urban schoolteacher, I also wish to share some reflections on three elements of educational practice that can build and sustain critical hope in urban schools.

Enemies of Hope

Hokey Hope

Optimism, Cornel West (2004) argues, "adopts the role of the spectator who surveys the evidence in order to infer that things are going to get better" (p. 296), even when the evidence does not warrant such a conclusion. This *hokey hope* is peddled in urban schools all the time. It is akin to what Martin Luther King Jr. (1963) referred to as "the tranquilizing drug of gradualism" (para. 5): an individualistic up-by-your-bootstraps hyperbole that suggests if urban youth just work hard, pay attention, and play by the rules, then they will go to college and live out the "American dream." I do not condemn this false hope because I doubt the importance of time and hard work for creating change. Rather, this hope is "hokey" because it ignores the laundry list of inequities that impact the lives of urban youth long before they get to the under-resourced schools that reinforce an uneven playing field.

Angela Valenzuela's *Subtractive Schooling* (1999) provides a profound examination of how hokey hope is manifested in Seguin High School, a predominantly Latino school in Texas. She argues that Seguin is indicative of a national culture of ineffective schools that is "structured around an *aesthetic* caring whose essence lies in an attention to things and ideas" (p. 22). Relationships between school officials and students become pragmatic, the teaching and learning process is strained, and an "impersonal and objective language, including such terms as goals, strategies, and standardized curricula, is used in decisions made by one group for another" (p. 22). This leads to a culture of false caring, one in which the more powerful members of the relationship define themselves as caring despite the fact that the recipients of their so-called caring do not perceive it as such. Valenzuela's aesthetically caring teachers drew heavily from the work-ethic rhetoric to describe "good" students and doled out care in proportion to students' willingness to be accommodating of an unjust society and an unequal school.

Ultimately, hokey hope projects some kind of multicultural, middle-class opportunity structure that is inaccessible to the overwhelming majority of working-class, urban youth of color. This, in turn, largely delegitimizes the pain that urban youth experience as a result of a persistently unequal society. It is a false hope informed by privilege and rooted in the optimism of the spectator who needs not suffer—a "let them eat cake" utterance that reveals a fundamental incomprehension of suffering.

Mythical Hope

Obama's election has the potential to contribute to *mythical hope*, what Roland Barthes (1972) might have described as a false narrative of equal opportunity emptied of its historical and political contingencies. The significance of the election of a black man as the president of this country is undeniable, especially given our past and present national failure to meet the challenge of racial equality. But immediately after an election that few would have predicted, the overstatement of its significance began; it became naturalized as the consequence of a fictitious color-blind society. In John McCain's (2008) concession speech, after referencing the white rage that followed Booker T. Washington's dinner with President Theodore Roosevelt at the White House in 1901, McCain proclaimed:

> America today is a world away from the cruel and prideful bigotry of that time. There is no better evidence of this than the election of an African American to the presidency of the United States. Let there be no reason now for any American to fail to cherish their citizenship in this, the greatest nation on Earth. (para. 6)

McCain's insinuation that this election signifies the "end of racism" (D'Souza, 1995) is mythmaking. His statement ignores the fact that people of color trail their white counterparts on virtually every indicator of social, political, and economic well-being. Educators must not use Obama's election as evidence that we have emerged victorious in our battle with racism or with any of the oppressions (classism, patriarchy, xenophobia, homophobia) that continue to cripple our society. Obama (2006) himself preempted this argument by pointing out:

> To say that we are one people is not to suggest that race no longer matters. . . . To suggest that our racial attitudes play no part in . . . disparities is to turn a blind eye to both our history and our experience—and to relieve ourselves of the responsibility to make things right. (pp. 232–233)

Perhaps this is why West (2008) describes Obama's election as sitting precariously between an example of the American dream coming true and "the grand exhaustion of the dream built on the success of any one individual" (pp. 58–59). Educators must understand that Obama's election gives us "hope on a tightrope," because a single event cannot, by itself, provide the healing and long-term sustenance required to maintain hope amid conditions of suffering. Obama's election *is* change, and he may even give us some reason to be hopeful. Time will tell. But he neither embodies nor can he produce a fundamental departure from the inequities our children experience in the classroom. No president, no policy, and no program can do this for us. To claim otherwise is to peddle a mythical hope.

Mythical hope is a profoundly ahistorical and depoliticized denial of suffering that is rooted in celebrating individual exceptions. These individuals are used to construct a myth of meritocracy that simultaneously fetishizes them as objects of that myth. Ultimately, mythical hope depends on luck and the law of averages to produce individual exceptions to the tyranny of injustice, and thus it denies the legitimacy of the suffering of the oppressed. Educators must avoid the trap of overstating the significance of Obama's election for teaching and learning in urban schools, because, at the end of the day, we are the ones who create classrooms that instill in our young people the "audacity to hope" (Wright, 1990).

Hope Deferred

Hope deferred, constructed on a progressive politics of despair, is a common justification for poor teaching. It hides behind misinterpretations of research that connect the material conditions of poverty to the constraints placed on schools. Many teachers feel overwhelmed by the challenges urban youth face in their lives and consider themselves ill-equipped to respond with a pedagogy that will develop hope in the face of such daunting hardships. They are liberal-minded enough to avoid "blaming the victim," turning instead to blaming the economy, the violence in society, the lack of social services, the "system." These teachers have a critique of social inequality but cannot manifest this critique in any kind of transformative pedagogical project (Solórzano & Delgado-Bernal, 2001). They "hope" for change in its most deferred forms: either a collective utopia of a future reformed society or, more often, the individual student's future ascent to the middle class.

However, according to S. Leonard Syme (2004), professor emeritus at the University of California, Berkeley School of Public Health, hope should be thought of as "control of destiny" (p. 3), an actively present sense of agency to manage the immediate stressors in one's daily life. He argues that recent research into the importance of hope for life outcomes is a "major breakthrough in thinking" for scholars in public health and epidemiology (p. 3). Syme attributes the genesis of this breakthrough to the groundbreaking Whitehall studies, which led to revelations that the distribution of "virtually every disease in every industrialized country in the world" (p. 3) was remarkably well-correlated with social class. For a growing number of scholars, the most likely explanation for the unequal distribution of health is the unequal distribution of hope along the social gradient.

At the bottom of this social gradient, where urban youth are positioned, this "control of destiny" is almost nonexistent. David Williams, of the Harvard School of Public Health, argues that this results in the

> accumulation of multiple negative stressors, and it's so many of them it's as if someone is being hit from every single side. And, it's not only that they are dealing with a lot of stress, [it's that] they have few resources to cope. (Adelman, 2008)

The exposure to chronic stress associated with living in these types of "socially toxic environments" (Garbarino, 1995) is now thought of as one of the most—if not *the* most—significant contributors to poor health. This research helps us understand that many of the health problems plaguing poor communities result from "unnatural causes" (Adelman, 2008), confirming what we have known intuitively for years: inequality *is* making us sick.

The implications of chronic stress for teaching and learning are profound. Consider Abraham Maslow's (1943) hierarchy of needs, which defined a person's primary human needs (food, clothing, shelter, and safety) as prerequisites for pursuing needs higher up on the scale (such as education). When we connect the dots between Maslow's framework and the latest research on inequality, a serious dilemma is revealed for urban youth whose exposure to unremitting stressors leaves most, sometimes all, of their primary human needs under constant attack. When we are unwilling to confront these harsh realities of social inequality with our pedagogy—to cultivate their "control of destiny"—all we have left to offer youth is hope deferred. This offer comes when we ask our students to set their sights on some temporally distant (and highly unlikely) future well-being. There is nothing wrong with setting long-term goals with students, but hope deferred advocates that students take a path that the educator is unwilling to help them find. This student path is almost always individualistic in nature and requires a level of sacrifice that most teachers themselves are loath to make. Eventually students come to perceive a significant gap between their most pressing needs and the education we offer them. When they figure out that the teacher is unwilling and/or unable to close this gap, their hope is deferred. And just as Martin Luther King Jr. foretold of justice, hope too long deferred is hope denied.

Critical Hope: The Enemy of Hopelessness

On the flipside of these false hopes lies critical hope, which rejects the despair of hopelessness and the false hopes of "cheap American optimism" (West, 2008, p. 41). Critical hope demands a committed and active struggle "against the evidence in order to change the deadly tides of wealth inequality, group xenophobia, and personal despair" (West, 2004, pp. 296–297). There are three elements of critical hope: material, Socratic, and audacious. Unlike the forms of false hope, which can operate independent of one another, these three elements of critical hope must operate holistically and, in fact, are mutually constitutive. I have wrestled them apart only for the purpose of analytic convenience.

Tupac Shakur (1999) referred to young people who emerge in defiance of socially toxic environments as the "roses that grow from concrete." Concrete is one of the worst imaginable surfaces in which to grow, devoid of essential nutrients and frequently contaminated by pollutants. Any growth in such an environment is painful because all of the basic requirements for healthy development (sun, water, and nutrient-rich soil) must be hard-won. The ability to control, in a material way, the litany of social stressors that result from growing up in concrete is nearly impossible for urban youth. Educators committed to *material hope* engage their work by tempering this reality with the acknowledgment that there are always cracks in concrete. The quality of our teaching, along with the resources and networks we connect our students to, are those cracks. They do not create an ideal environment for growth, but they afford some leaking in of sunlight, water, and other resources that provide the material justification to hope. The courage to pursue the painful path of bursting through those jagged cracks in the concrete is what I call *Socratic hope.* The solidarity to share in others' suffering, to sacrifice self so that other roses may bloom, to collectively struggle to replace the concrete completely with a rose garden is what I call *audacious hope.* The following sections discuss each of these elements in turn.

Material Hope

Material hope is one element of the critical hope that teachers can cultivate in their students, and it comes from the sense of control young people have when they are given the resources to "deal with the forces that affect their lives" (Syme, 2004, p. 3). It seems like a simple point, but teachers who want to build material hope must understand that quality teaching is the most significant "material" resource they have to offer youth. The best of the research in our field defines "quality" in teaching by our ability to produce student growth across assessment measures (grades, social development, test scores, student engagement, etc.). To accomplish this, we have to bust the false binary that suggests we must choose between an academically rigorous pedagogy and one geared toward social justice. An English teacher participating in my three-year study of successful urban educators in Los Angeles put it this way:

> Terms are not difficult to teach. The question, really, is will you take the time to make the things you teach relevant to students? The terms I teach are present in students' lives every day. But most people try to teach them strictly by using textbooks, worksheets, or the literature. I teach them using life and then it's much easier for students to connect them to what they are reading.[1]

The most effective urban educators, in every discipline at every grade level, connect the academic rigor of content areas with their students' lives (Duncan-Andrade, 2007). If we are serious about giving our children hope, we must reflect on how to connect our pedagogy to the harsh realities of poor, urban communities. An e-mail to me from Ms. Truth, a fourth-grade teacher in Los Angeles, reveals the magnitude of this undertaking:

> Today was an almost unbearably sad day at school. According to my students (all of which were SOBBING) two young men were sitting in a car yesterday afternoon. Some men in a car rolled up, got out and shot one in the eye (his head exploded) there was a 3-month old in the back seat (she was left "unharmed") the other got out and ran (they call him "baby" Marcus) the guys ran after him and shot him in the back and then more when he fell. . . . The nephew of one is in my class, the brother of the other is in Mr. [Randall's] class. This is a close community so word spread pretty rapidly yesterday. For an hour and a half [this morning] the kids all just talked and cried. I felt ill-equipped to handle a crisis like this but, we got through it. . . . I said as little as possible, I cried with the kids, we all consoled each other, and others began sharing different stories of violence and loss. In the end, I did what I thought (and hope) was best, tried to empower them with the belief that they must work to become the warriors who combat the senseless violence and madness on the streets. . . . We're making cards, and going to send a little money to the families. The kids all seem to feel a little better. How would you handle this? It looks as if many teachers didn't say or do much. Feeling a bit weary today.

In most urban schools, there is no formal structure to prepare or support teachers to handle such tragic events. The result is that, as Ms. Truth mentions, most teachers avoid or ignore tragedies that take place in the community. But the effective teachers I have studied do not.

Ms. Truth's class collected over $100 for the family. She delivered the money, along with several cards expressing condolences, at the funeral of one of the murdered young men. Here, effective teaching included literally generating material resources, and in my research I have witnessed underpaid teachers providing laptops, housing, food, supplies, car rides, and links to legal and medical services. But, more importantly, an effective teacher is herself a *material* resource: an indispensable person who can connect schooling to the real, *material* conditions of urban life.

Socratic Hope

West (2001) describes "Socratic sensibility" as the understanding of both Socrates' statement that "the unexamined life is not worth living" and Malcolm X's extension that the "examined life is painful."[2] *Socratic hope* requires both teachers and students to painfully examine our lives and actions within an unjust society and to share the sensibility that pain may pave the path to justice. In my research, effective educators teach Socratic hope by treating the righteous indignation in young people as a strength rather than something deserving of punishment; Freire (2004) called this a "pedagogy of indignation." The moments of despair and rage that urban youth feel are not only understandable, they are, as West (2004) proclaims, an "appropriate response to an absurd situation" (p. 295). He goes on to argue that youth

> are saying they want to see a sermon, not hear one. They want an example. They want to be able to perceive in palpable concrete form how these channels will allow them to vent their rage constructively and make sure that it will have an impact. (p. 296)

To show the sermon, rather than preach it, is the essence of Socratic hope.

Darnell, an eleventh-grade student of one of the effective teachers I have studied, explained that this type of teacher-student relationship forms as the result of pedagogy that prioritizes the humanization of students above all else:

> In [Mr. Lapu's] class we bonded because we all gave each other a chance to humanize ourselves and let us know each other's stories . . . [and] after that we looked at each other different. After I told my narrative, I humanized myself and then . . . they stopped looking at me as just a gang-banger and they started looking at me as a smart black man. I don't want you to acknowledge me as a gang-banger, which happened. I want you to acknowledge me as [Darnell]. He helped us humanize each other, and that's how it was.
>
> It was beautiful just knowing that my classmate that's sitting right next to me is fighting the same fight that I'm fighting. So, I got his back. That was beautiful, just knowing that we're going through the same shit. From the 'hood to school. When we walk to school, we gotta dodge a bullet like every day. That's your struggle? Well that's my struggle, too. Let's just handle this right here, so we don't gotta go through this four years from now. We felt comfortable that [Mr. Lapu] had our back, and that's just all it is.

Educators who foster this type of solidarity with and among students recognize the distinction between being liked and being loved by their students. As Ms. Truth explained, being liked comes from avoiding unpleasant situations, whereas being loved is often painful:

> Many of these teachers are so afraid that students won't like them if they discipline them that they end up letting students do things that they would never permit from their own children. They lower their standards and will take any old excuse from students for why they did not do their homework, or why they cannot sit still in class or do their work. Not me. You gotta work in my class. I can be unrelenting at times, probably even overbearing. Oh, I might give a student slack here or there, but most of the time I'm like, "go tell it to someone else because I'm not trying to hear that from you right now. We've got work to do."

For urban youth, their evaluation of which side of the loved-liked line an educator stands on is often based on whether we share the painful path with them: Do we make the self-sacrifices in our own lives that we are asking them to make? Do we engage in the Socratic process of painful scrutiny about these sacrifices? Do we have the capacity and commitment to support students when they struggle to apply that framework in their lives? Teachers who meet these challenges are beloved by students. The sacrifices they make and the solidarity it produces earn them the right to demand levels of commitment that often defy even the students' own notion of their capabilities. Teachers who fall short can be liked but not loved, and this means they are unable to push the limits of students' abilities; they cannot take them down the painful path.

With teachers I have studied, the move from liked to loved did not happen because of the demands they made of students. It happened because of the level of self-sacrifice, love, and support that accompanied those raised expectations. Sometimes this was simple encouragement, but many times it meant amplifying the material hope they were giving to students. This support took many forms: afterschool and weekend tutoring; countless meals and rides home; phone/text/email/instant messaging sessions; and endless prodding, cajoling, and all-around positive harassment. These additional investments of time and money clarified for students the idea that with raised expectations came the teacher's willingness to sacrifice in order to help students along the way.

The development of these trusting relationships also resulted in these teachers feeling indignant about student failure. They saw student failure as their own failure and, consequently, engaged in painful self-critique to determine more appropriate future actions. They never excused students from their responsibilities, and they never let themselves slip into despair—rather, the Socratic project contributed to their hope that they would be more successful next time.

Socrates said that "all great undertakings are risky, and, as they say, what is worth while is always difficult" (Plato, 2003, p. 220). As educators, we must take great risks and accept great challenges if we are going to be effective in urban schools. We must confront our failures and know that no matter what we do in our classrooms, there will still be forms of social misery that confront our students. This kind of self-reflection will be painful, but it is necessary all the same.

Audacious Hope

Our nation expends a good deal of effort trying to avoid what Carl Jung (1970) referred to as "legitimate suffering," or the pain of the human experience. The stockpiling of resources in privileged portions of the population so that they may be "immune" to suffering, while heaping the unnatural causes of socially toxic environments onto others, creates undeserved suffering while simultaneously delegitimizing it. In the face of these conditions, critical hope is audacious in two ways. First, it boldly stands in solidarity with urban communities, sharing the burden of their undeserved suffering as a manifestation of a humanizing hope in our collective capacity for healing. Second, critical hope audaciously defies the dominant ideology of defense, entitlement, and preservation of privileged bodies at the expense of the policing, disposal, and dispossession of marginalized "others." We cannot treat our students as "other people's children" (Delpit, 1995)—their pain *is* our pain. False hope would have us believe in individualized notions of success and suffering, but audacious hope demands that we reconnect to the collective by struggling alongside one another, sharing in the victories *and* the pain. This solidarity is the essential ingredient for "radical healing" (Ginwright, 2009), and healing is an often-overlooked factor for improving achievement in urban schools.

This is the inescapable challenge before us as urban educators, and it is often misunderstood. Too many of us try to create classroom spaces that are safe from righteous rage, or, worse, we design plans to weed out children who display it. The question we should be grappling with is not how to manage students with these emotions, but how to help students channel them. The way I take on this challenge is by thinking about my classroom as a micro-ecosystem. Ecologists would tell me that to build a healthy micro-ecosystem, I need to understand the principle of interdependency—in short, that both pain and healing are transferable from person to person inside the classroom. They would also note that the classroom is not a closed micro-ecosystem; I should be aware of external toxins that will be carried into it. I have virtually no control over the array of social toxins to which my students are exposed in the meta-ecosystem of our society, but I can control how I respond to them in my classroom. This gives me, and my students, the audacity to hope.

The pain that our young people carry manifests itself in my classroom in a variety of ways. Sometimes it takes an obvious form like an outpouring of emotion, which might even be directed at me or another student. Usually that pain reveals itself more subtly, in the classic forms of depression (fatigue, sadness, or self-deprecation). In these moments, when a child can no longer contain the pain she feels, my response has the potential to add to it or to begin the healing process. We may think that if we send out the "disobedient" child, we have removed the pain from our system. It simply does not work that way. Rather, when we exclude a child, we introduce another social stressor into the micro-ecosystem. We rationalize the exclusion by telling ourselves that we have pulled a weed from the garden, allowing for a healthier environment for the other children to grow. This ignores the fact that every student in our classroom is part of a delicate balance built on interdependency. K. Wayne Yang, an urban science and math teacher for more than seventeen years, and one of the finest educators I have known in my career, put it this way: "All my students are indigenous to my classroom and therefore there are no weeds in my classroom."[3] From this perspective, the decision to remove a child, rather than to heal her, is not only bad for the child but is also destructive to the social ecosystem of the classroom.

I have been teaching long enough to know the enormity of this challenge, particularly because these moments almost always happen when I am convinced we are doing something of the utmost importance in the classroom. But then I think to myself, how did I get to a place where I am prioritizing lesson plans over healing a child in pain? This choice not only ignores my most basic sensibilities as a teacher, it also disregards years of research documenting the importance of self-esteem, trust, and hope as preconditions for positive educational outcomes. As educators we tend to seriously underestimate the impact our response has on the other students in the class. They are watching us when we interact with their peers. When we become frustrated and punish youth who manifest symptoms of righteous rage or social misery, we give way to legitimate doubts among other students about our capacity to meet their needs if they are ever in pain.

At the end of the day, effective teaching depends most heavily on one thing: deep and caring relationships. Herb Kohl (1995) describes "willed not learning" as the phenomenon by which students try *not* to learn from teachers who don't authentically care about them. The adage "students don't care what you know until they know that you care" is supported by numerous studies of effective educators (Akom, 2003; Delpit, 1995; Duncan-Andrade, 2007; Ladson-Billings, 1994). To provide the "authentic care" (Valenzuela, 1999) that students require from us as a precondition for learning from us, we must connect our indignation over all forms of oppression with an audacious hope that we can act to change them. Hokey hope would have us believe this change will not cost us anything. This kind of false hope is mendacious; it never acknowledges pain. Audacious hope stares down the painful path; and despite the overwhelming odds against us making it down that path to change, we make the journey again and again. There is no other choice. Acceptance of this fact allows us to find the courage and the commitment to cajole our students to join us on that journey. This makes us better people as it makes us better teachers, and it models for our students that the painful path *is* the hopeful path.

License to Hope Audaciously

Obama has given us license to reinsert hope into the mainstream educational discourse. He has called for a "radical transformation" of urban schools, placing emphasis on the "recruitment and training of transformative principals and more effective teachers" (Obama, 2006, p. 161). This will require serious attention to revamping teacher recruitment, credentialing, and support structures so that schools can attract, reward, and retain educators who come to the profession with demonstrated commitments to critical hope. Can we meet such a challenge? Only with a hard look at what hope really means in the lives of urban youth.

There is a well-documented changing of the guard taking place in teaching (NCTAF, 2003) as upward of one million new teachers, mostly in urban schools, will join the profession within this decade. This brings with it an unprecedented opportunity to swing the pendulum toward educational equity. We can, if we so desire, invest heavily in refocusing our efforts to recruit, train, and develop urban educators who are committed to shifting the tide in urban schools from despair to hope. Research in other fields identifies hope as one of the most promising responses to the conditions of urban inequality (Syme, 2004; Wilson, Minkler, Dasho, Wallerstein, & Martin, 2008), suggesting that hope has major implications for successful teaching (and for raising test scores). Educational research suggests that we can know what makes urban educators effective. We can name the characteristics of effective practice. We can link those characteristics to increases in engagement and achievement. If we fail to significantly invest in the support and development of these characteristics in this new wave of teachers, it will not be for lack of know-how but for the lack of determination to provide hope to all our young people.

The radical transformation that Obama is calling for will not occur unless we treat every classroom as having the potential to be a crack in the metaphorical concrete that creates unnatural causes in the lives of urban youth. For those of us who will be working alongside this next generation of teachers, we must purposefully nurture our students, colleagues, and ourselves through the cracks, knowing we will sustain the trauma of damaged petals along the way. It is essential that we understand these damaged petals as the attributes of indignation, tenacity, and audacity. They are *not* the social stressors we are trying to overcome, and they must not be misinterpreted as deficits in our students. We must implore our colleagues to recognize that our damaged petals, and those of our students, are not what need to be reformed out of us; they are what need to be celebrated about us. Each time we convey this—the true value of the painful path—we are building critical hope in the person next to us who wonders if they, too, can make it through the crack. Obama's campaign has had this galvanizing effect for some, enrapturing the nation with a level of hope that we have not seen for quite some time, particularly among young people. But for me the success of his campaign has been yet another reminder that I teach teachers and I teach the youth in my community because I hope, audaciously.

Notes

1. Unless otherwise noted, quotes from teachers and students are from interviews and conversations that took place during my study of exceptional teachers in Los Angeles between 2002 and 2005 (see Duncan-Andrade, 2007).
2. In his 2001 lecture, West credits Malcolm X with this statement. Socrates made this point in section 38A of Plato's *Apology of Socrates.*
3. I am indebted to Mr. Yang for our extensive conversations about the development of the ideas presented in this essay.

References

Adelman, L. (Executive Producer). (2008). *Unnatural causes: Is inequality making us sick?* [Television Series]. San Francisco, CA: California News Reel.

Akom, A. A. (2003). "Re-examining resistance as oppositional behavior: The Nation of Islam and the creation of a black achievement ideology." *Sociology of Education, 76* (4), 305–325.

Barthes, R. (1972). *Mythologies.* London: Fontana.

Delpit, L. (1995). *Other people's children.* New York: New Press.

D'Souza, D. (1995). *The end of racism: Principles for a multiracial society.* New York: Free Press.

Duncan-Andrade, J. (2007). "Gangstas, wankstas, and ridas: Defining, developing, and supporting effective teachers in urban schools." *International Journal of Qualitative Studies in Education, 20*(6), 617–638.

Freire, P. (1997). *Pedagogy of hope.* New York: Continuum.

Freire, P. (2004). *Pedagogy of indignation.* Boulder, CO: Paradigm.

Garbarino, J. (1995). *Raising children in a socially toxic environment.* San Francisco: Jossey-Bass.

Ginwright, S. (2009). *Black youth rising: Race, activism, and radical healing in urban America.* New York: Teachers College Press.

Jung, C. G. (1970). *Psychology and religion: West and east* (G. Adler & R. F. C. Hull, Trans.). In G. Adler & R. F. C. Hull (Series Eds.), *Collected works of C. G. Jung, Vol. 11* (2nd ed.). Princeton, NJ: Princeton University Press.

King, M. L. K., Jr. (1963, August 28). "I have a dream." March on Washington. Washington, DC. 28 Aug. 1963. Retrieved February 5, 2009, from http://www.mlkonline.net/dream.html

Kohl, H. (1995). *"I won't learn from you": And other thoughts on creative maladjustment.* New York: New Press.

Ladson-Billings, G. (1994). *The dreamkeepers: Successful teachers of African American children.* San Francisco: Jossey Bass.

Maslow, A. H. (1943). "A theory of human motivation." *Psychological Review, 50*(4), 370–396.

McCain, J. (2008). "McCain's concession speech." Retrieved January 3, 2009, from http://www.nytimes.com/2008/11/04/us/politics/04text-mccain.html

National Commission on Teaching and America's Future. (2003). *No dream denied: A pledge to America's children.* Washington, DC.

Obama, B. (2006). *The audacity of hope: Thoughts on reclaiming the American dream.* New York: Random House.

Plato. (2003). *The republic* (D. Lee, Trans.). London: Penguin Press.

Shakur, T. (1999). *The rose that grew from concrete.* New York: Pocket Books.

Solórzano, D., & Delgado-Bernal, D. (2001). "Examining transformational resistance through a critical race and LatCrit theory framework: Chicana and Chicano students in an urban context." *Urban Education, 36* (3), 308–342.

Syme, S. L. (2004). "Social determinants of health: The community as empowered partner." *Preventing Chronic Disease: Public Health Research, Practice, and Policy, 1*(1), 1–4.

Valenzuela, A. (1999). *Subtractive schooling.* Albany: SUNY Press.

West, C. (2001). *Progressive politics in these times.* Mario Savio Annual Lecture Series. Berkeley, CA.

West, C. (2004). "The impossible will take a little while." In P. Rogat (Ed.), *The impossible will take a little while: A citizen's guide to hope in a time of fear* (pp. 293–297). New York: Basic Books.

West, C. (2008). *Hope on a tightrope.* New York: Smiley Books.

Wilson, N., Minkler, M., Dasho, S., Wallerstein, N., & Martin, A. (2008). "Getting to social action: The youth empowerment strategies (YES!) project." *Health Promotion Practice, 9*(4), 395–403.

Wright, J. (1990). "The audacity to hope." *Preaching Today.* Retrieved February 5, 2009, from http://www.preachingtoday.com/sermons/sermons/audacityofhope.html.

A Teacher's Quest for a Child's Questions

KATHE JERVIS

This description of one child in an urban third/fourth grade public school classroom is really about teaching. I was not the teacher.

Ideally, teachers should write about their own classrooms, but the time and energy demanded by teaching precludes this for all but a small handful of teacher-writers. I have written briefly about my own classroom[1] but in less detail and depth than I would have liked, so when the opportunity arose to write about someone else's classroom, I jumped at it. I had begun working in this classroom under the auspices of the Teachers and Writers Collaborative. The following year the class teacher, Karen (as I am calling her), welcomed me as a note-taking observer from September to June. I was not a participating teacher—we agreed that I would write and she would teach—but I was available to the children for conversation and help. Mine was the luxurious perspective of the undistracted eye.

Teachers know how to make good classroom decisions, but they often do not articulate their reasons. My goal was to understand and make explicit what Karen did in the classroom. We need to know more about how individual teachers operate, how they think about children, and how their philosophy influences what they do. We also need to know more about children's unique patterns.

I did not choose Karen's class at random. Aside from the good fortune of finding someone who welcomed my scrutiny and a principal who didn't prevent it, Karen was a good colleague for such a project. Language is central to her whole life. She writes journals, poetry, complaints, notes to parents, and narrative report cards when checklists would be sufficient. Yet, like most teachers, her decisions are intuitive. My presence forced her to state why she acted as she did.

Harvard Educational Review Vol. 56 No. 2 May 1286

Further, her teaching intrigued me. She operates from a particularly strong political and philosophical base; her value system is at the forefront of her classroom vision, influencing her every interaction, relationship, and decision about teaching. She strives resolutely for the goals her values dictate. She has a powerful effect on children, perhaps because she is so unconflicted about what she does.

Karen sees her classroom not in terms of an imposed curriculum, but as a group of individuals in a community. She registers, notes, and reveres nuances of how people relate to her and to each other. Her interventions start from these observations. She has an uncanny sense of when to support, when to insist, when to back off, and when to interpret for the child what she sees.

People with her values are not found frequently enough in the teaching profession. Because she frees children from large amounts of teacher-imposed work and allows them to choose their own activities, they seldom develop feelings of incompetence if they do not read or speak as well as other children. Karen does not praise children for good reading or good speaking. On the contrary, she is on a campaign: she passionately attacks those who overvalue verbal facility. She is vitriolic about teachers who reward children for their ability to speak well. It angers her that less verbal children are frequently ignored and overlooked. She notices and encourages strengths that are often undervalued.

The children in her school are diverse along many dimensions: religion, ethnicity, language, and economic status. Karen welcomes every child in this population, even the most difficult, without complaint. She is the one who takes children no other teachers want, and no one wanted Daryl at the time he entered her class. Some teachers might have recommended him for a special education class, but Karen refused.

While all children are extraordinary, Daryl would stand out in any class. His beginning stance was distancing, mute, and provocative; whatever mattered to him was unrecognized by the school community, as he gave no clue to his real self, his aspirations, or his strengths. Karen's focus on Daryl's "quest" (her word for any child's central concerns)[2] allowed him to move beyond the alienating, confrontational persona he presented at school.

Creating the opportunity to discover each child's own questions (the "quest" that Karen takes so seriously) is Karen's most compelling reason for structuring her teaching as she does. She believes children learn by investigating their own questions, "even though on some level all of our questions are the same; how we go about answering them—in what medium and with what materials—is significant in who we are and who we are going to be" (personal communication, 1985). The purpose of giving children class time to pursue activities of their own choice, as Karen does, is to give them more opportunities to show themselves. The more children are known, the more she as teacher can sense what their questions are. She believes that "once I understand a child's questions, I can see the learning in what the child has chosen, and the activities become more legitimate to me as the teacher. Most of the time children can't articulate their vital concerns. When I see what their questions are, then I can help them recognize what they are about" (personal communication, 1985).

Daryl's questions—Who is in control? Where do I fit in? What are my limits? Who is imposing them? How can I get around them?—are typical questions fourth graders ask as they grow toward autonomy. For some reason we will never know, Daryl needed more latitude to find answers than most children. For the two years he was in her class, Karen saw that he had it.

Daryl: A Child in Need of an Anchor

I first met Daryl in the middle of his third-grade year, when I came to teach drama. My early memories of him are filled with images of leaping or floating. His thin torso was loose and graceful, but his arms, just hanging, were magically attached and seemed unrelated to the rest of him. He appeared not to be anchored to the ground. He seemed to propel himself, gazelle-like, on and off the tables, as if the only way to get from one side of the room to the other was on the tops of furniture—a brown blur bounding through my line of vision on his way to nowhere.

During that third-grade year, the children nearby were as inaccessible to him as the floor beneath his feet. He had no friends and probably spent as much time roaming the halls as he did wafting about the classroom.

One thread, however tenuous, did connect Daryl with various adults. I vividly remember glimpses of him as I moved through the school. He would be standing motionless, silent, sleepy-eyed, an eight-year-old of average height, looking up at the grown figure facing him. The only sign that he was relating to this adult was a certain angular jutting of his chin—as if, despite his overwhelmingly passive body language, this was the one part of him that represented resistance to adult authority. Opposite Daryl's statuelike pose, the adult would be in a position of full-stage alert, rising to maximum stature, eyes flashing, often lecturing, threatening, or confronting. Undeniably, Daryl had difficulty with authority, but the symptoms usually showed up more dramatically in the adult response.

What we gleaned about his life out of school revealed the same detached child we saw in school. He came to school on the bus—a long ride each way—with other black children, none of whom he knew well. Opportunity for him to make friends on the bus was limited; early in the year he had angered the bus driver and was confined to the front seat, where he was admonished to sit silently. Restive under these constraints, he was always on the verge of being kicked off the bus. When he returned home each afternoon, Daryl went to a local after-school program, whose other participants went to neighborhood schools. This program provided no sanctuary. In a rare moment he confided the problem, "Kids at my after-school tease me 'cause I go to this white school." He was estranged from his most natural peer group and felt compelled to defend his "white school." Daryl was caught with no social anchor, uptown or downtown. Once again he was floating.

Karen believed that before Daryl could make any progress, he needed an anchor. He chose to anchor himself to her, characteristically on his own terms. Usually flexible about rules, Karen has one that is almost unbreakable—the classroom door is locked at lunchtime and no children may intrude on her privacy. Daryl, however, after knocking on the door and jumping up high to peek in the window, was reluctantly admitted one day during the sacred lunch period. He began to come up every lunch period on some pretext—he'd forgotten some food, his comic book, his jacket, something essential to his lunch hour welfare. Since no child so careful of his possessions would intentionally "forget," Karen let him in; he would retrieve the item and ask, "What are you eating?" or inform her of his fatigue and wait for her response, then leave. One day he hurt himself on the playground and came up to cry in her presence. Those tears were the first emotional connection he made to Karen; thereafter, lunchtime visits became a ritual, a singular point of relatedness in Daryl's day.

At the end of his third-grade year the entire faculty—except Karen—saw a child who was isolated from peers at home and at school, who was locked in passive battles with white authorities, who thumbed his nose at routines, who abstained from visible work, who exempted himself from group activities, and who, to tighten the noose around his own neck, did poorly on standardized tests.

Daryl's third-grade year, however, was more productive than it appeared on the surface. Though he irritated authorities as soon as he stepped outside the threshold of room 312, inside he had Karen's unconditional acceptance. He formed a solid relationship with Karen, his first attachment to an adult in the school, his first to any white adult authority figure, and maybe even his first important attachment to any adult outside of his family. No other task could have been more crucial. A sense of belonging, whether to the peer group or to part of the hierarchy, is a necessary condition for learning, especially in an institutional setting, and Daryl's relationship with Karen drew him toward the community, reducing his isolation from both children and adults. Karen communicated to Daryl that he was a valued person whether or not he fit into the class.

Daryl in Fourth Grade: Time and Resistance

By fourth grade, Daryl and Karen had a solid relationship, but having him in class was not easy. To a teacher in charge of children in large groups, one of his most exasperating characteristics was the immense quantity of time he took to change from one activity to another. He could run at top speed on a field trip to be the first person across the bridge or at the head of the line walking through Central Park, but he could also be the last, lagging far behind. Then he was like a twig lodged against a rock in the stream of classroom events. Daryl got stuck, though all reason dictated that he should have moved with the rest of the class. The excessive time he needed for adult-dictated transitions was unreasonable for any teacher who had to engineer complicated schedules for children in groups. Whether he was holding onto a shred of autonomy or executing a passive maneuver to make authorities angry, the result was disruptive.

Rather than nagging him to be prompt, Karen accepted his unsynchronized day because she felt he needed to be on the edge of any group, either first or last, so that he could explore the personal and institutional boundaries of which he was so unsure. She felt he was not ready for the conventional discipline which shapes mature classroom behavior.

Karen's attitude of acceptance extended to Daryl's academic work as well. Some researchers correlate time-on-task with measurable learning outcomes. Karen does not. She is unconcerned with children wasting this currency which teachers are always admonishing children not to squander. She believes that lasting significant results occur over the long term, that children cannot be forced to grow like hothouse orchids, and that their growth cannot be quantified. Measurements can identify only trivial, testable gains, but only elusive, not easily enumerated gains matter. And those, she believes, are nourished by an abundance of time. She felt Daryl needed time, measured in months, to make friends, and time, measured in years, to mature. Time would result eventually in more disciplined behavior and more learning. She was not in a hurry to measure progress, and she did not hurry Daryl to learn faster.

In any case, compelling Daryl to meet a classroom timetable would have been fruitless, as he resisted direct instruction. His unwillingness to learn in a group was extreme; sometimes it took all his energy just to conform outwardly and he could do no more than that. From my notes on November 19th:

> At the Metropolitan Museum, his small group stopped to look in detail at Cezanne's *Card Players*, which required all six children to face forward. Daryl refused and sat with his back to the painting. In a rare moment of insistence, Karen took the time to make an issue. "I ask so little of you. Turn around." Moved perhaps by the urgency in her voice, he oriented his body somewhat closer to the painting, but he volunteered nothing and as far as I could tell, looked a million miles away.

Standardized testing is the epitome of necessary compliance. He willfully resisted during the entire week. This is only one example:

> Every test section begins with two sample questions. For five days, three times a day, Daryl marked the answers to the samples where the first real answers were meant to be, making answers out of sequence from the beginning. On Mon-

> day it was understandable; by Friday it was willful. Some could be fixed, others couldn't. On one reading test Daryl's score was lower than chance.

Always the effort required to submit drained energy from the work itself:

> On June 4th, Karen asked Daryl to complete the math work on the board. The first problem is 164 × 20, and he has answered 2,128. Karen asks him to do it again and he argues, "But I have so much math. Can't I do it at home?" Karen insists. He protests, "I don't know how." She sets it up for him (100 × 20; 60 × 20; 4 × 20). He does it with her sitting next to him. When he gets the answer, he has a big, satisfied smile. He says, "finished," as if he has been working at hard labor for an hour rather than three minutes on computation.

The case for a steady diet of direct instruction is weak for many children and hopeless for children like Daryl. Assigned classwork only creates an arena for conflict as teachers lament, "I taught him, but he just won't learn." Some children resist learning when they have no control, but because their behavior is less extreme than Daryl's, a settled routine results; they have an unspoken contract with the teacher—"I won't cause trouble if you don't make demands"—and class time is spent copying off the board and completing other nonengaging tasks.

In some classrooms, Daryl's behavior would have been an obstacle rather than the platform on which further growth could take place. Rather than absorbing Daryl into the group and accepting his rhythm, Karen could have silenced him by demands to "hurry up," "be still," "get out," all of which might have kept him where he started: mute and outside the group. Karen accepted Daryl, unregulated as he was. By allowing him to contribute when he was ready and on his own terms, she enabled him to change from a silent isolate into someone about whom she could write in her final report, "Daryl has made enormous social growth this year. He is part of and central to the class. He is not on the outskirts, nor does he want to be."

Karen had an intuitive sense of Daryl's questions, though what they were and how she figured them out remained a mystery to me throughout the year. Only after studying my notes and Daryl's notebooks did I come to understand what Karen had been doing. My constant questions also forced her to articulate why she made the decisions she did. But it was Daryl who yielded evidence that her strategies supported his growth.

Choice, Drawing, and Shared Perspectives

How Daryl got from the outskirts of the class to its center is not one linear story of unimpeded progress. I have recorded dates and told the story chronologically, but Daryl's growth, like everyone's, is not of one piece.

Daryl's attachment to Karen and her acceptance of him were crucial, but their bonds were embedded in her classroom philosophy, especially her attitude toward choice. Karen believes that giving children freedom to choose how they spend classroom time enables them to make their own preferences clearer to themselves and others. The classroom then becomes a community of persons sharing their perspectives.

Karen describes what that means in vivid and idiosyncratic language. What matters to Karen is that children have a "place" (a secure sense of themselves in the group), that they "stand tall" (speak for themselves in the group), and that they do not hide behind masks or retreat from the give-and-take of peers. Nurturing these qualities in school requires a classroom where, as Karen recorded in her journal of December 16, 1980, "Children are getting angry and sharing it, finding solutions on their own without rage, becoming proud of their effort and work. The central theme of my class is living together and sharing perspectives." Karen strives for community, but not unity. The atmosphere in her class is not a medium which cultivates homogeneity. Ensuring a "place" for each child emphasizes diversity; differences make for choices. She does not question children's choices. Daryl chose to draw.

When Daryl gravitated to the drawing table, Karen assumed his reason would eventually be clear to her. The record surrounding Daryl's drawing demonstrates (often to my surprise) that what he drew and what he chose to say and write about drawing confirmed Karen's conviction that he needed extraordinary space to explore boundaries and find his own direction. When given this space, he thrived.

Initially I believed that any slice of the record would document Daryl's undeniable growth, and I chose to look at his drawing because he chose drawing. Now it is clear to me that drawing was crucially intertwined with his development as a person. Close observation at the drawing table turned out to be as important for my understanding as the resulting drawings. Often children's finished work is only a small, though significant, artifact of what transpires while they draw.

Daryl brought to drawing, as he brought to everything, his own style and rituals. He preferred cartooning, and in the beginning he traced characters from comic books. Then he taught himself to copy them and finally executed them freehand, a development which took several months. Persistence with the tracing book and freehand practice required effort. He persevered until he could draw what he called a "cartoon universe." His involved concentration and labor—more than he ever applied to assigned work—ensured a measure of skill and satisfaction. His drawing was a spontaneous outlet for self-expression and an exercise in disciplined self-teaching.

A teacher-chosen art activity might have served a similar community-building purpose, but Daryl's drawing was pressure-free, without any need to bend to group standards and demands. A class mural might have failed, because he would have resisted any external constraints.

Daryl's interest in drawing first surfaced in second grade, but because he refused to put his pens away and move on to other work, his drawing became an arena for confrontation with the teacher rather than a vehicle for growth.

In Karen's class, drawing was as legitimate as reading, receiving neither more nor less approval than any other activity.

While Daryl drew, he surveyed the classroom, positioning himself as if he were not going to be there long. From my notes in early September:

> He is perched on a picnic bench, balanced on his knees, which are crossed, leaning far over the table. He never sits solidly and looks as if he could either take flight or be wafted away at any moment. He is drawing in his Drawing Book and has a pencil, provided by Karen at his request. He is not uninvolved with his drawing; his mouth is slightly open in concentration and his expressionless eyes cast downward, but at the same time he is monitoring the action in the rest of the room. Others are drawing congenially in twos and threes, but Daryl is at a table alone.

Is he using drawing as an excuse to observe before participating? "Better to be checking out the action in the room than out in the hallway," Karen said.

Had Daryl been the only one to draw, the social benefits would have been less striking, but drawing is natural for children at this age. They often spend free time drawing at home or in the interstices of a class which permits it, usually after all the teacher-assigned work is finished. In Karen's class, drawing was an appropriate activity which allowed children enough time to focus on each other, meeting a need rarely recognized in most schools. The social nature of drawing enhanced Karen's goal that every child find a "place." Children chatted as they drew, asking each other questions and discussing their views on the world. This is what Karen means by sharing perspectives.

Drawing has two other components which were good for Daryl's growth. First, it anchored him to one physical location. As his noisy disruptiveness made him newly visible, a stationary position at the drawing table gave children the opportunity to make overtures to him that they could not make when he was floating around the room or out in the halls. Second, drawing calmed him and saved him from his old forms of misbehavior. When faced with a new situation, a test, or a transition, he drew. When the music was "scary" at a concert, he took his pens from his back pocket and drew on the program. Before standardized tests, he drew. He found safety in drawing: the act of sitting with pencil and paper helped him cope.

Karen felt Daryl needed exposure to his more social peers through the mutual exchange and conversation which accompanies drawing. He needed to learn to focus on others as he had not the previous year. This leisurely drawing time gave him the chance to be included in a small friendship group and, as Karen said, "learn how it's done."

His socializing developed tentatively. As he reached out to others, his overtures were not hasty. But over the fall I observed a progression. First, Daryl appears in my notes drawing in various places alone; then silently with Jason and Terry; then with Arnie and Jeremy; then with Jason, Arnie, Jeremy, and David. The following excerpt from my notes shows him making a rare, early overture to another child and quickly withdrawing, but in it are the seeds of future friendship:

> On October 5th Daryl is at a central table, knees on the bench, body resting on his crossed legs, tracing comic book characters from *Crazy Magazine.* Arnie is sitting next to him. Daryl says, "Play you a game of Space Invaders?" This is the first time I have witnessed such an initiative. Arnie nods, changes his position, gets out a clean piece of paper, and says, partly for my benefit, "I played last year every recess." Daryl adds, "I never played at all last year."
>
> Arnie is the acknowledged class expert at this game. It is played by two or more players and the point is to destroy an opponent's bases. The strategic location of bases can impede attack. The only constraint is a firmly held pencil which is manipulated as a bomb. The distance a bomb can travel is the length of one pencil mark, about 1 ½ inches.
>
> Daryl and Arnie draw their bases and agree on dividing their paper more or less equally. Daryl is using Karen's personal marker. "Can I use your pencil?" Daryl asks me. I trade with him, but he isn't satisfied (a stalling move?) with my wobbly eraser. He goes ever so slowly across the room to get three new pencils from his briefcase.
>
> Arnie masterfully holds his pencil poised to destroy an asteroid. Daryl is much more tentative and is clearly outclassed.
>
> After two or three rounds, lasting maybe four minutes, Daryl stops. All of a sudden, with no verbal communication, Daryl has retreated, and Arnie is playing alone.
>
> Kamal, who takes the bus with Daryl, sits down next to him and Daryl switches into his performing mode—louder voice, phonier tone. I sense he is playing to an audience. Kamal and Daryl begin to draw on one piece of paper. Kamal draws USA in red on one of Daryl's space ships. Daryl says loudly, "Don't do that." Kamal invites Daryl to draw on his ship. Daryl retorts, "We're playing our way," casting an eye on Arnie's deftly drawn game.
>
> Kamal and Daryl are sitting very close, their bodies touching. There is a cast of silliness to the whole enterprise, but it seems to me a genuine interaction and involvement with each other. Those are rare for Daryl. When Kamal stops drawing to put a Band-Aid on his finger, Daryl wordlessly helps him to get it on properly.

This interaction with Kamal would have been wholly gratifying had it not taken place exactly as Karen announced, "Time to line up for the yard." Daryl and Kamal played while the class complied with Karen's request. Mary, the student teacher, asked Daryl to line up and then grabbed his pencil away in an affectionate physical tussle. He acknowledged her with a smile but didn't move. Finally Kamal said in a parental tone, "Come on, Daryl, do it." But Daryl didn't budge, and Mary put down the pencil and left with the group. Only after more than four minutes of slow-motion organizing was Daryl ready to leave, but Kamal waited for him and they went out together.

Daryl's overtures, when they occurred at all, were usually awkward. They were often disruptive because the time or topic was inappropriate. He needed to learn, almost by successive approximation, how and when to initiate, but his attempts were complicated by his insensitivity to what was going on around him. "Time for him to know and become known," was Karen's prescription for his yet-to-be developed ability to relate to individual children.

A "black group" formed temporarily in the early fall, and Daryl's inclusion in it helped him cross the line from disruptive performance to more genuine friendship with a smaller group. Ten black children, four of whom were female, stuck together and to the black student teacher, as she put it, "like white on rice." This group spent long hours of uninterrupted time together, collaborating on stories, drawing, finding out about each other's favorite music, testing power relationships, making allies and enemies, computing math problems, and differentiating themselves from the rest of the class in an effort to feel safe in this primarily white environment. Daryl, while not an active force, hung on the fringes of the group and was included by virtue of his color. I saw him watching the wrestling on the gym mats or sitting in the corner reading his *Smurfs*, next to others who were oblivious to him but tolerant of his neutral presence. One day at the end of October, Daryl moved to the center of this group. It was two o'clock, time for writing daily logs. Six children were at the table.

> Easy transition from meeting to work. Daryl sits down with the "black group" who are assembled at a table in the corner of the room. He has written in his log during silent reading (though Karen said he could not), and he is proud of his long, finished entry. He is making a pretense of drawing, but he is really interested in distracting the group, telling elephant jokes and using street language. It is the first time I have seen him funny with words rather than slapstick gestures. Daryl is supplying the energy and a new impetus every time conversation lulls. There is much giggling and camaraderie among the boys. The girls are merely observers, but a crucial audience. Daryl has a kind of uncharacteristic charm, quite unlike his mute presence or the exaggerated ham I have seen before, and is clearly enjoying himself.

When Karen decided this "black group" felt secure enough for unity again, she said to them one afternoon, "What is this? The back of the bus?" Though she continued to ease these children gently back into the larger unit, Daryl took advantage of this ready-made group to begin to develop relationships. But a group could be a vehicle for Daryl's growth only when he contributed appropriately. His skill in drawing gave him a better opening than distracting others; it didn't, however, necessarily encourage better timing, as the following anecdote shows.

Under Karen's direction, the class composed an illustrated book of "Stories and Poems We Made Together" which could be given as a Christmas gift. Daryl volunteered his "friends" to do the illustrating, marking a point in the year when one could say he had a congenial group of peers with whom to draw. But characteristically he contributed on his own terms, insisting that his illustrations could be done only during silent reading: "I can't read—I hafta draw another picture to go with Terry's story because my first one got lost." Request granted.

The Christmas book was teacher-organized. By January, Daryl and his friends spontaneously produced a series of collaborative "Joke Books." The idea was to copy jokes from library books, make them up, or get them from classmates' joke books. The jokes were inscribed and then illustrated. "Welcome to the Daryl, Jamel, and Nick Joke Book" reads one, and then below, "Made by the Art and Joke Club." "The Jamel-N-Daryl Drawing-N-Joke Book" is nine pages of drawings and captions, no jokes. The theme of superheroes is emblazoned across each page, accompanied by smaller subtitles: "Justice vs. the Demons," "Justice vs. the Cosmic Craters," and "Justice in Death."

These collaborative efforts were contagious; they spread through the class and absorbed more children than just the "black group." They incorporated even the boys who usually played sophisticated pencil-and-paper war strategy games. As the most prolific of joke book producers, Daryl was becoming known for his cartooning skill and even sought after as a partner. In September he had not been capable of consistent participation—much less leadership—in a class discussion, on the playground, or even in the corridors. But drawing, matching as it did his own preferences, enabled Daryl to test out a more positive role instead of being typed as the class ham or the distracter par excellence.

This spate of joke books coincided with Daryl's beginning to behave differently, at least within the classroom. He communicated more openly, was out of the room less (though he almost always left when a visitor came), and more willingly risked new experience. There was a gradual shift in how he reacted to the rules. He still offered whiny resistance, or complained, "I'm too tired" or "Do I have to?" But he eventually lined up, joined the circle, or otherwise did what he was asked to do. These changes sprang from various corners of life under Karen's tutelage, but his improvement and his new social "place," carved out at the drawing table, seemed connected.

By March the joke book phenomenon had died down, but the pattern was set for shared art. Evidence of this shared activity comes from both the art room and Daryl's journal.

The art room was the only location outside the classroom where he did not invite antagonism. The lunchroom aide was quite specific, telling me one January day, "If you want to give me a nervous breakdown, just send me Daryl," but after lunch Daryl behaved like a "straight kid." During recess at P.S. 135, children can choose among gym activities, outside games, or the art room. The art room was a dream setup for a child like Daryl and provided essential support in much the way Karen did: no direct instruction, no lessons, just materials and a chance to explore. Students from grades K through 5 worked side by side. Daryl could enter and exit at will, float around to see where the action was, momentarily involve himself, and move on. He spent time there every day.

Excerpts from his daily log:

> 3/31 I went to the art room with Nick and he drew a space picture.
>
> 4/4 I went to gym and went to the art room and my friend drew me and my friend a picture.
>
> 4/20 . . . Then I went to the art room and drew space ships.
>
> 4/22 Then I went to the art room so then my friend drew me a picture.
>
> 4/29 Then I went to the art room with my friend and he drew me a Garfield and then I drew in my Drawing Book.
>
> 5/6 Then I went to the art room and my friend Hugh drew me a picture.
>
> 5/7 Then I went to the art room and drew my friend Tyrone something. Then I drew another picture for my friend Ebbin.

None of the children he mentions, except Nick, were in his class. This group regularly congregated in the art room; they were the school's most passionate artists. The fact that Daryl was a part of their reciprocal gift-giving ritual shows how far he had come out of his social isolation and how much he felt a part of the entire school community. This was major growth.

Pencils, Paper, and Daryl's Drawing Book

Karen and I have radically different attitudes toward classroom materials, so I paid special attention to basic supplies in her classroom. I am constantly provisioning and organizing; Karen leaves it up to the children. But far from being indifferent, her strong teaching values extend to pencils and paper.

In keeping with her philosophy that children need to contribute for the good of their own education, Karen provided few supplies. Supplies were the children's responsibility and, by extension, their parents', who, she believed, should be deeply involved in the classroom. Children were encouraged—even required—to bring in pencils for the whole class. "My own pencil" was not a phrase supportive of Karen's idea of community. Shared materials were the norm, and she considered children's use or abuse of them indicative of how far they had come toward her vision of community. Many teachers in this era of inadequate budgets resort to their own pocketbooks. When Karen contributed, she did so for the whole school. Through her mother's workplace she had access to a seemingly endless quantity of the highest quality eighteen by twenty-four inch white drawing paper, and the entire P.S. 135 population enjoyed that luxury. Her classroom depended on materials donated by its members to be used by everyone.

Daryl brought materials from home, and what he shared and what he hoarded provided an interesting commentary on his growth. He kept his collection of essentials in top condition: thin-tipped pens, a drawing notebook, and a pad of tracing paper. He stored his pencils in his cubby and frequently expressed surprise that anyone would "bring in pencils for the whole class when the class hadn't done nothin' in return." But he rarely used his own pencils, preferring to borrow one from an adult. He never loaned his pens and took such care of them that no one dared to ask. They were kept in his back pocket where he could get to them in a hurry, and he touched them often just to check their whereabouts. He followed the losses of other people's pens carefully, though he never lost his own or became involved in ownership disputes.

He owned an extensive collection of comic books which he brought each day. This meticulously cared-for resource became a necessary prop for his drawing, and possibly smoothed his entry into the class social life. Although he didn't lend his pens, he shared the precious comics; it was the combined activity suggested by comic books and drawing that provided his first collaborative work projects.

That he hoarded pencils and refused to contribute to the class supply, yet lent his comics, was curious. My sense was that he knew the comics were his and he would continue to own them, but he could not reconcile giving up consumables to others without any tangible return. This was true through the end of the year, but Karen says she has confidence that a fond dream of hers will come true—"that somewhere, in a classroom I will never hear about, Daryl will bring ten pencils for the whole class without being asked."

Some children use possessions to engage others in acts of friendship, but Daryl lent comics without ceremony to anyone who was interested. Early in the year he had no investment in any particular children, and those who gravitated to the drawing/cartooning activities were the natural borrowers. Karen was ever alert to children who "buy off" others and would not have allowed the comics to remain had Daryl used them to include and exclude.

Karen organized very little. "How can I organize for children I haven't met?" was Karen's response before school opened to my asking why she didn't devise procedures for organizing materials. Though she appreciated every scrap of writing or drawing and valued the thought and the child who created it, she just didn't value its corporeal manifestation—that it needed a place in the classroom on real shelves with real mechanisms for keeping it in order. As she pointed out in one of our heated discussions of this issue, "Those children for whom organization is important maintain that organization without me." Daryl was one of those children. The environmental chaos did not seem to touch him; he remained meticulously organized all year.

Despite the availability of all Karen's wonderful drawing paper, Daryl chose to draw in a lined composition book. He labeled it "Daryl's Drawing Book" and generally carried it with him or kept it in his cubby. He never left it lying around, nor did he ever misplace it or leave it at home. He did not date the pages but drew on them in order, leaving no pages blank. He never did math or wrote stories in this book (with one important exception), though he occasionally added fragmentary captions.

This Drawing Book was very much a part of him. When I wanted to Xerox it at the end of the year, he could hardly bear to part with it, even for an hour.

When I insisted, Karen rushed over. (She would have taken his side had any real dispute developed.) Daryl complained to her, "She thinks it's like a treasure." We both said in unison, "It is." He was pleased enough by my interest to consent to the book's absence during music, if I promised to have it back by recess. However, he had the last word. He pulled a straight-faced joke on me, making me promise not to return his book all white. I agreed without understanding, but when I gave it back to him, he said, "Good. I thought you were going to Clorox it."

The Content of the Drawing Book

The Drawing Book exudes energy and motion. Some figures are fully drawn, others are moving sticks achieved by swiftly dashed-off lines. Explosions pepper most pages. Some pages have captions, some don't. There are no stories or assignments. This is an artist's sketchbook with experiments, doodles, and half-finished work.

Daryl didn't start out drawing in this vivid way. At first he taped tracing paper to comic books and traced characters over and over until he felt ready to draw them freehand. He valued his tracing—and perhaps the confidence it gave him—so much that a substitute teacher once outraged him by insisting his tracing was "babyish." She had passed out tracing paper and colored tissue paper for children to tear up and make scenes of spring. Daryl matter-of-factly refused, saying, "I did this in kindergarten," and proceeded to trace from a book. The substitute continued to argue that tracing was "a crutch, and a mindless activity." His defense was weak—"Karen lets us trace." He was the only one who ever traced, but his use in late May of "us" bespoke his new community feeling. He stopped the tracing, but from that moment on he provoked this woman mercilessly, as only he knew how. Daryl's tracing was important to him; he depended on this safe method of learning that contributed to his pleasure and eventually to his skill.

In the Drawing Book, immobile cartoon characters without Daryl's special stamp are occasionally interspersed with his action drawings. When asked by a teacher to draw during class, he often returns to these stereotyped drawings, but the work he did for himself is much more expressive.

Karen saw his cartooning in a broader context. "Cartoon," she reminded me, "has other meanings, one of which is a preparatory design for a larger work." Daryl's larger work, according to Karen, was to explore his own questions. Looking in detail at one page in his Drawing Book illuminates his unique perspective, as would any slice of his drawing, writing, or behavior.

The drawing I have chosen to describe here was done during February, with a very thin Magic Marker. The nine furiously active figures are suspended in mid-air like trapeze artists, floating without visible ground to anchor them, but Daryl has supplied an imaginary floor to give them leverage to push or kick. Facial expressions (hard to study in a reproduced version) show anger,

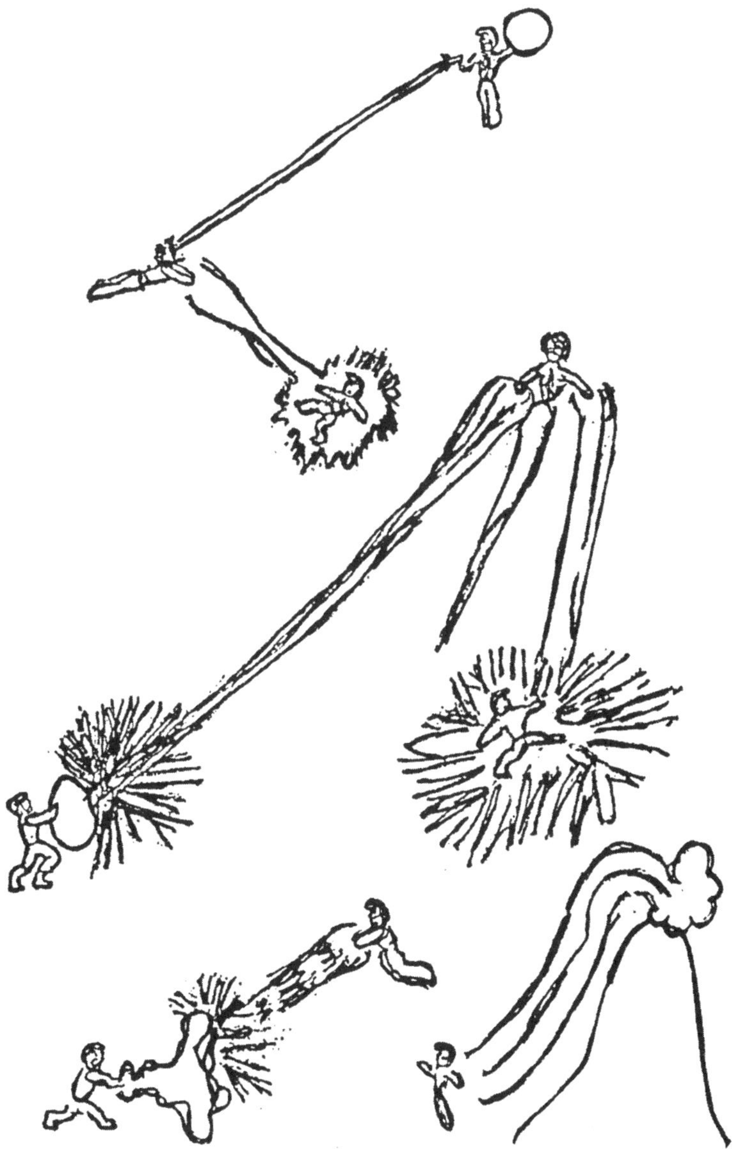

Daryl's Drawing

exertion, and concentration. Like many of Daryl's drawings, the triangularity stands out: three figures in each of three groups are connected by lines which instinctively cause the viewer to supply a missing hypotenuse. The top third of the page is blank, and these three triangular shapes plus an obscure figure in the lower right form a parallelogram.

Conflict is the subject, and ambiguity reigns. The muscular figures are neither clothed nor naked. Each of them deploys a weapon, superheroic body force, or both. Each emits a laser-like beam, or a defense against it. The essentially parallel lines which connect the figures either begin or end in short radiating bursts which might be devastating explosions or protective shields. Action dominates, but meaning is obscured. Is there a story? Are these the same figures over time? Is there any outcome? Hard to tell.

Power seems to be at issue, but unlike hand-to-hand combat this is power-at-a-distance. Who has the power? Is it two against one? Or one against two? The power is so symmetrical it is impossible to tell. Elegantly balanced, this is a collision of equals; no one conquers, and no one is conquered. The overriding impression is tension among the combatants as they challenge and resist.

Daryl's thought, as in all cartoons, is condensed, abbreviated, and conveyed by parsimonious lines. Cartooning is a tightly-bound medium. This is not the comic book plot of good prevailing over evil, but rather Daryl's perspective on attack and resistance. He has captured the tension between and among his characters without identifying his own viewpoint. This is a place where ambiguity and lack of clarity could exist within tight boundaries, an arena for Daryl's own explorations.

Every child's drawings are uniquely expressive, though some adults find it easy to dismiss children's cartoon-style drawing as trite, unoriginal, and repetitive. For that reason, Daryl's cartoons did not get the attention they deserved during the year from me or any of the other adults in his life, except Karen.[3] She valued his drawings and attended to his self-image as an artist.

Daryl approached institutional life so hesitantly but with such insistence on his own conditions that when he disclosed any part of himself at school, Karen took notice. Daryl first identified himself out loud as an artist when the dance teacher asked children what they were going to be for Halloween. After some coaxing, Daryl answered, "a artist." Though he wore no costume for the traditional school parade, Karen took it that "the thought was in his head."

Except for the Christmas books, Karen's role in how the children spent their free time was characteristically indirect, so any intervention took on a heightened significance. On January 19, sitting next to Daryl as he traced, she said quietly, "I knew someone who made a whole comic book and told a story with tracings. Maybe you could do that." No requirements, no pressure, just a casually tossed-off comment, but her tone conveyed conviction that he could do whatever he wanted to do. Daryl responded as if he were sharing a secret, "I know what I want to be when I grow up," he said, enumerating on his fingers, "a artist and a storyteller."

In January he wrote in his Drawing Book: "Daryl is not a drawer, he is a good drawer." In February he had expertise to share and added a PR touch at the end:

> Today kids we're going to draw cartoon people with Daryl.
>
> No. 1 You draw a head with some ears.
>
> No. 2 Then you start to draw some eyes with a nose and a mouth.
>
> No. 3 And then you start to draw the Body with some clothes and some shoes.
>
> No. 4 Then you write your name and tell your friends that you drew it. And that's all.

In June, modestly but with confidence, he announced to a group of peers, "I am a better drawer than some. In fact I'm a good drawer."

Karen picked up these fleeting references and made them more salient to Daryl, his classmates, and me. Between the art room and the classroom he was becoming known to other children for his cartooning.

In February, when he wrote an undisguised autobiographical story in his Drawing Book (the only composition to appear there), Karen took it as his effort "to make himself more visible to himself and others." She believes one function of written self-expression is to "hear yourself as you write." She said, "Daryl is addressing his family to make them see who he is and understand that he is a strong person in his own right, entitled to his own goals and preferences." This is the composition, corrected for punctuation to make it more readable, but uncorrected for spelling (he made no errors) and grammar.

> Once upon a time there was a boy name Daryl and he like drawing and wanted to be a artist. But his brother said "No, no, no, be a football player." "No, no, no, be a painter," said his mother and then his father said, "Wait a minute now. If Daryl wants to be a artist let him be a artist." "That's right mommy. I'm going on ten and you keep telling me to be a painter," said Daryl. "But don't you want to be like Rembrandt?" "No," said Daryl. "Why?" "Because I like to draw pictures," said Daryl. So one day Daryl made a picture and his father said "Wow, that's great. I'll go and show it to your mother." "No," said Daryl. "She might say 'he shoulda painted it.'" "So what. Don't let that get in your way," said the father. "Okay. She could see it, but I will show it to her." So Daryl showed his mother and his mother saw it and called Kirk and Kirk said "Daryl should be an artist after all," and Daryl got married and been a artist. —The End

The narrator starts out in the powerful language of the storyteller: "Once upon a time there was a boy named Daryl who wanted to be a artist." He names the boy Daryl, but puts some distance between himself and the story by choosing to write in the third person. Fairytale-like, the story begins with a goal for the future, poses obstacles to surmount, and has a happy ending.

Daryl's task is to overcome the "no, no, no's" showered on him by his mother and brother, which are not so much life-threatening as soul-threatening. His father is the enabler who runs interference, the catalyst for Daryl's growth:

"Wait a minute now. If Daryl wants to be a artist, let him be a artist." Three times his father intervenes, and each time Daryl stands up for himself and his increasing maturity. Daryl begins to argue for himself, and then, foregoing merely oral argument, he draws a good picture and proves his qualifications. Still, he is not yet strong enough to stand entirely on his own. The final arbiter is his brother Kirk, who gives the needed permission: "Daryl should be an artist after all." Daryl wins out. The story ends romantically despite a plot devoid of romance: "Daryl got married and been a artist."

From the first Daryl knows what he wants and persists until he engineers an agreement. He is caught in a typical preadolescent dilemma; he depends on his family's approval, even as he resists their advice. He is saying, "I'm going on ten years old and you are still telling me how to run my life." But he still needs their reassurance and approval.

"This composition," Karen says, "is about growing up, making choices, and having aspirations. Daryl is struggling with the coming of age that allows us to get onto the next stage." Karen has protected Daryl against the "no, no, no's" which thwart his own inner direction. She has been an enabler, giving him space and encouragement. In turn, Daryl has adopted one of her most characteristic sayings, "Don't let that get in your way." "If Daryl wants to be an artist, let him be an artist" is exactly how Karen feels about honoring children's preferences.

This writing could easily have been ignored, like his cartoons, or used to demonstrate sticky family politics, limited vocabulary, immature style, or puzzling confusion between painters and artists, rather than as an entry into how he views the world. Karen assumes that each act of self-expression, each spoken word, and each classroom choice is a significant statement and deserves respectful attention. To understand those choices is her quest.

Daryl's Questions

Conversation on June 3rd:

Daryl: I want to be the first and only one on the moon.

Jeremy: But you wouldn't have any friends.

Daryl: But then I'd see what the future is like.

Conversation on June 25th:

Daryl: Hey, what age would you be if you could be any age?

David: I don't know.

Daryl: I'd be old enough to drive. I would drive myself right home.

David: You wouldn't know the way.

Daryl: Yes, I would. I know in my head. I would just get in the car and go right there.

Excerpt from my notes, June 7th:

> On the way back to school, Daryl regards the rest of the field trip as his own personal shopping expedition. Even though thirty adults and ninety children are walking together through Midtown, Daryl is stopping at each store window to check it out, comment, fantasize. He runs way ahead, then lags until the group passes him. The adults are concerned that we will lose him if we don't wait, but miss the school bus if we do. I am nominally in charge and visibly exasperated. Just as I was too dizzy from keeping tabs on him to care whether he got lost or not, Karen passed by and without even making eye contact with him, calmly said, "If you miss the school bus, don't ask me for help."

And he did miss the school bus. And he did solve the problem, as Karen knew he would. He didn't call his mother at work or ask anyone for city bus money. He walked thirty blocks to his after-school program, though he had never gone on foot before. He found his way by remembering landmarks. The next day as he retold the story, he was proud of his effort, his good memory, and that "I wasn't even tired." Karen was proud on his behalf.

So much of Daryl's energy went toward deviating from what was expected that his potential had gone unnoticed, as had his startlingly strong sense of self-direction. To school authorities, Daryl appeared to be a classically oppositional child, fighting battles for the sake of fighting. On closer observation, Daryl knew exactly where he wanted to go, and how to find his way. Karen was the first adult in his school life to see this. She knew he needed to travel his own path, and her commitment to supporting him on that journey never wavered. She understood his questions.

When I first came to Karen's class, the image of Daryl floating silently around the classroom overwhelmed any other impression of him. By June he had ceased to float and had revealed his destination: he is bound for the moon, for home, and for his after-school program, all under his own command. He knows the routes and controls how he travels. He is self-reliant, not only in fantasy, but in reality. Karen, if only intuitively, understood all along, but it took me months of studying my notes to see that until he felt autonomous, Daryl was incapable of learning in a conventional classroom setting where institutional strictures and academic demands were beyond his control. As Daryl emerged from his silence, he was no longer an invisible child in danger of falling into the special education track; his deviant presence was no longer a nuisance. He was ready to move on within the mainstream.

Karen believed that had Daryl not been in her class, he would have continued to be "a child who spoke under his breath, never daring to raise his voice." He would have kept himself so enveloped in protective layers that no one would have ever known his true nature. In fact, Daryl changed from a contained, unknown child into a "straight kid" (Karen's word for a typical ten-year-old) whose wit, facility with language, and capacity for intimate friendship came as something of a surprise to everyone but Karen. Her skill was the ability to unite the issues of time, self-direction, and compliance with her acceptance of Daryl.

Daryl's slowness, recalcitrance, and need to ponder the world at his own pace were parts of his personality that Karen made no attempt to change. She insisted that the group include Daryl as he was and stretched the usual school and class rules so he did not feel boxed into situations from which he could not escape.[4] His stony resistance dissolved in part because Karen diluted institutional demands enough so that he began to see himself as a "straight kid," not as a deviant nuisance. Others began to see him more positively, too. Karen mediated external time pressures on Daryl because she felt that he could not yet comply and forcing him would lead nowhere. Even though his behavior could try one's soul, she never expressed distaste for the way he was. On the contrary, she appreciated him and took pleasure in him as his personality emerged over the year. Her willingness to allow Daryl some leeway in conforming gave him a chance to negotiate this unfamiliar school territory at his own pace and in his own way.

Karen understood that Daryl questioned personal, institutional, and physical boundaries. Boundaries obsessed him. He pushed adults to the end of their tolerance. Instinctively he moved to the fringe in any group, always toying on the edge of the barely permissible. He made tentative contact with his surroundings as if he weren't quite sure walls, chairs, and tables were solid. He chose the tightly bound medium of traced cartoons for his first disciplined activity. At first glance, an obvious teaching strategy would dictate setting firm limits, but any attempt to impose secure boundaries failed. Paradoxically the more closely drawn the external rules, the more Daryl overstepped them, but the less clear the boundaries were, the more anxious and provocative his behavior became. Karen saw him through this paralyzing conflict. She did not hold him to the rules and tolerated his provocations until they stopped. She created an environment in which he could be himself.

Conclusion

Good teachers are not all alike. Karen's approach is only one possibility among many, but unless teachers have the autonomy to apply their own philosophy and values, schools will continue to miss out on an enormous wealth of talent.

Karen's classroom, though unconventional and incomplete in some ways (the Cusenaire rods on the floor drove me crazy), is a success for many children because she teaches by her own idiosyncratic methods. For some children there is a greater chance of growth in this classroom than in other places in school. There are teachers and administrators who might think that this kind of teaching belongs in special education, but Karen disagrees for the same reason she refused to refer Daryl to special education classes: she believes the labeling and segregation of children is pernicious. She feels that daily, relaxed, sustained interaction among children of different backgrounds and temperaments is crucial to their knowing each other and breaking down the barriers which separate them. This is how understanding is built.

The structure of schooling must encourage differences rather than similarities in teaching styles if schools are ever to meet the needs of the unique children in their care. Schools need teachers like Karen for her passion, her ability to teach hard-to-reach children, her insight, and her acceptance of all children as they are.

Notes

1. Jervis, *Children's Thinking in the Classroom* (Grand Forks, ND: University of North Dakota Press, 1978).
2. One of Karen's core beliefs is in the existence of a "quest," a serious word in her idiosyncratic lexicon. I didn't see its importance until after my year of note-taking was over. Though I criticized much about her practice and we discussed every facet of her teaching, she never changed her views or flinched under my criticism. She simply said, "You are not seeing children's questions." She was right and the clues were there. An article by Beth Alberty so confirmed what she thought that she excerpted the following paragraph and sent it home as part of a notice on parent conferences and field trips (see "Children's Art: Where Art and Education Meet," *Artworkers News, 11*, No. 5 (1982), 20–21):

   > [Descriptions of children's artwork] are unfinished and partial, but at least they make more visible to us, as interested adults and especially as educators, a personal intentionality on the part of the child that is a form of questing. It is here, to my mind, that art and education meet in children's art, for in its deepest sense, education, like artmaking, is a quest, an inquiry into the world, self, and others from which personal understanding evolves.

3. During the year, though I saw his drawing as a mark of social progress, I did not look carefully at the content. I scooped the Joke Books off the floor, worried that they were casually treated by the children, and marvelled only that there were so many of them, a goodly number not finished. Karen was characteristically unconcerned. I took them, along with the "Cloroxed" Drawing Book, off to the Prospect Summer Institute and left them on my shelf, ignored, until a college-level children's art teacher pounced on them when she came to my room for a chat. We had been discussing her doctoral research, a once-a-week class with children where she determined the agenda. She had photographed and catalogued all the products beautifully, but she was dissatisfied. All the Institute participants had oohed and aahed over her slides, but she felt her children's work was "inauthentic." When she saw Daryl's work, she exclaimed, "This is what I mean by authentic. This work has the stamp of the child all over it. What I wouldn't give to have access to a class that did artwork like this." She made me take another look at what Daryl had invested in his drawing and to pay more attention to how important it was for him to have the opportunity to draw.
4. For my article on her strategies, see "Daryl: Becoming Part of a Group," *Outlook, 49* (Autumn 1983) 3–24.

I have been helped by talks about Daryl with Karen; with my Los Angeles Children's Thinking Seminar; with Lillian Weber; and with numerous Prospect Summer Institute participants, especially Pat Carini, Anne Martin, and Nancy Lambert.

On Jorge Becoming a Boy

A Counselor's Perspective

TRAVIS WRIGHT

Macho

One month shy of three years old, Jorge is well on his way to becoming a little boy.[1] He is said to be the mirror image of his father, with wavy brown hair, dark brown eyes, and a light beige complexion that reflects his Latino heritage. Besides mirroring his father's physical appearance, Jorge shares his nickname, Macho. A scratch on Jorge's left cheek, the remnants of a clumsy run-in with a classroom table, indicates that this is a child who likes to be in motion. Jorge is shorter than the rest of his classmates; his head rises only slightly above my knees. Yet, with a smile that lights up his entire face and eyes that twinkle with mischievousness, Jorge makes up in personality for anything that he lacks in physical stature.

I have known Jorge since he was sixteen months old, the first child I met while completing a counseling internship. While it is uncommon for children to participate in therapy at such a young age, Jorge was referred through his day-care center, which is the site of a university research project aimed at fostering the positive development of children and families living in poverty. Originally, Jorge was referred for therapy mainly as a preventative measure — his family's low socioeconomic status and his father's sporadic involvement in his life make Jorge particularly vulnerable to future challenges. However, in recent months, due to a contentious custody dispute between Jorge's mother and the father of Swahim, his six-year-old half-brother, therapy has helped Jorge deal with the unexpected departure of his own father and Swahim's removal from their home by the Department of Social Services. These events have had a great impact on Jorge's mother, who has become overworked and

[1] Pseudonyms have been used in this article to ensure the confidentiality of participants.

Harvard Educational Review Vol. 77 No. 2 Summer 2007

often appears depressed, sometimes struggling to maintain a consistent routine for Jorge and his five-year-old sister, Shanille.

Despite my initial reservations about working with small children, I was assigned to work with Jorge by Linda, the center's clinical director, who believed that "the little guy could benefit from a male presence in his life." For over two years, Jorge and I spent nearly ten hours a week together — in his classroom, on the playground, and in our weekly pair play-therapy sessions, where we were joined by Jorge's classmate, Goddess, and Linda. Pair play-therapy is a unique modality involving two children and two therapists, who all work together. The aim of pair play-therapy is to provide a relational context through which children develop the interpersonal competencies necessary to participate successfully in their social world (Selman, Watts, & Schultz, 1997). For approximately an hour each week, Jorge, Goddess, Linda, and I "played" together in the center's tiny therapy room, exploring play themes introduced by Jorge and Goddess that echoed their real-life experiences: loss, fear, joy, ambivalence, trust, anger, mastery, growing up, and figuring out what it means to be a little boy or girl. It has been rewarding to watch Jorge and Goddess become friends, developing a bond that sustains itself even outside of the supportive therapeutic environment.

Recognizing my special connection with Jorge, several teachers at Jorge's day-care center often jokingly referred to Jorge as my son. Despite my corrections, Jorge even called me Daddy for the first six months of our time together. I heard Jorge's first sentence, held his hand as he learned to hop on one foot, and supported him through the departure of his father and brother. Building a relationship with Jorge has been the most profound learning experience of my educational career.

Becoming part of Jorge's life has challenged me to confront parts of my own life. Our experiences and communities are different in many ways, yet I see much of myself in Jorge. I know what it is like to live in a home filled with both good times and worry. I was raised by a hardworking single mother in an underresourced southern community. I have felt unsafe. My father walked out on us when I was still a boy. I was able to connect with Jorge's experiences of abandonment, not necessarily understanding his experiences or knowing his feelings, but certainly able to imagine, empathize with, and try to interpret them. As in any relationship, one may never truly know how another is making sense of his or her world. However, as I have learned with Jorge, through time, connection, and listening we may come to a deeper understanding of others' perspectives. Reflection, on my own and in supervision with Linda, has helped me to understand better how my experiences could both help and hinder my understanding of Jorge. In this article I offer my perceptions, recognizing that Jorge's actual experience of events may be different.

In thinking about the kind of man I want to help Jorge become — my explicit charge from the day-care center's clinical director — I have been challenged to think about the kind of man I hope to be myself. Attempts to reconcile the values of my childhood, where good men are supposed to marry women, do physical labor, and conform to conservative religious traditions, with those of my life as a gay graduate student at an Ivy League institution, where liberal, intellectual nonconformity is prized, have allowed me to recognize that communities and cultures often have conflicting notions of what it means to be a good man and that failure to conform to the dominant standards may be painful for an individual. It has not been easy for my family to accept me as an urban, gay intellectual, as they often assume my path is a criticism of their own. I have often felt similarly marginalized as a proud, working-class, southern person of faith in the world of the privileged East Coast academic establishment. In both environments I have experienced rejection, dismissal, and misunderstanding. To overcome the sting of such marginalization, I have at various times worked to accommodate the values of my past (driving a pickup truck, playing sports, and making it a point to be conversant about NASCAR) and my present (reading *The New Yorker*, wearing blazers, and taking a wine-tasting course). Yet, I also wonder what is lost in conformity.

Many men in competitive patriarchal societies, like that of the United States, struggle to sustain close relationships, experience intimacy, and express emotions (Kaufman, 2001; Kindlon & Thompson, 1999; Kimmel & Messner, 2001). Theorists argue that these challenges are the result of the way dominant notions of masculinity are constructed in these societies (Kimmel & Messner, 2001). Although different patriarchal cultures have unique words (like *masculinity* in the United States or *machismo* in Latino culture) and traditions (like football or bullfighting) to perform and celebrate their particular interpretation of what makes a good man, scholars have posited that there are certain similarities across these traditions. Historically, the good man of Western patriarchy has been portrayed as strong, aloof, aggressive, competitive, and independent (Kimmel & Messner, 2001). For a man to be perceived as otherwise would result in his being ridiculed, ostracized, and perhaps even victimized by the dominant society (Kimmel, 1994). The prevalence of taunts like sissy, *maricon,* faggot, and queer on our playgrounds, sports fields, and in our schools speaks volumes about the pervasiveness of this masculine code, at the same time pointing to the antiwoman and antigay inclinations of our particular brand of patriarchy. Yet, women and men who do not conform to traditional notions of gender are not the only ones to suffer in such an environment. For even those who may be perceived by society as being effectively masculine, being a good man also comes at a cost. In cultures where men are expected to stand on their own, not cry, and be tough guys from a very young age, they simply do not have permission or the skills to feel close to others or vulnerable — a potentially lonely and frustrating existence. Coming to see my journey as one shared by Jorge and all men has forced me to question the kind of partner, father, and friend I will work to become. I have also been led to consider, as a child psychologist, what kind of boys and men I will support my clients in becoming.

I hope that my answers to these questions will support counselors, teachers, and other practitioners as they think about the ways their understanding of gender may influence their work with young children. In this portrait, I explore a question that I hastily scribbled in the corner of my therapy notes a few months into my work with Jorge: "How is Jorge, a two-year-old Latino child, called 'Macho' by his community, learning what it means to be a boy?" I use several guiding questions to organize my interpretation: How is gender represented in Jorge's day-care center, and how are such representations related to social and cultural perceptions of masculinity and femininity? What are the implicit and explicit values promoted in Jorge's day-care environment in terms of different expressions of masculinity? What strategies are used to facilitate gender socialization in this day-care environment? And, lastly, how might Jorge be affected when his behavior and emotional needs contradict the norms of his day-care environment, culture, and society?

Given the similar construction (if not performance) of masculinity across Western, competitive cultures, I focus for the purposes of this portrait primarily on the impact of gender socialization as a social phenomenon rather than a cultural one. I use the lens of culture not as a critique of a particular culture, but to better illuminate the way gender is represented and reinforced for Jorge within his cultural context. Indeed, the central aim of this analysis is to provide commentary on the impact of restrictive notions of gender, and on the ways that Western, competitive cultures perpetuate these notions, rather than examine the norms of Latino culture.

I utilize portraiture as the organizing methodological approach in this work. Pioneered by Sara Lawrence-Lightfoot (1983; Lawrence-Lightfoot & Davis, 1997), portraiture combines rigorous analytic and interpretive strategies with aesthetics to capture the complexity and subtlety of human and organizational experience. Lawrence-Lightfoot and Davis (1997) explain:

> Portraitists seek to record and interpret the perspectives and experiences of the people they are studying, documenting their voices and visions — their authority, knowledge, and wisdom. The drawing of the portrait is placed in the social and cultural context and shaped through dialogue between the portraitist and the subject, each one negotiating the discourse and shaping the evolving image. The relationship between the two is rich with meaning and resonance and becomes the arena for navigating the empirical, aesthetic, and ethical dimensions of authentic and compelling narrative. (p. xv)

The goal of the portraitist is to produce a "narrative that is at once complex, provocative, and inviting, that attempts to be holistic, revealing the dynamic interaction of values, personality, structure, and history . . . in context" (Lawrence-Lightfoot & Davis, 1997, p. 11). Consistent with the aesthetic considerations of this approach, portraiture does not typically include citations, although the interpretive framework of the portraitist is embedded in an understanding of the relevant research literature. In keeping with this approach, rather than explicating the findings of my analysis, I have organized this portrait conceptually, choosing vignettes and subheads to represent the various themes emerging from my data. I have found that the portrait can provide an alternative to the ways many of the objectivist disciplinary conventions of academia reduce the complexity and goodness of individual lives to patterns, trends, and problems.

In order to balance the aims of holism and complexity, I have chosen to use a temporal framework — one day in the life of my relationship with Jorge — to organize this portrait. However, the analytic and interpretive aspects of this work draw from a multiple-year relationship with Jorge within the context of his day-care center and community. Field notes, memos, my personal journal entries, direct observations, videos of our therapy sessions, and interviews with Jorge's teachers, social workers, therapists, and his family were the basis for analysis in this work.

The portraitist does not explicitly aim for her or his work to be generalizable, but a valid and deeply textured representation of his or her subject. However, it is assumed that by going deeply into the experience of another, a more essential experience of the world might be captured. Thus, my intention in this work becomes twofold. Through a deep exploration of Jorge, and of his interactions with me and his world, I provide insight into how sociocultural forces impact the development of children. Specifically, I explore the consequences of gender socialization that prioritizes a masculinity that is detached, hierarchical, and devalues emotion. I also comment on the importance of reflection and reflexivity in work with young children, presenting portraiture as a tool that both captures and supports this process.

Two Worlds

The alarm clock screams in the morning stillness. It's 5:55 A.M. I have woken early in an attempt to arrive at the day-care center before Jorge. He is usually the first child to be dropped off in the morning and is often playing with his mother and older sister in the center's parking lot when the staff arrives at 7:30. Jorge's mother, Susan, who works from 8:00 to 5:00 as an aide to a legal assistant, takes great pride in being at work on time.

As I walk to my pickup truck, my mind turns to Susan. It has taken me over an hour to ready myself and my five-year-old dog for the day. I cannot imagine what mornings must be like for her. Alone with two children who have to be ready before 7:15 A.M., Susan must have her hands full, yet she seems to have a knack for balancing complicated schedules. Despite having been a teenage mother of two, Susan graduated from high school in four years at the age of eighteen. She has since completed a technical skills certificate and given birth to her third child, Jorge.

Winding along the banks of the Franklin River, passing the spires, bell towers, and distinguished redbrick buildings of the university, I laugh to myself when I realize the seeming mismatch between the country music coming from my radio and the stoic reserve and understated self-importance of the university buildings around me. I cross the river and eventually drive onto Landing Road, a busy commuter route beginning to fill with morning traffic. A driver in front of me attempts to merge across three lanes and creates a gridlock of angry commuters. As I wait for the melee to diffuse, I feel myself getting anxious. It is now 7:29.

As soon as I cross Dickinson Avenue and into Jorge's neighborhood, the streets become narrow and the potholes more pronounced. The buildings in this part of the city seem smaller than they actually are, dwarfed by the shadows of skyscrapers from the downtown nearby. Rather than stately red, the bricks on these buildings are gray, which underscores their run-down appearance. Rusted air conditioners, a boarded-up window, and an old bicycle chained to the corner light pole suggest that folks here are just making ends meet.

Turning right onto Eastland Way, I am greeted by rows and rows of identical white, three-story duplexes. Replacing what was once the most dangerous and monolithic of the city's housing projects, the relatively new Fresh Start Housing Development is the shining star of the mayor's low-income housing improvement efforts. The calm façade belies the violence that often occurs here after dark.

Various scarecrows, holiday lights, pink flamingoes, and assorted yard art are scattered throughout the neighborhood, resisting the anonymity of its design. On most mornings as I drive to work, I see mothers waiting with young children on street corners as buses slowly crawl from stop sign to stop sign. Old men and women stand in their doorways, watching the world move outside. But not on this morning; it is still too early.

I turn left into the parking lot of the Child Works Early Childhood Development Center, located in the center of Fresh Start. The brown brick building, perched on a tiny rise, watches over the neighborhood. Rows of windows stretch across the front and sides of the building, giving it an appearance of grinning when viewed from almost any direction. The bright reds, blues, yellows, and greens of a tiny fenced playground, complete with slides, a bouncing bridge, and a toddler-sized playhouse, signal that this is a place where children are happy.

I quickly find a parking space, glance at my watch — 7:39 A.M. — jump out of my truck, and run into the building. I wait for the security guard, a tall, muscular Black man whom I do not recognize, to buzz me through two separate security doors. The guard and doors are a response to a violent incident between two angry parents inside the center just three months earlier. On my way to the front desk, I pass the parents' bulletin board. Along with a few announcements, photos of all registered sex offenders living within several miles of the center are posted. Mostly White males, these faces are the only ones that look like mine at Child Works. Self-conscious of this fact each morning as I enter the building, I wonder if this bulletin board reflects fears that students, parents, and teachers may harbor about me — or if it might actually create them.

Shirley, the toddler classroom teacher, has been recruited to monitor the front desk this morning. She greets me as I enter the foyer. "Hi, Travis."

"Hi, Shirley. How are you today?"

"I'm tired. Wish I could have taken the day off and enjoyed a three-day weekend," she responds.

"Well, thank goodness it's Friday. We're almost to the weekend," I respond, attempting to empathize with her. "Is Jorge here yet?"

"Yep, you just missed Susan," Shirley informs me, yawning.

"How was the transition?" I ask.

"It was not good. Jorge did not want to get out of the car and was crying when Susan brought him in here. He has been crying every morning this week. I don't know what's gotten into that boy."

"Guess he just misses being in your room, Shirley," I say with a smile. "Let me get into Happy Hornets and check on him."

Jorge's class is twice as large as the class he was in last year, and most of his classmates are a year or two older than he is. The Happy Hornets is regarded by the clinical staff as the best class at Child Works, and Linda and I lobbied the classroom teacher, Juan, to accept Jorge and Goddess into his classroom even though they are a year younger than most of his other students. Usually children at Child Works move from the toddler room to a classroom for three-year-olds before entering the preschool class. However, given recent staff turnover in the three-year-old classrooms, we believed that Jorge and Goddess would benefit from the stability of the Happy Hornets class. Though Juan agreed, in large part because he seems to get a kick out of Jorge's antics, I have had the feeling in recent weeks that this is a decision that he might be regretting. He has appeared stressed and recently asked me for extra help with Jorge. Supporting Jorge requires a lot of energy, as he is younger than the other children and less capable of independence. In the new preschool environment, where he is no longer allowed to crawl into laps when upset, to be rocked to sleep when tired, or lavished with hugs, kisses, and cuddling, Jorge seems to miss the close relationships he enjoyed with his previous care providers, mostly women. He is now learning to stand on his own.

This change has not been an easy one for Jorge. Used to being coddled when upset, Jorge is now expected to take care of himself. In the midst of one of his tearful mornings, I witnessed a staff member saying to him, "Hush up, Jorge. There's no use in crying, nobody gonna be able to do nothing about it." Reflecting on how he might make sense of such a response to his feelings, I wondered whether Jorge might become guarded and mistrustful, questioning if others were willing to support him and thinking he must take care of himself. Although such stoic posturing may prove protective in some dangerous areas of Jorge's environment, such as when confronted by a bully, deciding whom to trust, or risking abandonment by another person he cares about, I imagine that it could also get in the way of other relationships that require closeness. It makes me sad to think that Jorge could feel lonely.

A Little Man

The Happy Hornets classroom, the largest at Child Works, bursts at the seams with its enrollment of twenty students. Filled with a cubby for each child, four tables, a block area, toy kitchen, computer, goldfish tank, music listening station, and a reading loft known as the Treehouse, the classroom is always buzzing with the sounds of little children. Walls are covered with construction-paper masterpieces, laminated alphabets, and the occasional freelanced Crayola graffiti. Classroom shelves are labeled in both Spanish and English. Puzzles, books, and toys are assigned locations, and students are expected to clean up after themselves before moving to a new activity. Order and self-control seem valued in this place.

Jorge is crying as I enter the classroom. Looking like a little man with his brand-new black Timberland high-tops, navy cargo pants, and a yellow-and-blue rugby shirt, Jorge is dressed much like the teenage boys I see on the sidewalks outside the center. Yet, his clothes' diminutive size and the Tonka Toy jeep on the front of his shirt show that they are indeed made for a little boy. Jorge attempts to hide his head in his hands as he turns into the block shelf, which is only a few inches shorter than he. Jorge's teacher, Juan, is a Puerto Rican man in his forties who has been teaching at Child Works for almost twenty years. He is standing a few feet from Jorge and bends over him slightly, encouraging him in his accented English, "What's wrong, Jorge? Stop crying and be a big boy. Mommy will be back later." This regular intervention at Child Works — "Stop crying and be a big boy" — seems to be both a request and a statement of value.

The imperative usually results in the little guy attempting to swallow his tears and put on a stoic front. I often wonder if the sadness is truly redirected or just hidden, becoming anxiety, or worse. It may be especially hard for Jorge to trust that his mother will be back later, as he is still waiting for a brother and father to return. It is in these moments that I am most torn; I want to encourage Jorge to express his sadness, for he has experienced so much loss, but I understand the importance of standing back and respecting the classroom process.

Teachers at Child Works have complained that the clinical staff undermines their authority by not holding children to the more stringent classroom norms. This adult conflict has at times been played out through students. At one point I was not permitted to enter Jorge's classroom for almost three weeks because one of his teachers felt my presence was too disruptive for him. She later shared with Linda that she did it to teach me a lesson — that she was "in charge of the children." Consequently, I have worked to help students understand that the rules of the therapy room are different from the rules of the classroom. I know that it will be easier for Jorge if he becomes part of the group. Nevertheless, I fear that Jorge is being encouraged to let go of his desire for connection and dismiss his feelings of longing, and being rewarded for standing on his own.

Taking in this scene between Jorge and Juan, I am struck by the similarities in their appearances. Though much larger than Jorge, Juan is also dressed in navy sweatpants, Timberland boots, and a Boston Red Sox jersey. Rather than a toy truck, a large golden rooster emblazoned with the Puerto Rican flag sits on Juan's chest. Six feet tall and clean-shaven, Juan compliments his look with three golden rings, two on his left hand and one on his right pinky.

Originally a janitor at Child Works, his first job after moving to the mainland United States, Juan worked his way up to lead teacher of the largest preschool class. He knows most of the children and their families outside of the school, as he lives with his wife just down the street from the center. I have admired Juan's patience, consistency, and positive interactions with the children since my first days at Child Works — and have come to appreciate the treacherous terrain he navigates so deftly. Though spending his days doing what many regard as "women's work," Juan is perceived by those around him to be a "good strong man," a compliment given to Juan by the grandmother of one of his students. Indeed, to be thought otherwise would raise suspicion about Juan's intentions with the children, a fact not lost on Juan. Though he seems to take great pleasure in teaching the children, I sense that Juan is often restrained in his contact with them.

Once he realizes that I have entered the room, Juan smiles at me, tossing his hands into the air and shrugging his shoulders as if to say, "Our friend Jorge . . . another rough morning." Jorge, sensing my presence, turns his body away from the shelf and lifts his eyes to look at me. Now self-conscious, he is reluctant to walk toward me but will not look away. Though I want to comfort him, I watch Jorge and Juan for clues as to how I should respond. Until a few weeks earlier, I would have picked Jorge up and held him, but the teachers in the preschool rooms have requested that the clinicians not hold children in the classrooms. They believe that such behavior fosters dependence on caregivers. In a class of twenty four- and five-year-olds, there is simply not enough lap time to go around. It saddens me that Jorge, not yet three years old, is expected to handle his feelings alone — that he is expected to be a "big boy." Yet I fear that while Jorge may be developing a greater sense of agency and autonomy, he may also be learning that the world is a cold and insensitive place. He is too young to be cynical. Jorge and I are both adjusting to new rules.

Jorge walks across the room, meeting me halfway and making it clear that he wants me to come to him. I walk over and kneel, placing my arm on Jorge's back. He steps into me, letting his head fall on my chest. After a few seconds of consolation, Jorge moves closer into my body and sits on my knee. I try to help Jorge name his feelings and say to him, "It's nice to be close to Travis." I also say, "It's nice to see you, too."

After regaining his composure, Jorge takes my hand and leads me to the computer area. It is the nicest play area in the room and the most isolated. Though the only other child in the room at this hour is busy with Juan, it is clear Jorge is trying to have me to himself. While grunting for me to stay "right here," Jorge drags one of the adult-sized chairs, reserved only for teachers, over to the table. Placing his hands on the fronts of my legs, Jorge pushes me into my chair with a clear nonverbalized command. When I ask him to use his words, Jorge responds with something that sounds remotely like "sit down." Though his words are barely understandable, probably a bit delayed for his age, Jorge is a skilled communicator. Relying on grunts, giggles, smiles, smirks, and the occasional bossy push, pull, or pinch, one rarely has to wonder what Jorge is thinking. Nevertheless, "Use your words, Jorge," is a constant refrain from those of us working with him. But we all share the belief, echoed by his former classroom teacher, that once he starts talking, "Jorge will never stop."

After helping Jorge turn on the computer and navigate his way to the "Wiggles Wild Adventure" game, I take out a pen and begin writing observations of the last few minutes. Jorge also grabs a pen on the table and begins to write on my paper. When I attempt to redirect Jorge's attention to the computer, he refuses, instead grunting for his own piece of paper. Jorge does not like to be ignored.

As Jorge scribbles on the paper he is holding on my lap, I become momentarily lost in my notes. Unexpectedly, Jorge looks up at me, touches my chest, and asks, "Travis titties?" Taken aback, I utter a nervous laugh, smile, and then say to Jorge, "No, not titties. I'm a boy. This is my chest," while directing his hands back to his lap. Curiously, Jorge replies, "Mommy's titties?" Still somewhat confused, I respond, "Yes, Mommy has titties, just like other big girls. Boys don't have titties. I am a boy." Jorge then clutches his own chest, asking, "Jorge's titties?" I answer gently, "No. Jorge doesn't have titties. You are a boy." Perhaps sensing my nervousness and already possessing a keen wit, Jorge goes for a reaction this time and grabs my chest, "Travis titties." I counter with feigned frustration, "Silly, Jorge. Boys don't have titties." Jorge giggles before turning back to the computer, taking great pleasure in his joke's success.

Reflecting on this moment, I am reminded of a similar encounter several months earlier during one of our play-therapy sessions. The episode began with Jorge sitting beside me and listening to my cotherapist, Linda, and his play partner, Goddess, reading *That's My Mommy*, a book popular among young children. As Linda ended the book with her exclamation, "That's my mommy!" Jorge unexpectedly jumped out of his chair and gave me a long hug and kiss while saying to me, "That's my mommy!" Surprised by the spontaneity and sweetness of Jorge's outburst, Linda and I exchanged an amused glance. I followed it with a masked sigh of confusion, and some anxiety, wondering what sense Jorge might have been making of my relationship with him. Might these episodes reflect Jorge's understanding of what it means to be a woman or a man? Three months ago, maybe Jorge thought of a mommy as someone who loved him. Today Jorge is beginning to recognize differences in my body and his mother's, learning to segment the world into male and female, masculine and feminine. Perhaps more importantly, he is being socialized to the different expectations that come with each type of body — people who nurture and provide care have "titties."

I am sure my mind returns to this scene in part because it was personally challenging for me. Indeed, I have been replaying it to myself and in supervision for the last several weeks. A sensitive child, I was at times teased by other children, and sometimes by adults, for being "a sissy." Through the challenging years of childhood and adolescence I worked hard to develop a more traditionally masculine guise. Though I accepted Jorge's spontaneous affection as sincere, it made me feel exposed and vulnerable in the moment that it happened — I had risked letting myself get close to this little guy and now he thought me a sissy too. Though I could intellectualize it otherwise, Jorge's remark still felt like a judgment to me. Did this mean that other people think this of me, too? The last time people thought me too sensitive I was teased, judged, ostracized — a rejection that I was not eager to experience again.

Don't Talk

When other kids enter the room, bounding over to say hello, the sounds of Juan's favorite salsa music playing softly in the background, Jorge improvises a game to prevent me from talking to them. Jumping up from his chair, Jorge focuses on my face, drawing his attention to a blemish just below my lips. Placing one hand on my forehead and the other on my chin, Jorge looks me in the eyes and asks, "You got boo-boo?"

Determined to get my undivided attention, Jorge gently examines the imperfection. Letting me know that he'll be "right back," Jorge runs to the pint-sized sink, used mostly for hand-washing, and returns with a wet paper towel. A group of three or four preschoolers have crowded around to watch him care for me, asking me questions or telling me stories of their own "boo-boos." When I attempt to respond, Jorge places his fingers over my lips and tells me, "Don't talk."

After gently swabbing my blemish, Jorge, in what almost becomes spitting, attempts to blow on my sore. Though I appreciate the sweetness of Jorge's gestures, I am made a little uncomfortable by his intimacy and need. There is something sad about how hard he works to gain my attention; his clinginess seems to reflect his anxiety about our attachment. It should not be this hard for him to trust our connection, though I understand that he may feel others have betrayed his trust.

Or, maybe I am the one being challenged by Jorge's care, struggling to feel comfortable with another's dependence on me. I learned to stand on my own a long time ago and it is unsettling to know that someone else depends on me so much, although I am sure this is only part of my hesitancy. My biggest fear each day as I enter the center is that people will question my intentions and integrity with the children. Against the backdrop of the Catholic priest sex abuse scandal, in a world where prevailing stereotypes about gay men often portray us as child molesters, I worry about what might be said of me if I seem to care too much about my young clients.

Reminding myself to think about all of this later, I simply say to Jorge, "Thank you for taking such good care of me. You pay a lot of attention to your friend, Travis." When he finishes, Jorge draws in close to my face and asks, "Feel better?"

A few minutes later, when I say that I need to go to the bathroom, Jorge protests. He grabs my hand, kisses it, and then pulls the palm over his face. He does not want me to leave. I tell him not to worry and remind him, "I'll be right back." Jorge doesn't yet understand the difference between two minutes and two weeks. All he knows is that when I leave, I'm gone. Jorge protests mournfully, "Noooooo."

I try to comfort him, while still moving toward the door. When it looks like his attempts are going to fail, Jorge runs between two toy shelves, stops, and spreads his arms and legs to block my path. Though he is smiling, I know that if I attempt to outmaneuver Jorge, his eyes will quickly fill with tears. This is not the Jorge I knew six months ago.

Before his brother was unexpectedly removed from the home and his mother's subsequent depression, Jorge almost never cried. Self-confident, gregarious, and as funny as a two-year-old could be, teachers often made special trips by the toddler classroom to say hello to "Macho." For over a year, Jorge bounded over to greet me with a hug and giggle each Monday and Wednesday morning when I entered his classroom. Jorge could always be counted on to dance, wave, or make a funny face. Now Jorge no longer seems as happy. His social worker told me that Jorge's mother confessed to crying almost all the time since her other son, Swahim, was taken from her; Jorge's mother fears that he and his sister might also be taken from her. Jorge may not understand his mother's fears, but unfortunately he appears to have taken on his mother's sadness, partnering it with his own sense of loss and confusion. Jorge at times appears sad, angry, and tired. Perhaps he is wondering if he too might be taken away from his mother, or if he caused his brother's departure and mother's grief.

It is hard to know exactly how such a small child makes sense of any one moment and what he needs to overcome it. I wonder what it means to him that the people he has lost have been males. It must be hard for him to feel he has so little control. Is he learning to walk away from things that make him uncomfortable? Is he learning that leaving is a way to be longed for?

I eventually relent, giving in to Jorge's pleas for me to delay my bathroom break. I decide that if my absence will be so difficult for him, I can hold on a little longer. I tell Jorge, "I need to go, but I want to make it easier for you. Let me know when it's okay for me to go, and I promise I'll come back." We sit back down at the table. Jorge seems annoyed by my trying to write my notes, and he tries to get me to draw Barney on his paper.

When Rosita, the assistant teacher, arrives with the breakfast tray, Jorge bursts into a rough-edged rendition of the clean-up song. "Clean up. Clean up. Everybody everywhere, clean up. Clean up. Everybody do your share." From a distance, Rosita's long, straight brown hair, blue jeans, T-shirt, and white tennis shoes give her the appearance of a woman much younger than her forty-something years. Unlike Juan, Rosita wears little jewelry, only occasionally a thin gold necklace. Rosita is both more directive and more physically nurturing than Juan. The children adore her for sometimes obliging their requests that she rub backs at naptime. Rosita and Juan have a masterful partnership; they know each other's routines and responses so well that it often appears they are reading each other's minds. It is amazing to me that their efforts are unrehearsed.

Juan signals for the children, by now numbering almost twenty, to take their seats. The room is filled with the sounds of commotion: two girls skipping, a boy asking if he might bring his car to the table, and two parents entering the room to drop off their children. Jorge holds my hand, pulling me toward the table, and lets me know that I will sit by him. Only when most of the other children begin charging rambunctiously toward me, hoping that I might be available to sit with them, does Jorge realize that he may be in over his head. Rather than share me, Jorge decides it's time for me to go to the bathroom. "Go bathroom. Go bathroom," he says. He pushes me from behind all the way to the door. As I walk out of the room, he says, "See you."

When No One Is Looking

On my way back to the Happy Hornets, I decide to watch Jorge for a few minutes through a one-way mirror looking into the classroom. I realize how much he has grown, but as the smallest child in the classroom, it is still easy to think of him as the baby.

Rosita and Juan are occupied with breakfast clean-up and moving the children to an art project. Jorge, unbeknownst to either of them, decides to venture into the block area, a part of the room where children are not allowed at this point in the morning. Juan gently calls to him — "Jorge . . . Jorge . . . Jorge" — after noticing his absence. Jorge initially ignores Juan, perhaps attempting to test the boundaries of his independence. He eventually decides that he has seen what he needs to and just as unassumingly turns around and takes a seat next to Rosita at the art table.

Jorge rests his head on his hand while he watches Rosita carefully write his name on a sheet of construction paper. When she finishes and turns away, Jorge stares into space, softly rubbing his eyes. He looks sleepy to me, just as he has during our last few visits. I wonder if he's getting enough sleep. This could also explain why Jorge is having such a difficult time in the early mornings at school. I know things at home have not been easy for Jorge's family since Swahim was taken from them.

As Rosita and Juan again become occupied with other students, Jorge sneaks back into the block area. He carefully picks up a block, moves it to another pile, and then walks to the corner to see if his teachers have noticed him. They do not. Jorge repeats this cycle several times. In between his stacking and checking to see if he has been discovered, Jorge dances a jig of liberation. He spins around as he flings his arms out. Jorge kicks one leg into the air before running back to stack a block. He appears to be taking great delight in his recklessness.

It makes me happy to see Jorge having such a good time. I have been worried about his sadness and his level of need during my recent visits and therapy sessions, fearing that he might be lost in the shuffle. While transitioning from home to school or from one activity to another and not getting his way appears to be difficult for him, Jorge seems able to regulate his emotions quickly. This strong self-protective factor will be helpful for his continued positive development. In contrast to being told to stifle his emotions, which means to avoid or dismiss them, emotional regulation means that Jorge can regulate his level of emotional arousal. He is developing the ability to understand and focus his emotions, to experience feelings without becoming undone by them.

Perhaps recognizing that the room has become more settled, which makes his escapade in the block corner more risky, Jorge decides to use the bathroom. The bathroom consists of two miniature toilets separated from the rest of the classroom by four-foot walls. Although the children are too small to peer into the bathroom, teachers may easily monitor everything happening inside from almost anywhere in the classroom. From where I am standing, I am able to see Jorge's head sticking out of the potty area.

Rosita is solely responsible for monitoring bathroom breaks and all bodily functions in the classroom. Juan does not change children's diapers or supervise children inside the restroom area. I discovered this over a year ago when I first began working with Jorge in the toddler classroom adjacent to the Happy Hornets. As I was attempting to change Jorge's diaper, my first ever, I had clumsily removed his baby blue jeans when Rosita raced into the changing area, scolding me, "Don't touch that child." Incredulous, I asked why not, and she responded, "This is woman's work. It's not a man's place to change a baby's diaper." In field notes from this day, I indicate that I experienced the reaction as an assault on my own intentions rather than an attempt to honor my masculine privilege. Shirley, the lead teacher in Jorge's classroom at the time, intervened, stood beside me, and coached me through the diaper-changing process. I was permitted to change Jorge's diaper when he asked me only two more times in over a year, an effort on Shirley's part to keep the peace. In subsequent conversations with staff members and my supervisor, I came to understand that much of Rosita's reaction was informed by strong cultural attitudes about the roles of men in childrearing. Though Rosita seems to have forgotten this episode and has become more comfortable with me, at times bringing me homemade breakfast treats, it was an intense introduction to her perspective on male child-care providers. During more recent conversations, following her return to work after an extended hospitalization, Rosita told me that she "cooked, cleaned, and stayed on top of her children," even though she was supposed to be on bed rest. When I asked her why, she said, "The woman runs the house and the children." When I asked her why she thought this, she said, "That's the way my mommy did it, and that's the way it's supposed to be."

Though he attempts it, and much to Rosita's chagrin, Jorge cannot yet manage to stand up to use the potty. He pulls down his pants, lifts his shirt up over his head, and sits down. He reverses the process when he's finished, but can't quite get his Spiderman underwear adjusted. He exits the bathroom twisting and tugging at his clothing, though clearly taking great pride in the fact that he managed the situation by himself. When Juan notices Jorge, he smiles and says, "Are you having problems, Jorge?" Jorge laughs slightly and smiles back at his teacher, "I got Spiderman Underoos!" Juan grunts an amused laugh and then returns to his tasks with the other children.

Jorge is now at the sink, washing his hands. Over the din of the classroom, I can hear Rosita say, "Jorge!" She says it again, and it is now obvious that Jorge is playing in the water. Rosita calls to Juan. Finally, Juan says sternly, "Enough, Jorge." Jorge stops immediately. It interests me that in this instance Jorge ignores Rosita, whom I know he likes very much, and stops only when Juan intervenes. It was clear from the tone of his voice that Juan meant business, and Jorge responded to this.

As the morning continues, a frustrated Rosita calls out to Juan for assistance several times when her interventions with some of the boys have no effect. Other times, without being asked for help, Juan steps in to help Rosita in a challenging situation that does not resolve itself easily. Rosita seems to appreciate his assistance. Given that she is the mother of five children, a respected teacher in the center, and a strong personality in her own right, it is shocking for me to watch Rosita accept Juan's interventions so readily. I wonder how Jorge and the other children might be making sense of this dynamic and what they might be thinking about the role of women in relationship to men. Should men dominate women? Are women supposed to defer to men? Are people supposed to value the opinions of women? At times it seems that Juan's authority is the only one with consequence in the classroom. Though Rosita and Juan provide a positive example of partnership and connection, much of their interaction is organized around Rosita's accommodation and deferral to Juan and a strict, gendered division of labor. In two years working at the center, Rosita is the only one I have seen rock the children, sit them on her lap when they are upset, change dirty clothes, and braid the little girls' hair. While Juan seems to orient himself to the class or a group of children, it is usually Rosita who pays closest attention to them as individuals, kissing their "boo-boos," noticing new clothes and hairstyles, and reminding them to "be good so you don't get in trouble with Juan." During recess, while Juan usually sits on the bench supervising the children who have found themselves in a "time-out," Rosita pushes the others on the swings. For many of the boys who are raised by single mothers, this classroom is one of the few places where they may watch a man and woman interact so closely.

Only Girls Are Allowed

When I reenter the classroom, I am struck by how noisy it is, not realizing that it must have sounded the same just fifteen minutes before. The sounds of the pencil sharpener, crying, laughing, and bickering now seem almost deafening, but the children and teachers do not seem bothered. Jorge, along with several other children, comes over to say hello. I say, "I'm happy to see you, too," but then encourage them to go play, hoping to get a better sense of how Jorge might be getting along with his peers. Looking at Jorge, who is now attempting to pull me toward the block table, I encourage him, "Why don't you go play, buddy? I am really tired. I'm going to sit over there and watch."

Eventually, Jorge ventures away to play with a group of other children in the block area. As the girls and two boys are discussing the rules of the game, Jorge circles the group with a dump truck, listening for an opening. It is difficult for the younger children to find their place in the class hierarchy. Another child asking me a question temporarily intercepts my gaze, but my attention is soon drawn back to the block area when I hear the sound of crying. It is Jorge. One of the boys has hit him on the shoulder. Jorge's mouth is wide open with tears rolling down his face, and he looks for a place to go. Instinctively looking for his teachers, Jorge soon remembers I am in the room. He seems torn, hesitating in the middle of the classroom. He eventually moves in my direction, presumably because I am physically closer to him than the other adults. The tears are gone as soon as my fingers touch his face.

Goddess, who has just turned three and is Jorge's best friend and play-therapy partner, comes over to make sure that he is all right. Only a month older than Jorge, she is almost a full head taller. She has dark black skin, meticulously braided hair, and rhinestone-studded jeans. Sitting beside Jorge, they make quite a charismatic pair. Sensing his full recovery, Goddess leads Jorge to the art table. Both are generally willing to follow the other's lead, happy to have someone who understands their games.

Carefully placing his sponge in a pie pan filled with paint before dabbing it on a piece of vanilla construction paper, Jorge is meticulous with his art project. When he is finished, Juan asks Jorge to explain his creation. Jorge proudly describes to Juan what is going on in his painting, pointing animatedly to a particular blotch in the center of the paper. It is clear that Juan is unable to understand Jorge's words, but he nods emphatically to encourage Jorge's creativity.

When he is finished, Jorge again seeks out Goddess, who is now back in the toy kitchen. He crawls into the corner and "hides" beside the fake wooden fridge when Emily yells to Rosita that Jorge has invaded the kitchen. "Only girls are allowed," Emily protests, as she stirs a pot on the stove. With the teachers ignoring the outburst, play quickly resumes. I watch Jorge hug Goddess from behind, a scene he has surely witnessed elsewhere. I remember that I have seen Jorge's teenage uncle similarly hug his girlfriend in the center's parking lot, while waiting to pick up Jorge for Susan. Jorge soon ventures off to do his own thing.

When Jorge picks up the toy telephone just outside of the kitchen area and yells something undecipherable, though clearly angry, into the receiver, I wonder if it is due to boredom or if he is re-creating a scene he witnessed at home before his father left. I am not sure who he imagines on the other end, but it is almost always his "Mommy" when he has similar phone conversations in the therapy room. Jorge slams the phone into its base — and then repeats this episode of screaming into the phone and slamming it down again three more times. As his therapist, I have mixed reactions while witnessing Jorge's behavior. I am glad that he is finding a way to express some of his feelings. But I am also struck by the fact that Jorge may already have learned to use anger to defend himself from the pain of sadness and disappointment, a stereotypically masculine response to such emotions. Unfortunately, anger is an emotion that often pushes others away, while disappointment and sadness are usually resolved when people move closer to each other. I am afraid that in isolating himself from his feelings of sadness, Jorge will also isolate himself from others.

Learning the Rules of the Game

Soon Jorge returns to the kitchen area. With all of the other children now occupied in other parts of the classroom, Jorge has this area to himself. His back is to me and the rest of the room. Recognizing that a similar strategy had worked for Goddess earlier in the day, Jorge is engrossed in preparing the perfect party feast in hopes of luring some playmates to his gathering. He sets out five teacups and carefully pours some pretend tea into each. He takes a spoon, carefully stirring the cups one by one. It is striking to me that Jorge often attempts to accommodate other children in an effort to be close to them, something that most children are not able to do until they are much older. Many of the others in the classroom simply fight for what they want, leaving the details of compromise to Juan and Rosita. I wonder if this might be the way Jorge has learned to comfort Susan, or if the seeds of this behavior were sown by those of us who received so much happiness from his toddler antics? He has often been asked to perform.

While Jorge continues preparing his party, all of the other boys — except for the new child who is now sitting near the doorway crying for his mother — are playing blocks in two groups on opposite sides of the room. With no guests arriving for his party, Jorge leaves again to talk on the telephone. This time, he calmly lifts the receiver to his ear, greeting the pretend caller: "Hi, Mommy."

The crying boy has now wandered near the kitchen, observing that Jorge is also playing alone. Jorge ignores him, walking by on his way to the toy cash register. He picks up the price scanner, pointing it like a gun at the new boy. "Quiet!" he shouts.

One of the older girls in the room, much larger than Jorge, approaches and attempts to take away the cash register. Jorge says, "Stop!" his voice becoming less loud and more tentative with each repetition. The girl is now holding the side of the toy, tugging it away from Jorge. He finally resists softly once more before acquiescing. Returning to the telephone, Jorge may be complaining to his mother. As the smallest child in the room, Jorge sometimes finds it difficult to stick up for himself.

Finishing his phone conversation, Jorge puts a baby doll in the cart. I wonder if caring for the baby helps Jorge feel some sense of control after being humiliated by the loss of his toy. Fascinated by the rolling wheels, Jorge seems to find pleasure in the quick turns and jerky movements he performs around the classroom obstacles. Jorge parks his buggy in the doll corner after a few laps around the playroom and then heads to the block table where the oldest boys in the room are gathered. While he does not join in their game of "auto crash," he does sit beside them, stacking his own blocks. It is clear that Jorge is paying close attention to their make-believe scenarios, full of car crashes, dueling superheroes, and jockeying for supremacy. As the adults encourage Jorge not to cry and expect him to stand on his own in the classroom, it seems to me Jorge would appreciate some new strategies for gaining the attention of others. I wonder if Jorge, perhaps recognizing that these children, the toughest in the classroom, no longer play with dolls, may be attempting to figure out the rules of their games.

It's Hard to Say Goodbye

Realizing that it is almost time for me to leave, I ask Jorge if he would like to read with me for a few minutes. Given how difficult my departure has been for him over the last few months, I hope that a few minutes together might help him with my transition out of the classroom.

Jorge and I end the day together as we started, sitting together talking. No competing or crying, these are my favorite times with Jorge. As he turns the pages of a book, he is now pretending to read to me. I let Jorge know that I will be leaving in a few minutes. He responds simply, "No."

Jorge continues reading and then pauses to ask me to "find green parrot," a request that I have always made when reading this book to him in the past. I remind Jorge again that I will be leaving shortly, but he ignores me this time. To help with the transition, I begin singing our goodbye song softly, "Goodbye, Travis. Goodbye, Travis. Goodbye, Travis. We'll see you again next time." Jorge seems unmoved.

I then begin to sing, "Goodbye, Jorge . . . ," but he stops me by placing his finger over my mouth, "Shhh," he whispers. Maybe this means he is ready. I remind Jorge, "I'm leaving now, but I'll be back again. I always come back." To offer him some control over the situation, I ask Jorge if he would like to walk me to the door. He takes my hand, grinning, and then begins the march across the classroom. As we pass Juan, I offer my thanks for being allowed to spend the morning observing and, winking, let him know that Jorge is walking me to the door. Juan understands he needs to be ready and watches as Jorge and I enter the small hallway leading out of the classroom.

I offer high-fives to a few kids on the way out of the room, but Jorge appears unmoved. His job is to get me to the door. Once there, Jorge releases my hand and looks up at me. I lean down, placing my hand, which is now covered with purple crayon and blue ink, on his shoulder, saying, "Thank you for playing, friend. I'll be back again."

Jorge smiles, then wraps himself around my leg, clutching my kneecap. Juan starts toward us. Touching Jorge's back, I drop to one knee and offer a hug. I look into Jorge's eyes, tears now starting to well, and say, "It's hard for me to leave too, but I'll be back," attempting to say the words that Jorge might like to have heard from his own father. Words that I would have liked to have heard from mine.

Juan now stands behind Jorge, his knees touching Jorge's back. I open the door, turning to leave. Another child, Anthony, has now appeared, using his own back to hold the door for me. Distracted by Anthony as I walk from the room, I miss Jorge as he darts out the door toward me. Before I hear his plea, "Travis, don't leave," I feel his arms around my knees.

I lean forward, taking Jorge's hands, which I then pass to Juan, who has now joined us in the hallway. Juan says definitively to Jorge, "One more hug." I kneel down as Jorge throws his arms around my neck. As Jorge hugs me, Juan reminds him that I will return next week. He then takes Jorge's hands from around me, turning him toward the classroom. I am glad that Juan does not punish Jorge for needing to say goodbye, recognizing his need for relationship. I hope that Jorge will never feel bad for wanting to reach out to others.

Though I can imagine Jorge straining his neck to watch my departure, waving to me as I walk away, I do not turn around. I am shocked by how hard it is for me to leave, how drained I feel walking down the hallway. I think to myself that maybe it is time that I help Jorge to stand on his own, to depend less on me — although I am not entirely convinced of this. I know how hard it is to have someone leave, never looking back.

Conclusions

During my time as Jorge's therapist, I have become increasingly aware of how my own experiences, understanding, and biases have shaped my perspective of his journey as a boy — a dynamic that has proven both helpful and stifling at times. For example, my experience of abandonment has made me particularly sensitive to Jorge's anxiety around transition. However, I have also learned to consider that every behavior manifested by Jorge at school is not indicative of fearing loss. Rather, at various times, Jorge might be confronting challenges with control, jealousy, sadness, or experiencing more joyful emotions. In my evolution as a counselor, my reflections and observations have helped me understand his experience and allowed me to remain more open to alternative interpretations of Jorge's actions.

My work has taught me to navigate cultural, educational, racial, ethnic, and class differences, which has similarly underscored the importance of remaining open-minded, reflective, and aware of the potential for misinterpretation. While bridging such sociocultural divides in my interactions with Jorge and his community has been challenging at times, it has not proven impossible. Much of what Jorge and I have been able to accomplish together has been through resolving misunderstandings — about each other and the world. For example, while reading a book and taking a nurturing posture toward me, Jorge revealed his perception that people who nurture are "mommies." However, by confronting this misunderstanding during the course of our relationship, I hope I have helped Jorge develop a broader perspective on nurturing that provides permission for men to be connected and responsive to each other as well.

Indeed, interactions with Jorge have taught me to question lessons I learned a long time ago. Familiar refrains from my childhood — "Don't cry," "Keep it to yourself," "Be tough," "Only sissies make tears," and "Don't be afraid to finish a fight" — now seem insidious. In learning to become more understanding and responsive to Jorge, I have been challenged to confront the way I have traversed the confusing terrain of masculinity. My relationship with Jorge has underscored for me that becoming a boy — becoming a man — is a difficult journey. Independence, resisting one's desire for connection, and demonstrating fewer emotions — traits deemed necessary to become the strong, independent man so celebrated by society's dominant culture — are acquired at some cost. Almost as soon as he can literally stand on his own two feet, the little boy's socialization begins. In his second year of life, adults have instructed Jorge to "Hush up," "Stop your tears," "Get in line," and "Say goodbye."

My relationship with Jorge straddles the time in his life when the challenges of becoming less dependent on caregivers are most acute for a boy (Gilligan, 1982, 1996). Our connection has allowed me to study and empathize with the pain Jorge experiences in moments of conflict between his needs and the social/cultural demands of the world around him. The conflict between what I imagine Jorge feels and what he is allowed to express may require him to decide whether to honor his emotions or hide them in order to be accepted by others. Such contradictions between one's experience and social expectations may lay the structure for psychological suffering (Gilligan, 1996). In her relational theory of human development, Carol Gilligan posits how this is implicit in boys' psychological development:

> Early childhood for boys [is a time] of psychological crisis, because at these times in development voice and relationships come into dramatic tension . . . Young boys come under pressure from without and within to give up close relationships and cover their vulnerability — to separate their inner world, their self, from the outer world of relationships. The tension between desire and necessity, between the needs of the psyche and the requisites of civilization forces a compromise between voice and relationships . . . setting the connection between inner and outer worlds and thus establishing the structure of character, but also the structure of neurotic suffering. The . . . relational crisis of boys' early childhood pressures young boys to take into themselves the structure or moral order of a patriarchal civilization: to identify with fathers or with the law of the father, to internalize a patriarchal voice. (p. 250)

Such psychological instability may heighten the risk of being thrown off balance in times of stress.

For boys who experience early loss, like Jorge's being abandoned by his father and seeing Swahim be removed from the home, the demands of individuation are particularly insidious. In the midst of needing reassurance, support, and stability, Jorge confronts a world that pushes him away, expecting him to be macho, a little man. Though he feels like crying, Jorge is told that he should not. When he asks for connection, it is sometimes withheld. Given the importance of the early childhood years in laying a foundation for all sorts of future life outcomes, children's cognitive development (Bradley, Corwyn, McAdoo, & Garcia Coll, 2001), social competence (Jackson, 2000), self-esteem (McLoyd, 1998), and mental health (McLoyd & Wilson, 1991), to name but a few, shouldn't such vulnerable children be given more support and security than usual, rather than less?

Yet, this portrait of Jorge should not be viewed as one of risk alone. Through my interactions with Jorge and his world, I have witnessed many moments of resistance and resilience, and opportunities for hope. Though often told not to do so, Jorge does continue to reach out to others — a resistance that I hope will not be diminished. Similarly, individuals around Jorge have actively sought more connections for him. I have been invited to work with Jorge by members of his world, with the expectation of creating a space of unconditional positive regard, connection, and care.

I was able to observe how Juan's behavior communicates clearly to the children that he cares for them, which simultaneously challenges and confirms many patriarchal stereotypes. Though he may not change diapers, rub backs, or offer unsolicited hugs, Juan does clearly nurture his students. Juan shows up every day, speaks kindly, and takes delight in his students' learning. As an insider to Jorge's cultural milieu by his very presence, Juan is perhaps equipping Jorge with the skills necessary to navigate his world while also challenging the status quo to become more accepting of nontraditional modes of masculinity. Similarly, I hope that my relationship with Jorge will help him, as it has me, to imagine broader possibilities for connection, responsiveness, and strength in his journey toward becoming a man.

References

Bradley, R., Corwyn, R., McAdoo, H., & Garcia Coll, C. (2001). The home environments of children in the United States Part I: Variations by age, ethnicity, and poverty status. *Child Development, 72,* 1844–1867.

Gilligan, C. (1982). *In a different voice: Psychological theory and women's development.* Cambridge, MA: Harvard University Press.

Gilligan, C. (1996). The centrality of relationship in human development: A puzzle, some evidence, and a theory. In G. Noam & K. Fischer (Eds.), *Development and vulnerability in close relationships* (pp. 237–263). Mahwah, NJ: Lawrence Erlbaum.

Jackson, A. P. (2000). Single mothers in low-wage jobs: Financial strain, parenting, and preschoolers' outcomes. *Child Development, 71,* 1409–1424.

Kaufman, M. (2001). The construction of masculinity and the triad of men's violence. In M. S. Kimmel & M. Messner (Eds.), *Men's lives* (pp. 4–16). Needham, MA: Allyn & Bacon.

Kimmel, M. S. (1994). Masculinity as homophobia: Fear, shame, and silence in the construction of masculinity. In H. Brod & M. Kaufman (Eds.), *Theorizing masculinities* (pp. 119–141). Thousand Oaks, CA: Sage.

Kimmel, M. S., & Messner, M. (Eds.). (2001). *Men's lives.* Needham, MA: Allyn & Bacon.

Kindlon, D., & Thompson, M. (1999). *Raising Cain: Protecting the emotional lives of boys.* New York: Ballantine.

Lawrence-Lightfoot, S. (1983). *The good high school: Portraits of character and culture.* New York: Basic Books.

Lawrence-Lightfoot, S., & Hoffman Davis, J. (1997). *The art and science of portraiture.* San Francisco: Jossey-Bass.

McLoyd, V. (1998). Socioeconomic disadvantage and child development. *American Psychologist, 53,* 185–204.

McLoyd, V. C., & Wilson, L. (1991). The strain of living poor: Parenting, social support, and child mental health. In A. C. Houston (Ed.), *Children and poverty* (pp. 105–135). New York: Cambridge University Press.

Selman, R., Watts, C., & Schultz, L. (1997). *Fostering friendship: Pair therapy for treatment and prevention.* New York: Aldine de Gruyter.

Nicaragua 1980

The Battle of the ABCs

FERNANDO CARDENAL, S.J.
VALERIE MILLER

It is September 1980. Nicaragua is green from winter rains. The countryside that just two weeks ago was bustling with more than 50,000 young volunteer literacy teachers is quieter now. The National Literacy Crusade is over. The peasant-shirt, blue-jean uniforms of the young *brigadistas* ("student volunteers") can no longer be seen in the far-away hills and valleys. Their footsteps no longer mark the mountain paths between San Rafael and Yall, but their voices and spirit remain, transformed and replaced by those of their students. Local people from Waslale and Wiwill now conduct the community study groups begun by the volunteers. From cotton fields to the jungle valleys, reading and writing continues.

In the cities, the buses overflow, crowded again with teenage faces. Endless registration lines of students surround the high schools and universities. The country begins another school year, which on the surface looks like any other. Yet, Nicaragua will never be the same again. The National Literacy Crusade has broken the patterns of the past and has laid the foundations for the future. In five months, more than 400,000 Nicaraguans learned to master basic reading and writing skills, and tens of thousands of young people and their families learned about rural poverty and peasant culture.

Nicaragua recently celebrated an educational victory that a little over a year ago would have seemed impossible. On August 23, 1980, the nation applauded the success of students and teachers of the National Literacy Crusade. We saluted their achievements, and we also saluted thousands of people who could not stand with us, those who had given their lives in battle to free this land. The National Literacy Crusade was a living tribute to their sacrifice, commitment, and hope. Their dedication and faith in the future made the

Harvard Educational Review Vol. 51 No. 1 February 1981

campaign possible. Their memories live on in each one of us. This article is dedicated to them.

Nicaragua's struggle for self-determination had been going on for many years, but finally exploded on a massive scale in 1978. After decades of foreign domination, inequity, and military repression, the mounting rebellion could no longer be contained. As the battle intensified, young people went to the mountains and joined the liberation forces. Directed and organized by the Sandinista National Liberation Front (FSLN), they fought with an unshakable belief in victory and an uncommon courage against extraordinary odds. Civilians, organized into community-defense committees, added to their force. City people dug up the neighborhood streets to form barricades against tanks and troops. When the tear gas became too thick, housewives set out on their porches specially prepared tubs of bicarbonate of soda water for the young fighters to neutralize the burning chemicals. Women's groups organized clandestine hospitals in their homes. First- and second-graders served as couriers carrying important messages across battle lines. Businessmen led strikes and raised funds for arms. Market women hid ammunition at the bottom of baskets brimming with vegetables and carried out their missions walking confidently between rows of armored cars. Families carved out bomb shelters in their patios, using shovels and spoons. They created homemade hand bombs out of firecrackers and collected rocks to throw against Somoza's machine guns.

Despite this extraordinary display of courage and faith, the war was long and costly. Some 40,000 people were killed, 100,000 wounded, and 40,000 children orphaned. Somoza escaped with all the reserves in the Central Bank except $3.5 million, leaving an international debt of $1.6 billion. Yet, less than one year after victory, the nation was transformed from a violent war zone into one enormous school. The spirit and commitment of hundreds of thousands of Nicaraguans forged in combat became the moving force behind a massive literacy program. Young men and women who had taken up arms and gone to the hills now took up pencils and primers and returned to the mountains.

Where machine guns and bombs had filled the air such a short time ago, the sounds of ABCs and singing could be heard. Along the same paths where young fighters had rushed to battle, young literacy teachers set up blackboards and guided unsteady hands in writing their first words. In cornfields ravaged by war, beside the simple graves of fallen patriots, the literacy volunteers worked the land side-by-side with their adopted peasant families. In bomb-damaged factories, workers taught fellow workers the ABCs. The violence and destruction of yesterday had been replaced by the quiet pride of learning. A new nation was being born. One battle had been won and another begun. In these pages we will describe that second battle by explaining the origins of the campaign and its relationship to development. We will also examine some of the major problems that the Literacy Crusade confronted and the strategies developed to overcome them.

Origins of the Battle

On March 24, 1980, the entire country became engaged in a nationwide learning campaign. Student volunteers went to the countryside to teach literacy and learn the ways of peasant living, while urban workers and housewives taught and learned from people in the cities. The program was designed to help Nicaraguans acquire the skills, understanding, and empathy necessary for participation in a society undergoing rapid transformation.

The spirit that inspired the campaign had its origins in the early part of the century. The 1980 Literacy Crusade grew out of the liberation struggle begun by General Augusto César Sandino. The tensions that led to the struggle were related primarily to efforts to establish an interoceanic canal in Nicaragua. In 1909 Liberal President José Santos Zelays refused to grant canal rights to the United States. As a result, the State Department gave its support to the Conservative opposition which, when it took power, agreed to a permanent U.S. military presence and U.S. control of the economy through management of national bank, railway, and customs operations. In the 1920s the tension between the two parties escalated into open fighting. The buildup of the Liberal army in 1927 posed a serious threat to the Conservative regime. Fearing a loss of power and stability, the United States bolstered the marine presence. By a combination of political promise and military threat, the United States ambassador persuaded both parties to halt the fighting. General elections were agreed to and a National Guard was created to maintain the "peace." U.S. Marine commanders were put in charge of its training and organization, and Anastasio Somoza García was among its chosen officers.

However, General Sandino refused to accept the United States-negotiated accords. For seven years, Sandino and his peasant army battled against foreign intervention. Unable to defeat the increasingly popular general, the marines finally were forced to withdraw in 1933. With their departure, Sandino signed a peace treaty with the government, dismantled his army, and retired to organize peasant cooperatives in the north. The United States installed Anastasio Somoza as the head of the National Guard. In 1934 Somoza had Sandino assassinated, his cooperatives destroyed, and their members and families exterminated.

Throughout Sandino's struggle he had always wanted to assure his people's social and economic development. He set up cooperatives for agricultural production and, when possible, urged his troops to learn to read and write. He was especially proud of their educational achievements:

> I can assure you that the number of our illiterate officers can now be counted on fewer than the fingers of one hand. Unfortunately, due to a shortage of people who can teach, progress among the soldiers has been almost negligible.
>
> When General Pedro Altamirano first joined us he did not know how to read or write but . . . during the fighting and only because I insisted on it, Altamirano learned, stumbling and mumbling as he went along. Despite his age, he has

> made great strides since then, and now, as amazing as it may seem, he actually knows how to type — even if it is only with one finger.[1]

In the early 1960s, the FSLN took up Sandino's challenge. The struggle for both literacy and liberation was once again alive.

Development and Literacy: Yesterday

Under Somoza, Nicaragua was run as a family plantation. Development had been narrowly focused on modernizing the economy's agricultural export sector for the benefit of a small privileged minority. The promotion of universal literacy or adult education was irrelevant and potentially threatening. Under this economic system, national development programs were essentially used to enrich Somoza's personal fortune and to buttress the regime's power structure by providing his partners with lucrative business opportunities involving massive graft and corruption. While isolated sectors of the population benefited from the programs, the root causes of economic disparity and political injustice were never addressed. Ultimately, development projects led to the expansion of the government's corrupt patronage system and to the further impoverishment and repression of the majority.

Illiteracy was both a condition and a product of this system. In 1979 a special census revealed that more than 50 percent of the population was illiterate, a figure which soared above 85 percent in some rural areas.[2] This problem was never seriously addressed during the dictatorship because the promotion of universal literacy was neither politically advisable for the maintenance of the system nor economically necessary for its functioning. The development model of export agriculture depended upon a large pool of unskilled workers, and therefore it neither required nor encouraged an educated labor force. Politically, it was unwise for Somoza to undertake a genuine nationwide literacy program. Basic education would have provided the poor and disenfranchised with the potential tools to analyze and question the unequal power relationships and economic conditions under which they had lived. An illustration from the crusade underlines this point. A peasant is speaking during the dialogue section of the lesson:

> Somoza never taught us to read — it really was ungrateful of him, wasn't it. He knew that if he taught the peasants to read we would claim our rights. Ay! But back then, people couldn't even breathe. You see, I believe that a government is like the parent of a family. The parent demands the best of his children and the children demand the best of the parent, but a governor, like a parent, who does not give culture and upbringing to the child, well that means he doesn't love his child, or his people. Don't you agree?[3]

Under Somoza, literacy teaching was used as a cover for counter insurgency operations in the north. The "Plan Waslala," according to the Ministry of Education's own report in 1978, appointed more than 100 literacy teachers to act

as spies and identify peasants sympathetic to the FSLN. Many people singled out by this operation later disappeared. Waslala itself was the site of an infamous concentration camp where hundreds of peasants had been savagely tortured and killed.

Development and Literacy: Today

With the recent triumph of the Sandinista Revolution, the meaning of development and education changed radically. The ideas of Julius Nyerere, President of Tanzania, seem especially appropriate for understanding the change. In his writings, Nyerere stresses that development means freedom and liberation. Development means people. But, as he emphasizes, people cannot be developed, human beings can only develop themselves. In the new Nicaragua, we also believe that development means freedom, a freedom that is based on liberation and popular participation. Such a process rests on the redistribution of the nation's power and wealth and on the thoughtful, creative involvement of people in community organization. Development in Nicaragua today requires that all aspects of society be examined and recreated to respond to the needs and aspirations of the majority. It involves a profound transformation of the social system and the creation of structures which promote permanent opportunities for learning and enhance equitable forms of economic and political participation.

We believe that in order to create a new nation we must begin with an education that liberates people. Only through knowing their past and their present, only through understanding and analyzing their reality can people choose their future. Education, therefore, must encourage people to take charge of their lives, to learn to become informed and effective decision makers, and to understand their roles as responsible citizens possessing rights and obligations. A liberating education nurtures empathy, a commitment to community, and a sense of self-worth and dignity. It involves people acquiring the knowledge, skills, and attitudes necessary for their new community responsibilities. Education for liberation means people working together to gain an understanding of and control over society's economic, political, and social forces in order to guarantee their full participation in the creation of the new nation. Literacy and permanent programs of adult learning are fundamental to these goals. We believe they are essential to the building of a democratic society in which people can participate consciously and critically in national decision making. The struggle to achieve these aims is long, and we are just beginning.

Soon after the triumph, the Government of National Reconstruction and the FSLN proposed their first development plan. Education and literacy were among its top priorities. The program emphasized economic reactivation and national reconstruction and was founded on four major points. First, it established a socioeconomic policy based on a commitment to full employment, improved social services, universal literacy, land reform, self-sufficiency in basic food stuffs, increased production for the common good, and a mixed economy. Second, it encouraged popular participation through a network of citizens' and workers' associations, a representative legislative body, the Council of State, and a variety of public forums for open debate and dialogue between government and citizens. Third, the program called for the birth and affirmation of the "New Nicaraguan," revolutionary men and women, characterized by sacrifice, humility, discipline, creativity, love, generosity, hard work, and a critical consciousness. Finally, to accumulate the necessary capital for domestic investment and to pay the nation's staggering debt, it emphasized austerity. Salary differentials were drastically reduced, wages controlled, and luxury imports curtailed.

In their development plan, conducting a nationwide literacy campaign was one of the first priorities of the young government. In August 1979, just fifteen days after victory, Nicaragua's Literacy Crusade was born. The first goal of

the campaign was to eliminate illiteracy. Specifically, this meant reducing the illiteracy rate to between 10 to 15 percent, establishing a nationwide system of adult education, and expanding primary school coverage throughout the country. Other important goals were to encourage an integration and understanding among Nicaraguans of different classes and backgrounds; to increase political awareness and a critical analysis of underdevelopment; to nurture attitudes and skills related to creativity, production, cooperation, discipline, and analytical thinking; to forge a sense of national consensus and of social responsibility; to strengthen channels of economic and political participation; to acquaint people with national development programs; to record oral histories and recover popular forms of culture; and to conduct research in health and agriculture for future development programming.

Specifically, the Crusade was intended to help people acquire basic skills in reading, writing, math, and analytical thinking, and to develop an elementary knowledge of history and civics. Learning materials were chosen to acquaint people with the history of the Revolution, the national development plan, and the emerging political and economic structures. As a whole, the campaign was designed to sensitize the entire country to the problems and rights of the poor and to prepare citizens for their responsibilities in meeting the challenge of national development. The Crusade had one other important function: it gave the young people who had fought and suffered the traumas of the war a channel for their energy and enthusiasm. Their participation as volunteer teachers helped them make the transition between the violence of war and the challenge of transformation.

In its design and implementation, the campaign was eminently political and profoundly spiritual. First, it was aimed at giving the nation's poor and disenfranchised the skills and knowledge they needed to become active participants in the political process. In doing so, it consolidated a powerful new political force and challenged the power of large economic interests. Second, it was spiritual. The act of learning to read and write served to restore and nurture spiritual values which had for so long been suppressed. Dignity and self-worth took on new meaning as people began to gain confidence in themselves and their future. Literacy was considered much more than a basic human right. The FSLN called literacy "an apprenticeship in life because in the process the literate person learns his intrinsic value as a person, as a maker of history, as an actor of an important social role, as an individual with rights to demand and duties to fulfill."[4]

The means to carry out such an ambitious educational challenge emerged from both the philosophical principles and the practical experience of the Revolution. The actual strategies of battle provided a model for educational action. One of the fundamental tenets of the GRN and the FSLN was citizen participation: just as in war, victory rested on active community involvement. Triumph over illiteracy meant citizens learning from citizens, neighbors helping neighbors, an entire nation organized to educate itself. The specific strategy depended upon the network of citizens and labor associations that originally had been organized clandestinely for the war. The actual operation of the literacy struggle followed the same general lines as the liberation struggle — from isolated skirmishes and harassment of the enemy in the pilot project stage, to a national insurrection during the main implementation phase, on to the final offensive of accelerated study, and ultimately to the consolidation of the Revolution through the follow-up program.

The metaphors and terminology of the campaign were purposefully militaristic — "The National Literacy Crusade: Heroes and Martyrs for the Liberation of Nicaragua," "the war on ignorance," "the cultural insurrection," and "the second war of liberation." The literacy warriors, or brigadistas, of the Popular Literacy Army were divided into brigades, columns, and squadrons and were located along six battlefronts identical to those of the war.[5] They joined forces with the Peasant and Workers' Militias and the Urban Literacy Guerillas. Each battle unit chose the name of a fallen combatant as a means of honoring his or her memory.

In no way was the use of military terminology designed to glorify war or violence. Anyone who lived through the horror perpetuated by Somoza's guard was acutely aware that the pain and trauma of violence and repression were not worthy of glorification. On the contrary, the choice of military metaphors was designed to help young volunteers integrate the memories of the past, transforming terms related to the war into positive associations with teaching and sharing. Military terminology also helped the brigadistas see the Crusade as a vital part of the nation's continuing liberation struggle and understand that, as such, it demanded the seriousness, dedication, and discipline of a military offensive. In essence, we wanted to make clear that peace-time battles demanded the same selfless, disciplined commitment as did the war effort; in fact, they demanded more.

The use of military terms and the naming of fallen heroes had a deeply spiritual significance. The Crusade owed its very existence to the Revolution and to the sacrifice of thousands of men and women who fought and died for liberation. By calling forth their names and memories, the young volunteers kept alive the courage and example of their fallen compatriots. A spiritual bond joined the living with the dead. It inspired greater levels of commitment and compassion and it spurred people on in moments of difficulty. Over 40,000 Nicaraguans died in the struggle's violence. The Crusade and its symbols were a living testimony to their sacrifice, dedication, and faith in the future.

The Challenge and the Problems

The challenge confronting the Crusade staff would have discouraged most educational planners. At times we were overwhelmed. The lessons of the war, however, provided us with a special source of strength and inspiration. During the insurrection we had learned to take unimaginable risks. We learned about organizing, and about trusting in people's extraordinary capacity for daring, creativity, and perseverance. We were confident that we could translate that spirit into the Literacy Crusade. But, initially, we weren't quite sure how to prepare, organize, and mobilize the large numbers of people necessary for the battle or how to finance it. The problems appeared formidable.

Somoza had left the country destitute. We could not count on public financing. We estimated that we would need to raise approximately $20 million to support the effort. Since the war had affected much of the nation's transportation system, and years of government corruption had impeded the development of a rural infrastructure, new methods had to be devised to maintain communication with the isolated regions of the country, to transport the tens of thousands of brigadistas to the countryside, and to distribute massive amounts of equipment and teaching materials.

The long months of battle had destroyed industry so that supplying even the basic material necessities of the Crusade required herculean efforts. Machinery had to be imported, factories reorganized, cottage industries developed, and materials ordered from foreign markets to provide the necessary uniforms, lanterns, mosquito nets, boots, raincoats, malaria pills, water purification tablets, and study materials. Agricultural production had been interrupted, and scarcity in rural communities was commonplace. Basic foodstuffs first needed to be imported and then distributed to supply the brigadistas.

Because decades of repression had prevented the development of community groups and labor associations, the campaign had to depend on organizations that were still in their infancy for the crucial tasks of mobilizing and supporting the Crusade's volunteer personnel. Long years of neglect had deprived the poor of adequate health care and resulted in high levels of parasitic and skin infections, malaria, and malnutrition. Conditions in rural areas were especially severe. Medical supplies and basic health information would have to be provided to the brigadistas. To mount a campaign of such magnitude, a network of offices needed to be established. Since the number of trained and experienced administrators was limited, the Crusade would have to become a learning laboratory for educational managers.

Once launched, the Crusade confronted another series of problems. The rainy season began in May and continued throughout the duration of the campaign. As a result, many volunteers were isolated, and transportation and communication throughout the country were seriously impaired. Somoza sympathizers and former guardsmen created grave problems and tried to spread fear among the brigadistas and their families in an attempt to paralyze the Crusade. In certain regions, literacy teachers and personnel were threatened and harassed; nine were assassinated.

In the face of such complex difficulties, our inexperience weighed heavily on us. Out of the initial staff of seven, only two had worked in literacy programs, and none had ever been involved in a project of such magnitude. Our strategy for overcoming the team's lack of experience evolved over time. Basically it included study, long hours, hard work, collective problem solving, and hiring experts in adult education.

We spent the first month studying — reading about the experiences of other countries, discussing the small church-sponsored literacy projects that had been attempted in Nicaragua, talking with experts, writing position papers, and outlining a possible primer. We also had to spend time searching for desks and chairs. The Ministry offices had been left empty, and there were times when the team had to take turns using desks and either share chairs or sit on the floor.

To complete our national team, we hired selected experts in education from Argentina, Colombia, Costa Rica, Mexico, Honduras, Puerto Rico, and the United States. During the campaign they were joined by four Cuban specialists who had participated in the 1961 Cuban Literacy Campaign. As one of their first assignments, they were given a truck to pick up student desks from the university so that they would have a place to sit.

We also requested further technical assistance from a variety of organizations and institutions — UNESCO, the Organization of American States, the World Council of Churches, CELADEC (a Latin American ecumenical group working in popular peasant education), CREFAL (Regional Center on Adult Education and Functional Literacy for Latin America), and Cuba's Ministry of Education. Cuban teachers who worked in Nicaragua's primary schools participated in the Crusade after classes. Spain, Costa Rica, and the Dominican Republic sent delegations of teachers to participate in the campaign. During the course of the program, additional international experts joined, including people from Canada, Chile, El Salvador, Peru, Spain, and Uruguay. More advisors also came from Colombia, Mexico, and the United States.[6]

At the end of September the core team of seven visited Cuba for a week. We interviewed the former director of the 1961 Cuban Literacy Campaign and spent four valuable days delving into the archives of their Literacy Museum. During October 1979 we organized an intensive one-week planning seminar with a team of experts from Mexico, Colombia, and the United States. After a careful clarification and analysis of the Crusade's proposed plan, we developed some general operational guidelines and began to define program structures and tasks.

As the work intensified, the core team met daily to identify and study specific problems as they emerged, and to seek effective responses. The staff labored fourteen to fifteen hours a day, seven days a week. This combination of commitment, intensive study, group problem solving, and the elaboration of easy-to-follow operational procedures enabled us to overcome many of our initial shortcomings. Before any program could be launched, however, we had to face the legacy of debt, destruction, and corruption left by the dictatorship. Serious problems of financing, health, food, transportation, and communication demanded immediate solutions.

Financing the Crusade

The Crusade had to be financed from sources outside the government. We called in two specialists from the Ministry of Planning. After providing them with program details such as the Crusade's proposed scope, duration, and personnel and material needs, they developed a tentative budget calling for approximately $20 million (200 million *cordobas*).

We immediately set up a finance office. Requests for assistance were mailed to governments, institutions, and solidarity groups around the world. Official delegations were sent to the United States and to Europe. In Nicaragua, the Crusade established a program of Patriotic Literacy Bonds and encouraged community fund-raising efforts. Employees from all sectors, public and private, tithed one day's salary each month to the campaign. Marketwomen from Managua and peasants from distant mountain villages came to the national office in order to make their contributions personally. For example, three representatives of the Revolutionary Sports Committee of Chontales, two peasants and one young student, contributed 1,000 cordobas collected from community raffles. Enthusiastic high school students filled the city streets carrying tin cans. Following some of the same tactics used in the insurrection, they set up road blocks — to collect "pennies for pencils" — and called on radio stations to read official declarations of war against ignorance and to make appeals for financial help. Dances, song fests, concerts, and poetry readings all added to the fund-raising effort.

Including cash and materials, some 120 million cordobas were raised. Since the program had been carefully streamlined by cutting out all excess expenses, these funds covered the costs. Catholic and Protestant organizations were the first to contribute. The countries most generous in their donations were the Federal Republic of Germany, Switzerland, Sweden, Holland, and England, although people contributed from all over the world. In this way, they too formed part of the Crusade and shared in its achievements.

Health Problems

For decades, life in the countryside had meant poor health and early death. Malnutrition, malaria, measles, gastroenteritis, and mountain leprosy — a widespread skin infection that causes large scabs and scars — were common and sometimes deadly. To protect the brigadistas, inoculations were given, as well as basic health training which included malaria diagnosis and control. Each teaching squadron was provided with a first-aid kit with supplies sufficient for the duration of the Crusade.

Health problems, however, were more extensive and complicated than anticipated. Many older people attending literacy classes suffered from poor eyesight and therefore had difficulty reading. While eyeglasses had been ordered, their delivery was delayed, causing some people to withdraw, at least temporarily, from the campaign. Other program participants suffered from debilitating illnesses, making attendance sporadic. Volunteers suffered similar ailments. In some cases, disease prevented people from enrolling in the Crusade.

The first-aid supplies which had been carefully calculated to last five months usually ran out within two weeks. When confronted with the extent of illness and disease in the countryside, the brigadistas placed their first-aid kits at the service of the community. Medicine was immediately shared with their adopted peasant families. As a result, new supplies had to be ordered and special medical brigades formed. After a brief intensive training program, some 700 university medical students were placed throughout the country to serve as mobile health teams. Besides providing basic medical attention to volunteers, they

also prepared them to give community classes in elementary health education. In addition, the brigades gathered vital information on national disease patterns and health conditions to be used in future health programming.

Food was also a problem. Without the timely organization of an emergency distribution system, food shortages would also have affected the brigadistas' health. Through the Institute of Basic Grain Distribution (ENABAS) volunteers were provided with double rations of basic foodstuffs both to feed themselves and to assist their host families. Weekend visits by parents and care packages from home helped improve the community diet.

Transportation and Communication

Nicaragua's poor transportation system hampered many aspects of the Crusade. Mobilization operations, supply distribution, and communication were all affected. For the March mobilization, brigadistas were dispersed gradually, their departures staggered over a four-day period. To accomplish the massive operation, the Crusade worked in coordination with the Ministry of Transportation and the Farmworkers' Association. They located, employed, and coordinated every available means of transportation — buses, boats, ferries, trains, dump trucks, jeeps, ox carts, horses, mules, donkeys, canoes, rafts, and, finally, feet. Some volunteers had to walk for two or three days to reach their assigned communities. During the campaign, helicopters were used for emergency medical rescues. Vehicles from every ministry and government institution were pressed into service for the distribution of supplies. Food, boots, uniforms, notebooks, pencils, pens, primers, medicine, lanterns, hammocks, and mosquito nets had to be delivered to all 144 municipalities. As winter approached, an emergency plan was instituted to accelerate the distribution process in order to provide sufficient supplies to those areas which would be isolated by the rains.

At the conclusion of the Crusade, the poor networks of roads and almost total lack of bridges exacerbated the problems of demobilization. By August, the winter rains had made many roads and rivers impassable. The lovely streams that the brigadistas had crossed on foot in the dry season had become swollen torrents, and the dirt roads had turned into muddy swamps. What had been a two- or three-day walk in March became a five- or six-day journey.

A carefully orchestrated eight-day demobilization program was put into action. At each point along the way, community organizations provided accommodations and hospitality for the footsore brigadistas. From the farthest sites, the young volunteers walked to area transportation points. From municipal centers, they were transported to department capitals, and then finally to Managua for the August 23rd celebration. Although there were many blistered feet, everyone arrived home safely.

Communication, while always a problem, was greatly improved through a network of forty-eight shortwave radios. Department offices and selected remote municipalities were given radio equipment and their personnel provided with training. A rotating team of volunteers staffed the central office twenty-four hours a day from March 10 to August 22. Besides maintaining communication in technical and administrative matters, the network served as a lifeline in case of medical emergencies.

Establishment of Records

Since government statistics were outdated and notoriously inaccurate, one of the first campaign tasks was conducting a census to establish actual levels of literacy and to ascertain the availability of volunteer teachers. With expert assistance, the census was planned and executed. Teams of volunteer census takers were trained and sent out into the field, and the results tabulated by citizens and labor organizations. Since this was our first experience in mass mobilization, the effort was not without its problems. Because the volunteer response in Managua was much greater than anticipated, not enough public vehicles had been secured for the operation. It was Sunday and all offices were closed. Not wanting to dismiss needed recruits, the Crusade's administrative coordinator borrowed money from his mother to rent private transport. No one was turned away. In all, the volunteers surveyed 1,434,738 people. Since the census tabulation would have absorbed all the nation's computer capacity for two weeks, a group of 2,500 volunteers received special training, and the tabulations were completed in ten days. The results indicated that 722,431 Nicaraguans were illiterate.

In addition, the census gave us a more complete picture of the country's illiteracy levels and their geographic distribution. As the Crusade progressed, however, it became clear that people's notions of illiteracy varied. Some who classified themselves as totally illiterate could recognize the alphabet and read simple words, but could not write. Exact skills were not known until brigadistas gave program applicants a qualifying test. This brief exam was the first in a series of three given during the campaign. The initial test was designed to determine the actual skill level of each participant, beginning with a simple exercise — drawing a straight line. This step was included so that those unable to continue beyond the first question would have some sense of accomplishment and understand that they too possessed the potential to master the alphabet. The next level of skill tested was the ability to write one's name, followed by reading and writing exercises — single words first, then short sentences. The test concluded with a comprehension exercise. People who completed all sections successfully were considered literate, and those who could read and write a few words were classified as semiliterates. Illiterates included people who could not read or write more than their own name.

An intermediate test was given to assess learner progress and diagnose individual study needs. The ability to read and write different syllabic families was determined so that specialized review could be oriented toward practicing those that had not yet been fully mastered. The final exam was administered by the literacy volunteer under the guidance of a technical advisor. It consisted of five parts which tested reading, writing, and comprehension skills. To be considered literate, participants had to write their name, read aloud a short text, answer three questions based on the reading, write a sentence dictated to them, and write a short composition. They were expected to be able to read with comprehension, pronouncing words as a whole and not as a series of isolated syllables. They were to write legibly, leaving appropriate spaces between words, and to spell phonetically. With such skills, participants were prepared within their vocabulary range to read newspapers, application forms, technical information pamphlets, and books.

Records kept on each student included such general information as name, age, sex, date of enrollment, residence, occupation, and past school attendance. A monthly progress chart indicated the lessons and exercises completed in both the primer and math workbook, as well as the total number of sessions attended. Test results for each of the three exams were recorded, as were observations about individual learning difficulties, health problems, and areas of personal interest for future study.

These reports reveal the history and progress of the Crusade. They also indicate the poor conditions under which the majority of Nicaraguans have lived and the tragic human costs of underdevelopment. According to the 1979 census, Nicaragua had an overall illiteracy rate of 50 percent, 30 percent in urban areas and 75 percent in the countryside. Children between ten and fourteen years of age accounted for 21 percent of the illiterate population. In the course of the campaign we discovered other dimensions of the illiteracy problem. As much as we did not want to accept the fact, some people simply did not have the capacity to master reading and writing skills in the campaign. Reports from volunteers and technical advisers indicated widespread learning difficulties and cases of disability. Poor health was the principal cause. Extensive malnutrition handicaps many Nicaraguans, impairing sight and hearing, limiting memory, and often causing early senility. Health statistics indicate that 25 percent of all newborns fall into the high-risk category. Many do not reach five years of age, and those who do suffer serious mental and physical disorders. About 9 percent of the population had severe learning disabilities that prevented them from studying.

Despite debilitating health problems and extreme hardships, 406,056 Nicaraguans learned basic reading and writing skills — an achievement that testifies to the creative power and determination of students and teachers alike. But initial statistics revealed that Nicaragua still had an illiteracy rate of 13 percent to overcome (6 percent urban and 21 percent rural). We believe, however, that by 1981 the rate will decrease as a result of the Crusade's follow-up program and the campaigns in English, Miskito, and Sumo.

Structural Organization: From Mountaintops to Managua

The success of the Crusade's administrative and support structure depended primarily on the participation of the citizen and labor associations. Though we did not know the kind of structure that would facilitate their involvement or exactly how to organize it, we learned much from the process. Since the campaign was an intensive, short-run nationwide project, it required setting up a massive organizational network that could effectively reach from isolated mountaintops down to the neighborhoods of Managua. With that in mind, we tried to develop a system that would be flexible and responsive at the local level and yet maintain a clear central direction and control. A single national coordinating structure took on the general management functions. Operational responsibilities were decentralized through a regional institutional network. In the field, the teachers' organization, ANDEN, and the Sandinista Young People's Association carried out organizational and implementation functions. Citizen groups, labor federations, and public institutions participated and supported the work at all levels. Two national congresses were held which brought together participants and staff to discuss program needs, problems, and solutions. Conferences began at the community level, proceeded to the municipal, on to the departmental, and finally to the national. In all, over 100,000 people participated.

To coordinate the campaign structures, the Crusade functioned in consultation with a National Literacy Commission. Presided over by the Minister of Education, Carlos Tunnerman, the National Literacy Commission, composed of delegates from twenty-five public and private institutions, workers' associ-

ations, and citizens' groups, assisted with resource mobilization and coordination. Parallel commissions were established on both the departmental and municipal levels with representatives from the same institutions and organizations as the national structure. Subcommissions were formed at the comarca and neighborhood levels.

The Literacy Crusade was organized as part of the Ministry of Education and therefore could draw upon any of the Ministry's technical or administrative support services. The campaign itself, however, was coordinated and managed by a single executive structure, the National Coordinating Board, headed by a National Coordinator and consisting of six divisions: Technical/Pedagogical; Production and Design; Technical/Organizational; Public Relations; Financial Promotion; and Administrative. A special subdivision was also established to design and implement the bilingual program.[7]

This administrative and organizational network was complemented by the actual operational structure in the field. The field network was directed by a variety of organizations and coordinated by the Crusade. For the rural work, the Sandinista Young People's Association was responsible for the organization, enthusiasm, and discipline of the teaching brigades. Made up of high school and college students, this group, known as the Popular Literacy Army

(EPA), formed the bulk of the rural education corps. The Farmworkers Association (ATC) organized a small but effective teaching unit called the Peasants Literacy Militia (MAC) which worked alongside the EPA.

The Nicaraguan Educators Association (ANDEN) was in charge of the teachers who served as the technical support staff for the brigades and militia. Each squadron of about thirty volunteers was assisted by three professional teachers. ANDEN was also responsible for two of the Crusade's auxiliary activities, the Retaguardia, a summer daycare program for primary school children, and the Quincho Barrilete project, a literacy and basic education program for child street vendors. Cultural brigades for some 450 students were organized by the University and the Ministry of Culture to collect oral histories, promote popular culture, and conduct different types of research studies. In the cities, the volunteers were organized into two main forces: the Urban Literacy Guerillas, coordinated directly by the Crusade and made up of housewives, working students, professionals, and private citizens; and the Workers' Literacy Militia (MOA), coordinated by the Sandinista Worker Federation and composed of factory workers, office personnel, market venders, and government employees.

Pedagogy in Practice: Revolution and Education

In designing the materials and methodologies for the Crusade, the liberation struggle served as inspiration and teacher. Its lessons were many, some pedagogical and some philosophical. Educational experiences carried out over the long years of fighting and community organizing had demonstrated the validity of a variety of teaching approaches and learning principles. Small study groups had met throughout the struggle to analyze, plan, and carry out war-related tasks; clandestine literacy efforts had been conducted as well. Learning in this context had been based on action and reflection. Lessons had a direct, urgent, and immediate application to reality. These experiences had combined such methods and techniques as experiential learning, dialogue, group discussions, and collective problem solving. They also revealed the tremendous creativity and capacity for learning that existed within people regardless of their educational background.

These experiences were enriched by the ideas and practice of Paulo Freire and others. At the beginning of the campaign, Freire had challenged us to create the best learning program we could. He stressed the importance of providing opportunities for learners to practice their creativity and added that within a liberating revolutionary process people would learn to read and write even with mediocre materials. The revolutionary context and methodology were more important than any isolated study program or particular teaching techniques. Literacy, he said, could only "have a genuine meaning in a country which is going through a revolutionary process."[8] With his challenge in mind, we faced two technical questions: how to design literacy materials for use by volunteer teachers and how to translate young people's enthusiasm and commitment into a minimum set of pedagogical skills.

The Crusade's education team attempted to address these questions first by studying Nicaragua's experiences in clandestine literacy teaching and then by analyzing other countries' programs in light of local needs. Cuba's literacy campaign was examined closely, as was that of Peru and those of the African nations of São Tomé and Guinea-Bissau, both of which had been greatly inspired by Freire. His thinking along with many other lines of Latin American thought and experience influenced the campaign, but the most important elements of the program emerged from the reality and needs of Nicaragua and the creativity of the Crusade's national education team. In all, five intense months were spent in developing and pilot-testing materials and methods. The resultant education program was a product of their collective effort. It was founded on dialogue and on a standardized national literacy primer.

We believed, as did Freire, that dialogue is critical to a liberating education and that, combined with a phonetics approach to teaching literacy, it surpasses any other method. Since we were engaged in carrying out a national literacy campaign in the context of profound social transformation, we focused on themes that were concerns of the society at large rather than on narrow issues of interest only to individual communities. Because it offered participants the power of the word and of history, the dialogue was highly political. By expressing their own opinions about their lives, their culture, their past and future, people would begin to develop and strengthen their creativity and analytical abilities as well as to see themselves as makers of culture and history. As Carlos Carrión, the FSLN representative to the Crusade, expressed it:

> The literacy methodology is intrinsically political. How? It's not just that we speak of Sandino or of Carlos Fonseca, or of the Frente Sandinista. The most political, the most revolutionary aspect of this literacy approach is the fact that we are providing scientific knowledge and analytical skills to our brothers and sisters in the fields and factories who do not know how to read or write — the skills to reason, think, compare, discern and the ability to form their own human and political criteria, their own critical framework.[9]

To help volunteers promote the process of dialogue we provided them with concrete, step-by-step guidelines. The five-step process contained a series of suggested questions designed to help participants develop both analytical skills and a profound sense of social responsibility. The questions proceeded from simple to difficult and encouraged the students to describe the contents of a photograph; analyze the situation portrayed; relate the particular situation to the life of the learner, to the community, and to the problems facing them; solve problems around issues identified by the group; and engage participants in transforming reality, committing themselves to solving the problem, and becoming active in the national programs of social change. During the course of the Crusade, however, we came to realize the obvious — that dialogue occurred both during the literacy teaching process itself as well as in the daily living experience, and that the latter was perhaps the richer and more profound exchange. We discovered that photographs needed to be chosen with great care to stimulate a critical discussion. The team had been limited not only by a certain inexperience but also by a lack of photographs from which to choose. After experimenting with line drawings, they discovered that photographs, despite the limited selection, were far more effective in stimulating dynamic discussion.

After twenty minutes or so of dialogue, the direct study of reading and writing skills began — first with a sentence, then a word, and finally a syllabic family. We expanded Freire's single-word approach by using a short phrase or sentence based on the photograph's theme as the starting point for literacy practice. The team felt that a sentence provided a smoother transition from complex discussion to the concrete study of syllables. Because sentences encompassed a whole thought, they were considered more appropriate for adult learning as well as more flexible in generating the study of syllabic families. After reading the sentence, a key word from each phrase was chosen and divided into syllables, from which one family of syllables was selected and studied. For example, in the second lesson the name Fonseca was divided, Fon-*se*-ca, initiating a study of the syllabic family, sa, se, si, so, and su. Writing exercises were introduced and recognition exercises were used to help the participants identify the syllables as phonetic units. As learners mastered the individual syllables, they went on to use them to build new words, thus practicing their creativity and skills in manipulating the written language.

The specific teaching materials we used consisted of the elementary literacy primer, *Dawn of the People,* a teacher's manual, the *Teachers' Guide for Literacy Volunteers,* and an arithmetic workbook, *Math and Economic Reconstruction: One Single Operation.* During the Crusade, teaching games stressing learner creativity, such as a type of syllabic Scrabble, were developed and distributed. In addition, during the entire year of 1980, the national match factory produced all matches in special boxes decorated with the alphabet to be used as letter building blocks.

The primer was divided into twenty-three lessons, each accompanied by photographs and practice exercises, and was organized into three major areas: the history and development of the Revolution; the socioeconomic programs of the Government of National Reconstruction; and civil defense and community participation. Some of the specific lesson themes were "Sandino, guiding force of the Revolution"; "Work is the right and duty of every citizen"; "Spend little, save resources, and produce a lot — that is Revolution"; "The FSLN led the people to Liberation"; "With organization, work, and discipline we will be able to build the nation of Sandino."

The teacher's manual provided step-by-step instructions on the use of the literacy methodology and also contained detailed back-up readings for each of the twenty-three themes. It gave the brigadistas the necessary social, political,

Ejercicio C

1.- Leamos la oración :

La Reforma Agraria recupera la producción de la tierra para el pueblo.

2.- Leamos la palabra :

tierra

3.- Separemos la palabra en sílabas :

tie rra

4.- Leamos las sílabas :

rra rro rre rru rra

5.- Leamos y escribamos las sílabas :

rra rro rre rru rri

rre rri rro rru

6.- Formemos y escribamos palabras combinando las sílabas conocidas:

This sample exercise from the workbook, El Amanecer del Pueblo, *introduces a sentence to the student, its theme building on topics and ideas presented earlier by pictures and short readings. The student focuses on a particular work, its syllables, and a certain phonemic family. After writing those syllables in the workbook, the student then reads and uses them to write words and sentences.*

and economic information to generate a knowledgeable discussion and dialogue. Since the Crusade was considered a reciprocal learning process, the handbook also outlined a systematic set of study activities for the volunteers. The basis of their learning was their own living and teaching experience. As such, they were responsible for conducting a careful research study of their communities and keeping a field diary of their activities.

A Pedagogy of Shared Responsibility

To prepare the immense teacher corps to use the program's materials and methods, a national training program of short, intensive workshops was conducted. The first training materials explained to the brigadistas their revolutionary educational role as literacy promoters:

> You will be a catalyst of the teaching-learning process. Your literacy students will be people who think, create, and express their ideas. Together, you will form a team of mutual learning and human development. . . . The literacy process is an act of creation in which people offer each other their thoughts, words, and deeds. It is a cultural action of transformation and growth.[10]

Training, therefore, required that all participants take on new educational roles in what we called a pedagogy of shared responsibility. The traditional model of the active, all-wise professor and passive, ignorant pupil was specifically rejected and replaced by one in which the traditional teacher became a type of learning coordinator. The role of the workshop director was one of facilitator, a role that involved motivating, inspiring, challenging, and working with the participants who were encouraged to become active problem solvers. Participants were the foundation and wellspring of the process. Their responsibilities were to explore, research, and create. Small-group study, team teaching, and problem solving affirmed this new relationship. Under the coordination of two facilitators, workshop members were given a variety of educational tasks to accomplish. During the training, they reflected upon the group process and their progress, integrating both theory and practice.

Our primary purpose in training was to have people master the materials and methods while developing skills necessary to solve social problems creatively and sensitively. Methods were chosen to enhance the initiative and imagination with which people acquire and apply knowledge. The specific techniques used were simulations, role playing, group discussions, debates, murals, poetry, drawing, songs, and some artistic forms of expression from Nicaraguan folklore. Each workshop began with an introductory presentation exercise to acquaint participants with each other and to establish a congenial, dynamic learning environment. The participants were initially divided into working teams of about six people each, which formed the principal base of learning for the entire workshop. The small group chose the name of a fallen combatant for their symbol and wrote up his or her biography, hanging it on the wall for others to read. In their teams, participants then discussed the meaning of the Crusade and why they had decided to become volunteers, listing their responses on large sheets of paper and tacking them on the wall for presentation to the group. To conclude the first exercise, they were asked to create some two-line, rhyme-slogans which summarized their discussion. This technique had its roots in Nicaraguan traditional culture, where couplets are a popular literary expression, and in the war. During the long years of struggle, short chants which synthesized and captured the spirit of popular demands and aspirations had been used to animate demonstrations and harass the National Guard.

During the workshop, the rhymes took on a life of their own. Groups used their spare time trying to create new and more imaginative ones. They would practice them together in a corner and in a moment of relative silence between activities shout out their creation with great pride and enthusiasm. They then prepared a carefully written copy of their work so others could join them in shouting their couplet. The effort generated a spirit of lively rivalry and boosted energies when long hours of work became heavy and fatiguing. It also served as a positive means to gauge involvement and comprehension levels. If for example a group didn't understand an exercise or a reading, invariably a humorous couplet indicating their confusion and frustration would surface. At the end of the workshop the walls told the story of training. They were covered by summaries of group discussion and popular poetry.

To implement the training program, a decentralized four-stage model was designed. The program's success depended on its multiplier effect: beginning with seven national trainers, it was expected that in less than four months almost 100,000 people would be prepared. From December to March, workshops were held across the country. The driving force behind the training was the "group of eighty." Forty university students and forty teachers were specially selected for an intensive two-week preparation program and a one-month field experience. From their ranks, forty were chosen to train approximately 600 students and teachers in the next phase. During late February these 600 people prepared more than 12,000 people, most of whom were teachers. They, in turn, conducted the eight-day intensive workshops for thousands of literacy volunteers. Once the Crusade began, permanent training workshops were given for those people who still wished to enter the program. A radio show broadcast twice daily, together with special Saturday seminars conducted by squadron technical advisors, provided a continuing in-service training for the volunteers.

The Continuing Challenge

We are presently involved in designing and establishing a permanent system of adult education. In October 1980 three new Crusades began — in English, Miskito, and Sumo — for Nicaraguans who do not speak Spanish as their native language; and in 1981 we are hoping to launch a Health Crusade along the same lines as the literacy campaign. So much needs to be done. The hundreds of thousands of Nicaraguans who mastered basic reading and writing skills have just begun their studies. Their skills are still fragile.

The Literacy Crusade is only a first step in a long process of education and social creation. For the moment, we are in a transition that began in the final month of the Crusade — a time for people to practice and strengthen their literacy and math skills. The transition program arose from a natural phenomenon occurring in the literacy groups. As the most advanced students finished the primer, they began to concentrate on helping fellow students in mastering skills. When the campaign terminated, outstanding literacy graduates or educated members of the community were chosen to continue the work of the learning group. After being given some basic training by the Crusade's teaching supervisors, the new educational coordinators were provided with a carefully designed teacher's guide and a set of follow-up reading materials that stressed collective study and action as the fundamental basis for community learning. These community learning groups are supported by the network of mass citizen and labor organizations. The work of the coordinators is bolstered by specially selected traveling "promotors" who serve as liaisons to the regional adult education offices and provide the community groups with encouragement, orientation, and extra learning materials when available. Rounding out the transition program is a radio show for the study groups, broadcast twice daily on all national channels.

The challenge for the future is awesome. Expectations are great, problems complex, and resources scarce. In the face of new tasks, the example and lessons of the campaign provide the inspiration and hope for tomorrow. As one young literacy volunteer expressed in August, "The Crusade is like the source of a river of popular knowledge which will flow onward forever."

Life as a Brigadista

Before we conclude, there is one more aspect of the Crusade that needs to be presented — the experience of being a brigadista. Life as a volunteer in the countryside was hard work. Tasks filled the day. Mornings were spent laboring alongside peasant *compañeros;* late afternoons and evenings were dedicated to leading study sessions in homes, patios, or front yards. The experience can best be described by those who were there. We have gathered some quotes which convey how the brigadistas lived and worked and how the campaign touched their lives. No one can explain it better.

> Dear All,
>
> I arrived here on this mountain top yesterday on the back of a mule. . . . We left Saturday from Managua at 3 A.M. in a caravan of 70 buses and dump trucks, about 1,500 university students in all, complete with a gasoline truck and an

army escort to protect us during the 20 hour journey. We spent most of the time singing, shouting cheers, and waving. It was incredible, really! Even though it was nighttime in every village and town along the way, people left their homes to wave at us. Of course, they knew we were members of EPA. Women would offer us oranges and bananas and shout up at us, "Take care! See you when you return. We love you!" They would throw us kisses too. One old man, he must have been at least 70, ran beside the bus smiling up at us shouting EPA, EPA, EPA. I didn't know whether I was crying from the dust, the cold, or the wind, or the emotion I felt at seeing what a revolution can really mean. . . .

Many Hugs, Gabriella

* * *

I am really impressed how some of these kids came prepared and equipped. One of the boys looks like he is ready to fight the crocodile that always shows up in the jungle movies wanting to eat Tarzan. Another one has all the trappings of a walking Boy Scout Store. It's a sure sign of how ignorant most of us are about how people live in the countryside.

The hardest part for the volunteers is the loneliness and isolation, finding themselves suddenly living among strangers with whom, at least up till now, they have little in common. The feeling is one of anguish and insecurity. Thank God because of their political spirit and Christian faith, none of my brigadistas have deserted. Everyday they seem to adjust and find themselves enjoying life here more.

I can understand the horror of some of the parents from the capital when they come to visit their children and find them living in peasant "homes." What I don't understand is why they are so horrified that their kids will have to spend 5 months in these conditions and not that 70 percent of the Nicaraguan people have to suffer this misery their entire lives.

Educational Advisor
Los Santos

* * *

To my literacy teacher and compañero: Guillermo Briones Cisñero

My friends, Nicaragua is free.
The oppression of Somoza is defeated
For with the rumbling of bullets,
  Anastasio and son ran far away.
And now with the shouting of ABCs,
  Ignorance flees and joins them in Paraguay.
These verses I do recite
  in honor of Guillermo, my friend and compañero
Because I respect him like no other
  and love him like an older brother.

Anselmo Hurtado Lopez

* * *

Dear Mom and Dad,

I am fine. I arrived safe and sound but please send me 20 cans of grape juice. The well is filled with mud and the river is far away. . . .

Love, your son

* * *

Dear Folks,

I'm learning a lot. I now know how to milk a cow and plant vegetables. The other day I was with Don Demesio roping a steer but I'm so stupid that I frightened the thing and we had to work twice as hard to catch it again. . . . The rains are constant. The soles of my boots came unglued and I had to sew them with a needle they use to make sacks with.

Love, David

* * *

It's difficult sometimes. Tomasita is smart and wants to study but her baby cries a lot and she can't put him down. I visit her three times a day just on the chance she'll be free but . . . she's only on lesson 4. . . . Camilo doesn't seem to assimilate his sounds very well. Of course he does need glasses. He's 67. . . . Socorro and Joaquina are way ahead on lesson 14 but Julio left to pick coffee and Catalina's in bed with malaria. . . . Vicente has improved incredibly since he fell off his mule. He was really a lazy bum before. But now, with his broken arm, he's quite serious and dedicated, even though he's had to learn to write all over again with his left hand.

Guadalupe from the Brigade Enoc Ortez
in a report to her teaching supervisor

* * *

Eight ex-national guardsmen crossed the border from Honduras yesterday and murdered the literacy teacher Georgino Andrade.

Newsbroadcast, Managua
May 19, 1980

* * *

The struggle is long and sometimes cruel. What's needed above all, my dear friend, is love and commitment. Remember, "the freedom of a people is not won with flowers." We are young and we are called upon to build the new, to create what our heroes and martyrs would have wanted. Put yourself in the place of Georgino Andrade. You wouldn't like it, if out of fear, the cause you gave your life for wasn't continued.

Letter to boyfriend Brigadista
from girlfriend Brigadista

* * *

The Literacy Crusade taught us two things. One, what our own children are capable of doing and of becoming. Two, what our country is like and how gentle and how poor our people are in the countryside.

Mother of three literacy volunteers

* * *

We take our malaria medicine twice a week and we're supposed to use our water purifying tablets. . . . The sicknesses among the children are many. Eight children in the next valley died last month of measles, three from the same family. It's unbelievable the inhuman conditions these people live under. I feel indignation and rage at not being a doctor.

Brigadista
Atlantic Coast

* * *

The Crusade has been carried out by the kids of Nicaragua, the wonderful kids who under the leadership of the *Frente* fought the tyrant — intelligent kids, sacrificing, determined — idealists and realists all at the same time. For me the principal lesson of the campaign is that now Nicaragua knows that it can count on this treasure for its future. Not all the best children died in the war. With the living, we can carry out the other necessary wars to be fought, the war against social injustice, the war against poor health, the war against disease.

The Crusade is over. The People of Nicaragua and the commitment of the *Frente* made it possible. Thanks to their efforts Nicaragua will be totally different in the future. It will be a better nation, a nation that all Nicaraguans deserve. If that's not a triumph, excuse me, but then what the hell do you call a triumph?

Priest,
Squadron Teaching Supervisor

Reflections

Thinking back over the last year, the most important lesson we learned will probably be the most difficult for educational planners to apply. In the final analysis, the success of the campaign depended not on scientifically tested educational theories, or complex planning systems, or even sophisticated curriculum design. The ultimate success of the Literacy Crusade depended on a commitment of the spirit — a commitment of a people and a government born of a liberation struggle. Only that kind of creative force could generate and maintain the levels of sacrifice and dedication required to accomplish such a task.

For when all is said and done, the Crusade is not a story of complicated techniques or complex cost-benefit analysis. It is a story of people and the extraordinary potential for liberation and creation that exists within nations.

It is about thousands of problems, big and small. But most of all it is a story about the creative intelligence of people and the courageous sacrifice of thousands of Nicaraguans who gave their lives so that intelligence and creativity could flourish. It is a beginning.

Its promise can probably best be described by the words of a peasant speaking to the mother of his young literacy teacher: "Do you know I am not ignorant any more. I know how to read now. Not perfectly, you understand, but I know how. And do you know, your son isn't ignorant any more either. Now he knows how we live, what we eat, how we work and he knows the life of the mountains. Your son, ma'am, has learned to read from our book."

Notes

1. Quoted in José Román, *Maldito Pais* (Managua: El Pez y La Serpiente, 1979), p. 135.
2. Ministry of Educatión, *La Educación En El Primar Año De La Revolución Popular Sandinista* (Managua: Author, 1980), p. 162.
3. Auxiliadora Rivas and Asunción Suazo, conversation in literacy class, Masaya, Nicaragua, May 4, 1980.
4. Unpublished Report on Literacy Crusade by FSLN (Sardinista National Liberation Front), December 1979.
5. Brigades were made up of all those brigadistas in one municipality; columns were made up of four squadrons where possible and each squadron contained thirty brigadistas and one to three education advisors.
6. In all, the Crusade's national office employed the services of the following international experts: two Argentinians, one Canadian, one Chilean, five Columbians, one Costa Rican, four Cubans, two Salvadorians, one Honduran, two Mexicans, one Peruvian, one Puerto Rican, four Spaniards.
7. The Technical/Pedagogical Division had four sections — Curriculum, Research, Training, and Library/Museum — and was designed to provide the educational expertise for the program. The Technical/Organizational Division essentially served as a support-control structure for the literacy promoters and as a liaison to the different sponsoring organizations. It had four sections: Statistics and Census; the Popular Literacy Army (EPA) and the Urban Literacy Guerillas (GUAS); the Mass Citizen and Labor Organizations; and the Internal Technical Secretariat. The Administrative Division was separated into two departments: Logistical Support, which was made up of Supplies, Health, Food Distribution, Transportation, Communication and Maintenance, and Plant Maintenance; and the Department of Administration, which contained Control, Accounting, Personnel, and Budget. The departments and municipalities were each structured along lines similar to the national — Technical/Pedagogical, Statistics and Census, Logistical Support, and Publicity.
8. Paulo Freire in conversion with Fernando Cardenal, Nicaragua, October–November 1979.
9. Carlos Carrión, speech before First Congress of the National Literacy Crusade, June 17, 1980.
10. Cruzada Nacional de Alfabetización, *Cuaderno de Orientacions* (Managua: Ministry of Education, 1979), p. 1.

The photographs in this article were taken during the Literacy Campaign and were provided by the authors.

Coda: The Slow Fuse of Change

Obama, the Schools, Imagination, and Convergence

MAXINE GREENE

I began writing this essay the day after waves of euphoria swept over what appeared to be a profoundly altered public space. We had seen the most diverse gathering of people coming freely together to affirm a common purpose no one could quite yet define. No one had instructed them to come out in the cold of that inauguration morning; there was neither prize nor penalty involved. And yet, for their own reasons and moved by their own private hopes, they chose themselves as newcomers to a community-in-the-making, working to find what they had in common and what brought them to that shared space. Was it Barack Obama's charisma, his way of speaking, his choice of words? Was it the appeal of his family, the propriety of those little girls, the obvious bond he shared with Michelle? Or was it the sense that a time of apathy and felt powerlessness was over? Was there a promise in that iteration of *change*—a promise of direction, of hopes to be fulfilled at last?

Obama indeed expresses and embodies a concern for education—and an underlying hope. Such an interest by a federal leader makes it easy to forget that public education was long considered a responsibility of the states and localities. This meant that the inequities perpetuated by some state laws could only be overcome by federal action sparked in part by a growing sense of injustice among the people. In relatively recent history, a growing recognition of our schools' deficiencies and failures led to federal actions such as the Johnson administration's passing of the Elementary and Secondary Education Act—in large part a response to a new sense of injustice informing the "war on poverty" and the civil rights movement. Similarly, as difficult as it was to begin to overcome years of prejudice and discrimination, the 1954 decision outlawing segregation in public schools led to new hopes and collective activities among African Americans in the South. Little by little, the public became acquainted with images of youthful heroism and instances of breaking down

Harvard Educational Review Vol. 79 No. 2 Summer 2009

the walls of inequity. It seemed a moment of triumph for people of color and those similarly excluded. But the victories were incomplete. It would take time before those who believed in equality and justice—and still believe—would begin to see these values carry the force of natural law.

The necessity of natural law can justify a strong hand on the part of the federal government. However, the president can neither make certain promises nor answer all questions—and neither can we. Few of us are skilled enough to muster telling arguments or make sure predictions about how best to prioritize the work that must be done to repair infrastructures, reduce joblessness, expand health care, or strengthen and enrich the education of young people. What is necessary is to remind ourselves that education has much to do with power and with the opening of public spaces—spaces where people come together in their freedom to bring a democratic community into being. There can be, and must be, spaces of dialogue, spaces of diversity and mutuality and concern. There must be spaces of convergence.

Though we can make no sure predictions, we can weigh probabilities in a very uncertain time. I am interested in possibility—in what might be, in what should be, if things were otherwise. In one of her poems, Emily Dickinson wrote that, "the possible's slow fuse is lit by the imagination" (1960). To commit to imagining is to commit to looking beyond the given, beyond what appears to be unchangeable. It is a way of warding off the apathy and the feelings of futility that are the greatest obstacles to any sort of learning and, surely, to education for freedom.

There seemed to be clues in the euphoria, efforts to light that slow fuse of possibility. The presence of veterans of the struggle for civil rights at Obama's inauguration lit many fuses of memory. Images returned—of fire hoses; of beatings; of the little girls in Birmingham; of the Selma march and the other long, hot marches; of the Mississippi murders; of the killing of Dr. King. Perhaps it requires an act of imagination to make meaningful the suffering, the sacrifices. In classrooms, the question of what can be done now that we have a president who says *we* and who speaks of *our* responsibility may become central. How can we make it worthwhile, each of us feeling herself to be a participant in our schools and our colleges, just as we participated in that remarkable campaign? Can we imagine ourselves moving beyond simply being there?

There was the suggestion that the inauguration may have been a coming-true of Dr. Martin Luther King's dream—one of the most potent imaginative constructions in our history. And there was the evocation of Dr. King's prophecy that he might not be with his people when they attained their goal. Surely, for more than a few, his prophecy suggested that new young women and men would emerge to carry on, that we needed to imagine such a possibility. In our imagining, we might think of Barack Obama after his success at Harvard and at a turning point in his life, faced with the choice of what next. Able to secure any position of his choosing, he chose remarkably to become a community organizer. We might hope—and we might imagine—that those experiences in

Chicago can even now help him note the savage nature of the inequalities he found (Kozol, 1992) and must continue to find as he moves across our land. We might imagine him bringing community members together with teachers and learners to show that it is unendurable for a child to be expected to climb a meritocratic ladder when she lacks sneakers or lunch money—and, most importantly, has no notion of things being otherwise.

We need imagination.

We need visions of the possible and of the unexpected. We need to act on the promises of that cold morning, stimulus or no, obstacles or no. To educate, to change, we need to converge.

References

Dickinson, E. (1960). The gleam of an heroic act. In T. H. Johnson (Ed.), *The complete poems of Emily Dickinson.* Boston: Little, Brown and Company.

Kozol, J. (1992). *Savage inequalities.* New York: Harper Perennial.

About the Contributors

Montse Sánchez Aroca is an associate professor at the Universitat de Barcelona. Her work has been developed in the areas of research methodology, ethnic groups, and social and adult education. She is author of *The Inclusion of Other Women: Breaking the Silence through Dialogic Learning* (2005) and *Critical Communicative Methodology* (forthcoming, Peter Lang).

William Ayers writes about social justice, democracy and education, the cultural contexts of schooling, and teaching as an essentially intellectual, ethical, and political enterprise. He is currently the vice president of the curriculum division of the American Educational Research Association and a member of the executive committee of the University of Illinois at Chicago Faculty Senate.

Kathy Boudin is the director of the Criminal Justice Initiative: Supporting Children, Families and Communities, an interdisciplinary project located in the Columbia University School of Social Work. During her twenty-two years of incarceration she was involved in adult literacy, the AIDS epidemic, mother-child relationships and higher education in prison. Since returning home, she has continued those commitments and additionally works in the area of restorative justice with longtermers in prison. She has published in all of the above fields. She received her doctoral degree in education in 2007 from Columbia University Teachers College.

Fernando Cardenal, S.J. served as the national coordinator of the Nicaraguan Literacy Crusade and the minister of education for the Sandinista government. He is the current director of the Fé y Alegría ("Faith and Happiness") school system in Nicaragua. He is a Jesuit priest and liberation theologian.

Jeffrey M.R. Duncan-Andrade works closely with teachers and school leaders to develop classroom practices and school cultures that foster self-confidence and academic success. He publishes regularly on the conditions of urban education, urban teacher support and development, and critical pedagogy. He also teaches a ninth grade English class at Mandela High School (Oakland, CA). He recently completed *The Art of Critical Pedagogy* (2009) and *What a Coach Can Teach a Teacher* (2010) and is finishing a book on the core competencies of highly effective urban educators.

Marco Garrido was a senior at Boston College High School in Dorchester, Massachusetts, when he wrote his piece. He has since received a BA in English Literature from Harvard University and an MA in International Peace Studies from the University of Notre Dame. He is currently in Metro Manila, Philippines, conducting fieldwork for his dissertation in the field of Sociology at the University of Michigan.

Jay Gillen is the Baltimore City School's facilitator for the Baltimore Algebra Project. His teaching focuses on Ella Baker's question: How do people face a system that does not lend itself to their needs and devise the means to change it? He is currently studying youth employment in knowledge work as a constituent element in the right to education.

Maxine Greene teaches a course in the Arts and Humanities Department at Teachers College. As philosopher-in-residence at the Lincoln Center Institute for the Arts in Education, she conducts workshops on aesthetic education to teachers and teacher educators. She has a central interest in the power and significance of imagination in thought and action.

Kathe Jervis has continued to pursue her professional interests centered on daily classroom life, teacher research, children's thinking, and racial issues in schools. Among her many educational projects is a recent one in Iraq for RAND, where she used close observation to document a school started by the American military for eleven- to seventeen-year-old Iraqi detainees. She is currently volunteering for the New York Civil Liberties Union on a project monitoring data collection abuses.

Valerie Miller is cofounder of Just Associates (JASS), a global community of activists, scholars, and popular educators based on feminist values and committed to strengthening women's voices and power and their efforts to create a just and sustainable world for all. Coauthor of the book, *A New Weave of Power, People and Politics* (2007), her history with organizations such as the Highlander Center, UNICEF, Oxfam, ActionAid International, and the Institute of Development Studies enriches her online teaching and her work with Wings of the Butterfly, a feminist organizing initiative based on theater and resonance.

Nancy Uhlar Murray is director of education at the ACLU of Massachusetts, as well as the director of its Bill of Rights Education Project, which she founded in 1987. In this role, she has encouraged teachers, students, and the general public to think critically about the difficult issues being debated in society and the courts, and to work for a future in which civil liberties and civil rights are safeguarded and enlarged. Her recent writing includes several articles about the post–9/11 crisis in civil liberties and civil rights, a contribution to *Putting the Movement Back into Civil Rights Teaching* (2004) and a curriculum for middle and high school students, *Rights Matter: the Story of the Bill of Rights* (www.rightsmatter.org). She is also a member of the editorial committee of the periodical *Race and Class.*

Wendy Ormiston is a social worker living in Oakland, California. She pursues social justice efforts through work in two worker-owned cooperatives, mediation and therapy practice, and anti-racism activism. For fun, she loves to quilt, backpack, and play the harmonica.

Ana Y. Ramos-Zayas is an associate professor of Anthropology and Latino and Hispanic Caribbean Studies at Rutgers University, New Brunswick. Her scholarly interests include critical race theory, Latino studies, youth, and the anthropology of affect, sentiment, and emotion. She is the author of *National Performances: Class, Race, and Space* *in Puerto Rican Chicago* (2003) and coauthor of *Latino Crossings: Mexicans, Puerto Ricans and the Politics of Race and Citizenship* (2003). Her current book project, tentatively titled *Learning Affect, Embodying Race: Brazilians, Puerto Ricans, and Neoliberal Emotions in Newark, New Jersey,* focuses on everyday affective experiences behind racialization practices under neoliberalism among U.S.–born Latinos and Latin American migrants.

Arthur E. Thomas is currently the program manager of the California State University San Bernardino Integrated Technology Transfer Network Program (CSUSB–ITTN) at Morgan State University in Baltimore, Maryland. His professional interests are in educational administration, with a specific focus on the preparation of successful undergraduate science, technology, engineering, and math graduates and successful programs and strategies that address critical issues facing the African American male. At the time of the interview, Thomas was director of the Center for the Study of Student Citizenship, Rights, and Responsibility in Dayton, Ohio.

Vanessa Siddle Walker (originally published as Emilie V.) is a historian whose research has focused on the schooling of African American children in the segregated South. Her recent work examines the network of educational activity that undergirded the development of African American school communities. Her newest book, *Hello Professor* (2009), focuses on the leadership of black principals in the Jim Crow South.

Travis Wright is an assistant professor at the George Washington University Graduate School of Education, where he leads the Project on Risk, Resilience, and Urban Leadership. His current work explores risk and resilience in the lives of women and young children living in poverty, the effects of economic segregation on parenting and education, and the experiences of young people navigating commercial sexual exploitation. He continues his work as an early childhood mental health clinician, providing services to pre-school students attending public charter schools in Washington, DC.

About the Editors

Gretchen Brion-Meisels is a doctoral candidate at the Harvard Graduate School of Education, and one of the manuscript editors at the *Harvard Educational Review.* Her research seeks to explore holistic student support processes that build on the local knowledge of students and communities. She is the author of "Playing in the Light: Experiential Learning and White Identity Development" in the *Handbook of Social Justice in Education* (edited by Ayers, Quinn, and Stovall for Routledge, 2008). Before coming to HGSE, she taught middle school humanities in Baltimore, Maryland, Cambridge, Massachusetts, and Berkeley, California.

Kristy S. Cooper is a doctoral student at the Harvard Graduate School of Education, where she is working towards an EdD in education policy, leadership, and instructional practice. Prior to attending Harvard, Kristy taught elementary school in Los Angeles for six years and earned her National Board Certification as a middle-childhood generalist. Her doctoral research explores the link between classroom engagement and identity development among high school students. Kristy currently serves as the book notes editor for the *Harvard Educational Review* and is a coauthor of *Inside Urban Charter Schools: Promising Practices and Strategies in Five High-Performing Schools* (Harvard Education Press, 2009).

Sherry L. Deckman is a doctoral candidate at the Harvard Graduate School of Education and one of the cochairs of the *Harvard Educational Review.* Her current research explores how undergraduate students negotiate race, class, and gender difference. She is also interested in professional development opportunities for educators related to addressing inequity and diversity. She is a coauthor of "But What Can I Do? Three Necessary Tensions in Teaching Teachers about Race" (with Pollock, Mira, and Shalaby, *Journal of Teachers Education,* 2009). She is an alumnus of Teach For America and has been a high school teacher in Washington, DC, and Fukuoka, Japan.

Christina L. Dobbs is a doctoral student in human development and education at the Harvard Graduate School of Education. In an effort to understand the development of writing skills, her current research focuses on the discourse of school, academic language, and speakers of dialectal variations of English. Christina is an adjunct lecturer at Lesley University and reading specialist who works with preservice teachers and reading specialist trainees. Prior to coming to Harvard, Christina was a secondary English and journalism teacher in Houston, Texas. Christina serves as one of the manuscript editors for the *Harvard Educational Review.*

Chantal Francois is a doctoral candidate at the Harvard Graduate School of Education, where she studies the intersection of urban adolescent literacy, identity, and school culture. She serves as the solicitations editor of the *Harvard Educational Review.* Chantal teaches high school English in New York City and is coauthor, with Elisa Zonana, of *Catching Up on Conventions: Grammar Lessons for Middle School Writers* (Heinemann, 2009).

Thomas Nikundiwe is a doctoral candidate at the Harvard Graduate School of Education and one of the cochairs of the *Harvard Educational Review.* He is currently researching community and youth organizing for school reform and, in particular, the role that consciousness raising plays in shifting power relationships between youth and the various institutions they encounter. Previously Thomas worked as a math literacy youth organizer for the Baltimore Algebra Project. Prior to his organizing work, Thomas served as a teacher trainer in Uganda and as a secondary mathematics teacher for the Baltimore City Public School System.

Carla Shalaby is a former elementary school teacher and a doctoral student interested in ethnic and cultural justice for our youngest schoolchildren. Her work focuses on the everyday politics of identity and power in schools—elementary classrooms in particular. She is currently the visiting director of elementary education at Brown University, where she is committed to preparing teachers who are reflective in their stance, critical in their pedagogy, and ready to stand in solidarity with our children, families, and communities. She serves as vision editor for the *Harvard Educational Review.*